COURTROOM
COWBOY

COURTROOM COWBOY

THE LIFE OF LEGAL TRAILBLAZER JIM BEASLEY

RALPH CIPRIANO

Every man's work shall be made manifest . . .
because it shall be revealed by fire; and the fire shall try every
man's work of what sort it is. (1 Corinthians 3:13)

Cover and Book Design & Layout: Andrea Hemmann/GHI Design, www.ghidesign.com
Front Cover Photo: © 2008 Bill Cramer/Wonderful Machine
Back Cover Photo: Nicole Chabat
Photo Editor & Production: Jim Graham
Chapter Photography: © 2008 Jim Graham/Graham Studios Inc.
Photography Restoration: Kristopher Chain Harris & Danielle Nowack

Library of Congress Cataloging-in-Publication Data
Cipriano, Ralph.
Courtroom Cowboy: The Life of Legal Trailblazer Jim Beasley, by Ralph Cipriano.
First Edition.
ISBN: 978-0-9817133-0-4
Library of Congress Control Number: 20089285

Printed in China

Acknowledgments

COURTROOM COWBOY, WHICH TOOK THREE YEARS TO WRITE, WAS CULLED FROM A hundred interviews and thousands of pages of trial transcripts and court records.

The book could not have been written without the cooperation of the many Philadelphia judges and lawyers who generously shared their vivid memories of Jim Beasley, including: Richard A. Sprague, District Attorney Lynne Abraham, Superior Court Judge Stephen J. McEwen Jr., Chief U.S. Magistrate Judge James R. Melinson, Judge Mark I. Bernstein, Judge Sandra Mazer Moss, Judge Charles P. Mirarchi Jr., Judge Isador Kranzel, Temple University Beasley School of Law Dean Robert J. Reinstein, Thomas R. Kline, Shanin Specter, James E. Colleran, Arthur G. Raynes, James F. Mundy, David Cohen, M. Mark Mendel, Sheldon L. Albert, James J. Binns, James L. Griffith, Slade H. McLaughlin, Benedict A. Casey, Paul A. Lauricella, Michael A. Smerconish, James J. McHugh Jr., Dolores Rocco, Judge Thomas B. Rutter, Helene Christian, Elaine M. Ross, George L. Young Jr., Gerald F. Kaplan, Bernard Snyder, Daniel L. Thistle, Thomas W. Smith, Marsha F. Santangelo, David A Yanoff, William P. Murphy, Scott A. Bennett, Meyer A. Bushman, Kathleen L. Daerr-Bannon, James E. Foerstner, William Lytton, Gregory M. Harvey, Richard D. Hailey, Warren Ballard, Edward B. Joseph Michael Mather and James C. Stroud.

Former expert witnesses R. James Woolsey Jr., Laurie Mylroie and Wolfram Rieger gave me valuable insights on what it was like to collaborate with Jim Beasley in a courtroom, as did former clients Richards A. Sprague, Mark F. MacDonald, Joseph McGovern, Gale Greenberg, Eddie Scarborough, Patricia Scarborough, Scott Woodworth, Justice John Doe, Jane Doe, John Maddux, Elisabeth "Buffy"

Maddux Hall, Margaret "Meg" Wakeman and Mary Maddux.

I am indebted to several journalists, including Eugene L. Roberts Jr., James M. Naughton and Kent Pollock, for explaining what it was like to go up against Jim Beasley in the epic libel case known as *Sprague v. Walter*. Zack Stalberg and L. Stuart Ditzen were also helpful in detailing the challenges of covering Jim Beasley as a news subject. Mike Mallowe, Jim Nicholson and Dan Lynch provided valuable background for understanding the *Sprague v. Walter* case, as well as insight into what it was like to be a reporter working in Philadelphia during the Frank Rizzo years.

F. Lee Bailey also gave me perspective on the *Sprague* case.

Architects S. Neil Schlosser and Karl Krumholz, contractor Joe Brassell Sr., artist Michael Webb and Beasley business associate Michael DiPaolo were essential in explaining Beasley's grand conversion of the former Epsicopal Church House into a law office.

Villanova Law Professor Catherine Lanctot tutored me on the history of the Philadelphia lawyer.

I would like to thank Jim Beasley Jr., the originator of this project, who also functioned as editor, and steadfastly insisted that *Courtroom Cowboy* be an honest and unvarnished portrait of his father.

I am indebted to the women in the Beasley family — Helen, Pam, Kim and Liz — for showing me the softer side of the courtroom warrior. Nancy Beasley, Lynn Hayes and Gloria Fletcher were also candid in discussing Jim Beasley's early life. For further insights, I would like to thank Nicole Chabat and Heidi Peditto.

Beasley's first cousin, Walter Woodworth, was invaluable in recalling Beasley's childhood and teenage years. Beasley's fellow warbird pilots — Dan Caldarale, Dan Dameo, Joe Scogna and Ed Shipley — showed me another side of the Beasley persona, that of the barnstorming and thrill-seeking daredevil of the air shows. I also appreciated the comments of Dr. Bernard L. Segal and Dr. John Glick.

I would like to thank editor Yolanda Fuller for helping me plan and carry out this project, and also for doing some valuable trouble shooting along the way. I would also like to thank other careful readers who caught numerous mistakes in the manuscript and made some telling suggestions on how to improve it, including Jim Beasley Jr., Helen and Pam Beasley, David A. Yanoff, Robert Zausner, Julia Bibb, Rosemarie D'Alba and Bob Fowler. I am also indebted to Joel Tuckman, Susan Holbrook, Valerie Ross and Chuck Lee, for digging up countless court files and other documents at The Beasley Firm, and I would also like to thank Sue and Val for straightening out every computer problem that came along.

Lastly, I would like to thank Sal Paolantonio, who, when I needed a lawyer, told me to call Michael A. Smerconish, who introduced me to Jim Beasley.

Introduction

❖

"ANYBODY BUT BEASLEY"
OR HOW I LEARNED TO LOVE
THE ANTICHRIST

At the Philadelphia Inquirer, where I worked as a reporter, Jim Beasley was so feared and despised that my editors called him the antichrist. Beasley was the king of libel suits who had made a career out of suing the Inquirer; he was notorious for assaulting journalists on the witness stand and for scoring multimillion-dollar libel verdicts. So when I secretly went to see him in the summer of 1998, I felt like a traitor. But I was in trouble and needed his advice.

"The Beasley Building," at the corner of 12th and Walnut Streets, was a Gothic stone castle, the former headquarters of the Episcopal Diocese of Pennsylvania. Behind heavy wrought iron gates, the place still had the feel of a 19th-century church, with its leaded stained-glass windows, marble fireplaces, and glowing Victorian candle chandeliers.

The receptionist at the front desk told me to go right up, Mr. Beasley was expecting me. His executive office was a cavernous second-floor suite featuring 15-foot ceilings that once belonged to the bishop.

At first glance, I thought Beasley, in his early 70s, was the image of a distinguished trial lawyer, with his flowing silver mane, craggy face, and intimidating brown-eyed stare. But then I saw some rough edges: slightly crooked teeth, a gaudy brass belt buckle emblazoned with a famous World War II fighter plane — the P-51 Mustang — and, under faded jeans, a pair of cowboy boots.

I was in a jam; my boss, the editor of the Inquirer, had just called me a liar on the front page of the Washington Post's Style section. My boss was upset because a story I wrote about lavish spending by the Catholic archbishop of Philadelphia — a story the Inquirer had declined to print for political reasons — had just been published by another newspaper. When Howard Kurtz of the Post called my boss to ask why he hadn't run the story, my boss defended himself by trashing me, saying I wrote things that weren't true. He also refused to apologize, even though he had been urged to do so at a staff meeting attended by 45 colleagues.

So I was a reporter with a credibility problem, trying to decide whether the only way to restore my reputation was to sue my editor and my own newspaper for libel. And who knew more about suing the "Inky" than the antichrist?

Like many clients before me who sat in Beasley's office, I was overcome with anxiety. Did I have a case? If I did sue, would it be the end of my career? And if I didn't sue and got fired, and nobody else would hire me, how would I pay the bills and put the kids through college?

Beasley took charge, calmly asking questions, and listening intently to the answers. "I think you've got a good case," he said finally, in a voice with a hint of a Southern accent, but he warned that libel suits were never easy.

I didn't know much about the subject, so Beasley leaned back in his upholstered leather chair and rattled off an impressive synopsis of a couple hundred years of American libel law. While Beasley filled me in on the meaning of public figures and actual malice, I glanced around his cherry-paneled walls, at all the legal awards and plaques commending outstanding generosity to charities and to Temple University, Beasley's alma mater.

It was hard not to be impressed with Beasley, but I couldn't make up my mind whether I had the guts to hire him. "Thanks for your time," I said as I was leaving, "but I've got a lot to think about. Maybe my boss and I can work things out."

Beasley didn't think so, but he didn't want to talk me into anything. "Good luck," he said, sticking out his hand. "You've got a decision to make, buddy, and I can't make it for you."

Not many people shared my favorable impression of Jim Beasley. Besides being hated by journalists, he was also unpopular with doctors and lawyers, because of his work in malpractice law. This guy had a talent for making enemies all over town.

A lawyer friend of mine said he wouldn't hire Beasley if his neck was on the line. "Beasley's a gambler," my friend said. "Do you want to put your life in the hands of a gambler?" My friend advised me to go see another top city lawyer who had a reputation for being cool under fire, someone less reckless and unpredictable.

Friends in the newsroom also stopped by my desk to offer unsolicited advice about hiring a lawyer. The unanimous recommendation: "anybody but Beasley." Go ahead and sue us, they said, just pick another lawyer. So to mollify all the Beasley haters I knew, I went to see this other lawyer.

He was a slick Baby Boomer in a suit and tie who said I might have an interesting case, because my boss had certainly acted rashly. But he said I sounded like a hothead too, and he was worried that I might come off to a jury as some kind of nut. He also wanted to know if I had any skeletons in my closet, and then he referred to some big shots at the Inquirer by their first names, as if I was supposed to be impressed. But I left his office wondering whose side he would be on.

Sorry, guys. Why go to war with a waffler like John Kerry, when I could hire General Patton? Beasley, a member of the Greatest Generation, didn't see the moral universe in endless shades of gray; to him it was all black and white. "You're right," he told me; "they're wrong. It's as simple as that. And we're gonna win the case." That's the kind of talk I wanted to hear from my lawyer.

Beasley drafted a complaint charging that I was the victim of a "malicious defamation," and after many revisions, it was time to sign. It wasn't easy, I told Beasley as I scrawled my signature, to sue the paper I'd written more than 1,000 stories for. When I looked up, my lawyer was smiling. The case was a winner, he said. He picked up the complaint, rolled it up and waved it in my face. "This one," he said, "has my byline on it."

After I filed suit, my newspaper suspended me from work, even though the newsroom labor contract had no provision for suspensions. The first person I called was Beasley. Don't worry, he said; they don't know what to do with you.

They figured it out. Two weeks later, two editors showed up at my doorstep to fire me. Once again, I picked up the phone and called Beasley, who was as upbeat as ever. Don't worry, he said, they just made a big mistake. Beasley promptly filed an amended complaint charging that the Inquirer had fired me in retaliation for exercising my constitutional right to file a lawsuit, which Beasley claimed was further proof of malice.

With plenty of time on my hands, I started showing up at Beasley's office for early morning strategy sessions. His phone was always ringing. A judge called with a new lawyer joke that made Beasley laugh. U.S. Senator Arlen Specter was on the line, seeking support for his reelection campaign. "All right, Arlen," Beasley sighed, lowering his head. "I'll do whatever I can to help."

An airplane mechanic called to talk about one of Beasley's beloved P-51 Mustangs. Beasley's hobby was flying vintage warbirds on weekends; performing daredevil maneuvers in formation with other expert pilots, like his son, Jim Jr. "It veers to the right," Beasley complained to his mechanic. "How much is this costing me now?"

When we talked about my case, the main thing Beasley wanted to know was, what had I done to my boss, Robert J. Rosenthal, editor of the Inquirer, to make him angry enough to call me a liar in the Washington Post? Did I make a pass at his wife? I'm not that dumb, I said. "He drove through so many stop signs and caution lights," Beasley marveled.

One morning, Beasley told me he was going on vacation; a group of lawyers from his office was flying to Tibet, to climb Mount Everest. I looked at Beasley to see if he was kidding. Here he was twice the age of these young guys, yet he too felt he had to climb the mountain. I was worried he might take a tumble and break his neck before he could try my case, but Beasley shrugged it off. "You only live once," he said.

When you're a newspaper reporter, it's hard to break old habits. Even an unemployed hack could see that Jim Beasley was a great story. He was a warrior out on the battlefield every day of his life; a maverick misunderstood by the wimps in the press. On his desk, he kept a small metal sculpture of a Sisyphus-like figure pushing a big boulder up a hill. His motto, hand-painted on the walls of his extravagant Sistine Chapel of a law library, was a quote from George Bernard Shaw's "Maxims for Revolutionists":

> *The reasonable man adapts himself to the world; the unreasonable*
> *one persists in trying to adapt the world to himself. Therefore, all progress*
> *depends on the unreasonable man.*

So it was Beasley's mission statement to be a pain in the ass. And he was so good at it. I told Beasley if he hadn't pissed off so many journalists, they'd have already written several books about him. He laughed, and then we argued about freedom of the press. I told Beasley if guys like me got our facts straight, guys like him would starve to death. "You're absolutely right," he said, laughing again.

We also got into debates about religion and God. Beasley knew I was a skeptic who converted while reading the Bible and working the religion beat at the Inquirer. But Beasley didn't buy organized religion, and he advised me to read a Bertrand Russell essay he admired, "Why I Am Not a Christian." He also declared with characteristic bluntness that the only reason people believed in religion or God was that they were afraid to die. I told him religion might be nonsense, but God was for real.

Beasley didn't buy that either. "What did God ever do for you?" he snapped. I looked at him and smiled. "He gave me a great lawyer." For once, Beasley had no reply. It may have been the only argument I ever won in that office.

Through every stage of the legal war, Beasley was resolute, keeping the case tightly focused on the remarks my boss made to the Washington Post, remarks that Beasley knew we would disprove. Whenever I brought up an issue that was off target, Beasley would put us right back on course by yelling, "What the hell does that have to do with what Bob Rosenthal said to the Washington Post?" When the case dragged on, Beasley reassured me by saying, "Relax, all they can do is postpone the inevitable."

He was right. After 2½ years of litigation, the bosses at the Inquirer decided to settle the case and avoid an embarrassing trial by printing a public apology and paying a confidential sum. The settlement, however, still received plenty of attention in the press. Beasley, who loved free advertising, posed with me in his law library for a photo to illustrate a cover story in Editor & Publisher.

By then, I was so fond of my lawyer I didn't want to say goodbye. When he asked if I was interested in collaborating with him on a book about his favorite cases, I eagerly agreed. Beasley began pulling court files and judges' rulings. He talked about some of the characters he had met during his 48 years as a trial lawyer, and the many legal precedents he had set.

As he prepared to write his book, Beasley ruminated on a yellow legal pad about a lifetime of courtroom battles: "There are cases that I should have won, that I lost," he wrote. "There are cases that I should have lost, that I won. That, simply stated, is the practice of law. Conflict makes the law, it is true; the heart of the law is conflict."

When I leafed through Beasley's case files, and saw the amazing variety of lost causes that he had embraced over the years, I realized that my lawyer was a bigger story than I had imagined. This guy wasn't afraid to take on anybody, whether it was wily boxing promoter Don King, fugitive killer Ira Einhorn, or terrorist mastermind Osama bin Laden. Beasley would take a case simply because it was the right thing to do, and he didn't mind tilting at windmills.

My relationship with Beasley began to change. "I'm not your lawyer anymore," he said wistfully one night in a restaurant over a few glasses of wine. Now talking to his ghostwriter, Beasley began to loosen up.

He was a mystery to most of the judges and lawyers in town because he never talked about himself or his humble beginnings; even the lawyers who worked for him wondered what drove him to keep working so hard. Beasley gave me some insight when he said that before he went to college on the GI bill, he was a high school dropout driving a Greyhound bus.

His success, Beasley confided, was probably equal to how neurotic he was, and how deep his insecurities ran. Then he changed the subject, preferring to talk about his cases again. Beasley wanted each chapter of the book to tell a stand-alone story about one of his favorite cases, but I told Beasley that the book should also tell *his* story. When I tried to steer the conversation back to personal matters, however, hoping for further revelations, Beasley cracked, "Who cares about that shit?"

Beasley and I met one afternoon in his office with Michael Smerconish, to come up with a title for Beasley's book. Smerconish was a lawyer who had worked for Beasley before becoming a radio talk show host. He was also the one who had originally talked Beasley into writing a book. Beasley listened with a poker face as

Smerconish rattled off such dignified titles as "The Philadelphia Lawyer" and "The Lawyer's Lawyer," which was appropriate because Beasley was the guy judges and lawyers turned to when they were in trouble.

When Smerconish was through, Beasley glared at me and silently slid a copy of Philadelphia magazine across the desk. It was open to a full-page color portrait of Beasley standing on his desk in cowboy boots, under the caption "Courtroom Cowboy." I looked at Beasley, and he had a grin on his face. "Is that what you want?" Smerconish lowered his head and covered his face with his hands.

So that's what we had to call it, because I owe a debt to the man, even if he didn't hang around long enough to help me write the book. Because, if you were ever in trouble, you dreamed of having an advocate like Jim Beasley. As he told the young lawyers who worked for him, "Never take any shit from anybody, and that includes a judge."

In an age of tort reform and lawyer jokes, Jim Beasley was a throwback: proud to be a trial lawyer, because he saw it as a way to help people, right wrongs, and improve society. And he knew only one way to practice the law — go all out.

What follows is a biography of a great American trial lawyer. Rest in peace, Jim.

❖❖❖

Chapter 1

SEND A MESSAGE

THE LAWYERS IN THE HOTEL BALLROOM WERE YAWNING AND NODDING OFF AS THE seminar speaker, S. Gerald Litvin, droned on with his lecture about how to construct a closing argument. When Litvin was finally through, moderator Arthur G. Raynes got up to say a few words about the next speaker, who had pointedly asked for no introduction.

"He doesn't need an introduction," said Raynes, who proceeded to give him one anyway.

"When I was a second-year law student at Temple Law School, and clerking at Richter, Lord & Levy, we all knew he was gonna be great then," Raynes said. "And he became greater than we all thought he was gonna be."

"Here's a man who has a national reputation and still comes out to lecture to lawyers in Philadelphia, where he started," Raynes said of the man who had also been identified in the local press as having won more million-dollar verdicts than any other trial lawyer in the country.

"He has been recognized by his peers," Raynes said before ticking off a list of accolades: "Who's Who in American Law, Who's Who in the World, Who's Who in America, Who's Who, Men of Achievement."

"The only thing you haven't made, Jim," cracked Raynes, who was Jewish, "is Who's Who in Yeshiva."

When Jim Beasley came to the podium, however, he wasn't smiling at Raynes' joke, he was frowning, looking down at the ground, and carrying a white rotary telephone.

The seminar, sponsored by the Pennsylvania Trial Lawyers Association, was billed as "Masters in Trial Advocacy." Beasley's scheduled topic was the same as

Litvin's, the closing argument.

It was June 1984. Beasley, who had a silver moustache, was just a few days shy of his 58th birthday. He was dressed in a blue three-piece suit, white shirt and striped tie; a silver pocket watch dangled on his vest. He put his phone down on a nearby table and stood in front of his fellow trial lawyers. His hands were plunged in his pockets; his face looked grim.

"It's June 2, 1980," Beasley began. "It had been a warm, sunny day. It's 8:30 in the evening. You're in the living room in the home of Mr. and Mrs. Guanere. Joe Guanere and his wife are sitting out on the front stoop. The phone rings. We hear Joe say to Mrs. Guanere, 'I'll get it dear.'"

"We see Joe come in and he picks up the phone," Beasley said, grabbing the phone he brought to the podium. "'Yes, my name's Joe Guanere,'" Beasley said.

For the benefit of his audience, Beasley also provided the stern voice of the caller on the other end of the line:

"Are you the father of Joseph N. Guanere?"

"Yes, yes I am. Who's calling?"

"Is your son at home?"

"No — no, he's not, but tell me who's calling," Beasley said, as he imitated the father's nervous tone.

"This is the Lower Makefield Township Police. I'm sorry to tell you, Mr. Guanere, your son is dead. Your son was killed this evening about an hour ago in an airplane crash."

"Joe puts down the phone, unbelieving," Beasley said, lowering his phone. "His legs are rubbery; his heart is beating fast. And he denies it. 'There must be a mistake. Not my son. Not my oldest son.'

"And we step back and we watch him slowly walk to the front stoop and bring Mrs. Guanere in," Beasley said, staring at the audience. "It is the beginning, it is the end —"

It was also vintage Jim Beasley. Instead of giving a lecture on how to make a closing argument, Beasley decided to just give a closing argument instead. And not just any closing, but a re-creation of the one regarded by colleagues as the greatest of his career.

Just two weeks before his scheduled lecture to the trial lawyers, Beasley had tried the case of *Guanere et al v. Cessna* over at the federal courthouse in Camden, N.J.

Beasley was the lawyer for the lead plaintiff in the case, and after he gave his closing, the jury hammered the airplane manufacturer with a record verdict. And so Beasley decided to reprise that closing for the benefit of the lawyers on the other side of the river. And although the court files in the Cessna case have long since been destroyed, Beasley's reenactment remains on videotape. It's been an inspiration to many trial lawyers.

• • •

"BEFORE WE GO FURTHER, WE MUST GO BACK," BEASLEY SAID. "BACK TO 1966. AND WE have to go 2,000 miles away to Wichita, Kansas. And we're standing out on the ramp of Cessna's production line and we see a hangar door open," he said, sweeping his hand across the horizon toward an imaginary factory. "And we see an airplane, a brand new airplane, 3847 Lima, roll off the production line and out into the sun of a Kansas afternoon."

Beasley stared straight ahead at his audience, fidgeting with one hand. His presence was commanding, his voice slow and deliberate.

"It certainly is a pretty airplane," Beasley said, as if reciting a poem. "And it smells fresh, and it smells new," he said, pausing for effect. "And it smells of death."

While the new Cessna sat on the ramp in Kansas, Beasley said, 4-year-old Joe Guanere played on the street in South Philadelphia. Beasley asked the audience to recall where they were back in 1966. And then he talked about how the plane on the ramp would control "the destiny of the Guanere family," and also bring members of the jury, as well as Beasley himself, to "this very moment in time."

"And here we are," Beasley said. "There is another telephone call that will be made," he said, referring to the white phone that he had carried to the podium.

"Before we get to that, let's go to June 2, 1980, and the Cape May County Airport," Beasley said. "And let me shepherd you through what happened that day."

Beasley described a Cessna tied down on the ramp. "Look over there," he said, as he pointed off in the distance as if he could see Keith Harper driving into the airport. Harper, the 55-year-old superintendent of schools in Wildwood, N.J., was the pilot of the Cessna that day. He was taking his 20-year-old son, Brian, out for a ride, along with Brian's two 18-year-old friends, Joe Guanere and Thomas Cannuli.

Beasley described "some young happy men" spilling out of the car, and how proud Harper was that his son was going to fly with him that day. Harper was a conscientious pilot who "very carefully and methodically" went through a check list to make sure the plane was fit to fly, Beasley said. "What about you, Joe?" Beasley said, channeling the pilot. "You all buckled in back there?" Beasley wanted the jury to know that before he took off, Harper had checked everybody's seat belt and made sure the door was locked.

Beasley also wanted his listeners to feel the story as he told it. "You better get back a little because he's gonna turn," he said about the pilot of the Cessna. "And we don't want a lot of dust and dirt blown over us." Beasley described the plane taxiing down the runway and gently lifting into the air.

Imagine, Beasley told the audience, that they had hopped into an airplane "real quick" and were flying formation on Harper's plane, watching from above as the

Cessna flew "over the marshes and towards Wildwood Beach."

"You can almost see the young men laughing and joking and waving and point-ing to the things that they're seeing below," Beasley said. The plane hugged the shoreline before it banked inward toward land.

"Look very carefully down there," Beasley said, his voice rising, and one fore-finger pointing toward the ground. "Do you see it there on top of that house? There's a little shed and there's somebody waving, waving a white towel," he said, pantomiming the wave. "You can almost hear Mr. Harper say, 'Brian, there's your mother. See Mom down there?'"

Beasley described how the pilot gently wagged the plane's wings at Mrs. Harper, and then he banked towards the airport. A pleasant joy ride on a sunny day was coming to an end, and for the men in the plane, Beasley warned, "Time is slowly running out."

At the Cape May Airport, Keith Harper said over the radio that he was coming straight in. "Let's follow him," Beasley said. The camera videotaping Beasley's lec-ture panned the audience, showing wannabe trial lawyers leaning forward in their seats, chins on hands; some looked enthralled; others scribbled furiously in their notebooks.

Beasley described how the plane began a gentle descent as the pilot put on 10 degrees of flaps, reducing the power, and slowing the plane in preparation for landing.

"His descent is perfect," Beasley said. "He's about a hundred feet from touch-ing down on the runway.... You can see him put the throttle forward, and then the airplane takes a precipitous nose up."

Beasley rocked back on his heels; his hands were spread apart. His voice rose in volume as he described what was going on inside the cabin. "Without any warn-ing, the seat that Mr. Harper was sitting in came violently back with such force that it broke Mr. Cannuli's left leg," Beasley said. And the pilot lost control of the plane.

"The nose goes up and the airplane goes to the right," Beasley said. As for the cockpit, "We can hear the people in there screaming." The plane crashed in a wooded section off the runway. Over in the control tower, the controller called the police. Moments later, Beasley said, "we can hear the wail of a siren approach-ing the airport."

In the dense woods, a police officer needed the help of a helicopter pilot to spot the plane wreckage. Beasley described the sights and sounds in the aftermath of the crash: the helicopter hanging overhead in the sky; the "flipping of those blades in the air"; the copter pilot leaning out and pointing down at the wreckage.

Beasley described a panting police officer running through the woods, carrying a first-aid kit, as branches tore at his clothes and face. The officer reached the felled plane. "It's mangled and it's upside down," Beasley said. "We can smell gasoline. My God, what's going to happen?"

The police officer knelt beside the pilot, Keith Harper, lying beside a strut, and it was obvious that Harper was dead. So was Harper's son, Brian. The police officer administered CPR to a moaning Joe Guanere. The officer worked on Joe for several moments until his pulse was steady. The officer then turned his attention to Thomas Cannuli, whose face was "so distorted by the injuries," Beasley said, that it was impossible to perform CPR.

Joe Guanere moaned again, and his pulse faded. The police officer tried to bring him back, but it was too late. Eighteen-year-old "Joe Guanere died at that instant" in the officer's arms, Beasley told his listeners. The officer helped Cannuli, the only survivor, out of the plane, which Beasley described as a "distorted wreckage of metal and humans." Rescue workers showed up to remove the bodies.

And the police officer who had tried to save Joe Guanere's life picked up the phone to call Mr. and Mrs. Guanere and give them the bad news.

• • •

"I WAS SERVING SUBPOENAS," ARTHUR RAYNES SAID OF HIS DAYS AS A LAW CLERK AT Richter, Lord & Levy, "and Jim Beasley took me under his wing.

"It was unusual because Jim was like the angry young man of his office," Raynes said. "He didn't talk to everybody. He had his own mission that he wanted to go do. He had a little chip on his shoulder. But for some reason, he took to me."

As a young law clerk, Raynes was so shy and intimidated that "I was afraid to speak." But he was also eager to learn how to become a trial lawyer, so he latched onto Jim Beasley as a mentor. Even after Beasley left the Richter firm, Raynes would pay a visit to Beasley's home whenever he was preparing for a tough case.

"I wanted him to go over it with me," Raynes said. Beasley would review the files and then, "He started ripping me a new one," Raynes said. "You know, 'Why didn't you do this. Why didn't you do that?' That's the way he taught the things that had to be done."

Beasley also gave the young lawyer some personal advice. Raynes was the son of Russian immigrants whose given name was Arthur Rodensky, but Beasley thought it sounded too ethnic. "Why don't you change your name?," Beasley suggested. "You sound like my grandmother," Raynes said, but he took Beasley's advice. And so Arthur G. Raynes joined the ranks of Philadelphia lawyers.

In those days, the personal injury lawyers from the Philadelphia bar were "pretty rough-and-tumble guys," Raynes said. "Lots of Irish, Jews, Italians." And they didn't think much of the idea of sharing information with competitors.

Raynes recalled one old-timer's reaction to the idea of holding legal seminars.

"You're gonna give lectures to lawyers who refer us cases, 'cause they don't know how to handle them, and you're gonna teach them how to handle cases? What, are you crazy?"

But the idea slowly caught on. Local lawyers gathered at a restaurant in the same building on South Broad Street where Richter, Lord & Levy was located. "They would meet in the basement and talk about cases and the law," Raynes said. "It was the beginning of continuing education.

"They started giving lectures," Raynes said of the Philadelphia Trial Lawyers Association, founded in 1959. The Pennsylvania Trial Lawyers Association was founded a decade later, in 1968.

"The philosophy was, a pigeon on the shoulders of a giant sees farther than a giant," Raynes said. "Everybody should train everybody else."

Few trial lawyers were as generous with their knowledge as Jim Beasley. His only drawback as a speaker, Raynes said, was a lack of humor. "He didn't have the timing. I told him, 'Jim, stick to trying cases. You can't tell jokes.'"

• • •

JIM BEASLEY TOLD HIS FELLOW LAWYERS THAT CESSNA HAD MANUFACTURED MORE THAN 175,000 airplanes with the same defective pilot's seat that killed Keith Harper, his son, Brian, and Joe Guanere. An extensive paper trail documented the fatal defect, Beasley said, but Cessna chose to ignore it.

"I will not trespass on your time," Beasley said, to detail the 10 National Transportation Safety Board reports about pilots killed as a result of similar accidents, where seats came off track, causing the pilots to lose control of their planes.

"Nor will I trespass on your time," Beasley said, to go over all of the "airworthiness alerts" that repeatedly called to Cessna's attention "the inherent danger" of the defective pilot seats.

Beasley said it was his burden of proof to establish "a fair preponderance of the evidence" for compensatory damages. "What is a fair preponderance of the evidence?" Beasley took his audience back to the days when there used to be general stores on every street corner in Philadelphia.

Customers would walk into the store and ask for "five pounds of beans or sugar," Beasley said. The grocer would place a five-pound weight on one side of the scale, Beasley said. And then he pantomimed a low scooping motion, as he described how the grocer would fill a sack on the other side of the scale with beans or sugar. Beasley held up two level hands to show how the grocer kept scooping until the two scales were balanced.

If the grocer dipped his fingers into the bin and added an "imperceptible few grains" to the sack on the scale, Beasley said, wiggling his fingers for emphasis, it would cause the preponderance of weight to shift to that side of the scale. Beasley went through the evidence in his case, and said the testimony he presented to the jury showed that he had added "more than just a pinch of sugar."

Beasley described how he brought a more durable pilot's seat into the courtroom, one available to Cessna for 14 years, and he demonstrated "the absolute safety of the seat." He also brought into the courthouse the mangled wreck of the Cessna that Joe Guanere died in, so that jurors could inspect it

"Come, members of the jury," Beasley said, his voice booming, his hands beckoning. "I want you to come out of the jury box. Because I have this airplane here and I'm gonna point out things and I don't want anybody standing up looking over somebody else's shoulder. I want you to see it firsthand… Now you see why this airplane crashed on this day."

Beasley reminded the audience that at trial Cessna did not refute the testimony of any of his expert witnesses. He also spoke about how Cessna did not produce any of its own engineers to testify, but instead had relied on "hired guns," two outside experts from Florida "who neither investigated any of these accidents . . . and who only recently took the time to view this wreckage.

"Indeed," Beasley said, his voice rising in indignation, the jury "spent more time looking at this wreckage" than Cessna's "$80-an-hour experts."

When it came time to assess punitive damages, Beasley talked about the "clear and convincing evidence that this company requires immediate and severe punishment now for conduct that has existed for 16 years . . . conduct that has brought these young men to an early grave."

His eyes were blazing, and he repeatedly jabbed one finger toward the ground, pistol style, for emphasis.

It was time to talk money. Beasley said if he was worth $10, and the jury brought back a punitive verdict of $1, "that would hurt a lot." But if he had $100,000 and the punitive verdict was only $1, "I'd laugh at you," he said. It would be cheaper to pay the punitive verdict than fix the problem.

Beasley mentioned Cessna's net worth — $327 million — and said there were "327 million reasons why they should be punished." And then he instructed the jury on exactly how to punish the defendant: "You're going to do it by bringing in a substantial — and when I say substantial, I mean a *substantial* award of punitive damages," he commanded.

"It should be so substantial," he said, jabbing one hand in the air, "that when your verdict is announced, as it will be tomorrow, this lawyer sitting over there representing Cessna," he said, gesturing behind him toward Raynes, "is going to make that other telephone call that I told you about.

"He's going to walk out to the telephone in the corridor, and he's going to pick it up," Beasley said, grabbing his prop phone and walking across the stage. "And he's going to say, 'Operator, get me Mr. Cessna in Wichita, Kansas."

People in the audience chuckled, but Beasley didn't even crack a smile.

"Mr. Cessna, the folks from South Jersey have arrived at their verdict," Beasley said, as he paced the ballroom floor. Suddenly he stopped, and brandished the phone at the audience, waving it for emphasis.

"Now you talk to Mr. Cessna," he yelled at the trial lawyers. "You give him a message that makes *his* knees rubbery, that causes his heart to beat fast."

Beasley hung up the phone. "And you do it in a clear, precise way so that when your verdict is recorded, and you walk out into the street and you look up into the clear skies of New Jersey," Beasley said, pointing upward, "and you see an airplane go over, you can say I may have saved your life."

Beasley reminded the jury about the fate of 18-year-old Joe Guanere. "This young boy cries out from eternal darkness for justice," he said. "Thank you."

The audience erupted in applause. Beasley turned his back to the crowd and fiddled with the microphone around his neck. "I can't get this thing off," he said. A smiling Raynes, shaking his head in admiration, removed Beasley's mike.

"That's it," Raynes said from the podium. "I'm sure you enjoyed it as much as we did. Thank you."

• • •

ON JUNE 8, 1984, IN CAMDEN, N.J., THE FEDERAL JURY IN THE CESSNA CASE RETURNED a $29-million verdict against the airplane manufacturer, $25 million of which was punitive damages. At the time, it was the highest-ever verdict against an aviation company. The case subsequently settled for $13 million.

• • •

JAMES F. MUNDY USED TO HAVE HIS OWN VIDEOTAPE OF THE BEASLEY CLOSING IN THE Cessna case before he lent it to somebody who never gave it back. Mundy still drives around in his car listening to Beasley's audiotaped lectures. "This was my idol," Mundy explained. "Everything I am, I am because of Beasley."

Mundy, a partner at Raynes McCarty, was a former president of the Pennsylvania State Bar Association, a former president of both the Philadelphia and the Pennsylvania Trial Lawyers Associations, and a past winner of the Justice Michael A. Musmanno Memorial Award from the Philadelphia Trial Lawyers Association.

But in 1970, Mundy was just a 26-year-old law clerk at the Richter firm when he first saw Jim Beasley in a courtroom. It was a lasting impression.

Beasley was picking a jury for a case that involved the family of a brain-damaged infant that was suing a team of doctors. "In those days at Ninth Street, there was one big jury room," Mundy said. "All the juries got picked out of the same room, and ahead of us were Frank Shields [the top defense lawyer of the day] and Jim Beasley.

"And from the voir dire alone, I knew this case could not possibly be won by the plaintiff," Mundy said. "There was not a prayer."

Back at the office, the young law clerk excitedly told his boss, B. Nathaniel "Nate" Richter, about his day in court, and the long odds Beasley faced. Richter told Mundy to go back to the courthouse and watch the rest of the trial. "You'll be of more value to me if you go down and watch that case than anything you're doing around here," Richter told Mundy.

"For 10 days, I was paid to watch Jim Beasley," Mundy recalled. "I remember seeing things that amazed me."

The mother of the brain-damaged baby was about eight-months pregnant when she was brought into the infectious-disease ward of Albert Einstein Hospital with infectious colitis, Mundy said. The mother began a spontaneous delivery. A nurse crossed the mother's legs in a crude attempt to prevent the birth, until the mother could be wheeled to the obstetrics ward. The result: a brain-damaged infant.

"It was a very different world in those days," Mundy said. Beasley didn't have a claim against the hospital, because hospitals at the time were considered charitable institutions, immune from liability. So Beasley sued the woman's regular doctors, who had been called while she was in the hospital, and didn't bother to go see her.

Beasley didn't have much of a case, Mundy said, but he was incredibly well-prepared and quick on his feet. After a court recess, Beasley put one of the defense's expert witnesses on the stand and asked him, "Isn't it true when you were out in the hall, you went up to Mr. Shields during this recess and said, 'I've got some more goodies for you.' Is that true?"

The doctor began to hem and haw, saying he didn't recall using those exact words. Beasley, Mundy said, seized the moment: "Doctor, could you tell this court what are goodies in a case involving a 6-year-old brain-damaged boy? What's a goodie?"

Mundy scanned the jury's faces and saw looks of anger and disgust.

Beasley had a bookshelf in the courtroom covered by a big red blanket. He stood in front of it and challenged a defense expert to cite the medical textbooks that backed his testimony. The witness named five or six books. Beasley whipped off the red blanket, and all the books that the doctor had named, and many he hadn't, were right there on the bookshelf. "Now, you said *Agnes on Obstetrics*?" Beasley said, yanking out the text. Every volume on the shelf was bookmarked.

"Now, open to the bookmark, doctor, and read it out loud to the jury," Beasley said. The book, Mundy recalled, said "the opposite of what the doctor said."

Thirty-five years after the trial, Mundy could still see Beasley in that courtroom. "I still remember the suits that had a split on the side and the square shoulders," Mundy said. "He was in absolute command of that courtroom…. He was very handsome," Mundy said. And fit. "He was looking like he could go 15 rounds if he had to."

When the defense witnesses gave testimony damaging to Beasley's case, Mundy looked over at Beasley, sitting by himself at the plaintiff's table.

"He had a box of pencils" spilled out on the table, Mundy recalled. "He licked the erasers and he stood up the erasers one at a time until they [the pencils] all stood up and when he got to about 10, they would collapse and he would make no noise and grab them," Mundy said. "He'd put them down and start the process again. And the jury is looking at him and the pencils, and they're not even looking at this expert."

The jury of six men and six women told the judge several times that they were deadlocked, but the judge kept sending them back to deliberate. "In those days, everybody wore shirts and ties on juries, not like today," Mundy said. The jury came back to the courtroom to talk to the judge one last time. And the jury foreman had a huge brown stain covering the front and back of his shirt.

"The jury was deadlocked six-six," Mundy said. "The six women were for the plaintiff, the six men were for the defendants. And one of the women had gotten so angry," Mundy said, that she grabbed a pot of coffee — fortunately, it was cold — "and poured it over this jury foreman.

"And the jury foreman said, 'Your Honor, we are deadlocked,' and they were dismissed," Mundy said. In spite of the deadlocked jury, "Beasley told me years later when I talked to him that the case settled for a million dollars, and I believe him," Mundy said.

Mundy had no idea before the trial what he was going to do with his life. But after he saw Jim Beasley in a courtroom, Mundy decided he had to become a trial lawyer. He also found a mentor.

"I will tell you from that day on, whenever Jim Beasley's name would appear in a seminar, I was there," Mundy said. "I didn't care what the seminar was about," Mundy said. "If his name was there, I went."

Mundy showed up at so many events, he eventually became friends with Beasley. And that led to a plane ride.

About a year after Beasley's speech to the trial lawyers, Beasley, a veteran pilot, offered to fly Mundy and another lawyer back to Philadelphia from a conference they had all attended in Pittsburgh. On the ride over to the airport where Beasley kept his private plane, Mundy told the other lawyer about Beasley's re-creation of his closing in the Cessna case, and how great it was.

The three lawyers arrived at the airport, and Mundy saw Beasley's plane.

"Jim, that's funny, you're in a Cessna," Mundy said. "Isn't that the same kind that was in the —"

Beasley cut him off. "Exactly the same kind," he said.

Mundy looked at Beasley. "So you modified it so the seat doesn't come back?"

"Nope," Beasley said.

"You son of a bitch," Mundy said.

Mundy climbed into the back seat of the plane, directly behind the pilot, and jammed both his knees into Beasley's back.

"Get used to the knees, pal," Mundy told Beasley, "'cause they're not moving."

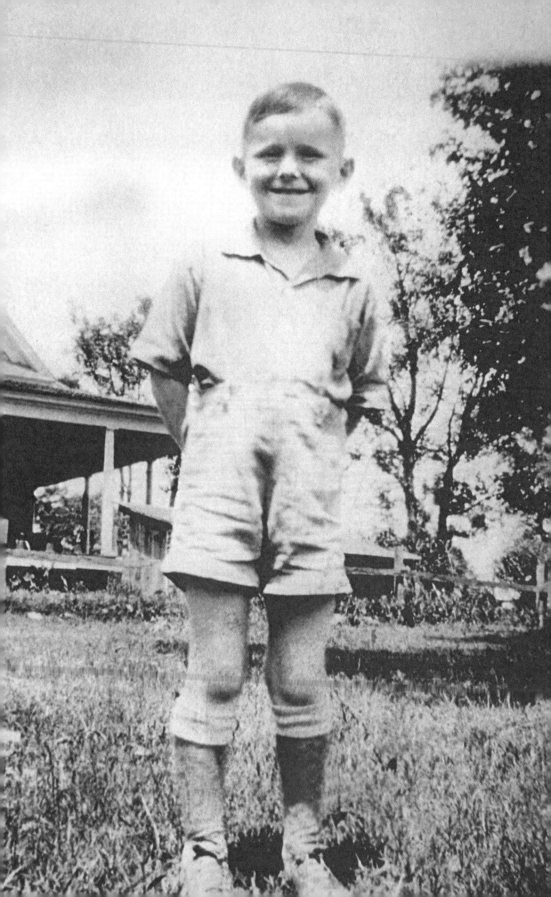

❖❖❖

Chapter 2

MISSISSIPPI HOT

IN THE COURTROOM, JIM BEASLEY WAS A SUPERSTAR WHO MADE IT ALL SEEM EFFORTLESS, whether he was charming a jury or cutting an expert witness off at the knees.

"It was like watching Willie Mays play baseball when I was a kid," said Philadelphia Common Pleas Court Judge Mark I. Bernstein. "I've had a lot of great lawyers in my courtroom. With the other lawyers, I could see them working and thinking." But when Beasley tried a case, the judge said, he was so relaxed, he acted "like he was sitting on a log, fishing."

When he spoke in court, Beasley didn't use notes, preferring to read people's faces. He was also big on making eye contact with individual jurors.

"I used to swear up and down that he practiced hypnosis, but I could never prove it," said James L. Griffith, a top Philadelphia defense lawyer. "He used to just stare at the jury."

And the jurors stared back. They watched and smiled or giggled as Beasley played tricks with the pencils on his desk. Or they talked about Beasley's whimsical collection of designer ties, like the one with the gold monkeys, or the blue pigs in blankets, or the blue ducks wearing red sneakers.

Outside the courtroom, however, Beasley could be aloof. "He was not a warm and fuzzy guy," recalled James E. Colleran, a top Philadelphia plaintiffs lawyer. Before he founded his own law firm, Colleran worked for Beasley for 25 years; at least half that time, Colleran occupied the office next to Beasley's. The two men didn't socialize much, but Colleran recalled one deep-sea fishing trip back in September 1969 at the Jersey shore.

They agreed to meet at 6 a.m. sharp in front of Beasley's house in Philadelphia. Colleran arrived a minute late, and Beasley was "already in his monster Cadillac, at the edge of the driveway, lights blazing, ready to roll." He took off without a word, and Colleran, driving a tiny French Simca, "could barely keep up." Beasley roared down the Atlantic City Expressway. Colleran had the Simca floored, but, "It was a struggle for me to keep him in sight."

Beasley got to the marina at Stone Harbor first; Colleran arrived 10 minutes later. They picked up Beasley's boat and went trolling for bluefish. "We were out in the middle of the ocean," Colleran said. "We'd go out there and just idle and wait for some fish to come on by. Jim, even in that relaxed recreational setting, was very shy and quiet. Oftentimes there would be periods of silence. . . . He was a very quiet, introspective individual."

But Beasley was also known for grandstand stunts such as posing as one of the figures on a five-story-high mural painted on the back of his office building, or standing on his desk in cowboy boots for the benefit of a photographer from Philadelphia magazine.

"He was constantly trying to show us he was the best there was, but we already knew that," said Sheldon L. Albert, a former Beasley law partner from 1960 to 1971, who subsequently became Philadelphia's city solicitor. Albert said he never understood what motivated Beasley to keep working so hard.

"You know that phrase 'driven by demons?'" Albert said. "I think that applies here, I mean in a good sense. But something drove Jim that was known only to himself. Money didn't satisfy Jim. Prestige didn't. Nothing satisfied him completely."

"I think that he was always trying to prove something," Colleran agreed. "And his clients benefited by that quirk in his personality."

If the defense had a witness on the stand who was killing him, Beasley maintained a poker face while he played with his pencils, as if whatever the witness had to say didn't really matter. He wanted people to think he was invulnerable.

When Beasley had triple-bypass heart surgery in 1992, he didn't even tell his family or his law partners. Colleran heard about it a week later, from a guy on the street. Beasley had secretly flown to Cleveland for the operation. "Nobody in the office knew he had bypass surgery," Colleran marveled. "He didn't want anybody to know he had any kind of a weakness. He was a very strange guy."

Beasley continued to try cases well into his 70s, working 18-hour days, and winning some of his biggest verdicts. He was always the first person in the office, typically arriving at 6 a.m. When a friendly judge asked if it was time to think about slowing down, Beasley said, "Don't you understand? This is what I do." Rivals joked he would die in the courtroom.

His son, who practiced law with his father, didn't do anything to dampen the speculation. "Dad's not gonna retire," Jim Jr. told rival lawyers. "We're gonna carry him out in a box."

Beasley's prickly personality and workaholic ways didn't make for a happy home life. He was divorced by two wives, and estranged at times from his five children.

Jim Jr. was often asked to explain the riddle of his father. "He was a combination of a hit man and a scared 5-year-old boy. It was one or the other," Jim Jr. said. "He was very sensitive. He would get hurt very easily."

Beasley, however, would take the stuff that gnawed at him and use it for motivation. "You should be glad that I'm neurotic," he told his daughter, Pam, a psychiatrist. "Well-adjusted people settle for mediocrity."

In his later years, friends and family saw more of Beasley's sensitive side: the flower nut who planted thousands of tulips at his Villanova estate; the romantic who picked out mushy cards and wrote love notes to the women in his life; the philanthropist who donated $20 million to Temple University to benefit the Law School, promptly renamed the Beasley School of Law.

Beasley wanted his epitaph to be the poor kid who made it so big he could afford full scholarships worth more than $20,000 annually for hundreds of needy law students, so they wouldn't have to struggle the way he did.

"I think his childhood was really traumatic," Pam said. Underneath the tough exterior, and all the success and relentless drive, she said, Jim Beasley was "a scared, traumatized kid" who hid his vulnerability.

He had plenty to run away from: the poverty and tragedy of his youth, a World War, and a legal scrape of his own that almost resulted in a military court-martial.

• • •

IN THE SUMMER OF 1936, "JIMMIE" BEASLEY WAS JUST A 10-YEAR-OLD STREET KID FROM West Philly riding in the back seat of his father's big black Cadillac LaSalle, staring out the window at passing sharecropper shacks, grazing cows and cotton fields.

Jimmie was out of school, but he wasn't on vacation. His father, Jim Sr., an out-of-work machinist and sometime taxi driver, was at the wheel, heading south on a 1,000-mile journey.

The elder Beasley was a slender six-footer with a blond pompadour and a long, thin face. He had moved from Buffalo, where Jimmie was born, to Philadelphia, looking for work, but he didn't have much success.

"In the middle of the Depression . . . the best my unemployed dad could do was a Pullman kitchen and a Murphy bed," Jim Beasley wrote in a brief memoir of his youth.

In a crowded one-bedroom apartment on 52nd Street in West Philadelphia, Jim Sr., his wife, Margaret, and their 8-year-old daughter, Peggy, all shared the same Murphy bed that unfolded from the wall. Jimmie Jr. slept on the couch. The Pullman kitchen was as narrow as the railroad car it was named after. The only air-conditioning in the place was a small fan that didn't always work.

"An unemployed dad has time on his hands," Beasley wrote. So Jim Sr. told his wife, "I'm taking the kids to Pontotoc for the summer." Pontotoc — an Indian word that meant "The Land of Hanging Grapes" — was in northern Mississippi, where Jimmie's grandmother lived on a 100-acre farm. The small agricultural town of 3,000 was tucked between Tupelo, home of Elvis Presley (born the year before, in 1935), and Oxford, home of the University of Mississippi.

Margaret Beasley, a waitress, stayed behind because she was the only family member with a job. Jimmie shared the back seat of the Caddy with his kid sister.

"In the hot summer, the trip on the two-lane road tortured and meandered endlessly through countryside, and it seemed to a 10-year-old that Pontotoc was beyond reach," Beasley wrote of his father's annual Southern migration.

Jim Sr. strictly observed local speed limits as he drove his box-shaped 1932 jalopy outfitted with running boards, clamshell bumpers, and bug-eyed headlights. The trip to Pontotoc began on a Friday night and didn't end until Monday morning. The Beasleys couldn't afford hotels. "The nights were spent in the car," Beasley wrote. "Dad slept in front; my sister and I stretched out on the seat in the back."

"At Al's gas station, we turned off onto a gravel road, and a mile and a half on the right was a yellow and white house with a Southern-style wrap-around porch," Beasley wrote. "It was not vacation time. School was in the fall, but now it was pickin' cotton time."

Jimmie walked between low rows of crops, dragging a sack along the ground, while his "less than nimble fingers" plucked cotton balls and tried to avoid thorns. It was a big adjustment for a city kid. "I wouldn't have known a cow before I got down there if I ran over one," Beasley said. "It was like falling into another world. You adapted."

The farm in Mississippi had an outhouse, and no running water or electricity. The weather also took some getting used to. "Philadelphia hot cannot compare with Mississippi hot," Beasley wrote. As the summer wore on, Jimmie milked cows, cut firewood, and fed chickens.

"The first Monday of the month was a treat," Beasley wrote. He hitched two mules to a wagon and rode to town, accompanied by the cows and chickens that he hoped to trade.

Jimmie was smaller than the Southern farm boys, and he also had a language barrier. "I couldn't understand this other English language and they couldn't understand me," he wrote. "I hadn't gotten the hang of 'you all' yet, and the Yankee 'tow truck' was a 'wrecker' down here."

The first time he said tow truck down South, "Everybody laughed," Beasley said in an interview. "I was humiliated."

Growing up in both Philadelphia and Pontotoc gave Jimmie Beasley a chance to explore two distinct cultures, and to learn how to talk to people from all walks of life. But it also cemented his status as an outsider. Jimmie was already undersized and dirt poor; down South, he was also a damn Yankee. And whenever he went back up North, they called him a damn rebel because of the Southern accent that had crept into his speech.

But Jimmie was resilient, a tough guy with a sturdy build, auburn hair and freckles. He wore knickers in family photos and flashed a mischievous smile along with a confidence that transcended his circumstances. Because, besides poverty, a dark shadow hovered over his family, especially the males named James Edwin Beasley.

The first James Edwin Beasley, Jimmie's paternal grandfather, was a local celebrity in the village of Ora, Miss., where he was "the mayor, sheriff and Elmer Gantry-style preacher," Jim Beasley wrote. The first James E. Beasley married Miss Nannie McGuffee in 1883, according to county records in Mississippi, and was appointed mayor of the lumber-mill town in a 1901 proclamation signed by Mississippi Gov. A.H. Longino.

"He was a helluva preacher," Beasley said of his grandfather. "He used to fill that tent." But he didn't live long. "He was young, close to 40, and my father was only 2 or 3 when he died. He was kicked in the chest by a mule."

Before the first half of the 20th century was over, two more James Edwin Beasleys would also die tragically, leaving Jimmie as the lone survivor of the name.

· · ·

JIMMIE DIDN'T HAVE A BROTHER TO HANG OUT WITH AS A KID, BUT HE DID HAVE A favorite cousin. Walter Woodworth was born the same day as Jimmie, July 2, 1926, although Woodworth always claimed he showed up 15 minutes earlier.

When Woodworth was 11, and again at 12, he made the annual summer trek down to Pontotoc, piling into Uncle Jim's LaSalle along with the rest of the Beasleys. "My Uncle Jim, he loved that car," Woodworth said.

Jimmie was a prankster, and many of his jokes were on Cousin "Walder," as Jimmie always referred to him, deliberately mispronouncing his name. Once, on the long trip from Philadelphia to Pontotoc, Jimmie talked Walter into opening the back door of the LaSalle while his father was driving, just to see what would happen. The back doors on the four-door LaSalle sedan were "suicide doors" that opened toward the front.

Cousin Walter opened the door and the draft sucked him right out of the car. He ended up "hanging outside, watching the highway go by," Woodworth said, while Jimmie's kid sister screamed "bloody murder." Uncle Jim calmly slowed down, got out of the car, and helped Walter back inside.

"He was a humorous character," Woodworth said of Jimmie, who was as close as a twin brother. "We just had fun all the time."

Down on the farm, Jimmie's grandmother, Nancy McGuffee Beasley, was a tiny, independent woman who dipped snuff and used to ring a chicken's neck by swinging the bird over her head. Jimmie idolized her, friends and family members said, and she in turn always stuck up for him.

After she was widowed at an early age, Jimmie's grandmother married H.Y. "Pa" Hardin, a pale former schoolteacher who wore a straw hat in the sun and suffered from high blood pressure. Jimmie's grandmother moved to Pa Hardin's farm with its three barns and smokehouse. Hardin rented out most of his land, but still tended to chores.

"I remembered his grandfather killed a cow," Woodworth said. "That terrified me. I thought the man was a gentle person. He took a sledgehammer and hit the cow in the head. I was mortified."

Jimmie had the messy job of slaughtering the hogs. "You'd shoot the hog in the forehead, hang him up by his feet, cut the throat, and let all the blood drain out into a 50-gallon drum," Beasley said. Then he'd drop the hog in boiling water to remove the hair.

When the city boys milked cows, Jimmie knew how to get a laugh out of his cousin. "'Watch this, Walder,' he would say, and he'd squirt the milk at me," Woodworth said.

Jimmie had a run-in with a Southern bully, whom he described as a "farm boy from the other side of town."

"He carried the name Darwin Beasley, and a Yankee was not about to be allowed the same name," Beasley wrote. "The fact that he was a head taller than me certainly gave him a confidence, which he didn't need, to challenge me to meet him in the town square Saturday night."

The scheduled bout got a lot of publicity. "It seemed that all 3,000 inhabitants got wind that the South would be coming Saturday night to get its revenge for the 1865 loss to the North," Beasley wrote. "That's a heavy load for a little kid."

When Jimmie's grandmother heard about it, she said "she had enough of that testosterone nonsense," and she reminded Jimmie about his legacy as the grandson of the former mayor, sheriff and preacher. "You are not about to track into town for an anti-Christian purpose, and besides, the Beasleys over yonder were poor dirt sharecroppers," his grandmother said. She wanted Jimmie to call off the fight, but he decided to go through with it.

"If I didn't trek into town, by default the South, at least in Pontotoc, would have redeemed itself" for the Civil War, Beasley wrote. When he saw Darwin

Beasley that night, his heart sank. "There he was in the middle of the square, now looking bigger than simply a head taller," Beasley wrote. But he didn't back down.

The actual fight was a disappointment. "As the crowd slowly melted away," Beasley wrote, "there was no winner; in fact it wasn't even a fight — more a boxing match. In a small way, I did win, I showed up. Very frightened, but there."

It was the same attitude Jimmie would bring into the courtrooms of Philadelphia, not intimidated by bigger opponents.

On the farm in Mississippi, bathing was a supervised activity. "You took a bath once a week whether you needed it or not," Beasley said. He would sit in a galvanized tub while his grandmother did the scrubbing. "You've got enough dirt behind your ears," she would say, "to grow potatoes."

At night, the kids played rook, a card game, by the light of the fireplace while Grandma played piano, or they'd listen to the Grand Old Opry on a battery-powered radio. Then it was time for Pa Hardin to read his Bible by the light of a kerosene lamp.

"We would all sit around," Woodworth recalled. "He'd read it for an hour. With certain verses, he would say, 'Listen up, boys.' And he'd read us a verse. 'Now, do you understand that?'

"Yes, sir," the boys would say. "When Pa Hardin closed that Bible," Woodworth said, "that was the cue for us to go to bed."

· · ·

In the fall, back in Philadelphia, Jimmie and Cousin Walter amused themselves by shoplifting from the Woolworth's five-and-dime. Walter distracted the cashier while Jimmie filled his pockets with candy. Then Jimmie engaged the cashier while Walter loaded up.

The boys also had a habit of snatching freshly delivered bottles of milk and loaves of bread off rowhouse doorsteps. An angry man once chased the two boys down the street, and pinned Jimmie facedown on the ground with a boot planted on the posterior.

Jimmie had to fake some tears and tell a tall tale about his poor starving mother to get him and Cousin Walter off the hook. Woodworth was amazed by Jimmie's powers of persuasion. "You're a good actor," Woodworth told his cousin. "You ought to go into the movies."

"He always had the smoothest talk," Woodworth said. "The adults, he would win them over. He would knock people dead with that smile of his: 'Please let us go, we'll never do it again.' He always got us into a predicament. But he always got us out."

When Jimmie and Cousin Walter got bored with big city life, they tried several times to run away to Mississippi on bicycles. Once, they packed some sandwiches and rode a few miles along what was then known as East River Drive, along the Schuylkill River in Fairmount Park, when they heard a horn blowing. "We stopped and turned around. It was my father," Beasley recalled. "That was another whipping we got."

The boys thought school was a bore, so they played hooky. When Jimmie and Walter were 13 and attending Gillespie Junior High, they were absent from school a total of 78 days, Woodworth said. The school sent a letter home to the Beasleys and the Woodworths, requesting that the adults accompany their sons to school every morning, to make sure they got there.

In the early 1940s, Jimmie moved to Mississippi to stay year-round. He attended school and helped his aging grandparents work the farm, according to a 1988 interview he gave Philadelphia magazine. The family was so poor that young Jimmie walked to elementary school in overalls and bare feet. School began every day with the Southern boys and girls standing and singing "Dixie."

"Of course, schools were segregated, and I felt segregated in language," Beasley wrote. So were the movie theaters. Jimmie and Cousin Walter used to sit with the whites down in front, watching cowboy movies, while all the blacks sat up in the balcony.

Growing up in Mississippi, Jimmie adapted to the seasonal rhythms of farm life. "I not only picked cotton, but when the spring came, you had to plant corn; that ground had to be turned," he said. "They had what was called a turning plow. You hitched the mule up to it and turned the ground over."

Jimmie's childhood came to an abrupt end, however, when his father contracted tuberculosis, the scourge of the day. The March 22, 1942, edition of the Philadelphia Record reported "an acute shortage of municipal hospital facilities for the tubercular," which amounted to a "standing menace to the public health."

The city's Hospital for Contagious Diseases had "too few attendants to keep the 'incorrigibles' from wandering away and mingling with the public," the newspaper said.

On Christmas Eve 1942, The Philadelphia Evening Bulletin reported that a new surge of tuberculosis was feared as local doctors and nurses were being drafted into the Army. At Philadelphia General Hospital, the newspaper reported, staffing was so low that approximately 400 tubercular patients had to share the services of five part-time interns.

Jim Beasley Sr. ended up in a tuberculosis ward in 1943 at the University of Pennsylvania Hospital. Young Jimmie was summoned back to Philadelphia, "Every Wednesday, we'd go to see Uncle Jim at the same hospital," Walter Woodworth recalled. Jimmie's father stayed in a big room with 50 beds on each side. "Everybody was sick with TB," Woodworth said. "Uncle Jimmie, he got thinner and thinner."

The visits were tough on young Jimmie, who was upset that his father was stuck in a pauper's ward and couldn't afford better medical care. "He always went there and tried to be happy," Woodworth said of Cousin Jimmie. "He thought it was his duty."

The elder Beasley "was coughing and he was gasping for breath," Woodworth said. "He'd get in a spell, and Jimmie would say, 'Let's go.'" But the weekly visits continued.

"We thought he was getting better," Woodworth said. "But then my mother told me to go to the hospital to say goodbye to your Uncle Jim, because he's dying."

"They took him out of the ward and put him in a private room," Woodworth said. Jimmie and Walter stood at the foot of the bed. "Aunt Marge was upset, and I started crying and ran out of the room," Walter said. "Jimmie came after me. I said, 'I'm sorry, Jimmie, I couldn't take it anymore,' and he said, 'I know, Walder.'"

Jimmie, however, shed no tears. "I knew he was angry, but he suppressed it. I knew he was really tormented by it," Woodworth said. James E. Beasley Sr. was only 42.

• • •

AFTER HIS FATHER'S DEATH, IN APRIL 1943, "WE WERE QUITE POOR," BEASLEY WROTE IN an autobiographical 1994 letter to the New York State Supreme Court. "I, as the only son, was now the man of the house. Being 16, with zero skills, it was a tough role to fill."

World War II was raging, and Jimmie decided to join the Navy, as his father had done, so he could send home a steady paycheck of $50 a month to his mother, or, in the event of his death, $10,000. The only problem was Jimmie's age.

Walter Woodworth was in the wood shop at Dobbins Tech when Jimmie, who attended nearby Overbrook High School, appeared in the doorway. "It was nothing unusual for him to show up at my school and signal to me, 'let's go,'" Walter said.

He thought his cousin wanted to play hooky again. "Where we going, Jimmie?" Walter asked. "We're going to join the Navy," Jimmie announced. Walter thought it was a bad idea, but Jimmie said it was smarter than waiting to get drafted by the Army and then getting slaughtered on some battlefield in Europe.

Jimmie and Walter went down to the Armory at 30th and Market Streets. "They told me to get undressed, 'You're gonna take a physical,'" Walter said. It took three hours and they had to strip naked. Walter didn't even have pubic hair yet. "I was so mortified," he said.

Jimmie used some ink eraser on his birth certificate to change his birthday from July 2, 1926, to Jan. 2, 1926, so he could be 17. An officer looked at the document and asked, "How old are you kids?" Jimmie's reply was, "None of your fucking business." The boys were rejected, but the officer said if they really wanted to join the service, they should come back 10 days before their 17th birthday.

When the boys returned to the Armory at the appointed time, they were told they still needed their parents' permission to enlist. "C'mon, Walder," Jimmie said,

"We gotta get these papers signed. C'mon Walder, we're gonna get in the Navy."

"What the devil are you getting us into?" Woodworth asked, but the plan was already in motion. The recruiter had promised the boys that they would stay together in the Navy. But Jimmie wound up as part of an armed guard on ships crossing the North Atlantic with cargos of high-octane gasoline, on the way to Russia, England and Scotland. Woodworth, meanwhile, was stationed on a destroyer in the Pacific.

·   ·   ·

IN AUGUST 1943, JIMMIE AND COUSIN WALTER WERE HOME ON LEAVE, DRESSED IN THEIR Navy whites. They were sitting at the counter of Walgreen's Drug Store, at 12th and Market Streets, drinking sodas when Jimmie spotted a couple of girls in a nearby booth, eating ice cream sundaes.

"They turned around and looked at us," recalled Gloria Fletcher, who was with her friend Doris. "I was facing them." Jimmie did the talking: "Can we sit with you?"

Gloria was the petite, dark-haired daughter of Phillip Facenda, a clarinet player who had changed his name to Phil Fletcher. His band was known as the Wild Canaries, and the musicians in the band, according to a 1922 photo in Downbeat magazine, included Jimmy and Tommy Dorsey.

Gloria was 19 and weighed only 89 pounds, but she had her admirers. A trio of fans, one of whom later became a priest, collaborated on a 1943 poem in Gloria's honor:

> *She's four-foot ten, her eyes are brown*
> *And she looks OK in a strapless gown*
> *Her hair is dark, and smooth as silk*
> *And her skin is as pure as a quart of milk…*

Jimmie was smitten; "Can we sit with you?" turned into "Can we take you home?" Gloria and Doris took the 36 trolley, which ran along Glenwood Avenue in Southwest Philadelphia. Jimmie turned to Walter and said, "Gloria wants to know if you're gonna take Doris home." Gloria, of course, had made no such request, but when Doris and Walter got off at 63rd and Elmwood, Jimmie rode with Gloria until the last stop, at 73st and Elmwood.

Jimmie had just lost his father to tuberculosis; Gloria's mother would die a month after they met, in September 1943, of the same disease. At the time, Gloria was working as a routing clerk for Western Union, riding around the office at 11th and Locust on roller skates. "You've got pretty legs," Jimmie told her.

"He was a nice-looking fella, but I was engaged to somebody else," Gloria recalled in an interview. "Can I write to you?" she remembers Jimmie asking. When he returned to the Navy, Jimmie sent her a letter, and she wrote him back, saying, "I don't remember what you look like."

"I have red hair," he replied.

• • •

ON CHRISTMAS EVE 1943, A HOMESICK 17-YEAR-OLD JIMMIE BEASLEY GOT INTO TROUBLE with the Navy brass. He had returned to Philadelphia on a three-day leave to check on his mother, spending her first Christmas as a widow.

"When I arrived home, I found my mother suffering from a severe depression and the doctor was quite concerned," Beasley wrote in his 1994 letter to the New York Supreme Court. Beasley wrote the letter to explain a summary court-martial listed on his service records in 1944 for being AWOL for 23 days. The matter came up a half-century later when Beasley applied for admission to the New York State bar. Beasley said in his letter that the records were mistaken, he had never been AWOL, and that he had informed his superiors of his whereabouts.

"My mother was admitted to the hospital for a few days to a week," Beasley wrote. "I tended to my sister, who was at home alone." Beasley wrote that his superiors told him to report his situation to a shore patrol officer, which he did. When he reported for duty, he was summoned to a hearing for "a summary offense, not a summary court-martial," Beasley wrote. "I told my story as set out above; a doctor's certificate was requested and produced."

The future lawyer could only watch helplessly on Feb. 22, 1944, while Navy officials deliberated his fate. It was a motivating factor no doubt in the way he would zealously represent his future clients. "There was quite a heated debate whether any charges should be heard at all," Beasley wrote. "I sat there, 17 years old, confused as to what was happening. I had done nothing wrong. I was told I was free to go and that a small fine would be levied."

"I returned to duty, not realizing that a distorted record was to remain," Beasley wrote. "I can only suspect that the original papers did, indeed, include a Summary Court-Martial offense. The matter went on to a hearing, and the records were not changed to reflect what actually occurred.

"I find significant support for this in the fact that there was a mitigation finding," Beasley wrote. "That could be the result of proof that what I did was right. At that time in our history, in the middle of the war, men who intentionally went AWOL for 23 days went to jail," Beasley wrote.

Instead, he was fined $33 a month for six months, but two members of the court made a "plea for clemency," according to Beasley's military records. The sentence was mitigated to $33 a month for four months, or $132.

"If whatever happened 50 years ago is sufficient to prevent me from being licensed to practice in New York State — so be it," Beasley wrote the New York Supreme Court. "I did nothing wrong then; I served my country honorably and well.

"I certainly was not privy to these records for if I was, I would not have allowed them to go unchallenged," Beasley wrote. After reviewing his letter, the New York State bar admitted Beasley to practice law.

• • •

JIMMIE AND GLORIA HAD DECIDED TO ELOPE WHEN JIMMIE CAME HOME ON LEAVE. THEY were married on Feb. 26, 1944, in Elkton, Md., before a justice of the peace. Gloria had bought a couple of $10 wedding bands and a $3 marriage license on her Western Union salary of $19 a week. Jimmie, listed on his military ID as 5-foot-9 and 140 pounds, wore his Navy uniform; Gloria, a blouse and a skirt borrowed from her older sister. "My knees were knocking," she said.

Jimmie had gotten better at lying about his age. He told 20-year-old Gloria he was 21, and she believed him, and that's what was printed on the marriage license. Jimmie's mother, Margaret, was the first person to tell Gloria the truth: "Jimmie's not 21, he's 17." Jimmie's mother was so upset that her son was getting married so young, she vowed to break up the marriage. The bride's father also refused to attend the wedding.

Jimmie, who was raised Episcopalian, tried to smooth some feathers with his Catholic in-laws by agreeing to convert to Catholicism, so that he and Gloria could remarry in the Catholic Church. The ceremony took place at St. John the Evangelist Catholic Church in Center City, Philadelphia.

The 17-year-old married man returned to the Navy and made several North Atlantic runs, before traveling to Casablanca, North Africa and Italy. Jimmie's unit was subsequently assigned to the Pacific Fleet, and he spent the rest of the war in the South Pacific, onboard submarines.

He became ill and ended up in sick bay. He was transferred to St. Albans Naval Hospital in Long Island with an admitting diagnosis of rheumatic fever.

"I remember this like it was yesterday," Beasley wrote the New York Supreme Court. "I must have walked over a mile to the bus, and when I arrived, my uniform was soaked in sweat to the point where it was as though I just stepped out of a shower.

"I was scared to death," Beasley wrote. His military records said that besides rheumatic fever, he also suffered from "psychoneurosis, anxiety."

"He is also bothered by insomnia, profuse sweating, and on two occasions he has been observed walking in his sleep," the service records said. "He worries excessively over home conditions, low finances, and the health of his wife, who is now pregnant."

But after Beasley recovered, he wrote, his doctors changed their original diagnosis of rheumatic fever. They downgraded his illness to something called "cat fever," and declared Beasley "perfectly healthy."

"I was given an honorable discharge" in October 1945, two months after atomic bombs were dropped on Hiroshima and Nagasaki, Beasley wrote. His highest Navy rank was boatswain, second class.

After the war, Jimmie moved to Florida, where he wanted to stay, and Gloria soon followed. Jimmie found work as a trash collector, but he had aspirations of becoming a motorcycle cop in West Palm Beach. He had two hurdles to overcome; he had never ridden a motorcycle before, and he had to memorize a thick manual of police procedures.

"How are you gonna read that book?" Gloria asked. "I'll do it," Jimmie said. "Your husband is a very smart man." He passed the test and rode a motorcycle for the West Palm Beach Police Department in 1945 and 1946. "They were desperate for any kind of body," Beasley told the Temple Review in 1999.

Jimmie, the converted Catholic, joined a new men's club and came home one night carrying a gold-trimmed Bible printed by the Masons. Gloria was aghast. "You can't be a Catholic and a Mason," she told Jimmie, but he didn't buy it. "I can do anything I want to," he said. And that included skipping Mass on Sundays.

Gloria was pregnant with the Beasleys' first child. "He really wanted a boy," Gloria said of her husband. She had the baby at St. Mary's Hospital in West Palm Beach. After the birth, Gloria asked the doctor to bring the baby to her, but the boy was born with the umbilical cord wrapped around his neck. Gloria wasn't allowed to hold the baby, because doctors were working to save his life.

"Bring the baby here," Gloria remembered pleading, "I'll make it start to breathe." Doctors worked on the infant for half an hour, without success. A nurse told Gloria that the baby looked "just like your husband, a very pretty baby boy," with red hair.

The only family member who got to hold the baby was the 19-year-old father. "It was a hard thing for Jimmie," Gloria recalled. "Jimmie was standing over me. He was really sobbing. 'My baby's dead,' he said."

Tragedy had struck a third James E. Beasley. Jimmie had to bury his infant son by himself in Hillcrest Cemetery, in West Palm Beach, while Gloria recovered in the hospital.

The infant's grave remained unmarked and untended for decades until 2003, when Jim Beasley's five surviving children chipped in to buy a tombstone for the brother they never knew. "James E. Beasley Jr. — Nov. 9, 1945," it says. "Our Little Angel."

Chapter 3

❖

SNOW IN THE
REARVIEW MIRROR

A DOZEN YOUNG MEN, MOST OF THEM WORLD WAR II VETS IN NEED OF A JOB, CLIMBED aboard a Greyhound bus idling at Philadelphia's Penn Station. It was October 1948. The men were training to become bus drivers, and after a week of classroom work, they filled the seats, anxiously awaiting their first road test.

"They called us up one by one," recalled James Gillespie, a former Marine who had fought the Japanese on the South Pacific island of Guadalcanal. The new recruits were asked to take turns driving around the city.

"They called Beasley," Gillespie said, and as he strolled up the aisle, the rookie driver made a lasting impression: "Short sleeves, big muscles, very determined," Gillespie rattled off 58 years later. "That was Jim."

"The rest of us were nervous" about driving a 37-passenger bus, Gillespie said. "I had never driven anything that large."

Many student drivers had trouble making turns on narrow city streets with a 35-foot-long bus. Several drivers ran rear wheels over curbs; others simply bailed after a disastrous turn behind the wheel.

"They lost their nerve," Gillespie said. Beasley, however, drove with ease, and by the time the Greyhound was parked back at Penn Station, he was the star of the class.

When Beasley and Gillespie finished the 30-day training program, they were issued gray-and-blue Greyhound uniforms and ID badges that they pinned to their caps.

• • •

FOR JIM BEASLEY, DRIVING A GREYHOUND WAS THE LATEST IN A SERIES OF BLUE-COLLAR JOBS he'd taken to feed his young family since he got out of the Navy. After they lost their son in Florida in November 1945, Jim and Gloria Beasley moved back to Philadelphia the following year, and Gloria gave birth to two daughters; Lynn, in 1946, and Nancy, in 1947.

Beasley recounted his early life on the road during a 1999 interview with the Temple Review. "Then I came back to Philadelphia, and the first job I had was driving a 1923 white truck with hard-rubber wheels for E.A. Gallagher, a rigging outfit that was located near the main post office. I drove a cab for a while, then landed a job driving a Greyhound bus."

The couple moved in with Jim's mother at 5404 Delancey Street in West Philadelphia. Margaret Beasley, a native of Great Britain, was a tiny, thin woman with a small nose and big blue eyes.

She came home on the trolley every night in her chocolate-brown waitress uniform after working the 4-12 shift at Horn & Hardart, at 54th and City Line Avenue. She would dump her tip money on the kitchen table, pour herself a beer, and light a cigarette. Then she would count her change while waiting for her favorite song, "The Bluebird of Happiness," to come on the radio at 1 a.m.

"Who gave you pennies?" Gloria would ask, upset that the customers could be so cheap, but her mother-in-law took it in stride. "Some people leave me nothing," she said.

Gloria spent a lot of nights with her mother-in-law, because her husband was usually on the road or working out at the gym. The lithe, tousle-haired, bare-chested Jimmie shown in Navy photos had bulked up as a civilian. At 5-foot-9, Beasley was used to weighing 145 pounds or so, but he ballooned to nearly 200, before he decided to turn the fat into muscle.

Beasley's cousin, Walter Woodworth, recalled walking in on Beasley at the local Y, while he was working out with weights. "What are you trying to do, look like Charles Atlas?" Woodworth asked. Soon, everybody noticed Beasley's bulging arms. "He was pumped," Gillespie said.

· · ·

IN 1945, THE PHILADELPHIA BOARD OF EDUCATION BEGAN AN ACCELERATED HIGH school equivalency program for returning veterans at Benjamin Franklin High School, at Broad and Green Streets. The program became a model for similar programs around the country, by allowing vets to obtain a four-year equivalency degree in just 12 to 14 months.

By 1947, the program had 83 teachers for 803 veterans, a student-teacher ratio of 10-1. Veterans from all three service branches ranged between 18 and 38 years old.

"Teachers in the Veterans School consider it a privilege to teach the former serviceman," Principal Charles H. Williams told the Philadelphia Inquirer on Dec. 29,

1947. The program attracted veterans from around the country; the first year alone, jalopies parked in the neighborhood belonged to veterans from a dozen states.

Jim Beasley was a 20-year-old truck driver in 1946 when he enrolled in the program. "I want to get somewhere," he told his wife. By December 1947, the year Beasley graduated, 5,000 veterans had gone through the program, and 1,800 had been accepted by colleges and universities around the country.

"It was the most unique preparatory high school in the world," recalled William Lederer, a classmate of Beasley's who would go on to become a city judge and a Pennsylvania state representative. Class size was limited to 20, with two teachers in every classroom, Lederer said. Students who flunked a test had to take a remedial one, and they weren't allowed to go on to the next lesson until they'd mastered the previous one.

Morale at the school was high, and so was the workload. The program ran from 8:30 a.m. to 3:30.p.m. five days a week. Students typically had 30 hours of class a week (with an hour off every day for lunch), plus 30 hours of weekly homework.

The school brought in motivational speakers such as former presidential candidate Wendell Willkie and Eleanor Roosevelt, wife of the late president. In September 1946, Eleanor Roosevelt attracted 1,500 listeners. "She sat down on the stage and everybody had to bring a bag lunch," Lederer recalled. "She was everybody's grandmother."

While most vets took 12 to 14 months to finish the program, Beasley claimed his degree in just six months. He was finally a success at school, but things weren't going as well on the home front.

• • •

JIM AND GLORIA DECIDED TO BUY THE HOUSE THEY WERE LIVING IN FROM JIM'S MOTHER. They handed Margaret Beasley $700 in cash and took over mortgage payments on a house that cost only $3,500. Jim's mother moved out, leaving the couple on their own, but the marriage was already in trouble.

Margaret Beasley was right about her son being too young to be married. He could have used a few more years to mature, and play the field. Instead, Jim was dating on the side, and he wasn't too discreet. "I've got to call my girlfriend," he once said in front of a female relative, who promptly told his wife, "He's running around on you."

While Jim had a problem with monogamy, Gloria had a temper. Walter Woodworth remembered walking in on one of the couple's many fights. Jim was walking downstairs, Woodworth said, while Gloria was upstairs, whipping a hairbrush at her husband's head.

"Gloria was a hellion," Woodworth said. "She was little, but she'd fight anybody. …She was a wildcat up there on the second floor, fighting and arguing." When asked about it a half-century later, Gloria said it was her wedding picture that she threw at her husband, and she added, "I have an Italian temper with men."

When Gloria decided she had had enough of her husband's affairs, she packed a suitcase for him and kicked him out of the house. Jim left without an argument, which his wife took as an admission of guilt. "I couldn't take anybody who was unfaithful," she said. "It would hurt too much."

None of the Beasleys' neighbors were surprised when the couple split up. Their fights had become so loud and violent, Gloria said, that neighbors thought "somebody was going to be killed."

While Beasley didn't see a problem with extramarital affairs, he held his wife to a higher standard. After they split up, Beasley accused his wife of cheating. "We weren't going together anymore," she said. "So I was going out with this guy from G.E.," where she worked. Beasley brought home a priest one day to remind Gloria that as a Catholic, she was not allowed to divorce.

But Jim and Gloria continued to lead separate lives. Beasley moved into a bachelor's apartment in West Philadelphia with Jim Gillespie and three other bus drivers from Greyhound. "I thought he was great," Gillespie said of Beasley. "Everybody liked him."

The two Jims lived together from 1948 until 1951. Beasley was a quiet roomie. "He didn't say much about his past, not even the Navy," Gillespie said.

Beasley also developed a useful hobby for a future trial lawyer: "He used to hypnotize people," Gillespie said. He watched many times as Beasley hypnotized friends at parties. "He'd put them to sleep and tell them to do things, like making faces or sounds," Gillespie said, and then they'd wake up and do just what Beasley had told them to do.

The bus drivers would hang out at their bachelor apartment, waiting for the phone to ring. "You were on call," Gillespie said. When the orders came in, "you'd be going in different directions."

Drivers typically worked six and seven days a week, averaging about 70 hours. In the days before interstate highways, it was a four-hour trip up Route 1 to New York City via Trenton, or 100 miles one way, for a grand total of $5 in wages.

Southern destinations included Baltimore, Richmond, Norfolk, Raleigh and Miami. Drivers on the road were expected to sleep at local YMCAs, and be able to change a flat.

At first, the job was fun for Beasley. "He loved to drive," Gillespie said. The drivers also had the responsibility on longer routes of escorting passengers to assigned seats. Beasley always put attractive young women on the right side of the bus, towards the front, so he could keep an eye on them in the rearview mirror.

Lou Rosof, one of Beasley's college buddies, recalled Beasley telling him the secret of where to sit a good-looking woman on the bus trip to Norfolk. "You put her where you can make eye contact with her for six or seven hours," Rosof recalled Beasley telling him. "If you get a good chick, put her in seat seven."

· · ·

BY DECEMBER 1950, HOWEVER, THE FUN OF DRIVING A GREYHOUND HAD WORN OFF. ON a blustery night, Beasley was on his way back from New York City to Philadelphia, driving a load of tourists through a heavy snowstorm. And as the diesel-powered GMC bus roared down Route 1 past Princeton, Beasley had a revelation.

At age 24, he'd been a man in perpetual motion — sailing on submarines, riding police motorcycles, and driving trucks, taxis and buses — and suddenly, he realized where it had all taken him: nowhere. His life was as directionless as the snow blowing in his rearview mirror.

"It was very early in the morning, 3 or 4 o'clock," Beasley told Philadelphia magazine in 1988. Most of the passengers were asleep. The only sound inside the bus was the steady click-click-click of the windshield wiper blades, whisking away heavy snowflakes.

"And I thought to myself, well, what the hell, 10 years from now I'll be doing the same damn thing," Beasley told Philadelphia magazine. "So I got back into Philadelphia and I quit."

Beasley pulled into the terminal and shut off the bus. He marched upstairs into the office and handed in his keys.

He had long daydreamed about going to college. "You know, I used to take the trolley into town from my home in West Philadelphia," Beasley told the Temple Review in 1999. "And I remember riding past the University of Pennsylvania and seeing all the kids walking the campus. I'd think, 'Geez, it must be great to be a college student here.' But I thought they never would have accepted me as a student."

Fortunately, there was a more practical alternative. Beasley's bus route in Philadelphia took him up North Broad Street, past Temple University. So Beasley applied to Temple. His bus driving buddies thought he was crazy. "I couldn't understand why he was leaving such a great job," said Gillespie, who would stay on at Greyhound for 37 years. "We were having a great time."

Temple admitted Beasley, and for the rest of his life, he was grateful. "I owe whatever I am to Temple University," Beasley told Philadelphia magazine in 1988. "They didn't have to take me in, a kid off the streets. But it turned my life around completely."

Chapter 4

❖

ACRES OF DIAMONDS

Iɴ ᴛʜᴇ ᴡɪɴᴛᴇʀ ᴏꜰ 1951, Jɪᴍ Bᴇᴀsʟᴇʏ ᴡᴀs ᴀ 25-ʏᴇᴀʀ-ᴏʟᴅ ꜰʀᴇsʜᴍᴀɴ ᴀᴛ Tᴇᴍᴘʟᴇ Uɴɪ-versity. His tuition was paid for under the GI Bill. But when Beasley needed money for food and clothing, he had to go back to Greyhound, and drive a bus part-time, after class and on weekends. He was the only student on campus, classmates said, who walked around wearing a Greyhound bus driver's uniform.

Shortly after he enrolled at Temple, Beasley donned another uniform, the cherry red and white of the freshman football team. The Temple Owls of the early 1950s wore helmets with no facemasks, and ran out of the T-formation.

Beasley, who had been working out with weights for years, made an immediate impression on the gridiron. "Jim was the meanest little guy you've ever seen; man, he could hit," recalled M. Mark Mendel, a former backfield coach.

"Beasley was fast and rawboned and tough," Mendel said. He wasn't big, "but God, he was made of steel. Even in practice, if he hit somebody, he would take them down and out."

"He was taking out his anger in other things in his football, and he was one of the fiercest competitors, I got to tell you," Mendel said. "He carried the ball frequently and he had good hands, so he'd go either way," meaning he played both offense and defense.

Beasley made the freshman team, and the following year he made varsity. "That's when he got hurt," Mendel said. "He got hit pretty fierce and went down on one leg, and he had a pretty substantial knee injury."

Beasley played a few more games before giving up the sport. "I think it was wise," Mendel said. "He had collateral ligaments that were shot. He was saddened by the fact that he couldn't compete."

As an assistant coach, Mendel carried around meal tickets for the Athletic Association dining hall. He always gave one to Beasley because they "had a camaraderie," and because he never knew if Beasley had enough money to eat.

Lou Rosof, a Temple classmate and Army vet, recalled that he and Beasley were always hitting each other up for money to buy food or gas. "You got a buck?" they would say. Usually, they didn't. The two men would visit the Horn & Hardart at 52nd and Market and order coffee. The restaurant featured a 35-cent beef pot pie that neither man could afford. But Beasley's mother was a waitress there, so she would bring out two coffees and two potpies, and a bill for just the coffee.

• • •

TEMPLE UNIVERSITY IN THE 1950S WAS PRIMARILY A NIGHT SCHOOL; THAT'S WHY ITS students were called Owls. Temple was known around the city as the only university that poor kids could get into. Its founder was Russell H. Conwell, a former union captain in the Civil War who went on to have several careers. He started out as a globe-trotting newspaper correspondent, then became a lawyer and a Baptist minister.

In 1884, when Conwell was pastor of the Grace Baptist Church, he began teaching a night class in the church basement to a small group of men who wanted to become ministers. Within four years, Conwell had hundreds of students, and a charter for Temple College.

That's when Conwell took up one last career, as a motivational speaker. The Baptist minister raised millions of dollars for his new college by giving the same lecture all over the country — "Acres of Diamonds." According to Professor Joseph C. Carter, Conwell's on-line biographer at Temple University, Conwell gave the lecture more than 6,000 times, becoming America's foremost platform orator.

The lecture was inspired by his newspaper days. Conwell had been a correspondent for the American Traveler, a weekly Boston journal, riding in a camel caravan in Mesopotamia when he heard a travel guide tell a story to entertain American tourists. It was the legend of a prosperous Persian farmer, Ali Hafed, who sold his own fruitful lands to roam the world in search of undiscovered diamond fields. Ali dreamed of finding an immense fortune, but he spent all his money on a futile search. He was so despondent he committed suicide by walking into the ocean. The punch line was after Ali's death, the man who bought Ali's farm discovered it contained acres of diamonds.

The moral of Conwell's lecture was: "Your diamonds are not in far-away mountains or in distant seas; they are in your own back yard if you will but dig for them." Besides the legend of Ali Hafed, Conwell used some real-life examples to prove his point. He told audiences about a California man who sold his ranch in 1847 to Colonel John Augustus Sutter in favor of going prospecting for gold. On the abandoned property, Colonel Sutter subsequently discovered $38 million in gold.

Conwell also talked about a man who sold a farm in Pennsylvania and left to study the oil business. The new farm owner was out walking one day when he found a plank that the previous owner had laid over a brook. The new owner lifted the plank and discovered a flood of oil worth hundreds of millions of dollars. The oil field became the city of Titusville, birthplace of the modern oil industry.

Conwell also used his famous lecture as a platform to preach a prosperity gospel. The Baptist minister told young Christians it wasn't pious to be poor.

"I say that you ought to get rich and it is your duty to get rich," Conwell declared. "I say, then, you ought to have money. If you can honestly attain unto riches in Philadelphia, it is your Christian and godly duty to do so…. Money is power…. In the hands of good men and women, it could accomplish, and it has accomplished, good."

The Bible, Conwell reminded his audience, did not say that money was evil, it said that "the love of money is the root of all evil."

Conwell, who died in 1925, never met Jim Beasley, born in 1926. But Beasley was just the kind of local diamond in the rough that Conwell had in mind when he founded Temple University.

•   •   •

BEASLEY GOT OFF TO A MEDIOCRE START IN THE SCHOOL OF BUSINESS AND PUBLIC Administration, taking six classes and 16 credits in the second half of the 1950-51 school year. He finished with two B's, in business administration and principles of economics; two C's, in history of the modern world and principles of accounting; and two D's, in English composition and general math.

Classmates recalled Beasley as rough around the edges, and a poor speaker. "Jim had a horrible vocabulary," said Bernard Snyder. "He would end his sentences with prepositions. Certain words he couldn't say. I guess when we met we were both 'dese and dose-ers,'" Snyder said, referring to the way he and Beasley pronounced "these" and "those."

Another vestige of Beasley's previous life no longer fit into his new world. On his right forearm, Beasley sported a tattoo of an American Eagle and a ship's anchor, a souvenir from his Navy days. Beasley became so embarrassed by the tattoo that he had it surgically removed, but the painful procedure left a three-inch-by-three-inch scar. For the rest of his life, no matter how hot it got, Beasley always wore long-sleeve shirts.

Beasley took 15 credits during the summer in 1951, earning two B's, two C's, and one D, in general math. In the academic year of 1951-52, his grades improved, as he took 12 courses and 36 credits, racking up four A's, two B's, and six C's. The following academic year, 1952-53, he took 12 more courses and 35 credits, earning 10 Bs, one C and one D, in statistics. He finished up his undergraduate course work with a typically heavy load, logging six courses and 18 credits during the summer of 1953, ending with two A's and four B's.

Beasley had to wait until the next commencement ceremony, February 1954, to graduate with his B.S. degree in general arts and sciences. He had completed a four-year undergraduate program in just 2 ½ years. And he did it while playing football, serving as commander of the campus ROTC unit, and working two part-time jobs. Besides driving a bus, Beasley also worked after midnight as a soda jerk at Schraft's, a restaurant at 15th and Chestnut.

Beasley wanted to go to grad school, but he hadn't decided whether to become a doctor or a lawyer. In the end, expediency won out. He figured he'd already lost enough time to the service, and all those blue-collar jobs. "I began to evaluate the situation," he told Counselor magazine in 1988. "Medical school meant four years plus residency. Three years of law school looked more attractive to me."

Beasley applied to Temple Law School in the summer of 1953. Two Temple law professors wrote letters of recommendation on Beasley's behalf to Benjamin F. Boyer, the law school dean.

"As an instructor in the Business Law Department of Temple University, I have had occasion to teach Mr. Beasley and have found him to be an extremely cooperative, intelligent and hard-working student," wrote H. Durston Saylor II. "He is aware of his responsibilities as a student, and I feel confident that, if admitted, he will be a desirable addition to the student body of Temple University Law School."

"Mr. Beasley, in my opinion formed from personal knowledge of him, is an intelligent, capable and serious student," wrote David H. Roberts, another law professor. "He has a very earnest desire to become a lawyer and will be, if given the opportunity, a credit to the school. His character is above question from the standpoint of morals, honesty and integrity."

On July 2, 1953, Beasley's 27th birthday, he received a letter from Dean Boyer, saying his application to the law school had been approved. When Beasley took a legal aptitude test, however, based on his responses he was projected to fail out. Beasley used the test results as motivation, keeping the document that predicted his imminent failure for the next 50 years.

A university photo taken in October 1953 showed Philadelphia Judge Theodore Reimel explaining legal procedures to law students in his Common Pleas courtroom. The judge was smiling, as were many students. Beasley, however, sitting in the second row, stared straight ahead, looking serious.

. . .

"From the day that he got into law school, that was the perfect fit for him. He loved the law," said M. Mark Mendel, Beasley's former assistant football coach, who was also a law school classmate.

Mendel said that both he and Beasley were lucky enough to be taught by one of the law school's top professors, George P. Williams III.

"He was a huge man, 6-foot-5 or 6-foot-6, the wispiest-looking scion of the Main Line that ever was, but he loved to teach torts and he did a fantastic job," Mendel said. "He was a real litigator, not a professor who never did it."

Professor Williams wore "gray flannel suits and Republican shoes," and drove a Lincoln Continental, Mendel said. He made a big impression on law students. "We thought that, *man*, this was what lawyering was all about," Mendel said.

Mendel recalled Williams' torts class as one long-running debate between the professor with the booming bass voice and Jim Beasley. "Beasley would take him on and George Williams loved it. Beasley would challenge everything," especially if it was a tradition, and people said that's the way it is, Mendel said. "Beasley would never accept that."

Beasley, however, found some of his theoretical classes to be a waste of time. "Jim used to shake his head and say, 'Jesus, how's this gonna help in a courtroom?'" Mendel recalled. "He saw very, very early he wanted to do litigation."

In his first year of law school, 1953-54, Beasley took 28 credits, making the dean's list with a 1.94 average, just slightly below a B average of 2.0. (Grades were weighted differently in those days, with an A worth only 2.75 points.) Beasley took three courses in the summer of 1954, racking up a C and two B-pluses.

Warren Ballard, a retired Temple law professor in his 90s, recalled in a 2006 interview that law school faculty members were "very much impressed with Jim Beasley's thoroughness. He left no stone unturned. …I don't think he was ever buffaloed by a problem."

Another law school classmate of Beasley's was Isador Kranzel, who would go on to become Philadelphia's city solicitor and an administrative law judge for the Pennsylvania Public Utility Commission.

Kranzel met Beasley as an undergrad. One day in class, "I was pontificating," Kranzel recalled, and Beasley yelled, "Izzy, for God's sake, will you shut up and let the teacher teach."

"I was not as driven as he was," Kranzel said. "It was very clear to me from day one that he was determined to be successful."

Kranzel said he didn't have to work in college because his father made a comfortable living in the hardware business.

"People like myself, at the end of a day in law school, wanted to relax and go home and do nothing," Kranzel said. "He didn't have that luxury. He wasn't out there boozing it up with the fraternity guys."

· · ·

TEMPLE LAW SCHOOL IN THE 1950S WAS SMALL AND "VERY SPARE; MANY OF THE undergrad classes were in old houses," Kranzel said. The class of 1956, of which Kranzel and Beasley were members, was the first to move into a former Gimbel Bros. office building.

"It was no-frills and all-business," Kranzel said. There were only a few class-rooms, and "Everyone was so uptight, so fearful of failure."

The drop-out rate was high. Kranzel recalled that of the 120 students that showed up for day classes, only about 60 graduated. In the night school, the pass-ing rate was even worse. Out of 120 students, only some 40 graduated, Kranzel said, "which also added to the anxiety.

"There was not a good esprit de corps because everyone was so insecure," Kranzel said. "You're dealing with a group of people who feel they really have to scramble and scrap to make it. That led to a competitiveness that I personally didn't like."

Kranzel recalled when he botched a contracts exam by not answering ques-tions in the proper order, and he received a failing grade. "Well," his fellow stu-dents clucked, "Izzy Kranzel won't be here long." But Beasley wasn't one of the detractors. "His competitiveness," Kranzel said, "never extended to putting down other people."

The pressure on the law school students was intense. "I was reading six to seven hours a day," Kranzel said. Each student was required to read about 50 cases a week, with each case running an average of 10 pages. That amounted to 500 pages of core reading material that professors expected students to master, plus several hundred pages a week of supplemental reading.

Beasley was one of the fastest readers in the class. He was known for holing up in an aluminum diner on Broad Street, where he would drink coffee and pore over cases. "It was almost like he was gonna teach the class," Mendel said. "He had this unbelievable zeal."

Beasley was also a copious note-taker with great penmanship, who made some extra money by selling his notes to other students for 10 cents a page.

"Some of the teachers were in awe of him," Kranzel said. "They realized how much he had sacrificed. . . . One of the reasons why he didn't want me shooting my mouth off in class was he wanted to hear what the teacher had to say. He felt he had lost something."

By the end of the first year of law school, Kranzel was No. 6 in the class, and Beasley was No. 7, out of 93 students. "He never let it happen again," Kranzel said. In the second year of law school, Beasley ranked No. 1 out of 39 students (the drop-out rate continued to be high). By the third year, Beasley was third out of 60.

"I never wanted to be in the study group with him," Kranzel said. "I thought they were crazy. They wanted to work day and night." Kranzel was amazed by Beasley's stamina. "He could work most people under the table."

Kranzel remembered Beasley as "powerfully built," somewhat shy and awkward. "He was really very modest," Kranzel said. "People were surprised because he didn't speak well. He spoke like someone from the working class. His diction wasn't perfect, but he was determined."

He was also broke. Beasley had financed his undergraduate education with veterans benefits and a ROTC allowance. He was still working blue-collar jobs while in law school, telling anybody who would listen that he was determined to succeed. On Jan. 13, 1954, a local businessman wrote the dean of the Temple law school on Beasley's behalf:

"I got acquainted with this young man when he was driving a taxi cab," wrote Laurence Saunders, president of the W.B. Saunders publishing company of Washington Square, Philadelphia. "He was very pleasant and seemed like a bright young man. Since he drove me home, he got my address, and since then, he has come to see me at the office and written me letters soliciting a loan in order to finish law school."

Dean Boyer wrote back a week later, telling Saunders not to cut any checks: "There are means at the University whereby Mr. Beasley can apply for a loan which could be available to worthy students, and I suggest that he do so."

• • •

BEASLEY HAD BEEN FORTUNATE TO ENROLL IN AN ACCELERATED HIGH SCHOOL FOR veterans. Then Temple opened its doors to him. But in his second year of law school, he really got lucky.

"Dean Boyer called me in one day and said there was a new federal judge and he needed a court crier," Beasley told the Temple Review in 1999. It was a new program unique in the nation, and Beasley was about to become its first beneficiary.

On Friday, July 2, 1954, Philadelphia residents were looking forward to the July 4th weekend. It was a sunny day when the temperature would hit 90. Jim Beasley was walking down Market Street in a jacket and tie, on his way to a job interview. It was his 28th birthday.

When he arrived at the federal courthouse at Ninth and Market, Beasley appeared lost. He stopped a pretty young woman in the hallway on the second floor to ask directions to a judge's chambers. Beasley had an appointment to see Judge John W. Lord Jr. of the U.S. District Court's Eastern District of Pennsylvania. Beasley told the young woman he was applying for the position of law clerk. She seemed impressed. "It's a wonderful opportunity for a young law student," she said.

Beasley went in to see the judge. "Now, I had never been in a courtroom," he would tell an interviewer years later. "I went down for an interview, but I really did not appreciate the significance of the job. I was in day school, and I didn't like the idea of working during the day crying 'oyez! oyez! oyez!' all day and going to school at night."

Beasley already had his law school schedule arranged; he was taking day classes and working nights, and he didn't know if he wanted to switch everything around just for the sake of a law clerk's job. After Beasley's interview with the judge, the dean asked to see Beasley a second time.

"The judge liked you, but he told me he hasn't heard back from you," the dean said. When Beasley explained he wasn't sure he wanted the job, the dean exploded. "Are you out of your mind? This is too good of an opportunity to turn down."

"I think that was one of the turning points in my life," Beasley told the Temple Review. "I took the job, splitting my courses between day and evening."

Beasley was appointed court crier and law clerk, a full-time position. He worked for Judge Lord from 1954 to 1956, when he graduated from law school. His grades actually improved while he worked full-time. Beasley took 20 credits in the 1954-55 school year and made the dean's list again. He finished No. 1 in his class with an overall average of 2.10, just above a B average.

In the summer of 1955, Beasley took three classes, and maintained a B average. But the courtroom experience he gained as Judge Lord's law clerk was more valuable than school.

"I saw how plaintiff and defendant lawyers prepare and try cases," Beasley told the Temple Review. The courtroom experience was "truly where I learned my trade."

• • •

ISADOR KRANZEL, NOW A RETIRED JUDGE, STILL RECALLS "THE ANXIETY OF THE BAR exam," which historically had been a problem for Temple law students.

"Temple had done dreadfully," Kranzel said. Only 40 percent of Temple's students passed the bar. "Our class shocked everyone by having a 57 percent result," Kranzel said. "People like Jim might have helped to make a difference. His example may have indirectly raised the competitive level in others."

In his final year of law school, 1955-56, Beasley took 24 credits, racking up six A's and four B's. He made the dean's list again, finishing with his highest average, 2.29. He ranked third out of 60 law students.

Beasley had blown through a program in just three years that usually took part-time students four years to finish. And he accomplished this while working part-time and full-time jobs. He topped it off in July 1956 by passing the bar exam, and being admitted to practice law in the state of Pennsylvania.

In just 5½ years, Beasley had gone from bus driver to lawyer.

• • •

BESIDES LAW SCHOOL AND WORK, BEASLEY ALSO HAD TWO KIDS TO TEND TO, AND ONE was accident-prone. Beasley's youngest daughter, Nancy, was just 2 years old when she fell off the second floor balcony of her grandmother's house. When she woke up, she had a concussion and swollen eyes, but she was safe in her father's arms. "I remember him holding me and just rocking me," she said.

When Nancy was 7, in 1954, she was swinging on a wrought-iron railing when she lost her grip and fell head-first on concrete. This time the top of her head split open, and she bled from her eyes and mouth, as well as internally. The police took her to the hospital, and when she woke up, she had no idea how long she had been unconscious. Her father was by her bedside, holding her hand, and singing "Beautiful Dreamer." "You're going to be fine," he told her. "Your dad's been here for a long time," a nurse said.

"My father was a very good father when we were young," Nancy said. "He used to come over and feed us breakfast. Mom was going off to work. If we were sick, he'd take off from school to take care of us. He was the most kind-hearted person you'd ever want to meet."

When Beasley became a law clerk, he took his wife and kids to see Judge Lord's chambers, furnished with big red chairs. "This is where I'm going to work," he said. He continued to live apart from his family, but still showed up on weekends to spend time with his daughters.

"We were back and forth," his wife, Gloria, said. "We were together and then we weren't." By 1955, Beasley and his wife had been married 10 years, but they had lived apart for the last seven.

Gloria decided she had had enough, so she filed for divorce. A boyfriend, she said, borrowed money from a loan shark to pay the legal bill. Gloria said her husband was surprised by the divorce filing and told her she would live to regret it. The divorce was granted in 1956, with no provisions for alimony or child support. Aside from the acrimony and bitter feelings, Gloria realized that her husband wanted a different life, and needed somebody to "make him feel important and big. I couldn't do that," she said.

A year later, Beasley visited his daughters at a summer camp in the Pocono Mountains. Nancy remembered the way her father stood out in the crowd. "He was so muscular," she said. "He would bend his arm to push back his hair, he had this auburn hair and it was so wavy, and these big muscles would pop up. I was so proud of him . . . . I thought he walked on water."

When Nancy and her older sister, Lynn, came back from camp, they had a surprise waiting at home. Their mother had remarried. Six months later, so did their father.

· · ·

THE PRETTY YOUNG WOMAN THAT BEASLEY HAD RUN INTO AT THE FEDERAL COURTHOUSE was Helen Mary Walsh, the executive secretary of Judge J. Cullen Ganey, chief judge of U.S. District Court.

Helen, 23, was a 5-foot-2 brunette with fair skin who weighed just over 100 pounds. She had such a knockout figure that many lawyers used to stop by Judge Ganey's office to chase her around the desk. (This was back in the days when men did not have to worry about sexual harassment charges.)

Helen was soft-spoken, classy, and an elegant dresser. A few years later, when a new president took office, many people would say how she looked like a petite version of the new first lady, Jacqueline Kennedy.

Beasley came up with all kinds of excuses to stop by and see Judge Ganey's secretary. When the judges weren't around, Beasley would stick his head into the next office and say, "Ahem, Miss, I'm having a problem with my typewriter. Could you come in and help me?"

"I'm busy now," Helen would say. "I'll come in when I'm able." Helen, however, was taken with the new clerk. "He was adorable," she said. "Strawberry blond hair, very muscular. He was very sweet. And restless. He always had to be going some-where. He was a man on a mission; he was in a hurry to be successful."

They had opposite temperaments; Helen was thoughtful and purposeful; Jim was impatient, and did everything at breakneck speed. When he asked if he could hypnotize her, Helen laughed him off. "Oh, no," she said. "This isn't going to happen."

They dated for four years. Beasley obtained a temporary pilot's license in 1955, and on weekends, when he and Helen had his two daughters with him, Beasley would rent a Cessna and fly everybody down to the Jersey shore. "I felt if I was going to be involved with Jim, I had to have a relationship with his daughters," Helen said.

Beasley was serious about Helen, but some of his pals wondered whether he would ever settle down with one woman. "Helen was a very beautiful girl," recalled Jim Gillespie, Beasley's bus driving buddy. "I wished her a lot of luck."

Beasley bought Helen a diamond ring, and they were married in Lansdowne by a Lutheran minister on New Year's Day, 1958. Beasley was a young lawyer just starting out, so he couldn't afford to take much time off. After a day of honey-mooning in the Pocono Mountains, he went right back to work.

He also moved into Helen's apartment. At the time, he was renting a $7-a-week room in West Philadelphia. Walter Woodworth thought Beasley made a smart move.

"She was very quiet and very demure," Woodworth said of Helen, but "she had a way with Jim." As far as Cousin Walter was concerned, Helen was the woman who civilized Jim Beasley.

Chapter 5

❖

THE ADVOCATE

THE ROOKIE LAWYER WAS TRYING HIS FIRST CASE. IT WAS JAN. 14, 1957, AT THE federal courthouse in Philadelphia, and Jim Beasley was on his feet before a judge and a just-picked jury. He was 30 years old; his auburn hair was cut short and neatly parted atop his high forehead. He was dressed in a brand-new gray knock-off of a Brooks Brothers business suit.

He called his first witness, a widow from Wilmington, Del., who was the plaintiff in *Nuttall v. Reading Co.* She had shown up alone in the courtroom, as Beasley had advised, to ensure maximum sympathy from the jury.

"Now, Mrs. Nuttall, I want you to keep your voice up so that the juror all the way over here can hear you, and then we can all hear you without any difficulty," Beasley said. "Will you state your name, please?"

"Florence M. Nuttall."

Beasley was about to ask the second question of his young legal career when he was interrupted by the judge. The Hon. George A. Welsh, then 78, was described by a retired city lawyer as "a wizened old man" prone to snide remarks. The judge must have thought Beasley hadn't been forceful enough.

"Just a minute, Mrs. Nuttall," the judge said. "See that young man over there at the far corner, Mrs. Nuttall?"

It was the same juror that Beasley had pointed to.

"Yes," the witness said.

"Now, you came all the way from home to tell us about this case," the judge lectured the widow. "They have to hear every word that you say, so will you kindly keep your voice up, please."

"Yes," the witness said. The judge turned to the rookie lawyer. "Will you repeat the question, Mr. Beasley?"

"Yes, Your Honor," Beasley replied. He had been a lawyer for only six months, spending most of that time in a mandatory training program known as a preceptorship that required new city lawyers to work as clerks before they were allowed to try cases. This was the moment that Beasley had been prepping for during all those days as a judge's law clerk and all those nights as a Temple law student. But his first trial was no slip-and-fall case.

In his courtroom debut, Beasley was trying a wrongful death case against the Reading Railroad, and its seasoned defense lawyer. John R. McConnell was a red-faced former World War II gunnery officer a decade older than Beasley. McConnell had already practiced law a dozen years at the Center City firm of Morgan, Lewis & Bockius, where he was a partner.

To make it even tougher on Beasley, his new boss, B. Nathaniel Richter, was popping in and out of the courtroom to keep tabs on the rookie. Richter was a legendary Philadelphia trial lawyer who knew *Nuttall v. Reading Co.* better than anybody, because he'd already tried the case twice.

The records from Beasley's first case were believed to have been destroyed long ago. A pristine 50-year-old trial transcript, however, was discovered in early 2007 in the files of the National Archives at Ninth and Chestnut Streets in Philadelphia, on the site of the old federal courthouse where Beasley originally tried the Nuttall case back in 1957.

The transcript shows Beasley making rookie mistakes as he takes up the cause of a hard-luck widow, while contending with McConnell and an old judge who keeps getting in the way.

• • •

FLORENCE M. NUTTALL HAD SUED THE READING RAILROAD ON BEHALF OF THE ESTATE of her late husband, Clarence O. Nuttall, a railroad employee of 37 years. On the morning of Jan. 5, 1952, Engineman Nuttall had tried to call in sick, but the yardmaster ordered him back to work. The yardmaster didn't have a substitute, and if he had to find one, the freight train that Nuttall was supposed to operate would have been 90 minutes late. So Nuttall reluctantly went to work, and the freight train ran on time, but by nightfall Engineman Nuttall was lying in a hospital bed. He died four days later, of pneumonia, at 59.

On the witness stand, Florence Nuttall told Beasley she was standing in her dining room at 5:30 a.m., when she called her husband down for breakfast for the last time.

"And did he come down?," Beasley asked.

"Yes, he came down and he said to me, 'I am going to call up the yardmaster and report off for I don't feel so well,'" Florence Nuttall told the jury.

"Before you go any further," Beasley said, "where is the telephone in the dining room?"

"It is at one end of the china closet."

"And where were you?"

"I was standing at the other end of it," Florence Nuttall said.

"And approximately how close were you to the telephone?" Beasley asked.

"Oh, about two or three feet," she said.

"Did you hear him say anything?"

"I heard him say, 'George, I won't be able to work today as I don't feel too well.'"

The judge interrupted to say he was having trouble hearing the testimony. Beasley turned to the soft-spoken witness: "Will you repeat that very loud?"

"'George, I won't be able to work today as I don't feel very well,'" the witness said in an amplified voice.

"You could not hear the reply?" Beasley asked.

"Oh no," Florence Nuttall said.

• • •

What Florence Nuttall overheard her husband tell the yardmaster had been the subject of two previous federal trials as well as a federal court appeal.

At the first trial, in January 1955, Judge John W. Lord Jr. agreed with Richter's contention that the widow's testimony was admissible, because it spoke to Clarence Nuttall's state of mind. The jury awarded Florence Nuttall $30,000, but the verdict was overturned, in part because of a battle over admissibility of evidence. At the second trial, in October 1955, however, Judge Lord changed his mind, siding with defense lawyer McConnell's argument that the widow's testimony was hearsay, and Richter lost the case.

Richter appealed, and on July 5, 1956, the same month that Jim Beasley passed the bar, the U.S. Court of Appeals for the Third Circuit ruled in favor of Florence Nuttall. "It matters not whether the evidence was hearsay," the appeals court decided. "One of the exceptions to the rule excluding hearsay is that a man's declarations as to his state of mind may be used to establish that state of mind . . . ."

"So, here, Nuttall's statements to his wife at the conclusion of the conversation on the telephone tend to prove that he thought he was being forced to do something he did not want to do," the appeals court said. "The account of the telephone conversation and the statement of Nuttall which followed it are admissible."

When it came time to try *Nuttall v. Reading* a third time, however, Richter was tired of the case, so he decided to let the new kid in the office take a shot.

"Nate took Jim under his wing," recalled Meyer A. Bushman, a former law clerk and lawyer from 1954 to 1960 at Richter, Lord & Levy, where Beasley went to work right out of law school. "Jim was one of Nate's favorites," Bushman said. "He thought Jim had all the makings of a great trial lawyer."

Beasley had a different view of why he ended up with the Nuttall case. "It was given to me, I think, because the firm thought it was a loser," Beasley told Philadelphia magazine in a 1988 interview. "I was the low man on the totem pole, so all of the dogs were given to me."

·   ·   ·

BEASLEY: "WHAT WAS THE NEXT THING YOU HEARD YOUR HUSBAND SAY?"

Nuttall: "I heard him say, 'But, George, why are you forcing me to work the way I feel?'

"And he was standing there with his fist clenched like that," Florence Nuttall said, raising her fist in the air and shaking it in front of the jury. ". . . He said, 'Well, I guess I will have to come out then as bad as I feel.'"

Beasley: "Then what happened?"

Nuttall: "Then he came over to me and he said, 'Florence, I guess I will have to go out to work.'"

The judge interrupted again: "What kind of a breakfast did he eat?" "He didn't eat anything," the widow Nuttall replied. "He wasn't able to eat breakfast."

Beasley: "Did your husband go to work, or did he remain home?"

Nuttall: "My husband went to work."

Beasley: "Let me get this straight, Mrs. Nuttall, in my mind. What did your husband say to you after he hung up the telephone?"

Nuttall: "He said, 'I guess I will have to go to work —" Defense lawyer McConnell was on his feet. "Your Honor, I object to any conversation after the telephone conversation."

"I sustain the objection," the judge said, turning to Beasley. "Can you get along without it?"

"Well, I would like the whole case to be before the jury and not just three-fourths of it," Beasley argued. "I think the plaintiff is entitled to have that information disclosed."

"Well, I am sure Mr. Beasley thinks that," McConnell told the judge. But the defense lawyer argued that if Florence Nuttall was allowed to tell her story in court, no cross-examination was possible because Clarence Nuttall was dead, and so was the yardmaster.

"Will you excuse me just a minute," the judge told the jury as he summoned both lawyers to a sidebar conference. During an off-the-record discussion, Beasley had a chance to cite the appeals court decision in Florence Nuttall's favor. The judge allowed Beasley to resume his questioning.

"After your husband hung up the telephone, what did he say to you?" Beasley asked.

McConnell was on his feet again before the widow could say a word. "If Your Honor please, I object —" But this time, the judge brushed off the defense lawyer's objections. "Yes," the judge said. "Your objection covers that."

Beasley turned to the witness: "You can answer, Mrs. Nuttall."

"He said to me, 'I guess I will have to go to work as bad as I feel,'" she told Beasley.

"There is no question in your mind that you could hear very clearly from where your husband was standing, talking over the telephone?" Beasley asked.

"I could hear very clearly," the widow said.

• • •

WHEN ENGINEMAN NUTTALL CAME HOME AFTER WORKING HIS LAST SHIFT, "HE COULD hardly walk, he looked just like the mask of death, his face was so white," Florence Nuttall told Beasley. Twenty minutes later, Engineman Nuttall was riding in an ambulance to Wilmington General Hospital, where he would last four days.

"Did he seem to be in any pain?," Beasley asked.

"Yes, he did," Florence Nuttall said. "He would take his fist and hit the oxygen tent like that," she said, demonstrating, "like as though he was trying to get his breath and trying to get out of there."

Engineman Nuttall had earned $5,190 in 1951, working six days a week for the Reading Co. When he died, after 37 years of service with the railroad, he left his widow a pension of just $65 a month.

After Florence Nuttall left the stand, Beasley called union boss Kenneth Myers, chairman of the Brotherhood of Locomotive Engineers. "Now, if you please, Mr. Myers, tell the members of the jury and the court what happens if a man has a job on which he is supposed to work, let us say, to a given hour," Beasley asked, "and he fails to appear, what is the practice and procedure of the railroad company?"

"If Your Honor please," McConnell interrupted. It was time to show up the rookie lawyer. "I think that question ought to be more specific," McConnell told the judge. "The case we have before the jury at the present time is what occurs if a man fails to appear because he is sick."

Beasley's question was too broad, McConnell said, because it asked what happened when an employee failed to appear "for any reason."

"All right," Beasley said. "I think that the —"

"Mr. Beasley," interrupted the judge, who promptly sided with McConnell. "I think that ought to be the first point of inquiry. That is our immediate task here." The judge instructed Beasley to narrow his question to the company's sick policy.

"Yes, Your Honor," Beasley said.

When Beasley got through with the sick policy, he asked Myers about the conditions that Nuttall had endured while operating the freight train on his last shift. As an engineman, Nuttall was required to stand by an open bay window with icy winter air pouring in, so he could peer out and see the train signals, Myers said. Meanwhile, the engineman's legs were being roasted by a heater placed directly in front of him that could not be turned off. Railroad engineers had long complained about the open windows and uncontrollable heaters, Myers said. Those design flaws were subsequently corrected, but not in time to save Engineman Nuttall.

While he was still questioning Myers, Beasley made the mistake of turning his back to the judge. "Mr. Beasley, there is some interference here," the judge admonished. "There is better interference here than we get on a football field. Do not talk when you are turning your back, making your round turn."

"All right, Your Honor," Beasley said.

• • •

DR. JOSEPH V. CASELLA WAS THE CHIEF PATHOLOGIST WHO PERFORMED THE AUTOPSY on Clarence Nuttall. He testified that the engineman died of pneumonia. The doctor also found that Nuttall suffered from arteriosclerosis, and had some scar tissue blocking his right coronary artery. Beasley didn't want the jurors to think that if he had survived pneumonia, Nuttall would have keeled over from a heart attack.

"Doctor, this condition of Mr. Nuttall's heart, would it have prevented him from living a normal life expectancy?" Beasley asked.

"In my opinion, Mr. Nuttall could have lived a normal life expectancy," Dr. Casella said.

Beasley brought the jurors back to the cause of death: "Now in the course of the treatment of pneumonia, grippe, influenza or a cold, would you recommend that a man go to work on a locomotive, where he is out in the cold, freezing, the cold air coming in front of him and in back of him, and a direct flow of heat towards his legs? Would you recommend that a man go to work if he had pneumonia, the grippe, influenza, or a cold?"

"No, I would not recommend it," Dr. Casella said.

Beasley had to endure one last embarrassment from the judge. He had just questioned his last witness, an actuary, about Clarence Nuttall's unfulfilled life expectancy, which the actuary estimated at 15 years.

On cross-examination, McConnell asked the actuary if his mortality tables were limited to just men afflicted with arteriosclerosis. No, of course not, the actuary said. But if they were, the defense lawyer asked, would the life expectancy be lower? "I should think so," the actuary replied. When it came time for redirect, Beasley stood to ask a question, but the judge interrupted him by cracking, "Has he stimulated your brain into activity, sir?"

Beasley was taken aback. "I am sorry, sir. I did not hear it."

"I say," the judge repeated, "has Mr. McConnell stimulated your brain into activity?"

"Yes," Beasley said. "Just for one question."

Beasley asked the actuary if his mortality tables included people who had diseases such as arteriosclerosis. "Oh, yes," the actuary said.

The witness stepped down, and after the defense put on its case, the jury came back with a $50,000 verdict on behalf of Florence Nuttall. In his first try, Beasley had outdone his boss, Nate Richter, who had been only able to score a $30,000 verdict for the widow. Beasley's victory had also established that a man's declarations regarding his state of mind could be admitted as evidence, even if the man was no longer alive.

"It was my first case, my first win, and it set a precedent that was used a lot," Beasley told Philadelphia magazine in 1988. "It was very significant for me."

Beasley took on several more cases that his bosses thought were dogs, and he won a string of victories. The rookie lawyer, earning only $6,000, decided it was time for a raise. He asked Nate Richter for $10,000, but Richter said no.

• • •

B. NATHANIEL RICHTER WAS 5-FOOT-8 AND OVERWEIGHT; HE WORE GLASSES, HAD A broad face, and a receding hairline. Despite his nondescript appearance, Richter was "very flamboyant and very aggressive" in the courtroom, recalled attorney Bushman. "His opening and closing speeches were just brilliant. He had juries crying."

It was Richter who showed Beasley how to talk to juries, cross-examine witnesses and dominate a courtroom. Richter, who died in 1974, was also a legendary character.

When he gave a summation, the Jewish lawyer would pace slowly in front of the jury box, and sometimes, a pair of rosary beads would spill out of his pocket. Richter would scoop up the beads and apologize to the jury, explaining that the beads were a good luck charm from his late Polish grandmother. But if the jurors were mostly Irish, then the grandmother became Irish.

"He had moxie beyond belief," recalled James F. Mundy, another city trial lawyer who began his career working for Richter. "He pulled every stunt in the world, including speaking to the jury in Polish."

During closing arguments, Richter would often talk about his Polish mother-in-law, recounting how just that morning he had sought her out for some folk wisdom on what to say to the jury to sum up his case. As Richter recounted these chats, they usually ended with his mother-in law kissing him on the forehead and saying in Polish, "God bless you, my son."

In reality, Bushman said, Richter's mother-in-law "wasn't allowed near his house."

Richter also had a reputation as a womanizer. Philadelphia District Attorney Lynne Abraham recalled visiting the Richter law office as a teenager, when Richter represented her stepmother in an accident case. "All of his secretaries looked like models," Abraham said of the bosomy women parading around in hats, gloves and short skirts. "It was like a harem."

"Nate was from a different era," Abraham said, adding that today, "he would be disbarred" or "locked up."

"He was a great lawyer, but he had poor judgment in the personal area," agreed Arthur G. Raynes, another prominent Philadelphia plaintiff's lawyer who spent a decade working for Richter. Raynes said that because of Richter's shenanigans, his best friend was the statute of limitations.

Bernard Snyder, a former classmate of Beasley's who later became a judge, recalled a trial lawyers' convention in Los Angeles where "they had to hustle Nate on a plane because the police were looking for him.

"He didn't think anything about accosting somebody," Snyder said. When asked if all the stories about Richter were true, Bushman said, "If just half of them are true, Nate is up there smiling."

But Richter wouldn't give Beasley a raise. So in 1958, two years after he joined the Richter firm, Beasley left to start his own firm with David Cohen, a 1952 Temple Law School alumnus, and Jerome E. "Jerry" Ornsteen, a 1956 classmate from Temple Law.

"I knew his days were numbered" at the Richter firm, Bushman said of Beasley. "He wasn't going to make any real money working for Nate." The pairing with Cohen made sense, because Cohen had just left a dissolved law partnership with some 50 liability cases.

"Dave Cohen had the business," Bushman said, "And he needed somebody to try his cases and bring in the bucks, and that was Jim."

Beasley continued his workaholic ways, working six days a week at the new law firm of Cohen, Ornsteen & Beasley. Poverty was a real motivator.

"My success as a lawyer, I think, is because I was poor," Beasley said in an interview for this book. "It wasn't until I was practicing law when I made any money at all."

FOOTNOTE: *Two decades after they had been courtroom opponents in* Nuttall v. Reading, *Jim Beasley and John McConnell teamed up during the 1978-79 academic year to teach a course on trial tactics at Temple University Law School. Beasley, who represented the plaintiff's perspective, was complimentary of McConnell's talents. And McConnell, who represented defendants, referred to Beasley as one of the finest civil trial attorneys in "the Eastern-speaking world," according to Scott A. Bennett, a student in the class, and a lawyer who worked for Beasley for 30 years.*

"And I make no doubt but your upright conduct, this day, will not only entitle you to the love and esteem of your fellow citizens, but every man, who prefers freedom to a life of slavery, will bless and honour you, as men who have baffled the attempt of tyranny; and by an impartial and uncorrupt verdict, have laid a noble foundation for securing to ourselves, our posterity, and our neighbors, that, to which nature and the laws of our country have given us a right — the liberty — both of exposing and opposing arbitrary power (in these parts of the world at least) by speaking and writing truth."

ANDREW HAMILTON, SUMMATION ON BEHALF OF
JOHN PETER ZENGER, AUGUST 4, 1735

❖

THE PHILADELPHIA LAWYER

J IM BEASLEY PRACTICED LAW IN A CITY HISTORICALLY RENOWNED AND REVILED FOR the skill of its lawyers. The first famous "Philadelphia lawyer" was Andrew Hamilton, whose eloquence in 1735 on behalf of a poor New York printer named John Peter Zenger was an early victory for freedom of the press in America.

Zenger was arrested by British colonial authorities on charges of seditious libel for publishing articles in the New York Weekly Journal that attacked William Cosby, provincial governor of New York, as "an idiot," "rogue" and lawbreaker. Cosby had upset New Yorkers by replacing a Supreme Court judge who ruled against him, and by taking questionable payments from the New York Assembly.

The governor responded to the public criticism by ordering the arrest of Zenger and the public burning of every copy of the Journal. Zenger, while serving eight months in jail, requested a court-appointed lawyer, but no attorney in New York would take the case. So Hamilton, the most famous lawyer in the colonies, came up from Philadelphia to represent Zenger pro bono.

It was a tough assignment. Under British law, truth was irrelevant in a libel case, and the only thing that mattered was whether the printer had published the libel. Under British law, the greater the truth the greater the libel, since officials believed that publishing a defamatory report that was true only increased the chances of sedition, or public unrest.

At Zenger's trial, however, Hamilton flat-out admitted that his client was guilty of publishing the articles in question. And then, over the objections of the prosecutor and the judge, the Philadelphia lawyer appealed to the jury to set a new precedent in the colonies that would uphold "the best cause…the cause of liberty." Hamilton argued the then-novel theory that a newspaper article could not be libelous if it was true, and that "Truth ought to govern the whole affair of libels."

"Power may justly be compared to a great river," Hamilton told the jury, as he proceeded to take a shot at the New York governor. "While kept within its due bounds, it is both beautiful and useful. But when it overflows its banks, it is then too impetuous to be stemmed; it bears down all before it, and brings destruction and desolation wherever it comes."

In the conclusion of his summation to the jury, Hamilton pulled out all the stops:

"And I make no doubt but your upright conduct, this day, will not only entitle you to the love and esteem of your fellow citizens, but every man, who prefers freedom to a life of slavery, will bless and honor you as men who have baffled the attempt of tyranny; and by an impartial and uncorrupt verdict, have laid a noble foundation for securing to ourselves, our posterity, and our neighbors, that, to which nature and the laws of our country have given us a right — the liberty — both of exposing and opposing arbitrary power . . . by speaking and writing truth."

The jury responded by unanimously acquitting Zenger. Spectators in the galleries reportedly exclaimed, "Only a Philadelphia lawyer could have done it."

Hamilton was honored by a dinner at the Black Horse Tavern and a grand salute of cannon fire as he left New York. His triumph inspired a popular saying in Great Britain, "It would puzzle a Philadelphia lawyer," as well as another saying in New England, "Any three Philadelphia lawyers are a match for the devil."

The fame of the Philadelphia lawyer, however, turned out to be a double-edged sword. Hamilton "actually got someone acquitted who was guilty" by skillfully arguing that the governor was persecuting his client, said Catherine Lanctot, a professor of law at Villanova University in Philadelphia who teaches courses in American legal history and legal ethics.

So, over the years, the term Philadelphia lawyer also acquired a pejorative connotation, as a smooth talker who would exploit any loophole to get his client off the hook. The negative perception "reflects an age-old disdain for what lawyers do," Professor Lanctot said, as well as the public's traditional "love-hate relationship with lawyers."

In other words, if you're guilty and your lawyer gets you off, you love him, but others may hate him for it.

Woody Guthrie wrote a 1937 song about a "Philadelphia lawyer" who, during a visit to Reno, tried to convince a woman to divorce a "gun-totin' cowboy" named Wild Bill. When Wild Bill overheard the Philadelphia lawyer attempting to sweet-talk the cowboy's wife into running off with him, the cowboy paused briefly to admire the lawyer's eloquence before drawing his gun. And, as Guthrie sang in the final line of his song, "There's one less Philadelphia lawyer in old Philadelphia tonight."

In the 1959 courtroom drama, *Anatomy of a Murder*, Jimmy Stewart added to the cavalcade of Philadelphia lawyer jokes by declaring, "There's only one thing more devious than a Philadelphia lawyer, and that's an Irish lawyer."

Besides being skillful (or devious), the Philadelphia lawyer also had a reputation for being a blueblood. The legends of the Philadelphia bar during the 19th century and first half of the 20th century were aristocrats named Binney and Biddle, Pepper and Pennypacker.

When Jim Beasley became a lawyer in post-World War II Philadelphia, old-time defense lawyers still wore silk stockings in the courtroom. Beasley used to look at the lawyers' fancy dress, scan the plain folks in the jury box, and wonder how he would ever lose a case.

It was a time in Philadelphia and across the nation when the ranks of lawyers were expanding at an unprecedented rate to include poorer classes and minorities. And Beasley, according to Robert J. Reinstein, dean of Temple University's Beasley School of Law, was a prominent member of a "really phenomenal group of trial lawyers" who would dominate Philadelphia courtrooms during a national movement toward plaintiff's rights.

Reinstein has been dean of Temple's law school for 18 years and also teaches courses in constitutional law and legal history. But he got to know Beasley as a courtroom adversary back in the 1980s, when Reinstein served as Temple's general counsel. It was Reinstein's job to play defense whenever Beasley sued Temple University Hospital.

"Jim did sue us a few times; they were good cases and we settled," Reinstein said. "Generally, Jim represented the little guy against big corporations. The person I compare him to was Clarence Darrow. He wasn't afraid to take on anybody. I generally regard him as sort of the people's lawyer."

• • •

THROUGHOUT HIS CAREER, JIM BEASLEY WAS ALSO THE LAWYER THAT OTHER LAWYERS turned to when they needed help. Bernard Snyder, a former classmate of Beasley's at Temple Law School, was a passenger in a car struck by a trolley on Rising Sun Avenue in North Philadelphia. "I hurt my back," Snyder said. "Jim tried the case in 1959 and got an $18,000 verdict. Of course, Jim wouldn't take any money."

So, Snyder bought him a new chartreuse Renault. "I left the car in his driveway on Christmas," Snyder said. "Jim was very thankful."

The two lawyers were so friendly that Snyder moved in with Beasley during the 1960s, sharing an office on Locust Street, although Snyder wasn't an official member of the firm. "I did my own thing," Snyder said. He was amazed at Beasley's work ethic. "Jim was working about 22 hours a day. He was an animal. Jim was tough to talk to because he worked all the time."

Another one of Beasley's early triumphs on behalf of his fellow lawyers was *Richette v. Pennsylvania Railroad*. Lawrence J. Richette was hired in 1958 by Elford W. Richardson, a barely literate railroad employee who cleaned train stations, to represent him in a damage claim against the railroad. Richardson, who suffered a broken ankle, was told by his union bosses, "You did the wrong thing" in hiring a private lawyer. The union bosses told Richardson if he wanted to keep his job and collect any damages, he had to get rid of Richette.

Richardson's union bosses then dictated a letter of discharge that was promptly sent to Richette. The spurned lawyer hired Beasley, who sued and won a 1961 verdict of $25,000. On appeal, the state Supreme Court in 1963 upheld the verdict for Richette, but reduced the award to $15,000. It was still more than Richette would have collected if he had retained the case. Richardson's injury claim settled for $8,500, so Richette's one-third cut would have amounted only to $2,833.

"The relationship between a lawyer and his client is a serious, vital and solemn one," wrote state Supreme Court Justice Michael A. Musmanno in upholding Beasley's case. Musmanno was famous for investigating the death of Adolph Hitler on behalf of the American government and also serving as a presiding judge in the Nuremberg war crime trials. In the case of *Richette v. Pennsylvania Railroad*, Justice Musmanno declared, "No third person may interfere with that relationship any more than he may with propriety intervene between a doctor and his patient."

Despite Beasley's successes, however, the new law firm of Cohen, Ornsteen & Beasley didn't last more than two years. The problem, according to David Cohen, was a dispute over Jerry Ornsteen's role. Beasley and Cohen were trial lawyers; Ornsteen, who died in 2003, aspired to be a managing partner, Cohen said.

"Jim wanted Jerry to have an equal partnership," Cohen recalled. "And I said, 'He's gonna be the highest-paid bookkeeper you ever had.'"

Cohen said that he and Beasley had a lot in common besides being Temple Law School grads: they were a couple of kids from West Philadelphia who had lost their fathers early in life. "We worked our asses off to get through college," Cohen said. "The only difference was, he drove a truck and I drove my own truck. I was in the live chicken business."

Cohen said that Ornsteen, the son of a prominent local psychiatrist, could talk a good game, but wasn't much of a trial lawyer. "Ornsteen was lucky he found the courthouse," Cohen cracked. He recalled a slip-and-fall case that Ornsteen tried for the firm that should have been a slam dunk, involving a blind man who fell through the door of an open cellar. "He lost it," Cohen said, still in shock four decades later.

Cohen left the partnership in 1959 to start his own firm the following year.

The remaining partnership of Beasley & Ornsteen wasn't a long-running act. The two split in 1963, and the parting ended in litigation. Cohen had lunch with Beasley shortly after the split, and he recalled Beasley telling him, "Goddamn it, you were so right."

"I regarded him as a great lawyer and I regarded him as my friend," Cohen, 83, said of Beasley in a 2007 interview. "I would have been happy to be Beasley's partner for the rest of my life."

• • •

ON JULY 3, 1963, DAVID COHEN WAS DRIVING A LINCOLN CONTINENTAL ON MONU-ment Road in Philadelphia when he slowed to a stop to make a right-hand turn onto Ford Road. Before he could make the turn, however, he was rear-ended by a Chevy driven by a sales representative for Gulf Oil Corp.

Cohen suffered severe whiplash. He had to wear a cervical collar and sleep at home in a hospital bed. The pain was so intense that he hung from a portable traction unit in his law office several times a day for relief, sometimes while talking to clients. Cohen required surgery on his neck, fusing three vertebrae, as well as surgery on his shoulder. His annual earnings took a dive.

So when Cohen needed a lawyer to represent him, he turned to his former law partner, Jim Beasley. *Cohen v. Gulf Oil Corp.* went to trial in 1967; instead of a jury, Beasley tried the case in front of the Hon. Theodore B. Smith Jr. The result was the first million-dollar verdict in Pennsylvania history.

The case turned on Beasley's cross-examination of the other driver in the accident. Peter J. King of Gulf Oil had made some damaging admissions in a deposition he gave in 1964, a year after the accident. When the case came to trial in 1967, King tried to change his story on the witness stand, but Beasley kept pointing out contradictions with King's deposition testimony:

Beasley: "And would you feel that your recollection a year after the accident was more clear than it is today, 3½ years after the accident?"

King: "...Having seen the results of that deposition for the first time this last week, candor forces me to admit that perhaps some of my observations were not accurate."

Beasley: "... OK. What did you tell us in 1964 the speed of your vehicle at the time of impact was?"

King: "I said about 25 miles an hour."

Beasley: "Now, that answer was not truthful?"

King: "It was not accurate."

Beasley asked King how far he was from Cohen's car when he saw it for the first time. In his deposition, King had estimated that distance at 200 feet. But on the witness stand, King hesitated: "Well, I am not sure of the distance now."

Beasley asked King about his deposition testimony that Cohen's car "was starting from a dead stop" when the accident occurred. And King changed his mind one more time.

Beasley: "You don't want the court to believe that the car was at a dead stop, do you?"

King: "I don't think that it was at a dead stop, no. I actually believe it was moving."

On May 17, 1967, Judge Smith awarded Cohen $1,100,000. "Suffice to say that we find the testimony of defendant's driver to be completely incredible," the judge wrote. "He was destroyed on cross-examination, and there were many contradictions in his testimony."

The case was on appeal when it was settled for $850,000.

• • •

BENEDICT A. CASEY WENT TO WORK FOR BEASLEY IN 1966, WHEN HIS LAW FIRM WAS known as Beasley, Albert, Hewson & Casey. Casey had spent the previous 10 years working in the trial division of a big insurance company. He was scheduled to start work with Beasley on a Monday, but he visited Beasley's office the Sunday before, to meet his clients in a slip-and-fall case.

Casey tried the case on Monday, and a day after the case settled, he tried a second case, which also settled during his first week on the job. Beasley wanted his lawyers to be in the courtroom most of the time, Casey said, trying cases that typically lasted less than a week.

"Cross-examinations for us were an essential part of success," Casey said. "We didn't do a whole lot of discovery." Lawyers were like firemen, Casey explained. "When the bell rings, you've got to go. Some fires are hard, some are easy. Doesn't matter; just go. Don't be a chicken."

In those days, juries were sequestered until they reached a unanimous verdict, so lawyers could be up until 2 in the morning, waiting for a jury to come in. The lawyers often passed the time, Casey said, by pitching pennies against a wall, to see who could come the closest.

Back at the office, Beasley had a habit of hiring attractive women, especially blondes. His longtime secretary was Donna Braun, a tall, leggy blonde who could type as fast as any lawyer could talk. Beasley's receptionist was Meryle Silver, a short, petite blonde and self-proclaimed Jewish American Princess, who usually came to work dripping in diamonds.

The boss knew how to bring in business. The standard referral fee at the time for taking a case from another lawyer was 25 to 33 percent of the lawyer's fee. The Beasley firm, however, paid 50 percent for referrals. "That was our way of broadening the base," said Sheldon L. Albert, a Beasley law partner from 1961 to 1971.

Beasley expected his lawyers to carry a heavy caseload. "The day I walked into the place, I was assigned 150 to 200 cases," said James E. Colleran, who joined the firm in 1969. "The vast majority of these were primarily automobile cases. There was lots more product liability work than there is now."

The half-dozen lawyers from Beasley's office usually went to lunch every day at the Locust Villa, a nearby hoagie and hamburger shop. Every night at 6, Beasley and Albert would gather in Beasley's corner office to "kick around" trial tactics and strategy. Then they'd hang out at the same bar on Locust Street. Some of their best friends and drinking buddies were the defense lawyers they had gone up against earlier that day in court.

Beasley also threw a Christmas party every year at the office for local orphans. Colleran dressed up as Santa and passed out toys and clothes to needy children.

The boss, however, wasn't always the sociable type. Casey recalled a trip he took with Beasley to Harrisburg in one of Beasley's fleet of leased Cadillacs. Beasley had been asked by a group of 19 state judges to try to overturn a provision of a new state constitution that imposed a mandatory retirement age for judges at 70. (The challenge would ultimately be unsuccessful.)

"He wouldn't let me drive," Casey said. "He was a peculiar guy. If you've ever been in the company of somebody where you had to carry the whole conversation . . . .

"On the trip to Harrisburg, I was doing all the talking, so I stopped," Casey said. "And so we rode in silence all the way out and all the way back. There was no meanness about it. It was like him living in his own world."

Casey decided to maintain a respectful distance from the boss. "If you get too close to Jim, he couldn't resist fathering people," Casey said. "That meant controlling you. So if you don't want to be controlled, you don't want to be too close. That didn't change my respect for him. He was undoubtedly the greatest lawyer I ever met."

On a plane trip out to Denver for a trial lawyers' convention, however, Casey discovered that Beasley was "a terrible poker player."

"Jim was always optimistic," Casey said. "He played poker like he was talking to a jury. He thought he could change the spots on the cards. He would just make outrageous bets whether he had the cards or not."

Casey ended up taking a few hundred dollars off Beasley. He also learned not to go to the boss for legal advice. "He's the last guy I would go talk to if I was losing a case," Casey said. "I already felt bad enough."

Casey recalled overhearing Beasley tee off on law partner Shelly Albert. "I hear these explosions coming out of Jim's office," Casey said. "He's yelling, 'God damn it, Shelly, how the fuck could you leave an accountant on that jury?'"

"I have no doubt that it happened," said Albert, who couldn't recall the specific incident. Albert, however, had a different view of Beasley:

"For 10 years, Jim was the best friend I ever had," Albert said. Every Friday night, Beasley hosted a poker party at his house in the Wynnefield section of the city with the same four or five lawyers. The menu was bourbon and pretzels. Albert, one of the regulars, confirmed Casey's assessment of Beasley as a poker player: "Jim was a bad bluffer."

But Beasley could be counted on in an emergency. When Albert's wife gave birth to a baby who quickly died, "Jim didn't want me to be alone," Albert said. Beasley had suffered a similar tragedy. While Albert's wife stayed in the hospital, Beasley had Albert move into his house for a week.

"He spent every day with me," said Albert, who left the firm in 1971 after a dispute he declined to discuss. "What happened afterwards," Albert said, "it doesn't undo things like that."

OUR LITTLE ANGEL
MARY ANN
1955 — 1962

COLLING

❖

Chapter 7

A PRESCRIPTION FOR DEATH

FOUR-YEAR-OLD MARY ANN INCOLLINGO HAD A SORE THROAT, A RUNNY NOSE, AND a slight fever of 99 degrees. Her mother took the dark-eyed girl with the long hair and olive skin to see the family pediatrician who had treated her since she was 5 days old.

Dr. Domenico Cucinotta peered down the little girl's throat and detected a bad case of tonsillitis. It was Jan. 22, 1960. The doctor took out a pad and wrote out a prescription for a drug that had done wonders for Mary Ann in the past — Chloromycetin. The popular antibiotic came in the form of a "pleasant, custard-flavored liquid." A warning label on the two-ounce bottle said, "Do not refill."

When the prescription ran out, however, and Mary Ann had a relapse, her mother, Connie, asked another doctor to write out prescriptions for two more bottles of Chloromycetin. Before the second refill was finished, Mary Ann had broken out in large bruises and nosebleeds that wouldn't stop. It was the start of two years of horror.

Mary Ann Incollingo of North Philadelphia was just 6 years old when she died in 1962 of a cerebral hemorrhage, after taking prescription medication for a sore throat. Her death would permanently change the way doctors in Pennsylvania practiced medicine.

Before the 1967 trial of *Incollingo v. Ewing*, doctors facing a malpractice case in Pennsylvania could hide behind "the locality rule" of 1903. This protectionist legislation was modeled after similar rules in Kansas and Massachusetts that dated back to the 19th century, and originally were created for the benefit of rural country doctors who didn't measure up to the standards of their big-city counterparts.

Over the years, the locality rule in Pennsylvania was interpreted to require only a level of care up to the standards of neighboring physicians. But after Jim Beasley spent a decade fighting *Incollingo v. Ewing,* a state Supreme Court justice wrote in a 1971 opinion that the locality rule was "an anachronism" that should be abolished.

· · ·

CHLOROMYCETIN, ACCORDING TO ITS MANUFACTURER, PARKE, DAVIS & CO., WAS A "broad-spectrum antibiotic" that cured a wide range of infectious diseases. Parke Davis first put the drug on the market in 1949. It became a big seller because it worked fast and, unlike other antibiotics of the era, didn't cause nausea or vomiting. In 1958, the first year that Dr. Cucinotta prescribed Chloromycetin for Mary Ann Incollingo, Parke Davis sold $80 million worth of the wonder drug. A company official subsequently told Beasley that Parke Davis manufactured 11 tons a year of Chloromycetin.

When Mary Ann got sick again in February 1960, her mother couldn't get Dr. Cucinotta on the phone, so she called Dr. Samuel I. Levin, Connie Incollingo's diet doctor, and asked him to refill her little girl's prescription.

Whenever Mary Ann coughed or sniffled, her mother gave her another teaspoonful of Chloromycetin. When the refill ran out, Connie Incollingo had her diet doctor write another prescription for a third bottle of Chloromycetin.

"She was a very good patient of mine, and the child was ill," Dr. Levin explained on the witness stand during the 1967 trial. "I felt, OK, I would do a Good Samaritan deed and refill the prescription for her."

The doctor's defense was consistent with the state locality rule. Dr. Levin testified that it was a reasonable and accepted practice by Philadelphia physicians at the time to prescribe antibiotics over the phone, without seeing the patient. Some patients were too sick to come to the office, the doctor told the jury, or the weather was bad.

Parke Davis, in its sale literature, had warned that Chloromycetin was a drug that "should not be used indiscriminately or for minor infections" because it was associated with certain abnormal blood functions. "Warning," the drug packaging said, "blood dyscrasias [disorders] may be associated with intermittent or prolonged use. It is essential that adequate blood studies be made."

Mary Ann had taken the drug three times during a 16-month period between October 1958 and January 1960, but no blood studies were ever done. When Mary Ann developed large bruises and severe nosebleeds, Dr. Cucinotta finally ordered a blood count. It showed decreased levels of red blood cells, white blood cells and platelets. Dr. Cucinotta's diagnosis: acquired aplastic anemia, caused by Chloromycetin.

Beasley sued Dr. Cucinotta, Dr. Levin, Parke Davis, and the pharmacist who had filled all the Chloromycetin prescriptions — Peirce G. Ewing, owner of the Ewing Pharmacy on Germantown Avenue in Philadelphia. Ewing died before the case went to trial, so lawyers read his deposition testimony into the record.

At the seven-week trial, the defense table was crowded with lawyers representing the four defendants. But over at the plaintiff's table, it was just Jim Beasley.

Beasley put Mary Ann's father, Vincent, on the witness stand, and asked about his daughter's bruises. Vincent Incollingo was a native of Italy with a fifth-grade education who dug sewers for a living.

"It was like blood was just about coming out of the skin," Vincent Incollingo told Beasley. The nosebleeds were even worse.

"She used to sleep with us most of the time," Incollingo said. "All of a sudden… she said, 'Mommy, I am all wet.' …And so we put the lights on. There was blood coming out from her nose… . I plugged her nose with cotton."

Dr. Cucinotta wanted to build up Mary Ann's blood count, so he prescribed vitamins and painful daily injections of steroids. But the steroids caused Mary Ann to sprout hair all over her body. Then the little girl developed acne, boils, coarse skin, and lesions all over her face. She also gained 20 pounds, displayed fits of temper, and became swollen and grotesque-looking.

"Her voice became like a man's voice," Vincent Incollingo told Beasley. "And she began to become very strong."

"What do you mean by that?" Beasley asked.

"Strong just like — when she got so big, she used to even wrestle with her brothers," Incollingo said. "Her brothers were pretty big and she used to beat [them] because this drug was such a powerful drug. It made her that way."

Then the seizures started. "She was laying on the sofa," Incollingo said. "All of a sudden she began to . . . twist her eyes and she began to shake just like you pull a fish from the river."

The seizures grew more powerful. "She was in convulsions [for] an hour," Incollingo told Beasley. "When the rescue squad came in, she was still in convulsions. …She was shivering just like electricity in you all the time."

James T. Weston was the forensic pathologist who performed the autopsy on Mary Ann Incollingo. He testified that the hemorrhage that killed Mary Ann was caused by Chloromycetin. The doctor also told Beasley that the drug was overprescribed, and that some 40 million doses were given annually to "practically every patient who came into the hospital for just about any condition."

Beasley asked Dr. Weston about the pharmaceutical salesmen of the era, known as "detail men," who would visit local doctors and pass out free samples. Dr. Weston testified that when doctors asked about the harmful side affects of Chloromycetin, the detail men responded that the "danger was so minimal that you shouldn't worry about it."

· · ·

CARMELLA INCOLLINGO – "THEY CALL ME CONNIE FOR SHORT" — QUIT SCHOOL IN THE 10th grade to become a hairdresser. She told Beasley that she trusted her doctors when she gave her daughter repeated doses of Chloromycetin.

"Did anybody give you any warnings about the medication?" Beasley asked.

"No, no warnings," she said. "It just said, 'This cannot be filled,' but they gave it to me. . . . Nobody told me how dangerous it was."

When Mary Ann developed nosebleeds, "she was a mess of blood," Connie Incollingo told Beasley. "It was just like you would turn a spigot on and let the water come out. She was just hemorrhaging from her nose… . And she bled, oh, my God, for a couple of hours."

Throughout her testimony, Connie Incollingo kept smiling and laughing at inappropriate moments, such as when she told Beasley that her daughter usually vomited after taking other medicines, but not Chloromycetin. Beasley called her on it, saying, "You are smiling now, but you don't think that is funny, do you, Mrs. Incollingo?"

"No," she said. "I lost a daughter. Do you think that is funny? I can't live since she died."

"Were you in the hospital during the time?" Beasley asked.

"Yes, sir, I was," Connie Incollingo testified. "I was in the hospital three times. I had psychiatric care."

"…Did you during any of your hospitalizations receive electrical shock therapy?" Beasley asked.

"Not at Temple," she said. "They were giving me injections."

In his summation to the jury, Beasley said the death of Mary Ann Incollingo had doomed her mother to a life of hell, prompting a defense objection and a warning from the judge about using prejudicial statements. Beasley then told the jury that Vincent Incollingo blamed his wife for his daughter's death, and that the couple's subsequent divorce "all flows from the Chloromycetin." That resulted in more objections from defense counsels. The judge sustained the objections and Beasley had to withdraw the statement.

The jurors, however, had made their minds up. They found the two doctors liable, as well as Parke Davis; only the late pharmacist was acquitted. The jury awarded the Incollingos $15,000 for medical expenses, and $200,000 to cover the loss of what Mary Ann Incollingo would have earned during her lifetime.

When the Pennsylvania Supreme Court upheld the decision in 1971, the court said it would not express an opinion about "the current validity of this geographical limitation" known as the locality rule. Judge Samuel J. Roberts, however, in a concurring opinion said the locality rule probably had made sense a century earlier. But because of "widespread dissemination of medical literature" and improved medical education, "the locality rule is an anachronism. Massachusetts, one of the original locality rule jurisdictions, has recognized this and abandoned the rule," Judge Roberts wrote. "We should do likewise."

The Pennsylvania Supreme Court's Civil Standards Jury Instructions Committee finally made it official in 2003, by declaring that "the committee believes the locality rule no longer has a viable justification."

weeping incessantly,

fear of ending in State Hosp. a little

—anger— equiled to dead—

Berlin 0.8 - 1-14. 8mgm.

C

I am really going to kill myself

weeping

—— shouting a bit — I'm angry,

50 - Rit 20mgm

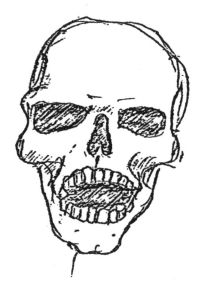

= Vφ

ne
in
for the first

P - 4

J.O. 12/2/

Chapter 8

❖

SEX AND DRUGS ON
A PSYCHIATRIST'S COUCH

JIM BEASLEY CALLED AS HIS FIRST WITNESS THE PSYCHIATRIST HE WAS SUING FOR MAL-practice. Then Beasley proceeded to cross-examine the psychiatrist about the affair he had with a young woman who spent a lot of time on his couch.

"Did the original training that you had in psychotherapy condone sexual relations with a patient?"

"I don't believe so," the doctor said.

Dr. Donald Lee McCabe was a slender man with gray hair and a white goatee. Behind his glasses, he had what his former patient described as pasty white skin and a piercing stare.

"When is it in your recollection of the facts that you first had sex with Gale Greenberg?" Beasley asked.

"The latter part of '69," the doctor said.

"Do you recognize or did you recognize then that when sex between a thera-pist and the patient occurs, that that can be a tremendous psychiatric problem for the patient?"

"No," the doctor said.

The trial of *Greenberg v. McCabe*, held in September 1977 at the federal courthouse in Philadelphia, was one of the most sensational in Beasley's career. The testimony dwelled on therapy sessions where Dr. McCabe injected his young female patient with uppers, downers or hallucinogens, and then had sex with her on his couch.

Beasley didn't fully believe his client's stories until he subpoenaed the doctor's notebooks and discovered that the bizarre sessions were thoroughly documented in the doctor's own notes and sketches of his favorite patient.

Beasley asked the doctor about the moment when Gale Greenberg went from patient to lover, if "the therapy should have been terminated right then and there?"

"No, I don't think that was necessary," the doctor said.

". . . Is it your opinion that having sexual relations with a patient . . . in analytical psychotherapy is an exercise of reasonable medical care?" Beasley asked.

"I don't think that the sexual involvement that I had with Gale had to do with therapy," the doctor explained. "It was outside the world of therapy as far as I'm concerned. It was a private matter between lovers."

The doctor, who had flown in from his new home in Sacramento, Calif., seemed annoyed by Beasley's questions, but did his best to keep his professional demeanor. He was not at all repentant.

"I do not think it traumatized her," the doctor said of his affair with his patient. "In fact, I think you will find some statements where she says that she could not have endured some of the thoughts and emotions that she had in therapy if she hadn't had such a strong attachment and feeling toward me."

"Is that known as transference?" Beasley asked, evoking the main theme of his case.

"It may be called transference," the doctor replied coolly. "It might even be called love, too."

• • •

GALE GREENBERG WAS A 25-YEAR-OLD "HARRIED HOUSEWIFE" FROM ALLENTOWN, PA., in 1968 who suffered from a combination of asthma and anxiety. That's how the 5-foot-2, 105-pound woman with the teased blonde hair ended up on the psychiatrist's couch.

Dr. Donald Lee McCabe was a married, 44-year-old doctor of osteopathy in Harrisburg, Pa., who also practiced a little psychoanalysis on the side, even though he had never completed a residency in psychiatry and was not certified in the discipline.

But the doctor was meticulous about recording his therapy sessions, which featured heavy drug use and the skillful drawings of a dirty old man. In March 1969, for example, the doctor wrote that he began a session with Greenberg by giving her a shot of Amytal, a barbiturate. As he waited for the drug to kick in, McCabe drew Greenberg lying barefoot on his couch. "If you care, you will help me," she said. Meanwhile, Dr. McCabe was peering down Greenberg's dress and sketching her cleavage.

In August 1969, the doctor began a session by injecting Greenberg with another shot of Amytal. Then he recorded his patient's reaction. "Don, what did you give me?" the patient laughed. "My brain doesn't seem to be working too well." Meanwhile, the doctor was sketching the patient's dazed eyes, short skirt and bare legs.

Within the first year of therapy, doctor and patient were having sex on the office couch while the doctor's wife and kids were upstairs. "Do you want me to fill the emptiness?" the doctor asked his patient, according to his own notes.

Greenberg begged the doctor for more injections, saying she never felt better. Greenberg, according to courtroom testimony, was also able to help Dr. McCabe overcome a case of impotency, but there were strings attached. "I don't want sex, I want love," she told the doctor, according to his own notes.

Kathleen L. Daerr-Bannon, now an administrative judge, was Beasley's cocounsel in 1977, when she worked for 18 months on *Greenberg v. McCabe*. In a 2006 interview, Daerr-Bannon recalled the central question of the case: "Why is this ditzy lady having sex and drugs with this ditzy doctor?"

It wasn't just "two human beings having human foibles" outside the medical arena, Daerr-Bannon explained. Instead, according to the legal theory advanced by Beasley and his expert psychiatrist, Dr. Wolfram Rieger, "It was a doctor purposefully abusing the psychological phenomenon between a patient and a psychiatrist known as transference," Daerr-Bannon said. That made *Greenberg v. McCabe* a medical malpractice case.

"Transference gave you the theory of the case, plus insurance," Daerr-Bannon said. "The medical malpractice [insurance] company couldn't get out of it."

Other lawyers might have shied away from taking on Gale Greenberg as a client because of her mental problems, naiveté, and many bad decisions. Beasley, however, was outraged by McCabe's conduct, and felt that it was his duty to expose him.

Beasley also wanted to help Greenberg. People with psychiatric illnesses don't forfeit their rights to be treated as human beings, Beasley once explained to a young lawyer. "Just because someone's crazy doesn't mean they haven't been hurt."

Beasley had one other big hurdle in the case. Greenberg, the defense said, had filed suit two years after the Pennsylvania statute of limitations on personal-injury cases had expired. But Beasley found a way around that issue as well.

• • •

GALE GREENBERG, THEN 34, SHOWED UP AT THE TRIAL WITH DARK CURLY BROWN HAIR cut short. She wore a simple brown suit and a white blouse buttoned to the throat. "She looked like a victim," recalled Daerr-Bannon.

"What was it that brought you to Dr. McCabe?" Beasley asked.

"My asthma was very bad," Greenberg testified. "And a friend of mine recommended me to Dr. McCabe because she thought I might be having psychological problems because of the asthma."

"Would you tell us what it was that you did as far as performing the duties of a housewife and mother during that period of 1962 to 1968?" Beasley asked.

"Did the laundry, the shopping, took care of the children, made all the meals," Greenberg said. "I was a normal housewife."

"When you had your first visit with Dr. McCabe, would you tell the members of the jury and the judge what occurred at that time?"

"… Dr McCabe told me that I was very, very ill," Greenberg said. "He said that I didn't know if I was a man or a woman and that I had a lot of sexual hang-ups."

Greenberg explained how the doctor told her she needed to see him at least twice a week for therapy, at the 1970s price of $25 an hour.

"Would you tell us what the central discussion of the therapy sessions was about?" Beasley asked.

"Sex," Greenberg said. "Dr. McCabe said that I would have to act out my sexual fantasies…. Whatever I said had a sexual connotation to it. Whatever dream I had, he would interpret it sexually."

"… How would the session begin?" Beasley asked.

"With an injection," she said.

"What would you be injected with?"

"Ritalin and Methergine, or just Ritalin," she said of the stimulant used to treat attention deficit disorder; Methergine was a blood-vessel constrictor.

"Where would the injection be given?"

"Intravenously.

"Where?"

"Anywhere," she said. "Anywhere he could find a vein."

Beasley asked about the effects of DMT, a hallucinogen comparable to LSD.

"Well, first when it was injected, it would start burning the back of my head," Greenberg testified. "And then that would go away and I would start to hallucinate. I would see things all over the room."

"What things did you see?" Beasley asked.

"Skeletons and eyes and faces, all different kinds of things, in color."

"… Was there any other explanation for the use of the drugs that he was using other than what you have already told us?" Beasley asked.

"He said it would help me break through my sexual hang-ups," Greenberg said.

Beasley asked Greenberg about her first sexual encounter with the doctor.

"Dr. McCabe gave me an injection of Ritalin and I started to talk," Greenberg said. "I was very high and I got up from the couch and I was pacing and talking…. He grabbed my arm and pulled me into the chair and started to kiss me and fondle my breasts."

Greenberg testified that she then performed oral sex on the doctor, who had claimed he was impotent. But even before that incident, she told Beasley, "I had become very emotionally dependent upon him and the drugs."

"… Did he ever give you any explanation as to why you and he were engaging in this type of conduct?"

"He said it would be good therapy for me…. It would be good therapy for me to be able to have a normal relationship with a man," she said. "Dr. McCabe would come on the couch and we would have intercourse and then he would get back in his chair and we would continue with the therapy session."

"Did you believe that this was legitimate therapy?"

"Yes," she said.

"…How were you feeling?"

"I was feeling awful and guilty," she said.

"What was going on at home?"

"My husband and I were continually fighting about my having therapy and not being able to take care of the children and the house," she said.

"Why didn't you just break away from McCabe at that point?"

"He became a god," she said. "I was dependent on him. I didn't think — he made me believe I was so sick that nobody else could help me but him. I was petrified."

"… Did he ever say anything to you about … acting out any fantasies?" Beasley asked.

"Yes," she said. "He told me to ask my girlfriend if she would engage in a homosexual relationship with me."

"Did you do that?"

"Yes," she said.

"How did that make you feel?"

"Disgusting."

"Did you tell Dr. McCabe about that?"

"Yes."

"Did you at any time ever want a sexual relationship with McCabe?"

"No."

"What was it that you wanted from him?"

"Love. Drugs. Love."

• • •

Dr. Wolfram Rieger, Beasley's expert psychiatrist, looked like a ski instructor, the press said, and spoke with an Austrian accent. "He was a wonderful witness," Daerr-Bannon said. "He was Sigmund Freud, only newer and improved." It was Dr. Rieger's job to explain to the jury how Dr. McCabe had trampled on the normal ethical standards of psychiatry.

The psychiatrist, Rieger told the jury, "more so than in any other specialty of medicine, has an obligation not to get involved in any personal way with his patients. That means that he cannot even touch the patient in a friendly gesture," Rieger said. "The most that is permitted would be a handshake, and that only upon initiation by the patient.

"He cannot socialize with the patient in any manner," Rieger said. "This is something that every young psychiatric resident gets taught from the very first day he enters training."

Rieger explained how in psychotherapy, patients go back to their childhood. "This phenomenon is called regression," the doctor said. "While they are regressed like that, they tend to project feelings they once held towards significant adults in their lives. They may be parents, sometimes it may be a grandparent, uncles, aunts, what have you, teachers. They project those feelings onto the therapist."

"The relationship between the psychiatrist and the patient is very much fiduciary," Rieger said. "It is a trust relationship precisely because the patient becomes in therapy child-like, and the therapist becomes father-like. Sometimes he is, you know, seen like an all-powerful person, almost god-like, that you know, can't do no wrong."

"In Mrs. Greenberg's case, the sexual encounter that was experienced between her and Dr. McCabe, in your opinion was that part of transference?" Beasley asked.

"In my opinion, this is a direct outcome of her transference, and unfortunately, also of his counter-transference that he could not control or did not choose to control," Dr. Rieger said.

". . . Does a patient who is experiencing this transference have free will and freedom of choice in engaging in the sexual act with the psychiatrist?" Beasley asked.

"…The patient at that point is almost in a trance, almost as if [she] were hypnotized by the psychiatrist, and would obey any order or suggestion that the psychiatrist would make," Dr. Rieger said.

Beasley asked Dr. Rieger what the patient's original diagnosis was when she showed up in Dr. McCabe's office.

"She was suffering from a mild neurosis, what we call, in jargon, 'the harried housewife syndrome,'" Dr. Rieger said. "She was a housewife with some asthma. This would be known as a psychic-physiologic disorder."

Beasley asked Dr. Rieger to give the jury his professional opinion of a psychiatrist having sex with a patient.

"It is like going to bed with your own father, which is in all peoples, and all cultures, in all religions, the worst possible or one of the worst possible crimes or sins," Dr. Rieger told the jury. "Therefore, she will be haunted for, probably, for the rest of her life by the thought of having transgressed this ultimate taboo."

Beasley asked Dr. Rieger about a bizarre drawing in one of Dr. McCabe's notebooks that juxtaposed a vagina with a skull baring its teeth, a psychiatric symbol known as "vagina dentate," or a vagina with teeth.

"Would you explain that to the jury?" Beasley asked.

"… It is a fantasy that pertains to men and little boys," Dr. Rieger said. "These men who have been too much mothered, not to say smothered, perceive women as a crypt with vaginas that have teeth, and these are men that very often then, because of this fear, become homosexuals and thus avoid this dangerous organ of the woman… ."

"You know he [McCabe] was impotent when he first wanted to consummate intercourse with her," Dr. Rieger testified. "He told her that he was impotent with his wife. He obviously had a lot of sexual hang-ups, and here they are in clear evidence by his own hand, skillfully drawn, and that is what he wanted to cure. . . . He wanted to cure himself at her expense."

• • •

DR. MCCABE GAVE GALE GREENBERG $13,530 WORTH OF TREATMENTS THAT INCLUDED injecting needles into veins all over her body, including her breasts.

The treatments began in 1968. The defense contended that McCabe's therapy formally ended in 1972, when Greenberg became the patient of another psychiatrist. That same year, Greenberg abandoned her husband and two young sons, and moved in with Dr. McCabe, who split up with his wife.

Pennsylvania has a two-year limit on filing a personal-injury lawsuit, and in Greenberg's case, it would have expired in 1974, the defense contended. Greenberg, however, had waited until 1976 to sue.

Beasley argued that during the two years that Greenberg lived with McCabe, the doctor still functioned as her psychiatrist. Greenberg testified that while she shared a house with McCabe, he continued to psychoanalyze her, as well as supply her with Quaaludes and injections.

The defense countered that during the two years that they lived together, Greenberg and McCabe were no longer patient and doctor, but boyfriend and girlfriend. But Beasley used Dr. Rieger to rebut that argument.

"Now, I would like to direct your attention to that period of time after 1972 or starting in 1972 when Mrs. Greenberg testified that she 'moved in' with Dr. McCabe, and I use 'moved in' in quotes," Beasley said. "Do you have an opinion based upon reasonable psychiatric certainty as to whether Mrs. Greenberg recognized at that time that there was a termination of the psychiatrist-patient relationship?"

"She could not possibly have realized this, because the relationship continued," Dr. Rieger told the jury. "Dr. McCabe continued being her treating physician, what he called a psychiatrist. He did not only give her written prescriptions, but continued giving her injections in many different areas of her body."

"Well," Beasley said, playing devil's advocate, "why wouldn't a reasonable person realize that when she moves into his house that that no longer constitutes a patient-physician relationship? Why would she continue to believe that her therapist-patient relationship existed?"

"…The patient-therapist relationship by far outweighs the boyfriend-girlfriend relationship," Rieger declared. "It is all-powerful, and once you are someone's psychiatrist, you are their psychiatrist 24 hours a day, 365 days a year.

"My patients, if they were to run into me in the supermarket or in a movie house or a restaurant, would always perceive me as their psychiatrist, and I would certainly refrain from any kind of prolonged small talk or any kind of social encounter in such a seemingly casual situation."

Greenberg's affair with McCabe ended in 1974, when, according to Greenberg, the doctor woke her up and demanded sex, and when she refused, he beat her so badly that he fractured her skull and sexually abused her. By that time, Greenberg had twice tried to commit suicide.

On the witness stand, Rieger referred to the 1974 confrontation as the harvest of the "ultimate grapes of wrath sewn along in the course of therapy. Any therapist knows that patients who have positive transferences will also have negative transferences, and if you teach a patient to act out the positive transference, she will have to act out the negative transference as well," Rieger said. "And if you then retaliate, then you have an altercation."

• • •

"Before you first saw Dr. McCabe, did you ever have any thoughts of suicide?" Beasley asked.

"Never," Gale Greenberg said.

Beasley asked about her second suicide attempt, which took place in the presence of her two young sons and Dr. McCabe.

"I don't remember what he said to me, but he made me feel hurt and angry," she said of Dr. McCabe. "I just went into the bathroom and I cut my wrists. He came in after me, he wrapped a towel around my wrists and he took me to his office and sutured me without anesthesia and with each, with each suture, he was going, 'I'll teach you, I'll teach you.'"

Beasley asked Greenberg about the end of the affair in 1974, when the doctor allegedly beat and sexually abused her.

"Was there any involvement by McCabe with your genital area?"

"Yes."

"What happened?"

"He shoved his fist in my vagina," she said. "I was back over the bed, and he twisted my cervix."

"Were you admitted to the hospital as a result of that?"

"Yes."

"Did you sustain any other injuries?"

"A fractured skull, concussion, bites, abrasions."

Beasley showed the witness pictures of two young boys. "Can you tell me, can you recognize those children?"

"Those are my children," she said.

"When you and your husband were divorced, who was it that obtained the divorce?"

"I did," she said, and then she began crying.

"What happened to the children?"

"I'm sorry," she said, wiping her tears. "I could not have them. Dr. [Lawrence L.] Altaker told me if I tried to take them with me, he would have to stop me because I couldn't take care of them."

"Have you had any sexual encounters with men since 1974 until now?" Beasley said, asking about the last three years.

"Yes," she said.

"How many?"

"I stopped counting at 60," she said.

"Why, Mrs. Greenberg?" Beasley asked. "Why do you have these encounters?"

"I don't know," she said. "I was so filled with grief and pain I didn't care, didn't care about my life; just didn't care. It wasn't for sex. I don't know."

Beasley asked about the side-effects from the drugs that Dr. McCabe had given Greenberg.

Have you had any experience from 1974 until now with hallucinations?"

"Yes."

"How often?"

"Every day."

"What are they?" Beasley asked. "Can you describe them for the jury?"

"I have experiences of leaving my body," she said. "One time I was lying down and all of a sudden I was in a field with Christ."

"…Was this a dream?"

"No."

"Well, what happened in this field with Christ?"

"He was saying, 'You have to get your life together.'"

"…How did you know this was not a dream?"

"Because I was wide awake."

"Were there any other experiences about leaving your body?"

"Yes," she said. "Another time I was lying on the bed awake, and I felt myself leaving my body, my spirit or whatever, going down over the bed and touching the dresser."

"…Then what did you do?"

"I got petrified and went back."

"Went back into your body?"

"Yes."

. . .

BEASLEY'S TRIAL SCHEDULE WAS SO BUSY THAT HE HAD TO GIVE UP HIS EARLY MORNING rows in a single scull on the Schuylkill River. Philadelphia magazine, however, in a long story on *Greenberg v. McCabe*, noted that the plaintiff's lawyer still had "the look of a long-distance rower" with his thick wrists, powerful chest and shoulders.

"The wrong kind of fighter, if he'd been a fighter, to mix with in close," wrote authors Matt and Garree Lang Quinn.

But when he cross-examined McCabe, Beasley didn't pin the demented doctor against the ropes, and pound away on any particular subject. Instead, he moved quickly from one tawdry topic to another, using skillful questions to cut through the doctor's professional cool and reveal him for what he was.

"Is it your testimony, Dr. McCabe, that Gale Greenberg was very sick when you first saw her?" Beasley asked.

"Yes, I think she was," Dr. McCabe said.

"…Well, did her condition get better or did it get worse under your care?"

"I think it got better," the doctor said.

"…Well, didn't you feel that the sex relations that you had with her were to her advantage therapeutically?"

"I think when one feels that somebody cares about you, it certainly benefits you and it makes you able to face things that you weren't able to face," Dr. McCabe said. "I think you must have experienced in your life —"

"Your Honor," Beasley said to the judge. "May I have the witness just answer the question instead of trying to analyze me?"

"I am not trying to analyze you," the doctor said.

Beasley asked the doctor what caused him to draw the vagina with teeth in his notebook.

"Well, I don't think it was relegated just to this session," the doctor said. "I think it's a time frame that we were working in," McCabe said before muttering about "her hostile use of her vagina."

"Her hostile use of her vagina," Beasley repeated, for the benefit of the jury.

"Yes," the doctor said.

"…What was the therapeutic value of calling her, your patient, a cock tease?" Beasley asked.

"…We are dealing here with her provocative hostile nature," the doctor said. "And a cock-teaser is a provocative, hostile person."

Beasley asked the doctor about his impotency.

"I mentioned that I was impotent. All right?" the doctor snarled at Beasley. "I answered that question before."

Beasley asked Dr. McCabe about a couple of famous sex therapists. "Do you know what Masters and Johnson say about the therapist having sex with a patient?"

"Not off the top of my head, no," the doctor replied. "What do they say?" "It's a rape," Beasley said, while the doctor just sat there, without making any reply.

Beasley asked about the doctor's method of injecting drugs. "Wasn't there a time in your therapy with Gale that you couldn't find a vein, so you injected into her breast?"

"No, that is not true," the doctor said.

Beasley asked the doctor to turn to his patient's notes from Jan. 12, 1972, and he instructed the doctor to read his own handwriting.

"Amytal 3¾ grams IV. Mammary shot – no apparent effect," the doctor read.

"What do you mean by a mammary shot?" Beasley asked.

"That is a mammary vein," the doctor said, vainly trying to split hairs. "That is not the breast."

Beasley pressed McCabe. "Why couldn't you get it into the arm or the wrist or the ankle where superficial veins are? Why did you find it necessary to go to her breast to get a vein?"

"Well, I didn't think it was that much of an issue," the doctor said dismissively. "A vein is a vein."

Beasley asked about the doctor's alleged physical and sexual abuse of his patient. "Did there come an occasion in 1974 that you beat Gale?"

"No, I did not beat her," the doctor said. "I had a tussle with her, a confrontation. We had a scrap."

"Did that scrap lead to her going to the hospital?"

"I don't know," the doctor said. "She entered a hospital subsequently, but I don't know that that scrap per se was the reason."

"…And you bit her, didn't you?"

"At one time she was biting me," the doctor said. "And I decided to give her some of what she was doing to me, so I bit her back just to let her know what it feels like."

"…What about the vagina?" Beasley asked. "Did you grab her anywhere in that area?"

"At one time, I think I grabbed her by the pubes," the doctor said.

Beasley asked the doctor about Greenberg's allegations that after a suicide try the doctor had sewed her slashed wrists back together without anesthetic.

"Did you use that suturing as a form of punishment for that girl?"

"Of course not," the doctor shot back.

· · ·

WHEN HE GAVE HIS SUMMATION TO THE JURY, BEASLEY DESCRIBED GALE GREENBERG AS a "pathetic and lost human being" who had "such a desperate need for attention and affection" that she had drifted from one affair to another, seeking "an emotional lift, just as if it were another shot of Ritalin.

"She has wandered from man to man," Beasley told the jury. "She is a wandering, aimless soul that in her, there is no redemption."

"But she didn't do it, McCabe did it," Beasley said. "And he did it day after day, shot after shot, until she had nothing left. The nakedness, the physical nakedness that she displayed on the couch to McCabe was nothing compared to the total nakedness that she has now."

"Her future is one heartbreak after another," Beasley said, because Dr. McCabe "stole this woman's soul."

When defense lawyer Edward B. Joseph gave his summation, he told the jury that underneath the tawdry tale of sex and drugs, there was still a two-year statute of limitations on personal injury cases in Pennsylvania, and that Gale Greenberg had missed the boat.

Joseph told the jury that Greenberg's involvement with McCabe during 1973 and 1974, when she lived with him and accompanied him to medical conferences, was not as a patient, but as a paramour and "a willing participant."

"She did not come to this court until it was too late," Joseph said. So the jury was entitled, Joseph said, to "send her through that door without a nickel."

Judge Joseph S. Lord III, however, did not take such a narrow view of the state statute of limitations for personal injury lawsuits. The judge instructed the jury that the clock on the two-year limit did not necessarily begin from the date of injury, but from the moment when the plaintiff realized "that the defendant's conduct was causing her harm."

The judge also left it to the jury to weigh the plaintiff's mental condition and "whether it amounted to incapacity." The judge also allowed the jury to "take into account mental disabilities caused by the drugs" that McCabe had given Greenberg.

. . .

THE JURY OF FIVE MEN AND THREE WOMEN DELIBERATED FOR TWO HOURS BEFORE coming back with an award for Gale Greenberg of $275,000 in compensatory damages, $300,000 in punitive damages, and $90,000 for future medical care, for a total of $665,000.

Gale Greenberg "cried softly when the verdict was announced," the Philadelphia Daily News reported. Beasley grabbed Greenberg's hand and squeezed it.

'I rarely talked to jurors, but I did in this case," said defense lawyer Edward B. Joseph in a 2006 interview. "They said, 'You stood no chance.'"

The defendant's appeal in the case was once again based on the statue of limitations issue, and once again it was a loser. Judge Lord in his U.S. District Court decision of 1979 said it was proper for the jury to consider mitigating factors, such as "the plaintiff's mental disabilities insofar as they were caused by the defendant."

The court, however, did side with the defendant on another issue, ruling that the plaintiff did not present sufficient evidence to prove that Greenberg would need $90,000 in future psychiatric care. Greenberg had testified that she would not want to undergo therapy again because she wouldn't trust another doctor. So the judge reduced the total verdict by $90,000, to $575,000

Dr. McCabe still believed he had gotten a raw deal for being such a soft-hearted guy. "Did you ever hear of falling in love?" the doctor told the Sacramento Union in 1979. "That doesn't have any bounds. There's no reason to love. It's a very irrational state."

Dr. McCabe lashed out at Beasley in the newspaper, saying: "He has a very ugly destructive mind. The guy must be sick." McCabe told the newspaper that he had bent over backward to help Greenberg, "and then some SOB like Beasley comes along and twists it into an ugly fairy tale."

The next party to sue Dr. McCabe was his insurance provider. The doctor had $250,000 worth of malpractice coverage from Aetna Life and Casualty Co. The insurance company, however, argued that McCabe's behavior with Greenberg was not medical treatment, but at best "an indulging of McCabe's own perversions and 'hang-ups,'" and at worst "a scheme of experimentation" that "involved the intentional infliction of injury."

Aetna lost the case in federal court in 1983 and had to pay the $250,000 as part of the jury verdict for Gale Greenberg. It was the only money Greenberg would ever collect because Dr. McCabe was able to successfully claim in court that he was broke.

Greenberg went on to pursue a career in nursing, including a stint as a trauma nurse. She also worked as a private detective, learned martial arts and how to shoot a Glock. She referred to Dr. McCabe in an interview as Hannibal Lecter, and expressed regret that he had gotten off easy for what he did to her. "He ruined my life."

Donald Lee McCabe has a book, *Handbook of Basic Clinical Manipulation (Clinical Handbook of Psychotropic Drugs)* that lists for $64.95 new on Amazon.com. When contacted in 2006, Dr. McCabe declined to discuss the Greenberg case. His current wife, Jean, however, had plenty to say. Dr. McCabe was never allowed to face his accuser at trial, his wife said. "And that to me isn't right."

"I hope you enjoy the money that you make and the discomfort that you give to others," she said before hanging up the phone.

Chapter 9

❖

A TRIP TO THE JUNKYARD

A<small>T THE REQUEST OF</small> J<small>IM</small> B<small>EASLEY, THE JURORS IN THE FEDERAL CASE OF</small> *D*<small>AWSON V.</small> *Chrysler* were riding a bus, on their way to a junkyard.

"I think the record should reflect that the Court is now reconvened at Marty's Auto Parts," U.S. District Court Judge Stanley S. Brotman announced on Sept. 26, 1978, after everybody had gotten off the bus.

"I think the procedure that should be followed is that questions should be directed to Marty [Hogan] as to what exactly is here," the judge said, referring to the owner of the junkyard. "Mr. Hogan, you are still under oath."

"Mr. Hogan, keep your voice up because we are outside and all the jurors should hear you," Beasley further advised the witness.

The jury gathered around the upside-down wreck of a police car that had been spray-painted to show its underlying steel frame.

"Tell the members of the jury whether this represents police pursuit car number 203," Beasley instructed the junkyard owner.

"This is a police car towed in from Cherry Hill Dodge," Hogan said.

"That car has not been changed in any way since it's been here?" Beasley asked.

"Negative, no," Hogan said.

"That represents the damage as it was when you picked it up at Cherry Hill Dodge?," Beasley asked.

"It came in on the flatbed," Hogan said, nodding.

"Now, I want you to pay specific attention to this damage that is shown here, the spring, the axle and the gas tank," Beasley said. "Is that the damage on that vehicle when you picked it up?"

"Yes," Hogan said of the wreck. "It can't move."

"Let the record reflect that the jurors have approached the vehicle and are looking at it," the judge said. "This was the vehicle that was involved in the accident. You look at it, ladies and gentlemen, and inspect it. It's here for your perusal."

• • •

ON THE RAINY NIGHT OF SEPT. 7, 1974, PENNSAUKEN, N.J., POLICE OFFICER RICHARD F. Dawson was responding to a burglar alarm at 1 a.m. when he lost control of his patrol car. The 1974 Dodge Monaco was traveling between 25 and 30 miles per hour when it slid off the highway, went over a curb and struck a 15-inch-diameter steel pole.

The pole pierced the car on the driver's side, near the left rear wheel well, and then ripped through the body of the Dodge at a 45-degree angle. When the pole hit the front seat, it propelled the officer headfirst into the roof, dislocating his left hip and rupturing his fifth and sixth cervical vertebrae.

The burglar alarm Officer Dawson was responding to turned out to be a false alarm. Officer Dawson, who wasn't wearing a seat belt, was left a quadriplegic, paralyzed from the neck down. He was 31 and married, with a young son.

Dawson, at 5-foot-11 and 175 pounds, was a seven-year veteran who was a member of the police scuba-diving team, and loved to play touch football with his fellow officers. After his accident, the crippled cop spent a month in intensive care, where doctors operated on his hip. He subsequently underwent a neck operation, and eventually regained some arm movement, but his legs remained paralyzed.

"Sooner or later, I'll get back to work," Dawson told a Philadelphia Evening Bulletin reporter in 1975. "And I want to get back on the street." But it was not to be.

When Beasley filed *Dawson v. Chrysler* in U.S. District Court in Camden, N.J., he alleged that although Officer Dawson's patrol car had been advertised as a special "police pursuit vehicle," it did not offer as much protection as many passenger vehicles. Beasley claimed that the patrol car was defective because it had gaps in its steel frame. The steel pole that pierced the car had actually ripped through one of those gaps, near the left wheel well. To protect the driver, Beasley argued, the car should have had a continuous steel frame that would have included steel posts in the door panels, and a crossbeam running through the floor boards.

With the added protection, Beasley argued, the police car would have bounced off the steel pole, and Officer Dawson would have walked away from the accident with only bruises.

It was a daring move back in 1978 for a lawyer to sue a major auto manufacturer over an alleged design flaw. It was also a novel idea to transport a jury to a junkyard so they could see the car with the alleged design flaw. That's why there was such a buzz at the Camden County Courthouse over *Dawson v. Chrysler*.

"This guy Beasley gave us a helluva performance in the courtroom," Francis M. Lordan, then a reporter at the Philadelphia Inquirer, recalled. It was Beasley's first visit to Camden, Lordan said; nobody at the courthouse had heard of him before. "I remember everybody was astounded."

It was also a coup that Beasley was able to talk the judge into allowing the field trip.

"He made an impression on me," Judge Brotman said in an interview. "I felt he was a pioneer" regarding presentation of evidence.

• • •

BACK AT THE JUNKYARD, JURORS HAD FINISHED VIEWING THE WRECKED POLICE CAR, SO the judge turned to Beasley: "What's next?"

"This would be the next vehicle, sir," Beasley said. "If we could, Marty, could you come over here? Would you identify the vehicle?"

"It's a '69 Mercury sedan," Hogan said.

Beasley had paid the junkyard owner to rip out steel frames and crossbeams from other wrecks and transport them on a flatbed to the Camden County Courthouse, so that jurors could see the advantages of a continuous steel frame.

"The maroon parts that were in court were cut off of this car?" Beasley asked.

"Yes, sir," Hogan said.

The six jurors moved on to the next wreck.

"Would you identify this vehicle, Mr. Hogan?"

"It is a '74 Mercury," Hogan said.

"The parts that are in the courtroom come from this vehicle?"

"The green parts came from this vehicle," Hogan said.

"Do you want to take another look, ladies and gentlemen?" the judge asked. "I guess we are finished here. Ladies and gentlemen, we will go back to the bus and return to the courtroom."

• • •

AT THE CAMDEN COUNTY COURTHOUSE, HARRY SHORT, CHRYSLER'S DEFENSE LAWYER, objected to Beasley's attempt to bring Officer Dawson's young son into the case. But Beasley had filed *Dawson v. Chrysler* on behalf of not just the officer, but also the officer's wife, Diana, and young son, Bryan. And Beasley wanted the jury to know all about the emotional problems the son had suffered because of the father's accident.

It was a typical Beasley maneuver, pulling anything he could to extract maximum sympathy from the jury, but the judge was skeptical.

"Do you have a case that shows that that's part of the case?" the judge asked during a sidebar conference. "Do you have a citation you can point to that says that this is an appropriate element of damage in this case?"

"Not right off the tip of my finger," the 52-year-old Beasley told the judge. "But I can tell you something that I think is better than case law. And that's common sense. I've got an 11-year-old son. I try too many cases. He's growing up and I don't know it."

Beasley was drawing on the tensions in his home life to make a point with the judge. Those tensions, to Beasley's regret, would be fully aired a few years later in divorce court, but on this day, the judge wasn't buying it.

"We've all gone through that, gentlemen," the judge told the lawyers at sidebar, as he sustained Short's objection. The judge acknowledged that being a workaholic was an occupational hazard for lawyers.

"We all spend very little time with our families," the judge said. "I did, too."

· · ·

DR. WILLIAM M LICKFIELD, OSTEOPATH, TESTIFIED TO THE JURY ABOUT OFFICER DAWson's injuries, and how he had to be fitted with a catheter, which had to be replaced every two weeks. Beasley asked about the officer's wife, who had also filed a claim for loss of consortium and loss of services.

"Have you ever treated Mrs. Dawson for any problems related to her husband's condition?," Beasley asked.

"Yes, I have," the doctor said.

"And would you tell us what they are?"

"On various occasions, she has come to the office complaining of muscular aches and pains or sprains, whatever," the doctor said. "The history usually given is she has to lift Richard for a lot of reasons, and sometimes she hurts her back or hurts some part of her body in doing so."

Beasley's next witness was Pennsauken Police Chief Nicholas J. Petitte. Beasley had called the chief to explain to the jury why Officer Dawson wasn't wearing a seat belt. Chrysler's lawyer had alleged that the lack of a seat belt was the main reason why the officer's injuries were so severe.

The chief, however, testified that most cops didn't wear seat belts.

"The fact that seat belts are a drawback to police work . . . has been substantiated due to the fact that a number of times patrolmen have not had freedom of movement," the chief told the jury. "And it also interferes with their weapon and other attached equipment to their belt. . . . Most policemen do not participate with seat belts, nor is there any regulation ordering them to."

• • •

STEVEN C. BATTERMAN WAS A PROFESSOR OF MECHANICAL ENGINEERING AND APPLIED mechanics at the University of Pennsylvania. Beasley asked the professor if he had an opinion on what would have happened to Officer Dawson's patrol car if it had a continuous frame that extended through the side door panels.

"Yes, I have such an opinion," the professor explained. "If the vehicle were designed to provide impact resistance at the side, the pole would not have intruded into the passenger compartment… ."

"All right," Beasley said. "What in your opinion could have been done as far as the structural integrity of this vehicle is concerned, which would have made it capable of resisting that 30-mile-an-hour impact with the pole?"

The basic problem," the professor explained, was that the police car lacked "a full perimeter frame" that would have extended behind the left wheel well, as well as a crossbeam that would have run through the floor boards.

"Are you saying you don't have to be an engineer to figure that out?" Beasley asked, leading the witness. The defense lawyer, however, had already been warned by the judge that he had spent too much time cross-examining one of Beasley's previous expert witnesses, so he sat silently and watched.

"Yes," the professor said.

Beasley brought up the frame of a wrecked 1969 Mercury that had been brought to court as an exhibit, and placed on a tarp, to show jurors the superiority of a continuous steel frame.

"Are you suggesting, sir, that this type of frame … is a much more secure design?"

"Yes, I am," the professor said.

Beasley asked the professor to explain what had happened when the steel pole hit the car's left wheel well.

The car "split apart," said the professor, who offered an analogy. "If you just took a straw and you tried to force a pencil down the straw, eventually you might just split the straw."

The professor testified that if the police car had had a continuous frame and a crossbeam in the floor, the steel pole that ripped through the car would have only been able to penetrate "less than 10 inches."

Beasley noted the price of the Chrysler — "in the neighborhood of $5,700" — and asked whether the cost of the extra steel would have been worth it in terms of the extra protection it would have afforded Officer Dawson.

This time the defense lawyer objected, but the judge overruled him. "Well, there would have been a cost increase on the order of approximately $300," the professor said, adding that "$300 is a very small amount of dollars for additional safety."

"Do you have an opinion as to what object stopped his [Dawson's] rearward movement and then caused him to go forward to cause a dislocation of the hip?" Beasley asked.

"Yes, I do," the professor said. "…It's clearly the pole intruding into the passenger compartment and impinging on the back of the front seat."

"You saw the front seat, didn't you?" Beasley asked.

"Oh, yes, I've seen the car," the professor said.

"And you saw that front seat right up against the steering wheel?" Beasley asked.

"That's correct," the professor said.

"You couldn't even put a jack of spades in there, could you?" Beasley said.

"That's right," the professor said. "The front seat is impinging against the steering wheel."

Beasley asked if the police car had a continuous frame, "what would have happened to Mr. Dawson?"

The defense lawyer objected again, but the judge overruled him one more time. The professor responded that Officer Dawson "would not have suffered the crushing injury to the cervical spine. He would not have suffered the dislocated hip, and to be sure, he would have been bruised on his left side, but he would not have suffered the injuries that brought him here today."

• • •

AFTER A FIVE-WEEK TRIAL, THE JURY CONCLUDED THAT THE STRUCTURE OF THE 1974 Dodge Monaco was defective and unreasonably dangerous, and not fit for use as a police vehicle. The jury also decided that Dawson's failure to use a seat belt did not result in his injuries.

The jury awarded Dawson $2 million for his expenses, disability, pain and suffering; his wife was awarded $60,000 for loss of consortium and loss of services.

The size of the award, court officials told the Philadelphia Evening Bulletin, was "one of the largest in memory in South Jersey." After the verdict had been read, the judge turned to Officer Dawson, who had sat through the trial in his wheelchair. "No money can compensate you for what happened," the judge said. "Life is not easy for you, but the money you received today should make it somewhat easier in the future."

The Dawsons asked the judge for prior interest on the award, in the amount of 8 percent a year, from the time the officer had filed the suit until the verdict. The judge responded by granting $388,012 in interest to Dawson, and $11,274 more to his wife, boosting the total award to $2.4 million.

Beasley was elated. He had told the jury that the officer's medical costs amounted to $32,900 a year and that Dawson's lost wages were $18,900 a year, for a total monetary loss of $51,800 annually. The $2.4 million award was 46 times that amount.

Chrysler appealed, arguing that it was not required to build a crash-proof car. Because the car met federal safety standards, Chrysler argued, a New Jersey jury should not be allowed to award liability damages based on a design failure.

The Third U.S. Circuit Court of Appeals, however, upheld the award in 1980, saying that compliance with federal laws does not exempt manufacturers from liability under state laws. Chrysler appealed again, but in 1981 the U.S. Supreme Court declined to review the verdict.

Lucinda Fleeson, a Philadelphia Inquirer reporter, stopped by Dawson's "tidy suburban kitchen" in 1981 to record his reaction to the end of his six-year legal battle.

"Dawson betrayed neither bitterness nor pleasure as he talked quietly about the case," Fleeson wrote. "But as his wife sipped coffee, her eyes occasionally brimmed with tears."

"Yes, we're glad if it's finally over," Diana Dawson told the reporter. "But even if it was $10 million, I would rather have my husband the way he was before.

"We seem fine now," she said, "but no one else is around when I'm . . . crying at night and Richard is talking about it."

Dawson, then 38, said he hoped that after he got through paying his medical and legal expenses, he would have enough money left over to support his family and send his 11-year-old son to college.

When the reporter called Beasley for comment, he told the newspaper that Chrysler had been punished for manufacturing an unsafe police car. "Bandits, burglars and bad guys have more protection in their cars than the cops had."

• • •

THE PENNSAUKEN POLICE DEPARTMENT MAINTAINS AN "OFFICER DOWN MEMORIAL PAGE" on the Internet, for "remembering all of law enforcement's heroes."

On March 7, 1999, the police department reported that Officer Dawson had died of injuries related to his 1974 accident. He was 56, and was survived by his wife and son.

Chapter 10

❖

BLOOD ON THE TRACKS

THE FINAL BELL HAD RUNG ON THE LAST DAY OF SCHOOL, AND 9-YEAR-OLD EDDIE Scarborough was out celebrating by playing basketball with his friends.

The kids were shooting at a milk crate and a wooden backboard nailed to a telephone pole at the corner of 13th and McFerran, two dead-end streets in North Philadelphia. They were playing "roughhouse," where the object was to score 32 points. And, as Eddie would subsequently testify in court, "I was about to win."

Eddie was at the foul line with 30 points. But since the object of the game was to hit 32 points on the nose, it was in Eddie's best interests to miss the one-point foul shot, grab the rebound, and hit the two-pointer that would give him the game-winning score.

So Eddie threw the ball a little harder than usual, and his shot ricocheted off the backboard and rolled a few feet down the street to a dilapidated chain-link fence. The ball slipped through a gaping hole in the fence and tumbled down an embankment, toward the railroad tracks below owned by the old Reading Railroad.

Eddie climbed through the fence and went down the embankment after the ball. He grabbed it, threw it to his friends, and started back up the hill. But then he heard a freight train coming.

Instead of returning to the basketball game, Eddie made an impulsive decision that would forever change his life: the fourth grader hopped the train for a youthful joy ride. It was June 24, 1974. Eddie was only on board a few minutes before he tried to jump off. But one of Eddie's pant legs got caught on the train, and in the process of trying to loosen it, Eddie slipped and fell under the wheels.

Both of Eddie's legs were severed just below the knee. He lay helpless and bleeding on the railroad tracks for at least 15 minutes before police arrived.

• • •

SEVEN YEARS AFTER EDDIE'S ACCIDENT, THE CASE OF *SCARBOROUGH V. READING CO.* finally came to trial in Philadelphia's Common Pleas Court. The trial was on a break in April 1981 when Jim Beasley rushed back to his office to call a potential surprise witness.

"I represent this little black boy," Beasley said on the phone. And then Beasley asked Frank Rizzo, the former mayor of Philadelphia, to do him a favor, namely testify in court on behalf of his client, Eddie Scarborough. Only the way Beasley talked, he was doing Rizzo a favor.

"This will be very good for you, Mr. Mayor," Beasley said. Rizzo was just a few months out of office after serving two consecutive four-year terms as mayor, and he was bored silly sitting around his big house in the Chestnut Hill section of the city. Everybody knew that Rizzo wanted to run for mayor again, and when he did, the champion of the white ethnics would need more support from the black community. That's where Beasley came in. He told the former mayor he could make him look good in the black community by standing up in court for "this little black boy who lost his legs."

Thomas R. Kline, Beasley's cocounsel, was in the office that day and could only hear one end of the conversation. Kline was waiting for Beasley to explain to the former mayor that by testifying on behalf of their client, Rizzo would have to testify *against* the City of Philadelphia.

"Do you remember Police Directive 38?" Beasley asked. As the former police commissioner during the 1960s, Rizzo was very familiar with it. "I'm not saying you have to testify against any particular cop, but what's right is right," Beasley told Rizzo.

Rizzo and Beasley were used to playing on the same team. In 1979, when Rizzo was still mayor, the U.S. Justice Department had filed a headline-grabbing lawsuit that accused Rizzo and the entire Philadelphia Police Department of systematically abusing private citizens. Rizzo hired Beasley to defend the city's police commissioner, and federal officials subsequently dropped the suit.

That same year, Rizzo also hired Beasley to research whether the mayor should file a libel suit against PBS for a critical documentary about the mayor, but after Beasley did his research, no lawsuit was filed.

So Rizzo was used to taking advice from Beasley, but this time, it seemed like a hard sell. Kline heard Beasley repeatedly pressing the former mayor. "I want you to think it over," Beasley said before hanging up.

• • •

AS FAR AS BEASLEY WAS CONCERNED, THE RAILROAD EMPLOYEES WHO RAN OVER EDDIE Scarborough were negligent because they had plowed through an area where kids were known to hop trains and play on the tracks. The railroad employees were supposed to be on the lookout for kids whenever they went through that area, but the day Eddie got hurt, the flagman wasn't up in his usual perch, on the caboose, and the employees didn't even notice that someone had climbed on board. The employees also didn't stop the train after they ran over Eddie to offer emergency assistance, a violation of railroad regulations. So Beasley was confident he had a solid negligence claim against the railroad.

But Beasley was all about pushing boundaries. And the grandstand stunt he would pull in *Scarborough v. Reading* would delight jurors for a day and leave city officials fuming for nearly a decade.

Beasley knew that a year before Eddie's accident, neighbors in North Philadelphia had complained to city officials about that hole in the fence above the railroad tracks, and the city had done nothing about it. So when he filed his lawsuit against the railroad, Beasley also named the City of Philadelphia as a defendant, charging that the city was guilty of negligence for not fixing the fence.

Lawyers from the city solicitor's office, however, argued in court that besides the hole in the fence, there were several other ways for the neighborhood kids to get down to the railroad tracks, including just walking around the fence. But city lawyers said that ultimately it didn't matter how Eddie got down to the tracks, because Pennsylvania state law clearly stated that no property owner was required to protect trespassers from a dangerous condition located on somebody else's adjoining property.

But Beasley believed he had found a way around state law with Police Directive 38, which required Philadelphia cops to report dangerous conditions that they observed on their beats. The way Beasley saw it, city employees had a responsibility to fix the hole in the fence. And Beasley believed the city proved his point in 1976 by finally repairing the fence, two years after Eddie's accident, for a cost of $328. So Beasley was looking for a witness who could sell Police Directive 38 to a jury.

Assistant City Solicitor Dolores Rocco, however, objected to Beasley introducing a copy of Police Directive 38 to the jury without first proving the copy was authentic. Beasley responded by threatening to call the current Philadelphia mayor, Bill Green, as a witness to authenticate the directive and say it was still in effect.

The witness list was already handed in when Beasley got his brainstorm to cold-call Frank Rizzo. "Who'd be better to authenticate Police Directive 38 than the former police commissioner?" Beasley told Kline.

. . .

BEASLEY'S LAW OFFICE IN THOSE DAYS WAS A SUITE OF ROOMS LOCATED ON THE FIFTH FLOOR of the city-owned Stephen Girard Building at 21 S. 12th St. Beasley drove to work every morning like a drag racer from his Villanova estate. He left his smoking-hot VW Rabbit in a VIP spot outside the parking garage adjacent to his office building.

It was a short walk from Beasley's law office over to 5 Penn Center, where the Scarborough case was being tried that April. At 54, the red-haired and musta-chioed Beasley still had a powerful upper body and a flat stomach. He walked to court every morning with Kline, more than two decades younger, and almost a half-foot taller than the 5-foot-9 Beasley. But Beasley strode so fast the two lawyers were dead even. Beasley thrust his chest out like a runner at the finish line, just about to hit the tape.

The bushy-haired Kline was a former sixth-grade teacher from Hazleton, Pa., and a recent law school graduate. Kline started working for Beasley in December 1979, about a year and a half before the Scarborough case. When a junior associate backed up Beasley in the courtroom, it was known as "baggin' for Mr. B," a reference to the two heavy leather trial bags that the younger attorney was responsible for lugging to court. Kline was following Beasley around so he could learn from the master. And one of the first lessons Beasley taught Kline was what to do when you discover that your client has lied under oath. Such was the case with Eddie Scarborough.

Beasley was the second lawyer to take the Scarborough case. And when he ques-tioned Eddie about the accident, he discovered that the youngster hadn't told the truth about how he lost his legs because, as Eddie would later admit in court, "I was scared that I would get a whipping."

Eddie had been repeatedly warned by his mother before the accident not to play on the railroad tracks. So when the railroad summoned Eddie for a deposi-tion, Eddie told railroad lawyer E. Parry Warner that he had never hopped the train. Instead, Eddie claimed that he was just an innocent bystander, standing next to the railroad tracks, when the train roared by and sucked him under the wheels.

Patricia (Pat) Scarborough, Eddie's mother, said that Beasley was the first person to get the real story out of Eddie, six years after the accident. Beasley did it by drawing on his own boyhood experiences. Like Eddie, Beasley was a poor kid who had jumped trains for joyrides, and he knew Eddie's story didn't make sense.

Beasley told Eddie he was facing an uphill battle, and that his lawyer was the best friend he had in the world. And that the only way Eddie could help his best friend was to be completely honest. Beasley also called Eddie "son" whenever he talked to him.

"That's what moved Eddie," Pat Scarborough said. "You don't mess with JEB. We thought he was God."

Beasley wrote railroad lawyer E. Parry Warner a letter on Sept. 2, 1980, explaining that Eddie's deposition from three years earlier hadn't been truthful. "For whatever reason, Eddie did not explain how the accident really happened," Beasley wrote. "What actually happened was that on the day of the accident, Eddie did go under a fence after a basketball, but then proceeded to attempt to hop the freight car. I believe that the matter should be set straight now, rather than there being any doubt as to how Eddie's injuries really occurred. Should you wish to schedule Eddie's deposition again at this time, I have no objections. Very Truly Yours, James E. Beasley."

• • •

ON THE MORNING THAT FRANK RIZZO WAS SCHEDULED TO APPEAR IN COURT, HE SAT IN a shabby waiting room at 5 Penn Center, making small talk with Tom Kline. Meanwhile, out in the courtroom, Assistant City Solicitor Dolores Rocco was having a bad day. Rocco wanted to see the judge in chambers, but Beasley objected, so they had a conference at sidebar. "What's the problem?" asked Judge I. Raymond Kremer.

Rocco was fuming. "The problem is the following: Mr. Beasley has brought in former Mayor Rizzo to testify concerning Police Directive 38. This is nothing but a Barnum and Bailey showmanship effort… ."

Rocco had been handed the Scarborough case file eight weeks before trial, because, she said in an interview, nobody else in the city solicitor's office wanted to go up against Beasley. Rocco was also upset that Rizzo's name wasn't on the witness list. And that Judge Kremer had overruled her previous objection about allowing Beasley to present Police Directive 38 to the jury, a directive that Rocco believed was irrelevant.

The judge, however, was known among his fellow lawyers as a plaintiff's lawyer at heart. He reminded Rocco that Beasley had warned her that he might call Mayor Green as a witness to authenticate the police directive and that Rocco hadn't seemed too concerned.

"Your Honor, Mr. Beasley came over to me last week and said, 'I'm going to subpoena the mayor in,' " Rocco told the judge. "I said you can do whatever you want. . . . The fact that I said bring him in does not mean that I consent to his testifying or whether it's proper, Your Honor."

But the judge was on Beasley's side and seemed eager to have Rizzo appear in his courtroom. "I not only think you consented to his testifying, but you challenged him to bring him in, and I will admit it," the judge scolded Rocco.

The sidebar conference was over; the witness was summoned to testify. Beasley loved grand entrances, and Rizzo didn't disappoint. As jurors watched with rapt eyes and open jaws, Rizzo marched into the room and headed for the witness stand. At 6-foot-2½ inches, and at least 250 pounds, "The Big Bambino" had what was often described as a commanding presence.

He was immaculately groomed, in an expensive suit, size 52-long, and gleaming shoes, size 11-E. It struck Dolores Rocco like the entrance of a movie star. She knew the jurors would all go home that night and tell their friends that they had just seen Frank Rizzo in court. And she also knew her chances of winning the case had just gone from slim to zero.

"In December of 1973, what was your occupation, sir?" Beasley asked. "I was the mayor of Philadelphia," Rizzo responded. Beasley asked Rizzo if he was familiar with Police Directive 38. "Yes, sir, I am," Rizzo said. Beasley asked Rizzo to read the directive to the jury.

"All police personnel are responsible for the prompt and accurate reporting of any dangerous highway condition, defective or damaged property, either city or privately owned, which may in any manner endanger the health, welfare or safety of the public," Rizzo read. "Personnel are also responsible for taking action to eliminate or minimize all dangerous conditions."

"Would you explain to the jury how that policy was to be implemented by the Philadelphia Police Department?" Beasley asked.

"This is a guide to the men and women who serve in the Philadelphia Police Department," Rizzo said. "The purpose of the directive is to give them a procedure and a policy direction so they will know what to do when they see something that would cause a hazard to the people who live in the city."

Beasley asked if Rizzo was familiar with the intersection of 13th and McFerran, above the Reading Railroad yards. "Very familiar," Rizzo said. He had patrolled the area as a cop "many, many years ago."

"Mayor, was there any particular policy in your administration concerning notifying the responsible city department if children were playing around railroad tracks?"

"Well, when I was the Police Commissioner, this [was] a very important directive, not only in this case, but in all cases," Rizzo said. "As you know, there are many hazardous conditions in the city such as holes, walls, fences down, poles that could cause a problem to the passing public, but also to the children who play in the areas of the various parts of the city, particularly railroads," Rizzo said. "And that fence, if it was down, it was the responsibility of the policeman in that area to report it." Rizzo added that he believed the fence belonged to the Reading Railroad.

"Now, would that directive apply even if this fence was assumed to be private property?" Beasley asked.

"Yes, sir," Rizzo said.

When most lawyers finished with a witness, they usually said, "No further questions." But Beasley's style, picked up by protégés like Kline, was to challenge his opponents. Beasley turned to the defense lawyers. "Cross-examine."

Warner, representing the railroad, asked Rizzo if he knew for sure if the fence belonged to the railroad. "No, sir, I do not," Rizzo said. "Thank you," Warner said, and he promptly sat down.

"Now, sir," said Assistant City Solicitor Dolores Rocco, trying to be good-natured with the popular former mayor; "The policemen are not required to go around the city . . . with microscopes, are they?"

"Yes, they are, counsel," Rizzo said.

Rocco tried again to reason with Rizzo: "So therefore if there was something dangerous, and policemen are trained as well as we all know they are, they would have reported the dangerous condition?"

Rocco knew no paperwork existed that showed any cop had ever notified the city about the hole in the fence, but Rizzo refused to budge from his talking points. "If there was a dangerous condition, it should have been reported," he said.

Rocco decided to ask one last question and get Rizzo off the witness stand as fast as possible. She was curious about Rizzo's professional relationship with Beasley, so she decided to ask about it, even though she wasn't sure what the answer would be.

"Doesn't Mr. Beasley represent you in your private capacity?" Rocco asked.

"Mr. Beasley never represented me," Rizzo said.

"Only the court," interjected Judge Kremer. Rocco had misfired; it was the judge who had once represented Rizzo in a lawsuit, not Beasley. Judge Kremer turned to the witness. "That's correct, isn't it, Mr. Mayor?"

"Thank you, Your Honor," Rizzo said.

As Rocco watched in amazement, the judge, who had a reputation for meddling, then proceeded to stage a mutual love fest with the plaintiff's surprise witness.

"I was a very good lawyer, wasn't I?" the judge asked. "The best," a beaming Rizzo replied. "You did represent me, Judge, and you won that case."

"I didn't want to tell them that I know more about Directive 38 than anybody in the room," the judge told Rizzo.

Rocco was still trying to coax the former mayor off the witness stand. "I have no more questions," she said. But that didn't stop Judge Kremer from continuing his chit-chat. The judge asked the former mayor if Police Directive 38 was ever repealed. "Not to my knowledge," Rizzo said. The judge asked Rizzo how long he was police commissioner before he was elected mayor. "Five and a half years," Rizzo replied.

"Thank you," Beasley said, ending the sideshow. Rizzo was excused. The former mayor had only been on the witness stand for a few minutes. But Rocco and other city lawyers would spend the rest of the three-week trial, as well the next eight years of appeals, trying to undo the damage.

· · ·

BEASLEY CALLED EDDIE'S MOTHER TO THE WITNESS STAND. PAT SCARBOROUGH WAS A payroll clerk who earned $5 an hour at the Army Depot in South Philadelphia. She was also a single mom who testified that after she heard about the accident, she rushed to see Eddie in the hospital. Beasley asked her to describe her son's condition.

"Well, he was — his legs were gone, and they had him wrapped up in gauze, and he was crying," she told Beasley. "And he was saying that he was just hot, you know," she said. "And he was just in pain. He was just laying there, you know, he was like moaning and complaining that he was so hot, he wanted water, he was thirsty."

Beasley asked Pat Scarborough about the first day Eddie got his prosthesis. "The first time I saw him with his legs on, he was really proud," she said. "He said, 'Look Mom, I can walk.'"

Beasley asked how Eddie got around without his artificial legs. "On his knees, on his hands, his knuckles," Eddie's mother said. "He has marks on his knuckles from walking. He would get sores from the prostheses... . They would erupt. I would have to either bandage him or put some kind of medication on and try to stop it, but he couldn't wear his legs."

"Does Eddie complain?" Beasley asked. "He is not a complainer," Pat Scarborough said. "He didn't complain when he was in the hospital the whole time. He would rather just try to take care of it himself."

It was Eddie's turn to take the stand. Beasley asked the 16-year-old to describe what happened seven years ago, when he had hopped the train.

"My pants leg or something got caught and I couldn't get away," Eddie said. "And I slipped under."

"And then what happened?"

"I got my legs cut off."

Eddie described how an older boy named Terrell pulled him out from under the train, "because it was dragging me."

"Did you holler or shout or cry at that time?" Beasley asked

"I was crying, but I wasn't hollering," Eddie said. "I just felt like it was burning, I felt like it was hot." Eddie described the phantom pain that woke him up every night. "It feels like my foot is there, but it's not."

Beasley asked Eddie to show the jurors how he had to take his prosthetic legs off every day. "Would you do it, son?"

"Yes," Eddie said. The boy got down from the witness stand and walked over in front of the jury. He turned to Beasley. "Do you want to show them my legs?"

"Please," Beasley said. "Do you want to take your pants off, son?… Is that something you have to do every morning?"

"Of course," Eddie said.

When his artificial legs were off, Beasley asked, "How do you get around?"

"On my knees," Eddie said.

"How do you take a shower?"

"I stand on my knees in the shower," Eddie said.

"You can't wear the legs in the shower?"

"No," Eddie said.

Eddie's demonstration left the jury in tears. And they weren't the only ones. The judge had watery eyes; so did Beasley. Kline saw Warner, the railroad lawyer, wipe a tear from his eye. Kline felt a chill run up his spine as he dried his own tears.

The only dry-eyed person in the courtroom was Rocco, who said in an interview for this book that she noticed several jurors staring at her. Rocco said she was used to seeing such sights, because she had formerly dated a Vietnam vet who lost a leg. But she also didn't want to appear cold-hearted. So Rocco said she turned away from the jury and poked herself in the eyes a few times so that she would also tear up.

· · ·

WILLIAM TROUT WAS BEASLEY'S EXPERT TRAIN WITNESS, A CRUSTY FORMER CONRAIL freight conductor and flagman with 37 years of experience. From the witness stand, Trout chipped away at the credibility of the flagman of the 82-car freight train that ran over Eddie.

"As far as I could see, he didn't do his job properly," Trout said. Since the train was passing through "a known trouble spot," Trout said, the flagman "should have been on the lookout for these children hopping trains." The section of tracks where Eddie got hurt was the site of two previous train accidents in the last four years. Two other kids lost legs in that same area before Eddie; incredibly, one of the victims was Eddie's second cousin.

The flagman also should have radioed ahead and ordered the train to slow down, Trout said. He cited railroad regulations that said if a train ran over somebody and caused a loss of limb, the employees were supposed to bring the train to an immediate stop, and offer emergency assistance.

The stage was set for Beasley to call George McReynolds, the freight train flag-man. The train that ran over Eddie was on its way to Harrisburg, McReynolds testified. McReynolds told Beasley he was used to seeing kids playing on the tracks, as well as hopping trains. The flagman said he tried to use his portable radio to no-tify railroad officials when Eddie got hurt, but the radio wasn't working properly. So the flagman had to wait until he passed a railroad tower in the Nicetown section of the city, at least a quarter-mile away. McReynolds said he yelled to the signalman: *"That there was a kid sitting on the eastbound with his legs off east of Broad Street."*

The flagman admitted that the train should have stopped after it ran over Eddie. But the flagman blamed his radio again, claiming it had conked out three different times when he tried to send out a Mayday alert. So the train kept rolling for seven more miles until the next scheduled stop, at Gladwyne, Pa.

From the witness stand, the flagman tried to mitigate the damage. He told Beasley that some of the kids playing on the tracks were throwing rocks at him, and that's why he wasn't in his usual perch atop the caboose. The flagman said he also was worried that the train might derail, if it was brought to a sudden stop.

Beasley called Capt. Thomas Crowley of the Reading Railroad to show how dangerous the section of railroad tracks was where Eddie got hurt. Crowley testi-fied that between June1973 and August 1974 the railroad had 72 registered com-plaints of trespassing in that area. So many neighborhood kids had access to the tracks that the area was supposed to be under 24-hour patrol by railroad police.

Beasley showed jurors a scale model of the intersection in the courtroom, so they could see where the train had left Eddie lying on the tracks. Beasley also had aerial photos of the accident site taken from his private plane, a World War II flight trainer known as a T-6. Beasley had repeatedly flown over the area, banking the T-6 so it could swoop low enough for Kline, riding in the passenger seat, to squeeze off a roll of film.

Beasley called Police Officer Ishmael Plaza to testify how he found Eddie lying on his back on the railroad tracks.

"And did you put him on the stretcher?" Beasley asked.

"Yes, we did," the officer said.

"And where were his legs?" Beasley asked.

"His legs were lying on the adjacent track," the officer said. "We put them with the stretcher, brought him up the hill again." The officer described Eddie as scared, in pain and crying, but "conscious all the time."

• • •

THE JURY WAS STILL OUT DELIBERATING WHEN DOLORES ROCCO PICKED UP THE Philadelphia Daily News to check her horoscope: "You will not fare well in legal matters this week." She showed it to Beasley, who laughed and said it was confirmation that she was going to lose.

Sure enough, the jury came back with what was then a record verdict against the city and the railroad: $3 million for Eddie Scarborough, and an additional $300,000 for his mother. City officials were furious.

"It's a travesty, a miscarriage of justice," Dolores Rocco told the Philadelphia Daily News. An editorial in the Philadelphia Evening Bulletin was headlined "More compassion than judgment." The Bulletin complained that the jury's award was "three times what it should have been." The editorial writer called on Judge Kremer to reduce the verdict to $1 million.

Shortly after the verdict, Rocco ran into Judge Kremer at a cocktail party and had a chance to register her displeasure. The judge, who died in 1999, had made the mistake of asking Rocco to describe for the other lawyers at the party what it was like to try a case in front of him.

"You really want to know?" Rocco asked. "And you won't hold it against me?" The judge promised he wouldn't. So, while the other lawyers watched, Rocco let the judge have it.

"You were the only man I thought who could ever get me pregnant, 'cause I never got fucked so much in such a short period of time, with no way to protect myself," Rocco told the astonished judge.

• • •

THE CITY APPEALED THE CASE, AND TWO YEARS LATER, WITH THE VERDICT STILL UNPAID, Judge Kremer found the railroad and the city liable for delaying the proceedings, and he raised the total jury award from $3.3 million to $3.79 million. The city responded by filing motions that accused the judge of bias. In its appellate brief, the city ripped Judge Kremer's conduct during the trial, particularly his decision to engage "in a warm, personal and self-aggrandizing exchange with former Mayor Frank Rizzo." The city said the jury might have taken the exchange as "a judicial endorsement of the witness's credibility."

While the city was still battling Judge Kremer, the railroad opted to cut its losses and settle its share of the case for $1.3 million. The city kept on fighting. Barbara R. Axelrod of the city solicitor's office argued one more time that the city was not liable for negligence on adjoining property that it didn't own or control. This time, somebody listened. On Oct. 16, 1989, the state Supreme Court agreed with Axelrod, vacating the jury verdict and dismissing Eddie and Pat Scarborough's claims against the city.

"Case law would appear, at first blush, to have imposed a duty on the city to erect a barrier along the dead end of Thirteenth Street," wrote state Supreme Court

Justice Stephen A. Zappala. The justice, however, said the law was originally intended to protect vehicles from falling down steep cliffs or embankments.

"In this case, Edward Scarborough, after climbing through the fence and retrieving the basketball on his own volition, returned to the railroad tracks to hop a train," Justice Zappala wrote. "This unsupervised activity of a minor child was not the danger sought to be avoided by the creation of a common law duty to erect barriers along a roadway."

Also, the judge noted, "It is well settled that the law imposes no duty upon a possessor of adjacent land to erect fencing or provide warnings so as to deter persons from entering a third party's property on which there exists a dangerous condition not created or maintained by the landowner and over which the landowner has no control."

Beasley wrote a brief letter on Oct. 20, 1989, to notify Pat and Eddie Scarborough about the state Supreme Court decision, saying, "I think this ends the case."

Michael Mather was chairman of the litigation department in the city solicitor's office when the Scarborough case was tried. Twenty-four years later, he was still angry.

"There basically was no way he [Beasley] was gonna connect the city with it unless he came up with something," Mather recalled. "I thought this was an imaginative way to do it.... A lot of lawyers would have said, I'll never get that one to fly, but he had a lot of guts."

Mather said for the city, the Scarborough verdict was "a thorn in our side" for eight years until it was finally pulled by the state Supreme Court. But Mather didn't hold any hard feelings, because in 2005, when he was interviewed, Mather was an adjunct professor at Temple University's Beasley School of Law.

As for Beasley, he didn't appreciate having his $3 million jury verdict vacated by the Supreme Court. But he did take notice of the city lawyer who beat him. And then he hired Barbara Axelrod to write appeals for him.

• • •

EDDIE SCARBOROUGH DIDN'T LET THE LOSS OF HIS LEGS STOP HIM FROM LIVING A FULL life. He learned how to ride a bike and drive a car. He kept playing basketball, and even on artificial knees, a witness said, he could still glide like Clyde Frazier. He also fathered three kids.

Tom Kline never forgot the lessons of the Scarborough case. In 1999, as the head of his own Philadelphia law firm, Kline & Specter, Kline represented Shareif Hall, a 4-year-old who lost his foot in a defective escalator underneath a city subway station on North Broad Street.

Kline sued the elevator manufacturer and the Southeastern Pennsylvania Transportation Authority (SEPTA). The elevator manufacturer decided to settle the case, but Kline stuck SEPTA with a $51-million jury verdict. SEPTA subsequently settled for $7.4 million.

The climax of the trial, according to the Philadelphia Daily News, came when Shareif Hall "limped into court, his mother removed his prosthesis and revealed his butchered limb. Some jurors looked away in horror. Others cried."

Kline, however, was used to such courtroom theatrics. "It was Eddie Scarborough two decades later," he said.

J.E.B. Loses Initial Ruling
But Noted Lawyer Wins Round Against Wife

By JULIA LAWLOR

James Beasley, a prominent Philadelphia trial lawyer who may have won more million-dollar verdicts than any other lawyer in the country, has chalked up another court victory — but this time as the plaintiff in a case against his wife, Helen Beasley's lawyer, Richard Sprague, filed a petition in Montgomery County Court in an effort to force Helen Beasley, 50, to return an estimated $75,000 to $90,000 worth of furniture she took from the couple's Main Line home last Oct. 30.

Montgomery County Judge Anita Brody on Friday called Mrs. Beasley's action "despicable." The judge ordered her to return everything within two weeks ...

Beasley

lanova where the Beasleys have lived for more than 10 years with their three children, Pamela, 21, Kimberly, 18, and James Jr., 14.

HELEN BEASLEY, a softspoken and attractive woman, testified last Friday that her husband left her for three weeks in 1978 for another woman, and that he ordered her out of the house last February while he was "intoxicated," calling her "stupid and a moron." She said she returned several months later at his request and agreed not to file for divorce, but to try to reconcile.

She said she returned under the condition that he would no longer "see or communicate with" another woman he had been teaching to fly in one of his private planes for the last three years. But, she said she was told on Oct. 13 that her husband had been talking to the woman, and three weeks later she took the furnishings and moved into a two-bedroom apartment.

Divorce proceedings were filed on Oct. 29.

Beasley, 55, glared at his wife from the witness stand last Friday as he

... in the home she plans to ... were wedding gifts before the marriage or, like the Rembrandt and an Oriental rug, were gifts to her from her husband.

After the call on Oct. 13, Beasley said he and his wife did not communicate, except to discuss bills. But on Oct. 18, she said her husband told her: "I expect you to continue doing my laundry as long as you're just sitting around here."

SHE SAID SHE decided to leave "because I was afraid. I didn't want to have any argument."

Sprague, a former first assistant district attorney who is being represented by Beasley in a libel suit he has brought against the Bulletin, was able to list the case using only the initials H.M.B. (Helen Mary Beasley) and J.E.B. (James Edwin Beasley). But Judge Brody issued a temporary order against using the initials in upcoming court proceedings.

"We are not accorded the right to do this for our own judges," Brody said.

Beasley refused to discuss the case. "My lawyer closes but want anyone to know about this matter," Hurowitz explained. "He's going to be very embarrassed."

described what he saw the night of Oct. 30, when he first discovered the furniture was gone.

"I came home ... there was a little furniture, my son, the dog and the cat," he said.

He said his wife had taken many expensive antiques, including the good silverware, a Rembrandt painting, several Oriental rugs, dressers, tables, chairs, and most of the living room furniture.

"The only thing left in the living room is the piano," he said.

Beasley also complained that his wife had taken "two or three" sets of dishes and left him and his son, the only child still living at home, with "the old chipped dishes that were around for 20 years." He said he noticed that a "thing I used to cook sausage" was not in the kitchen after she left.

WHEN NEIL HUROWITZ, a Montgomery County attorney representing Helen Beasley, asked him if he would be willing to give his wife $80,000 to furnish the apartment, Beasley replied: "If the dollars would balance out, I would furnish the apartment."

Hurowitz claimed that most of the furniture his client took ...

Jim Esmond on Main Street in Peabody, Mass.

Porter: His Life Changed

Continued from Page 2

Jim and Ray were put into a cell overnight. The next day, they were taken to plainclothes detectives in Woodland Estates, to an area behind some businesses. Two of the detectives held the two while a third inspected the doors and windows.

The windows were barred. Finally, the detective shouted back to his fellow officers, "I can't see any signs here. I'll be back in a minute," he said. Finally, he returned and stood out near the sidewalk with another man, near the sidewalk with another man. The officer was talking hurriedly and gesturing with one hand. The other man was listening intently and was nodding as though in agreement or understanding.

The two boys were taken back to a cell. A day later, the man who had talked with the detective in Woodland Estates visited Jim and his friend out of a lineup. They were arraigned the next day on charges of attempting to break and enter with intent to steal from a ... which is most of the ... Woodland Estates.

And on March 7, 1979 — a day after they were indicted, one less than a week after they got off the bus in Philadelphia — Jim stood before a Common Pleas judge who was not willing to permit it, to ask ... Corrections Institute for ... fine.

TOMORROW: A Boy Behind Bars

What Bag? 334G Find Is News to Us, Purolator Says

Robert Rowick and Robert Bisceviti, at the find of East County Line Road, Hatboro, returned a falling over bag containing $334,714 in canceled checks over the weekend, and there hasn't been a word of thanks.

"Nobody's offered anything," Rowick, 26, of the 100 block of West Street Road, Warminster, said. "We're a ...

The problem might be that no one is willing to claim responsibility for losing the bag, which Rowick and Bisceviti found on City Line Bridge Sunday.

according to detectives, the checks were placed in the bag by Purolator Courier Service after being sent from the ABC Warehouse branch. The checks were given to the guard at ... since it's 4 p.m. Friday ever ever to be delivered Sunday. But it was Purolator Courier Service ...

Rock officials have said the ... bag is a Purolator courier. The Purolator sounded nothing said ... of a Purolator courier ... Police Department Bureau.

"It was a Purolator vault. Our Courier ... February, nothing to show for that," Purolator ...

A child peers at the grave of Main President John F. Kennedy ... newspaper reporter at ceremonies ... of his assassination in ...

Chapter 11

❖❖❖

SHE LEFT ONLY THE PIANO

I̲ T WAS A STRANGE PLACE TO SEE JIM BEASLEY IN A COURTROOM, ON THE WITNESS STAND as a defendant. And many people noticed, including the press.

Somebody made sure the newspapers knew all about the divorce case of *Beasley v. Beasley*, then before the Montgomery County Court of Common Pleas. Jim Beasley read to the court a copy of a note addressed to the Philadelphia Inquirer. The anonymous tipster had also sent a copy to Beasley:

"Gentlemen. A master's hearing is scheduled for Tuesday, March 5, 1985, at 9:30 a.m. in the domestic relations courtroom, fifth floor, Norristown, Pa., on a nonsupport of Mr. Beasley's minor son and support of Mrs. James E. Beasley. Mr. Richard Sprague is representing Mr. James E. Beasley."

That wasn't the only time reporters showed up at the Beasley divorce proceedings. "There were reporters in the courtroom" at the previous hearing, Beasley complained.

"How do you know they were reporters?" asked Larry I. Haft, representing Helen M. Beasley.

"Because they carried with them the classic reporter notebook which has the line down the center as a stenographer's notebook," Jim Beasley said. He testified that he also saw the suspects "taking notes during the trial."

"Mr. Beasley," Haft asked, "what makes you think the press is interested in this?"

"I probably have more litigation with the Philadelphia Inquirer and the Daily News," Beasley grumbled. Either newspaper "would do anything it could to embarrass or reduce my reputation. That's why I think they would be interested."

Dick Sprague asked Beasley if the publicity over his divorce had caused him any professional harm. Beasley's answer was more about annoyance.

"I've had people who have been clients of mine who have called me and mentioned that they heard about the divorce proceeding," Beasley testified. "If these matters weren't put in the newspapers, a lot of these clients would never have known about it."

The press, however, knew a good story when it saw one. And it got even better after the reporters left the courtroom, to chase other stories. Because before the Beasley divorce case was over, Beasley's extramarital adventures would be exposed, along with the inner workings of his law firm.

• • •

THE HEADLINE ON NOV. 23, 1981, IN THE PHILADELPHIA DAILY NEWS: "J.E.B. LOSES Initial Ruling." The subhead: "But Noted Lawyer Wins Round Against Wife."

"James Beasley, a prominent Philadelphia trial lawyer who may have won more million-dollar verdicts than any other lawyer in the country, has chalked up another court victory — but this time as the plaintiff in a case against his wife, Helen."

The story said that Beasley's lawyer, Richard A. Sprague, had filed a petition in Montgomery County Court to force Helen Beasley "to return an estimated $75,000 to $90,000 worth of furniture she took from the couple's Main Line home."

Beasley, 55, glared at his wife from the witness stand last Thursday as he described what he saw the night of Oct. 30, when he first discovered the furniture was gone.

"I came home . . . there was a little furniture, my son, the dog, and the cat," he said.

He said his wife had taken many expensive antiques, including the good silverware, a Rembrandt painting, several Oriental rugs, dressers, tables, chairs and most of the living room furniture.

"The only thing left in the living room is the piano," he said.

Beasley also complained that his wife had taken "two or three" sets of dishes and left him and his son, the only child still living at home, with "the old chipped dishes that were around for 20 years." He said he noticed that a "thing I used to cook sausage" was not in the kitchen after she left.

The story said that 50-year-old Helen Beasley, described as "a soft-spoken and attractive woman," testified that her husband left her for three weeks in 1978 for another woman. But after a stay at the Drake Hotel, Beasley returned home and he and his wife tried to reconcile.

Helen said her husband had promised her he would no longer "see or communicate with" a second other woman that he had been teaching to fly in one of his private planes. But Helen said she was told on Oct. 13, 1981, that her husband had been talking to the woman again, so three weeks later, Helen took the furnishings and moved into a two-bedroom apartment. Then she filed for divorce.

Helen testified that many of the items she took were hers before she was married, and that the Rembrandt panting and Oriental rug were gifts from her husband.

The Daily News story described how Sprague had listed the case by initials, *H.M.B.* (Helen Mary Beasley) *v. J.E.B.* (James Edwin Beasley). But Montgomery County Judge Anita Brody issued a temporary restraining order against using initials in forthcoming court proceedings. "We are not accorded the right to do this for our own judges," Judge Brody said.

Beasley, the Daily News reported, "refused to discuss the case."

"Mr. Beasley does not want anyone to know about this matter," Neil Hurowitz, a Montgomery County lawyer representing Helen Beasley, told the newspaper. "He's going to be very embarrassed."

• • •

THE LEAKING OF THE COURT SCHEDULE IN *BEASLEY V. BEASLEY* WAS DONE "IN CAHOOTS with the press, and it was a very terrible thing," Dick Sprague charged in an interview for this book. "It was just part and parcel of getting the guy," Sprague said, adding, "They [the press] wanted to have him sort of punished."

Sprague said the media attention weighed heavily on Beasley.

"It had a big impact because he was really deadly serious and fearful that by telling the world about his financial condition, it would lead to robberies, burglaries and kidnapping of his children," Sprague said. "That's why he was just as upset as he could be."

Sprague said in his opinion, the Beasley divorce wasn't even newsworthy. "If it was somebody that was a favorite of the paper, say [Main Line blueblood] Robert Montgomery Scott, there would not be a word of it" in the papers, he said.

The longtime editor of the Daily News, Zack Stalberg, disagreed. "We certainly had no grudge against Beasley. In fact we loved him in a Daily News kind of way," said Stalberg, who ran the Daily News from 1984 to 2001. "In a town without celebrities, Beasley was a colorful, successful, rich attorney and that made him the kind of individual we loved to cover."

So when it came to the Beasley divorce, Stalberg said, "we were just doing our job. As far as Bobby Scott goes," Stalberg added, if Scott had been caught in a messy divorce trial, "we would have been Johnny-on-the-spot as well."

Beasley was high profile for another reason. Both the Inquirer and the Daily News had run stories that identified Beasley as a member of an elite new social club for American super lawyers known as the Inner Circle of Advocates. The 96-member club admitted by invitation only trial lawyers who had won million-dollar verdicts. The Daily News reported in 1980 that Beasley had more verdicts in excess of a million dollars than any lawyer in the country.

By the mid-1980s, the Inner Circle's membership had expanded to 115 lawyers. The club tracked million dollar verdicts around the country from 1960 to 1985. According to the club's private records, Beasley led the nation with 30 million-dollar verdicts. Thomas A. Moore of New York City was second, with 23 million-dollar verdicts.

Beasley didn't mind having his Inner Circle membership publicized, but the stories about his divorce case only served to embitter him toward the media.

"I think that it solidified his view," Sprague said, that the press did not always act in the public interest, but behaved like "press lords who have a monopoly in terms of the news and use the press for their own purposes."

• • •

BEASLEY V. BEASLEY DRAGGED ON FOR SEVEN YEARS, AND LIKE MANY OTHER CASES involving James E. Beasley, it set a legal precedent. At issue was whether the "good-will" aspect of Beasley's multimillion-dollar law firm should be considered marital property subject to equitable distribution.

In legal terms, goodwill meant future earnings, and Helen Beasley's lawyers thought she was entitled to half. Sprague objected, however, and warned that any attempt to appraise the firm's value — by rummaging through case files and clients' names — would violate lawyer-client confidentiality.

The issue had never come up before in Pennsylvania, until *Beasley v. Beasley*. The Pennsylvania Superior Court in a 1986 decision sided with Jim Beasley, deciding that the goodwill of the Beasley law firm wasn't marital property. The court also ruled that the law office's records did not have to be turned over to an appraiser hired by Helen Beasley's lawyers.

The law firm, however, was a frequent topic of courtroom testimony. While he was on the witness stand, Jim Beasley gave some insight into how the firm operated. The sign on the door may have said Beasley, Hewson, Casey, Colleran, Erbstein and Thistle, but as the court records put it, "Mr. Beasley operates practice strictly as a sole proprietorship."

The record of a hearing before the Common Pleas Court on Sept. 21, 1983, elaborated:

"Mr. Beasley described his law practice and the way it conducts business. He employs 14 or 15 attorneys and additional support staff. He owns all of the physical assets of the proprietorship, including typewriters, word processors, a computer and all of the automobiles he provides his employees. His firm practices negligence law, including 'a lot of medical malpractice, product liability . . . a lot of defamation, a few automobile cases.' "

If that wasn't blunt enough, Beasley himself cleared up any ambiguities when he took the stand.

"I do not have a partnership at all," Beasley testified. "I do not pay or make bonuses on the number of cases that are brought into the office, nor is it on a win-loss basis," he said. "We have no office meetings. If one of my associates brings in a file… he does not come to me and say, I brought this file, therefore give me a credit. Because no credits are given. There is no 'You brought in the file so you get 20 percent extra of the fee.' "

Beasley alone set salaries and decided what discretionary bonuses his employees would receive. There was no procedure for appeals.

· · ·

HELEN BEASLEY TESTIFIED THAT BETWEEN 1978 AND 1981, SHE AND HER HUSBAND WERE separated three times. The second separation, when Helen left with the children for four months, began in February 1981.

Attorney Larry Haft: "And was there an attempted reconciliation following that separation?"

Helen Beasley: "Yes . . ."

Haft: "And was there any understanding you thought had been reached with regard to that reconciliation?"

Helen: "Yes. I said that I would return if he promised not to see Nicole Chabat anymore."

Haft: "Who was Nicole Chabat?"

Helen: "Nicole Chabat, she worked for the Cancer Society, which was in the same building as my husband, and he had been teaching her to fly for a couple of years."

Haft: "And what promises were made to you regarding Ms. Chabat?"

Helen: "He promised me that he would no longer see or communicate with her."

Haft: "Mrs. Beasley, you mentioned October 1981. Was that the third and final separation?"

Helen: "Yes, it was."

Haft: "Who left the marital abode at that time?"

Helen: "I left."

Haft: "Why did you leave?"

Helen: ". . . I had a conversation with my husband about Nicole Chabat. And he said that she had been coming down to the office… . She had continued to come down to the office. After he promised me that he wouldn't see her anymore."

Haft: "Were there other factors that led to your departure in October 1981?"

Helen: "This was just a culmination of many years of abuse, being treated with contempt, indifference... ."

Haft: "Were there other circumstances which led to your leaving in October 1981?"

Helen: "Yes, there were. Early in the marriage, my husband told me that if he weren't married to me, he would have an apartment in town and have a different woman every night."

Haft asked about Jim Beasley's track record as a father.

"When our daughter, Kimberly, was born, he was too busy to bring me home from the hospital," Helen said. "About six weeks before our son was born, [Beasley] went on a safari to Africa, and returned 10 days before Jimmy was born.

"We never socialized," Helen Beasley continued. "He never took me to cultural events, theater. He was indifferent towards me."

Haft: "Did you experience with your husband any difficulties regarding alcohol abuse?"

After an objection from Sprague that was overruled, Helen replied, "My husband did not have dinner with the family for many years. He would have dinner in town and come home late, intoxicated frequently, and abuse the children and me and make the children cry."

· · ·

"I can still envision the headlights coming up the driveway at 8 o'clock at night," recalled Jim Beasley Jr. in an interview. "All of us would run upstairs because we were all in trouble."

Jim Beasley Sr. was the family disciplinarian, and his shift began when he came home from work every night. "He would get pissed," his son recalled. "He was working so hard."

Beasley wasn't the kind of dad who had heart-to-heart talks with his kids. "Dad never was a guy who displayed insight," Jim Jr. said. "He was a behaviorist: 'I don't like what's happening. Stop it.'"

Beasley's conversations with his kids sometimes became cross-examinations. He needed only a few choice words to dice somebody up. He made one remark to his daughter, Pam, when she was 6 or 7, about how fat she looked in a bathing suit, and it led to a lifetime obsession about not gaining weight. "We were all very weight-conscious," Jim Jr. said.

As a young man, Beasley had overcome his own weight problems by becoming a fitness addict. He didn't have much sympathy if his kids gained a few pounds, and he told them so. He also didn't want them getting into trouble, as Jim Jr. did when he became the class clown and got himself kicked out of Philadelphia's William Penn Charter School.

"You're fat," Jim Jr. remembers his dad telling him. "You shouldn't be. You're an asshole. You shouldn't be."

Every morning at 5 a.m., Beasley rose to work out in his own private gym that he had installed in the moldy, unfinished basement of his Villanova home. The gym was strictly no-frills, and featured "an old, unreasonably dangerous Sears bench press that was rusty and missing some bolts," Jim Jr. recalled. "Dad's exercise regimen was like Mr. T's in *Rocky III*."

Beasley also didn't understand why his kids didn't apply themselves like he did, 18 hours a day, seven days a week.

"I can't get along with you," Beasley once blurted to his son. "I can't get along with your sisters. I can't get along with your mother. What is wrong with you people?"

The son looked at the father and said, "It kind of answers itself, doesn't it?"

A boyfriend of Pam's once described Beasley as a "Jewish mother with a moustache." He would go to extraordinary lengths to bust his kids.

When Jim Jr. was 15, and didn't have his driver's license yet, and his father was at the airport, Jim Jr. would "borrow" his dad's Honda Civic and take it for a spin. The son did so much driving, he put 15,000 miles on the Honda before his 16th birthday. Sometimes, Jim Jr. and a buddy would hitch a trailer to the Honda and drive their dirt bikes over to Blackwood, N.J., to roar around a racetrack.

It got to be a cat-and-mouse game. Beasley would fly over the house in his Mustang and see that the Honda was gone. Then he would fly over the Blackwood racetrack and spot his son driving the car with a trailer, and a couple of dirt bikes loaded in back.

Dad would walk in the house at night and say, "So what did you do today?"

"Nothing," his son replied. "Just hung out."

Only then would Beasley share the intelligence he had gathered from his fly-overs. He also had a habit of telling his kids he was going away for the weekend, and then he would show up later that night to surprise them.

One Saturday night, Beasley returned to his Villanova estate and found the house crowded with 50 partying teenagers, the smell of marijuana in the air, and kegs of beer floating in the swimming pool. The kids scattered as soon as they saw Beasley. "Get the fuck out of here," he yelled.

• • •

IT WAS BEASLEY'S TURN TO TESTIFY IN HIS DIVORCE CASE. WHILE HE WAS ON THE witness stand, Dick Sprague gave Beasley a chance to present himself as a high-powered lawyer who had many demands on his time, including his own appetite for adventure, but he was still a loving parent.

Sprague: "Your wife testified as to the circumstances that early in the marriage you had said to her if you weren't married to her, you would have an apartment in town and have a different woman every night. Did you ever make such a statement?"

Beasley: "That never happened."

Sprague: "Your wife testified that when your daughter Kimberly was born, you were too busy to bring her home from the hospital. Will you tell the court what occurred at that time?"

Beasley: "Judge, I was in the operating room for each of my children. I would not have missed that for the world. If I were not available to bring my daughter and wife home, it was because I was on trial. Nothing short of that would have prevented it."

Sprague: "Your wife testified that about six weeks before your son was born, you had gone on a safari to Africa . . . and returned 10 days before your son was born. . . . Is that correct?"

Beasley: "It was something that happened at the moment. It was not a pre-planned thing, but it was an opportunity of a lifetime. . . . When I got on safari, there was no way I could communicate because it was out in the Serengeti Plain."

• • •

AN AMERICAN BAPTIST MISSIONARY SPONSORED BY THE BAPTISTS OF KING OF PRUSSIA, Pa., was driving a van in 1967 when he got into an accident on the outskirts of Nairobi. A female passenger was killed, the van impounded, and the missionary locked up on a homicide charge. That's when the American Baptist Mission called Jim Beasley and asked if he would fly to Nairobi to defend the missionary.

Beasley took the case. The first thing he did when he arrived in Nairobi was to have the missionary's van inspected by a mechanic. Beasley then argued in court that a manufacturing defect had caused the accident. "I got him off," Beasley said in an interview for this book. With the case over, Beasley had time to kill so he wandered into a store that advertised safaris for tourists.

Beasley tried to arrange a safari before he left Nairobi, but a "very proper Englishman... looked up with disdain" and told Beasley that reservations were made years in advance, Beasley recalled. Just then the phone rang, and a hunter called to cancel a reservation. Beasley suddenly had the chance of a lifetime to go on a safari. He called home to tell his wife about the big adventure, so she could share in the excitement. But Helen was nine months' pregnant, and not happy to hear that her husband would be coming home a few weeks late. So she hung up on him.

Some husbands would have canceled the safari at that point, but not Jim Beasley. He went off to the Serengeti and came back with a collection of big-game trophy heads and a bunch of stories that would last a lifetime.

"I hunted out there for two weeks," he said in an interview for this book. "I shot a lot of game and brought it home."

Photos taken on the trip show Beasley in bush country with a scoped rifle in hand, kneeling over freshly killed big game. He looks like the late American actor James Whitmore, sporting a cowboy hat and sunglasses. Beasley is shown patting the side of a wide-eyed zebra, grabbing a gemsbok by its horns, holding a leopard by its ears, posing with an antelope, and finally, patting the side of an enormous cape buffalo.

When Beasley came home, his wife greeted him by saying, "So the great white hunter has returned."

• • •

On July 17, 1986, Jim Beasley, who had just turned 60, was on the witness stand at the Montgomery County Courthouse in Norristown, testifying in the ongoing case of *Beasley v. Beasley*. The Hon. S. Gerald Corso was presiding. It was time for cross-examination. Larry Haft, Helen's attorney, was going line by line through the couple's household finances when he came to Jim Beasley's beloved P-51 Mustang.

"My airplane, this P-51," Beasley said, warming to the topic. "I have restored it back to the condition that it was that if you were to walk on an airfield in England in 1944 — '43 or '44 — this airplane would have been sitting there," he said proudly. "So it has intrinsic value."

Haft asked about a 1924 Renault that Beasley bought in Europe for $10,000. This time there was no pride of ownership. "It's a dog," Beasley said of the antique sports car. "It never would run. It's in a garage and has absolutely no value."

Haft went through the couple's vacation itinerary, trying to portray Jim Beasley as a man who led a life of luxury, but Beasley refused to play along:

Haft: "Have you ever vacationed at Greenbriar?"

Beasley: "At a convention there."

Haft: "How would you describe that?"

Beasley: ". . . I describe it as a hotel that has rooms, a golf course. I don't play golf. I'm a very informal person. I don't particularly like formal atmospheres, so if you're saying is it a place that I would go back to, I would not."

Haft: "Let me ask you if you would agree with me that these resorts, Breakers, Beach Club, Greenbriar, are among the most luxurious in the world? . . ."

Beasley: "Are they expensive? If you equate that with luxurious, yes. Are they luxurious in the sense that I enjoy them, no."

Haft: "What do you enjoy for luxury?"

Beasley: "Flying airplanes."

Haft: "And that's your hobby, flying airplanes?"

Beasley: "That's my salvation. It keeps me sane."

Haft: "For the two airplanes you've identified, the annual cost of that hobby is about $70,000, is that right?"

Beasley: "Whatever the figures show, it's cheap for me."

Haft: "It's cheap for you?"

Beasley: "Yes, sir. I worked hard to afford that. Nobody gave it to me."

• • •

HAFT WAS GOING THROUGH MORE HOUSEHOLD EXPENSES AT BEASLEY'S VILLANOVA estate, with its 12 rooms and six baths. The bills included $10,500 for a new radiator for the P-51; $18,000 for a 1969 Mercedes; and a grand total of $59,961 spent in 1985 on planting flowers, and replanting the lawn and flowers after extensive septic tank work.

"I have difficulty with your definition of luxury," Beasley told Haft. "My house is not Versailles, if that's what you're comparing it to."

Beasley recalled that when he first got married to Helen in 1958, he was earning $6,500 a year. By 1983, his net worth was listed at $3.4 million.

"I grew up in an entirely different environment than I'm living now," Beasley acknowledged from the witness stand. "And that has always been something in the back of my mind."

• • •

THE SUBJECT WAS MARITAL INFIDELITY, AND FOR JIM BEASLEY, THE WITNESS STAND became a confessional of sorts. It would not be Beasley's shining hour in a courtroom. Like many men, when the subject was sex, he had a hard time telling the truth.

"I had made a mistake, and I told her that, by having an affair," Beasley told Dick Sprague and the judge. "I don't know really what precipitated that, you know, the mid-life crisis or whatever it was. And she [Helen] said to me early on, she said, 'You know, if you're honest with me about that' — and then she kept nagging me about it.

"And I felt bad about it and I finally — my conscience bothered me, and I told her about the affair," Beasley testified. "She kept saying we'll put it behind us, et cetera. After that it was a constant reminder about the affair. And we were at a restaurant downtown . . . and she kept it up that evening. And I said to her, 'You're never going to let this go. You'll never let it die.' And I got up and left, because it was just too much."

Beasley, however, didn't sound like a guy who wanted a divorce.

"I came back because I did want the marriage to work," Beasley said. "I was very much in love with my wife then.

"She then accused me of having an affair with another woman, which I tried to explain to her that it was just not so, but she left the second time and was gone four months," he said. "During that period of time, I again pleaded with her to come back."

Beasley was a tough guy to argue with, but Helen knew how to get through to him. "I would try and talk to her, and from the very day we were married, she had a way of dealing with problems and that was not talking," Beasley said. "She would absolutely ignore me, no matter what occurred."

Beasley described how he changed his work habits to make it home every evening promptly at 6 o'clock, so he could eat dinner with his family, and he did that for a year and a half. It was something new in the Beasley household, where everybody was used to Dad working late at the office.

But then Helen found out that Beasley was still seeing Nicole Chabat. That's when Beasley came home and found the furniture missing, but he tried once again to get his wife to come back. "When my wife left, I was very much in love with her," Beasley testified. "I sent her flowers twice a week for over a year and tried every way to get — to have a reconciliation."

Beasley also left his living room empty. "I did not purchase any furniture because I didn't — I just didn't believe that the marriage was through, because I was very much in love with her," he testified. "I tried every conceivable way, even to the point of getting down on my knees in the driveway and begging her to come back," he said, but Helen said no.

• • •

Haft: "You mentioned a woman who worked for the Cancer Society with whom you had the affair. Is that Nicole Chabat?"

Beasley: "I did not have an affair with her."

Haft: "Who is the woman you mentioned you had an affair with?"

Beasley mentioned the name of a young lawyer.

Haft: "Was that an employee of your office?"

Beasley: "She was."

Haft: "How old was she?"

Beasley: "I don't know how old she was. Thirty-five?"

Haft: "How long have you known Nicole Chabat?"

Beasley: "I can't remember when I first met her, but I met her through going to the American Cancer Society to get pamphlets and brochures and information on breast cancer. Ten years? I just don't know. I'm not quite sure, Your Honor...."

The first time I met her wasn't really a monumental day in my life that I would have any cause to remember."

Haft: "Was she the woman that accompanied you to Europe on your recent trip?"

Beasley: "Yes."

Haft: "Whose fare you paid?"

Beasley: "Yes."

· · ·

"IT WAS NOT AN AFFAIR," NICOLE CHABAT AGREED IN A 2006 INTERVIEW; IT WAS A relationship that went on for more than a dozen years.

They met in 1977, in an elevator at the Steven Girard Building, where both worked. Nicole, a native of Paris, was going for her American citizenship that day and she was wearing yellow and blue, Jim Beasley's favorite colors.

Chabat, described by a former female colleague as "slender, lovely, elegant," was a petite blond 20 years Beasley's junior. She was also separated from her husband.

A few months after they met, a lawyer in Beasley's office called to ask Chabat if Beasley could obtain copies of the American Cancer Society's publications on breast cancer to show how a doctor had been negligent in a medical malpractice case. Chabat declined, because it was against the American Cancer Society's rules to get involved in a lawsuit.

Within a half-hour, Beasley had Chabat served with a subpoena. She was summoned to a courtroom, where she waited several hours for a judge to eventually decide that the Cancer Society publications would not be admitted as evidence.

During a break, Beasley apologized to Chabat for "taking me prisoner for a couple of hours," she recalled. "He was charming when he wanted to be. He talked about flying, which was his cachet." Chabat had never flown a plane before. So Beasley made her an offer: "To make up for what I did to you, I'll take you flying."

Chabat began taking lessons from Beasley in 1980, and she said a romance began the following year. Chabat loved flying and eventually got her pilot's license. Beasley even taught her how to fly one of his warbirds, the T-6 Navy Trainer.

Beasley also talked Chabat into going back to college and getting her degree, then going to law school for two years, but Chabat insisted on paying for it herself. She said she had always been an independent career woman, but that Beasley had a powerful influence on her.

"If you hung around him long enough, either you hated flying or you adored flying and were fascinated by what he did," she explained. Or as Jim Jr. put it, "Dad tried to turn all his girlfriends into pilots and lawyers."

Chabat went to work for Beasley as a paralegal, and flew with him on many trips in his vintage P-51 Mustang out to Nevada, while he was representing U.S. Senator Paul Laxalt in a libel case against the Sacramento Bee.

"He was always impeccably dressed," Chabat recalled. "He flew that airplane in a three-piece suit like the Englishman that he was. He never had any sign of perspiration. Jim never sweated. He would walk out of that warplane in a three-piece suit and a tie just looking like he had come out of a bus."

So Beasley knew how to dress, Chabat said, but he had some bad habits. He was a smoker, and he was also using Grecian Formula to color his hair.

Chabat, who ran the quit-smoking clinics with the American Cancer Society, said she talked Beasley into giving up cigarettes, and letting his hair go gray. She also expressed horror at the "cheap wines" he was drinking, and eventually got him to appreciate finer wines.

Beasley was also a lousy cook, Chabat said. He made the same dinner every night for himself and Jim Jr.: "Five pounds of spaghetti" topped with sauce and meatballs "right out of a jar," Chabat said, followed by a "ton of ice cream" for dessert. Chabat wasn't much of a cook either, so she talked Beasley into hiring a chef.

Beasley and Chabat had breakfast together every morning. "I was divorced, he was separated," she said. When Chabat wasn't staying at Beasley's Villanova estate, the couple shared a city condo that they bought in 1987. She described their relationship as volatile, because of Beasley's moods.

"If he wanted to kill you, one look would do it, but if he wanted to charm you, he could be very charming," she said. "We had a totally immature relationship. He couldn't bring himself to discuss most things. You had to be on your toes because you didn't know which way the wind was going to blow."

Chabat said that during their relationship, she wasn't the only woman in Jim Beasley's life. "I don't think he was ever faithful for very long," she said. "The conquest was energizing for him. He really liked that."

"He had women all over him in the office. He had women coming to him all the time," Chabat said, laughing. "Why would he turn them down? . . . There was a bit of the cat in him, and he loved to play with the mice."

Keeping up with Beasley was a challenge. "Jim wanted to live life to the max," Chabat said. "Our time together was adventure, work, traveling and just sheer exhaustion.... It was almost a competition to see who was going to wear out the other, and he won."

• • •

Larry Haft: "Were you ever unfaithful to your husband?"

Helen Beasley: "No, I was never unfaithful to my husband."

• • •

As the Beasley divorce case dragged on, Beasley realized that Helen wasn't coming back. He finally decided it would be better for everybody if the decree was granted.

Dick Sprague: "Mr. Beasley, beyond professionally, has the continuation of the marital status here between you and Mrs. Beasley been harmful emotionally to you?"

Beasley: "It's been terribly harmful."

Sprague: "Can you describe in detail?"

Beasley: "It's just been difficult — had been for many years — difficult for me to deal with, but it's been particularly difficult for the children. They constantly ask me, 'Dad, when is this going to end? Dad, why is it going on like this? Why can't we get this behind us?' "

Beasley testified that the divorce was especially tough on his son.

Beasley: "I think, sir, over the years my son has somehow or other blamed me for a lot of things that have occurred. I think I have spent in excess of $15,000 in psychiatric care for him. It has affected our relationship. I love my son very much, and it's been very difficult for him to deal with this divorce, extremely difficult for him to deal with it."

Sprague: "Is it your feeling that if the divorce was granted now, that at least that would be helpful even though the economic issues are being fought out, a resolution of the divorce and getting it over with would be helpful to you professionally, socially, emotionally?"

Beasley: "Absolutely."

Sprague: "Do you think it would be helpful to your children? All of them?"

Beasley: "I think the children would celebrate the day that divorce was final. I think that's the thing that has been bothering them so long, all of the children."

• • •

As a result of his parents' separation, Jim Jr. was the only one living at home with his father. The feuding parents decided that in order to help Jim Jr. learn to cope with the situation, he needed counseling.

"Look, I'll go, but why am I going?" Jim Jr. complained. "You guys need the counseling, not me."

But his parents insisted, so Jim Jr. used to drive himself to the psychiatrist's office in Wynnewood in his dad's Honda Civic. The only problem was, Jim Jr. was still 15. "How'd you get here today?," the doctor would ask. "Same way I got here last week," Jim Jr. replied.

The psychiatrist looked at his patient "like I had three heads," and then he lectured him about underage driving. Jim Jr. explained that Dad was at work and Mom had been driven out of the house by Dad.

· · ·

ON JULY 18, 1988, AFTER SEVEN YEARS OF LITIGATION, THE 193RD ITEM ON THE DOCKET for the case of *Beasley v. Beasley* noted that a divorce decree had finally been granted in favor of Helen M. Beasley.

The agreement called for Jim Beasley to pay his wife of 30 years a lump sum settlement that amounted to a bargain price of $1.7 million, considering that Beasley could make that kind of money just by winning a single case.

Court records said the couple "have decided that their marriage is irretrievably broken [and] that it is their intention to live separate and apart for the rest of their natural lives."

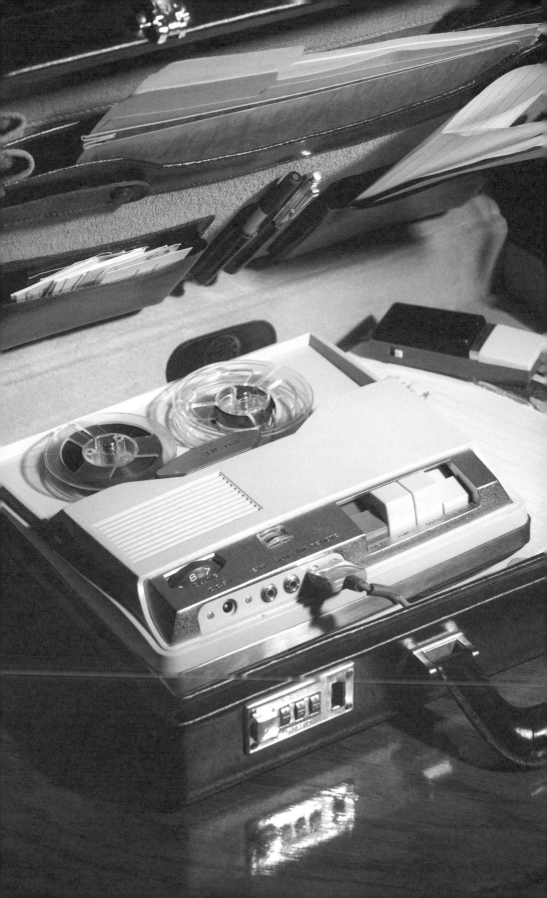

Chapter 12

❖

THE MOTHER OF ALL LIBEL CASES

J IM BEASLEY DIDN'T CARE MUCH FOR REPORTERS, BUT WHEN GREG WALTER SHOWED up at his office on Oct. 1, 1981, to give a deposition, Beasley went out of his way to make the notorious local muckraker feel at home.

"Mr. Walter," Beasley said, "you can take your coat off, relax. If you need anything, I will get it for you."

Walter was a tall and awkward-looking relic from another era, an investigative reporter with slightly stooped shoulders who wore a trench coat and Clark Kent-style heavy-rim glasses. He could dig up dirt on anybody, and the people he wrote about often ended up disgraced or in jail, or both. But while he racked up journalism awards, Walter also dealt with personal problems.

Walter was a recovering alcoholic who was thirsty, so Beasley dispatched an associate to get some water. Walter was also a diabetic on a strict feeding schedule, so he needed to take a lunch break in 90 minutes.

"Perfectly OK," Beasley said.

"Mr. Walter," Beasley said, turning to the reporter. "If at any time during this deposition you feel that you cannot continue for reasons of health, let me know."

"Surely I will," Walter responded.

"I want to try and be as considerate as we can," Beasley said.

"I appreciate that," Walter said. He had a habit of cocking his head and smiling while he made disturbingly direct eye contact. Beasley, however, seemed unfazed as he flashed his own patented glare. "You don't know me," he said, staring down the witness. "My name is James Beasley. I represent Mr. Sprague."

And Walter was on Beasley's turf. Acting on a hunch, Beasley brought the questioning around to the reporter's personal life, asking what happened 30 years ago when Walter was contacted by his draft board: "Did you avoid the draft?"

"No, I did not," Walter nervously replied. "I reported.... I was found unfit psychologically. I don't want to imply it was simply a physical reason.... Can I have an ashtray?"

"Certainly," said Beasley, ever the gracious host. He handed Walter a super-sized model. "That will hold a lot of cigarettes," Beasley said.

Walter, lighting up, was uncomfortable being the subject of an interrogation. He was usually the one asking the tough questions, often with a secret tape recorder running in his briefcase.

Walter was so good at intelligence-gathering that he was sought out for his expertise by investigators for the Pennsylvania State Crime Commission. But he was also reckless, and didn't always get his facts straight, which made him even more dangerous. Just ask Dick Sprague.

Richard A. Sprague, a spectator at the deposition, was a hawkish, squinty-eyed former prosecutor famous for the cold and predatory way he dissected witnesses. Even hardened cops on the stand were known to tremble when Dick Sprague asked the questions. Once, after Sprague left a courtroom, a newspaper columnist wrote, "You could almost see the icicles hanging from the woodwork."

Sprague had a spotless reputation as the top homicide prosecutor in the Philadelphia district attorney's office, winning convictions in 59 out of 60 murder cases. But after Walter got through with him, Sprague felt he'd been tarred in the press as a fixer, and that as a consequence his career in government had come to a premature end. That's why he went to court to sue Walter and the Philadelphia Inquirer for libel.

Now, the tables were turned. Greg Walter was on the hot seat, as the lead defendant in Sprague's libel suit. And Jim Beasley was doing the interrogating.

• • •

COPS AND POLITICIANS WEREN'T THE ONLY ONES AFRAID OF GREG WALTER; HIS FELLOW writers had reason to fear him as well. "Greg was a scary guy," recalled Mike Mallowe, an award-winning investigative reporter at Philadelphia magazine, and briefly a colleague of Walter's. "You knew if you got in his way, you were gonna get thrown under the bus."

Walter didn't give up much information, not even to fellow journalists. "He'd never give you a straight answer," Mallowe said. "Greg always gave the sense that 'I am the keeper of the secrets, and in my time and in my way I'll reveal them.'"

Walter first became known in the 1960s as a writer for Philadelphia magazine, and then in the 1970s, when he worked for Life magazine and two Philadelphia newspapers, the Evening Bulletin and the Inquirer.

It was a time when investigative reporting was in vogue, and no town was more in need of exposure than "corrupt and contented" Philadelphia, as Lincoln Steffens famously described the City of Brotherly Love in his 1904 *Shame of the Cities*.

Walter's first big hit was on a fellow journalist: Harry J. Karafin, then an ace investigative reporter at the Inquirer. Karafin had pals at City Hall who let him rifle confidential files to come up with incriminating information that led to one front-page scoop after another. But instead of printing everything he knew, the reporter decided it would be more profitable to use the information he gathered as blackmail. Karafin went around town threatening people, forcing them to pay him exorbitant fees as a public relations "consultant," so they wouldn't be exposed on the Inquirer's front page.

The shakedowns went on for years until Karafin was exposed in a 1967 Philadelphia magazine story, "The Reporter." Writers Gaeton Fonzi and Greg Walter asked how, on a newspaper reporter's salary that averaged $11,000 a year, Karafin could afford to take European vacations, buy furs for his wife and pay cash for two brand new Buicks. "How did he do it?" Fonzi and Walter wrote in Philadelphia magazine. "He did it by prostituting the power of the press," and pocketing hundreds of thousands of dollars in extortion payments.

Karafin wound up getting fired, indicted for extortion, and dying in jail. And Philadelphia magazine won an award for the exposé from Sigma Delta Chi, the national society of journalists.

Walter's next big victim was famed novelist Pearl S. Buck, winner of a Pulitzer Prize and a Nobel Prize in literature for *The Good Earth*. Walter had been a student of Buck's when she taught a writing class at Columbia University. "She took an intense interest in the daily lives and problems of her students," Walter wrote in Philadelphia magazine. Walter told Beasley that Buck had even provided him with "financial help" while he was at Columbia. But that didn't prevent Walter from exposing Buck in the pages of Philadelphia magazine.

Buck owned a farm house in Bucks County, where she raised six adopted kids. She also set up a nonprofit foundation to arrange for American adoptions of the unwanted children of U.S. servicemen and Korean mothers. The Pearl S. Buck Foundation was run by Theodore Harris, a former Arthur Murray dance instructor who first met Buck when he came out to her farmhouse to give her private ballroom dancing lessons.

Plying Buck with flattery, Harris became a confidante and then the president of her foundation. Harris used his new position to tap charitable funds and buy himself new suits and exotic pet birds. Harris also molested some of the boys he was supposedly trying to help, Walter wrote.

After Walter's story, "The Dancing Master," was published in 1969, Harris was forced to resign as foundation president, and the Buck Foundation lost its license to solicit charitable funds. Walter's story won a National Magazine Award, and another award from Sigma Delta Chi.

• • •

GREG WALTER WAS A STAR AT PHILADELPHIA MAGAZINE, BUT HE HAD A HABIT OF MISS-ing deadlines. "He was trying to research to the very end, and I thought that was the one technical problem . . . that would catch up to him," Mike Mallowe said. "He used to wait till the bitter end and then send a telegram" to the subject of his story, seeking comment.

Sending threatening telegrams is a tactic sure "to incense people," Mallowe said. One of those telegrams was delivered to Dick Sprague.

On March 14, 1973, Sprague, as Philadelphia's first assistant district attorney, was in Erie, Pa., getting ready to prosecute the biggest case of his career: the murder trial of three alleged contract killers of United Mine Workers leader Joseph "Jock" Yablonski, his wife and daughter.

The brutal killings had attracted national attention. The Yablonskis were shot to death on New Year's Eve 1969, in the bedrooms of their home in Clarksville, Pa., after Jock Yablonski had waged an unsuccessful reform campaign for union president.

Sprague was getting ready to prove in court that the murders were contract hits authorized by the president of the mine workers, W.A. "Tony" Boyle, and paid for with $15,000 in union funds.

But the telegram from Inquirer reporters Greg Walter and Kent Pollock gave Sprague a deadline of less than 48 hours to respond to a list of questions about a 10-year-old homicide case:

"DEAR MR SPRAGUE: REPEATED ATTEMPTS TO CONTACT YOU BY TELEPHONE AND IN PERSON HAVE FAILED. MESSAGES REQUESTING THAT YOU CONTACT US HAVE GONE UNANSWERED BY YOU. WE RE-SPECTFULLY REQUEST ANSWERS TO THE FOLLOWING QUESTIONS IN REFERENCE TO THE DEATH OF JOHN R. APPLEGATE, 1415 CLEARVIEW STREET, PHILADELPHIA, ON MARCH 3, 1963.

SHOULD WE NOT RECEIVE ANSWERS TO THESE QUESTIONS BY 12 O'CLOCK NOON FRIDAY, MARCH 16, 1973, WE WILL BE FORCED TO REPORT THAT YOU ARE UNWILLING TO COMMENT ON THE CASE."

Sprague dashed off a letter on March 15, 1973, to Eugene L. Roberts Jr., the executive editor of the Inquirer, saying it was impossible for him to meet with the reporters because he was trying the Yablonski case. When Sprague's libel case against the Inquirer went to trial, Beasley had Sprague's letter and the telegram from the Inquirer reporters blown up into four-foot-high courtroom exhibits.

In his letter to Roberts, Sprague charged that it was a conflict of interest for Walter to be investigating him, because Sprague had recently prosecuted Walter for a violation of the Pennsylvania state wiretapping law, namely tape-recording phone calls without permission. Walter had been convicted, and the case was on appeal.

"I think it appropriate to bring to your attention that since the time I successfully prosecuted Greg Walter, it has been reported to me by numbers of reliable individuals in Philadelphia that Mr. Walter has been stating that he was 'out to get me' and 'smear me,' " Sprague wrote Roberts. "It should further be pointed out that Mr. Walter is yet awaiting trial in a matter in which I am the prosecutor."

"I trust that The Philadelphia Inquirer would not permit itself to be used by a reporter who obviously has personal reasons for attempting to smear the prosecutor in his case and who has expressed such purpose as well."

• • •

SPRAGUE V. WALTER ET AL WAS AN EPIC FOUGHT IN THE COURTS FOR 23 YEARS. IT BEGAN in 1973, when Walter and the Philadelphia Inquirer ran a series of stories that accused prosecutor Sprague of being involved in illegal wiretapping and allegedly fixing a decade-old murder case for a friend who was a cop. Sprague filed his libel suit 18 days after the last story ran, claiming he'd been the victim of a journalistic vendetta.

If they ever made a movie out of *Sprague v. Walter*, it would be as wacky as *The Front Page* and as murky as a film noir. The case was set back in an era of Philadelphia politics when a huge, tough-talking former cop named Frank Rizzo ran City Hall, and didn't take kindly to snooping reporters. The subplots featured a couple of disco-era hookers who got caught trying to bribe an honest cop, and a bunch of cops who got caught spying on their fellow cops.

Beasley entered the saga in March 1981, when he took over the case at Sprague's request from another eminent city lawyer, Edwin P. Rome. At that point, *Sprague v. Walter* had floundered in the courts for eight years. But just seven months after he took the case, Beasley turned it around when he deposed Greg Walter.

The investigative reporter was known for making other people crack. Beasley, however, used the deposition to break Walter and expose him for having his own closet full of skeletons. The Inquirer never recovered.

"He [Beasley] was excellent in the deposition," Dick Sprague recalled in an interview. "Jim was bringing out an awful lot of info about his [Walter's] unstable background. The questions kept coming and coming. It was great and when it was over, I said, 'Jim, my God, how did you get all that information?'"

What information? Beasley said.

"That's how good Jim Beasley was," marveled Sprague, himself a master at the craft. "He felt something, and he developed it along the way. I was sure he had done an unbelievable investigative job, and he didn't have one iota.

"So, in any event, I enjoyed watching Jim," Sprague said. "I enjoyed being his client. Jim and I, through the years, he was my client, and I represented him. I was his lawyer, and he was my lawyer."

. . .

BEASLEY HONED IN ON WALTER'S REJECTION BY THE ARMY: "WAS THAT THE FIRST TIME . . . your psychology, your personality and mental attitude, however you want to describe it, ever came in question?"

"Well, Mr. Beasley," Walter stammered as he rambled. "If I may. I would like — I would be willing to — I realize that you want this history and I will tell you why I was found unfit."

"Will you answer my question first?" Beasley asked.

Walter looked at Beasley. "What is your question?"

Beasley asked the court reporter to read back the question, namely, when was Walter's mental condition first called into question. "Were you a teenager?" Beasley asked.

"No, at the age of 10," Walter replied, when he was institutionalized at the Deveraux School in Devon, Pa., a place for emotionally disturbed children. Beasley asked for details, and Walter, in between drags on a cigarette, said he would be happy to divulge all, "if I could start at the beginning."

Walter's attorney, Samuel E. Klein, a First Amendment expert, could only sit and listen with a poker face as Walter proceeded to bare his tortured past to Beasley, as if he was one of Walter's many psychiatrists.

Walter was born in Great Britain during World War II; his father was a cellist, his mother a prostitute. He was sent to America to escape Nazi bombs and was adopted by a wealthy foster family in Pittsburgh. His foster parents put him in boarding schools, but Walter kept running away.

"Will you tell me now what were the circumstances that led to the Deveraux School?" Beasley asked.

"In an act of rebellion, I had stuffed up the drains of the men's room in the dormitory at the boarding school I was attending," Walter replied. He told Beasley how he had "turned on the faucets and left the building and it resulted in . . . quite a bit of damage. I was immediately thrown out of school."

"My [adopted] father was an alcoholic and was hospitalized at that time," Walter continued, without waiting for a new question. "My mother didn't know what to do and on the advice of the master who threw me out, he told her that he felt I was retarded and needed special education at an institution."

Beasley asked Walter where he went to school after Deveraux, and Walter replied, "I went to West Chester Sanitarium." Walter told Beasley how he struck a teacher at Deveraux who hit him first, and ended up in the sanitarium, where they put him on phenobarbital, a powerful barbiturate used to control epileptic seizures, and then a dozen psychiatrists took turns evaluating him.

"When was the last time you saw a psychiatrist?" Beasley asked.

"Two years ago."

"What was his name?"

"I am sorry," said Walter, who seemed to be having a delayed reaction to Beasley's questions. "I was a little bit upset. You have gotten into an area that is very personal."

"I understand," Beasley said.

• • •

THE DEPOSITION OF GREG WALTER TOOK PLACE IN JIM BEASLEY'S SPACIOUS CORNER office on the fifth floor of the Stephen Girard Building at 21 S. 12th St. "Jim was behind his desk in a position of authority," recalled William P. Murphy, who in 1981 was a newly hired assistant at the Beasley firm in his first few months of practicing law.

Walter was on the other side of the desk, with his lawyer from the Inquirer, Sam Klein. The reporter seemed dignified and eager to please, Murphy said, and quickly fell under Beasley's spell. "My impression was he was a little bit enthralled by Mr. Beasley," Murphy said. "He gave up a great deal of information which to this day still astonishes me, and he did it with little resistance."

"I think he was a vulnerable character," Murphy said. "He behaved a little bit like he was looking for sympathy. It almost seemed like he was giving more info so that Jim would go easy on him."

Walter died of a heart attack in 1989, but his former private lawyer is still around. Gregory M. Harvey met Greg Walter when both men worked for the Evening Bulletin. Harvey, a First Amendment lawyer, did prepublication reviews of several Greg Walter stories while Walter was a Bulletin staff writer. Walter subsequently hired Harvey as his private lawyer.

"He was fearless, he had a crusading zeal," Harvey said in an interview. "He was brilliant at marshaling facts that others might have felt were collateral and immaterial. With adequate legal support he [Walter] was brilliant at investigative reporting."

Harvey faulted the Inquirer's attorney, Sam Klein, who died in 2002, for allowing Beasley to question Walter about his personal life. "He [Klein] should have terminated the interview," Harvey said. But Beasley kept asking questions, and Klein didn't object.

Gene Roberts, former executive editor of the Inquirer, said in an interview that Klein believed Walter would come across to a jury "as a sympathetic witness." Roberts said Klein was also confident that when the full truth came out about the dirty tricks employed against Walter by the Rizzo administration, it would be a trump card for the Inquirer. But Sam Klein turned out to be an unlucky poker player.

· · ·

BEASLEY ASKED WALTER WHAT HAPPENED AFTER HE WAS DRAFTED, AND WALTER REPLIED, "I had a nervous breakdown." That was in1957. The next time Greg Walter ended up in a mental hospital was 1972.

"What led to that hospitalization?" Beasley asked.

"I was extremely upset," Walter said. "I was on the verge of a nervous breakdown, and I had just been arrested for wiretapping, for a violation of the Pennsylvania wiretapping law."

The 1972 arrest came during a low point in Walter's career. Walter had just left Philadelphia magazine after the publisher refused to print an exposé he had written about former Police Commissioner Frank Rizzo, then a candidate for mayor. Walter told Beasley all about the unpublished story, and how it documented Rizzo's involvement with organized crime figures, kickbacks and "unnecessary beatings" of crime suspects.

Walter told Beasley that the publisher of Philadelphia magazine, Herb Lipson, refused to run the story because he was a political supporter of Rizzo's. Walter also accused Lipson of giving a copy of the unpublished story to Rizzo.

In an article about the unpublished story that ran in a 1972 journalism review, Lipson told author Joe McGinnis: "Greg built this up into something of the first magnitude, and then he gave birth to a mouse."

Another reporter who read Walter's unpublished story about Rizzo was Mike Mallowe. "It was crap," Mallowe said in a 2006 interview. "It was nothing but rumors and innuendos. I don't think there was a direct source named. [The editor] would have been insane to run it."

Walter, however, cursed out the editor of Philadelphia magazine before he quit, and then he jumped to the Philadelphia Bulletin, where he continued to investigate Rizzo and the Philadelphia cops.

Walter's unpublished Rizzo story resurfaced during the 1971 Philadelphia mayoral election, when someone anonymously mailed lengthy excerpts to several newspaper reporters. Dan Lynch, a former Inquirer political columnist, recalled sitting down with another local reporter and grilling Rizzo about Walter's allegations.

"Look, commissioner," Lynch said, "is it true you never paid for a suit of clothes in your life? Is it true you never paid for a meal in your life? Is it true you were keeping a woman in an apartment in West Philadelphia for 15 years?"

Rizzo, Lynch recalled, who weighed more than 250 pounds, just sat there while the reporters continued to ask their questions, swelling with indignation "like a blowfish." When the reporters finished, Lynch said, "Rizzo exploded like Vesuvius," and yelled, "Lies, lies, a pack of fucking lies."

Rizzo slammed the table with one hand, which Lynch described as "the size of a Hormel ham," and then Rizzo quickly added, "except for that broad in West Philly."

Rizzo was elected mayor, but Walter was still on his tail. The reporter agreed to help the state Crime Commission set up a sting operation to see if Rizzo's cops would take payoffs from prostitutes.

Investigators for the state Crime Commission recruited two hookers and got them jobs at a local lounge as exotic dancers. The investigators told the hookers to contact Greg Walter and "follow his instructions on what to do," according to a petition filed in court by an assistant district attorney. Walter, according to the petition, gave the hookers a tape recorder and a telephone jack to record their interviews and phone calls with police officers. Taping phone calls was a standard practice among investigative reporters of the era. In Pennsylvania, however, recording phone calls without the permission of the person on the other end of the line was and still is illegal.

"I knew that Greg was working with Crime Commission investigators," said Harvey, his lawyer, who described the two hookers as "informants." The whole scheme collapsed when one of the hookers got arrested for trying to bribe an honest cop. She told police that she was working for Greg Walter and the state Crime Commission. As proof, she turned over the tape recorder and telephone jack that Walter had given her.

Unfortunately for Walter, the tape recorder he gave the hookers contained a used tape. On the tape, the cops found a half-dozen calls that Walter had recorded with a cop, two investigators from the state Crime Commission, and "Peaches," the other hooker in the sting operation. District Attorney Arlen Specter, another big Rizzo supporter, indicted Walter for wiretapping and issued an arrest warrant. That caused a big stir in the press, and not just at the Bulletin where Walter worked.

"After Greg Walter was arrested, all hell broke loose in the media," Sprague recalled. "Arlen got attacked like you wouldn't believe….The heat was tremendous on Arlen."

The press said the arrest was unprecedented in Pennsylvania, and that law enforcement officials had conspired to use a little-used state wiretapping statute to muzzle Greg Walter. The Inquirer led the charge, with articles and editorials that condemned the district attorney. Sprague was Specter's first assistant, a homicide prosecutor who usually handled only big-time murders, but since Specter was taking so much heat, he asked Sprague to prosecute Walter.

At Walter's trial in Municipal Court, Sprague played the tape that Walter had secretly recorded. The first voice heard on the tape was that of Walter's lawyer, Gregory M. Harvey, so Sprague called Harvey as his first witness.

"He [Harvey] should have objected," Sprague said in an interview. But since he didn't, Sprague asked Harvey whose voice was on the tape, and Harvey said it was his. Sprague asked Harvey if he had given Walter permission to tape him, and Harvey said he hadn't.

Sprague called the other people on Walter's tape as witnesses to see if they had given Walter permission to record them, and nobody had. Sprague glanced over at the defense lawyer. "I could see Greg Harvey was still trying to ponder what happened," Sprague recalled. "That was basically the trial."

Harvey said there had been no sense objecting, because he knew he was going to lose the case. Sure enough, Walter was convicted and fined $300, plus $50 in court costs. Harvey filed an appeal.

Harvey defended Walter in an interview by saying the reporter had been investigating payoffs to police, and at the time "the police hierarchy very much desired to have that investigation terminated."

The police also were guilty of violating the same wiretapping statute that snared Walter, Harvey said, because they routinely taped all incoming calls, including calls from lawyers to clients. So Harvey filed a motion to dismiss the case against Walter, saying it was a discriminatory prosecution. Harvey also filed a motion to compel the police and the district attorney to turn over tapes of all recorded phone calls.

The district attorney responded in 1973 by dropping the charges against Walter and dismissing the case. Walter's legal headache was over, but his health and personal problems remained.

• • •

BEASLEY: "WAS THAT THE LAST INSTITUTIONALIZATION?"
    Walter: "No."
    Beasley: "When was the next one?"
    Walter: "To the best of my recollection, 1974. . . ."
    Beasley: "What was the admitting diagnosis?"

Walter: "Alcoholism."

Beasley asked whether there had been any other hospital stays, so Walter talked about his open-heart surgery in 1976. And how after the surgery, he developed "drinking problems," high blood pressure and diabetes. He was also being treated for depression.

Beasley asked Walter about the most recent time he had been institutionalized, in 1979. "I had gone into a deep depression and again I was worried about my drinking," Walter explained. "I had just gone through a divorce, lost my house."

"…Did the Bulletin know that you had a mental breakdown, or did you tell them you were on vacation?" Beasley asked.

"They told me to go home and stay there," Walter snapped. He could not contain his resentment. "I wasn't about to tell the Bulletin anything," he fumed. "As far as I was concerned, they were completely chicken-shit about it. I didn't feel they were standing behind me…. I felt they stuck a knife in my back."

• • •

GREG WALTER HAD A LOT OF ENEMIES ON THE PHILADELPHIA POLICE DEPARTMENT, AND over at City Hall, Mayor Rizzo had ordered all city employees not to talk to the investigative reporter. Then, in 1972, the city medical examiner subpoenaed Walter's medical records from the University of Pennsylvania Hospital, supposedly to help identify a skid-row corpse that police suspected was Walter's. The only problem was, Walter was still alive. And Walter's medical records, including his psychiatric records, were suddenly in the hands of his enemies. And they were mailing excerpts to the mayor, the district attorney, and executives at the Inquirer.

Mayor Rizzo wasn't sympathetic. "He [Walter] has made a career out of espionage and spying on the people," Rizzo told reporters. "Isn't it amazing he's screaming because somebody's looking over his shoulder?"

The records obtained from the psychiatric unit of the University of Pennsylvania Hospital showed that the newest patient, Greg Walter, had been admitted and placed on tranquilizers after he told a psychiatrist he was "on the edge of a breakdown."

Walter, according to trial testimony, was drinking up to a fifth of whiskey a day, plus wine. At the hospital, Walter told the psychiatrist he had been on a three-week bender since he had been indicted by a grand jury for wiretapping. His life had become "pure hell," he said. Besides his legal woes and his drinking, Walter was also having marital problems.

Walter told his psychiatrist that a month before, when he was "drinking especially heavily," he "went downtown looking for a hooker and picked up what turned out to be a transvestite." Walter told the psychiatrist that he willingly performed oral sex on the transvestite. And after that episode, Walter told his doctor, he "lost interest in his wife sexually" and "became totally disgusted with himself."

Walter may have been in the psychiatric ward, and on the outs with his wife and his employer, but he had a new advocate: Gene Roberts, the recently hired executive editor of the Philadelphia Inquirer. At the Inquirer, the Bulletin's main rival, reporters and editorial writers pursued the story of Walter's arrest with more outrage than did Walter's own newspaper.

Gene Roberts was a former New York Times reporter whose formative journalistic experiences were in the South, where he was the paper's chief Southern correspondent covering the civil rights movement, and in Saigon, where he was the Times' chief Vietnam War correspondent. Roberts took a dim view of government officials arresting reporters.

So when the Bulletin fired Walter in October 1972, Roberts decided to hire him, and two months later Walter started work at the Inquirer. His conviction for wiretapping was still on appeal. After only two weeks on his new job, Walter told Beasley, he was looking into Dick Sprague's background, investigating several alleged scandals as possible stories for the Inquirer.

He was also hanging out in bars. Walter's psychiatrist wrote in his journal in April 1973 that the reporter "still cannot control [his] drinking."

"It was so extensive that at times he would black out," Walter's former girlfriend, Carolyn Byrne, would testify in court after Beasley convinced her to come forward as a witness. "He would become extremely unruly. He would start arguments with people...."

"He would start drinking in the morning," Byrne told the jury. "And if he would stop at lunch time, he would be able to get back to the office for a while and leave early and go to the bar again and drink [some] more. This went on just about every day of the week."

· · ·

Still smarting from his wiretap arrest and conviction, Walter sat down in February 1973 to interview somebody who hated Dick Sprague more than he did. Jacqueline Sprague was Dick Sprague's ex-wife who had hired a private detective to follow her husband around before their divorce, because she suspected he was cheating on her. Jackie Sprague showed Walter her diary.

The diary said that one night in 1963, Rocco Urella, then a captain in the state police, made an urgent call at 12:55 a.m. to Dick Sprague's house. Sprague wasn't home so Jackie Sprague talked to Urella. The next day, Jackie Sprague said, her husband told her the call was about a homicide that involved Urella's son. Jackie Sprague asked what he had done about it, and her husband replied, "Everything was taken care of." To Jackie Sprague, Walter said, that meant her husband had "fixed the case."

(Jackie Sprague, however, had credibility problems. A judge had ruled against her, granting Dick Sprague a divorce on grounds of adultery. In a July 28, 1972 opinion, Judge Frank J. Montemuro wrote that Jackie Sprague's credibility had been impeached, and that her actions toward her husband showed "it is quite clear that she was venting her spleen in a desire for vengeance.")

A disgusted Beasley asked Walter if he saw any psychological similarities between Sprague's ex-wife peddling an alleged 10-year-old scandal about him, and Walter's drive to get his anti-Rizzo story published. The implication was that both the reporter and Sprague's ex-wife were out to get somebody when they teamed up to go after Sprague.

Greg Walter wasn't offended. "That, Mr. Beasley, that is a lovely psychological theory," he said. "It would be nice to have a drink with you and discuss it, but it's not anything."

· · ·

WALTER AND ANOTHER INQUIRER REPORTER, KENT POLLOCK, WERE SOON INVESTIGAT-ing a closed 10-year-old homicide involving the son of state Police Commissioner Rocco Urella.

It happened on a Saturday night in 1963, at Charlie's Bar in North Philadelphia. Two college boys from LaSalle College, Donald Scalesa and Rocco Urella Jr., were drinking screwdrivers. According to what the two college boys told police, here's what happened next: An older man at the bar, John Applegate, a clerk for General Electric Co., approached the young men and invited them to a party at his place, saying a lot of girls would be there.

Why not, they said, and they followed Applegate back to his apartment, just up the street from the bar. When they got to Applegate's place, however, there was no party, and no girls. Just Applegate's roommate, Franklin Funk, a gay, former Episcopal priest who was so drunk he was incoherent.

The young men tried to leave, but Applegate blocked the door; his fly was three-quarters open. "You're not leaving till I blow you," he said, lunging at Scalesa. Scalesa dropped Applegate with one punch to the jaw, and then he and Urella Jr. ran out the door, knocking Funk out of the way.

The following Monday, Scalesa and Urella read in the paper that a 48-year-old man had been found dead in his North Philadelphia apartment. The victim's address was the same apartment that the two college boys had visited.

Urella Jr. called his father and told him what had happened. Rocco Urella Sr., then a state police captain, advised both students to turn themselves in. Next, the senior Urella called Dick Sprague and asked for help. The two men had met a year earlier when they were both investigating a prison riot. Both the senior Urella and Sprague were at the homicide unit when the two students surrendered. Sprague read the students their rights. He asked the cops to give the students lie detector tests, as well as Funk, and then he left.

Donald Scalesa told police that he tagged Applegate with one punch to the jaw, and as proof, he displayed a bruised right knuckle. Urella confirmed Scalesa's account, and both LaSalle students passed lie-detector tests.

The medical examiner did an autopsy on Applegate and concluded that the death was consistent with the one punch Scalesa had admitted to throwing. The medical examiner also told Sprague that Applegate had drunk nearly enough booze that night to kill himself. (Applegate's blood-alcohol level was .29; a fatal dose was .01 percent higher, at .30.)

Sprague asked an assistant district attorney in the homicide unit to review the case. The assistant DA concluded prosecution was unwarranted because the one punch thrown by Scalesa was justifiable defense. The assistant DA did not think the case would result in a conviction.

Sprague agreed. The police, however, did not want to assume responsibility for letting Scalesa off scot-free, so they arrested him for murder. At a preliminary hearing, a homicide detective read a summary of the facts. Sprague told a magistrate that in his view the punch was justifiable. The magistrate agreed and dismissed all the charges. Scalesa was free to go; he thought his ordeal was over.

· · ·

GREG WALTER HAD CARRIED A LEATHER BOOK BAG INTO BEASLEY'S OFFICE, AND WHENEVER he walked out of the room on a break, he left the bag behind. The lawyers who knew Walter's penchant for secretly taping interviews kept staring at the open bag, wondering what was inside.

Walter wasn't the only investigative reporter in town who packed a hidden tape recorder. Jim Nicholson was a veteran investigative reporter who worked at all the same places that Greg Walter did in the 1970s, the Inquirer, the Bulletin and Philadelphia magazine. "Every cop, investigative reporter and politician kept a suction cup on their phone," Nicholson said in an interview. "It was like nukes, we all had each other, so nobody used the tapes. This was before Watergate, before we all became virgins."

Nicholson recalled when he was at the Inquirer in 1971, and the big story in town was contract negotiations between the city and its public school teachers, which were at a standstill. Nicholson said one of his editors asked him to plant an electronic bug in the room where the teachers were negotiating. A news blackout was on, but Nicholson talked his way in by claiming that his editors only wanted a picture of the empty room where the negotiations would take place. Nicholson still has the unpublished photo an Inquirer photographer snapped of Nicholson planting a bug behind the official seal of the Philadelphia Board of Education.

The next day, Nicholson waited outside the building with a tape recorder in his briefcase, but the signal couldn't penetrate 20 inches of stone and steel. "When they arrested Greg," Nicholson said, "all the investigative reporters knew what they got Greg for wasn't anything we hadn't done."

The Inquirer twice nominated Nicholson for a Pulitzer Prize; he later became well-known as an obituary writer for the Philadelphia Daily News. One of the obituaries Nicholson wrote was Greg Walter's, when he died in 1989, of a heart attack, at age 55.

"He was a controversial writer," Nicholson recalled. "There were people who were solid behind him, really strong." But Nicholson characterized Walter as "a hip shooter," somebody who "draws quick and shoots from the hip."

Nicholson had some experience investigating Walter's work habits. Nicholson was on a sabbatical from journalism in 1975, working as a private investigator, when the editor of Philadelphia magazine asked for help on a libel case. James "Reggie" Edgehill, an Atlantic City nightclub owner, had sued the magazine after Greg Walter wrote in 1971 that Edgehill was "one of the biggest dealers in town (a specialist in cocaine)."

It was a throwaway line near the end of a long story about political corruption in Atlantic City. Nicholson made two trips to Atlantic City and found that the nightclub owner "didn't even have a whiff of marijuana on him." Walter's alleged sources, Nicholson said, were a hooker and a priest, but both sources had supposedly left town and couldn't be found. Nicholson told the editor of Philadelphia magazine to settle. "It was indefensible," Nicholson said. "This was neon lights saying, 'Pay me.'"

But the magazine kept on fighting and lost a 1983 trial that ended in a $7-million verdict. The verdict subsequently was overturned, in favor of a new trial.

In 1989, on the eve of the new trial, and 17 years after Reggie Edgehill originally filed his libel case, Philadelphia magazine admitted it was wrong, printed an apology to Edgehill, and paid him a reported $4 million.

• • •

WALTER WAS "OBSESSED" WITH THE APPLEGATE MURDER STORY, "TO THE EXCLUSION OF anything else," Carolyn Byrne, Walter's former girlfriend, testified to the jury. "He was out to get Mr. Sprague. He was out to kill him."

Walter didn't just tell his girlfriend. In the city's tap rooms, the reporter openly bragged that he was "out to get" Dick Sprague, and that he would "destroy" the prosecutor.

William Wolf Jr., a former assistant district attorney, testified that he and Walter had been friends for seven years until Sprague prosecuted Walter for wiretapping. Wolf testified that he ran into Walter at a bar, and Walter said of Sprague, "'He's got me now... in his court... but you'll see, I'm going [to] destroy him.'

"And he pointed at me and said, 'I'm going to destroy you as well if you do anything to help him. I know you're Sprague's man....'

"He was standing — he's a tall fellow — he was standing about an inch away, and I got away from him because I thought he was going to slug me," Wolf testified. "He was like a man on fire. He was just so angry."

• • •

THE STORY OF THE SPRAGUE CASE THEN TOOK ITS MOST BIZARRE TURN. IN NOVEMBER 1972, state police investigators were stationed at the George Washington Motor Lodge in Valley Forge, located about 20 miles west of Philadelphia. The investigators assigned to the state Crime Commission were using the motor lodge as an undercover command post to secretly bug the phones of the Philadelphia police. The state cops were investigating allegations first raised in the Inquirer that Rizzo's cops were taking payoffs from bookies and numbers writers.

But upstairs, in another rented suite above the state cops, another group of rogue state cops was secretly bugging the buggers. The rogue cops were members of state Police Commissioner Rocco Urella's so-called palace guard, and they were keeping electronic tabs on the state police investigating Rizzo's police force. And somebody in the know was telling Mayor Frank Rizzo all about how his cops were being spied on.

Meanwhile, the state police investigating the city police were told by a maid that their phones were being bugged. The state police lifted their phones and discovered wires that led upstairs. When they followed the wires, the state cops ran into the rogue cops, who were attempting to escape the motor lodge, and a fight broke out.

The Inquirer was all over the police spying capers at the motor lodge. Reporters Greg Walter and Kent Pollock were also working on a story about the decade-old Applegate murder case.

Dick Sprague sent Gene Roberts another letter, charging once again that Walter was out to get him. This time, Sprague named names, listing four people who had allegedly overheard Walter publicly threatening Sprague. But that didn't stop the Inquirer from running its stories.

. . .

"Witness Ties Sprague to Mystery Figure in Trooper Wiretap Case," Tuesday, March 27, 1973. By Howard S. Shapiro, Inquirer Harrisburg Bureau.

The witness that the Inquirer used to "tie" Sprague to the illegal wiretapping at the George Washington Motor Lodge was a state police sergeant who testified at a court-martial of the rogue state police officers caught bugging their fellow cops.

The witness, Sgt. Matthew Hunt, was commander of the state Crime Commission unit investigating allegations of police corruption in Philadelphia. At the court-martial, Sgt. Hunt reluctantly testified on cross-examination that a confidential informant had once told him that Dick Sprague may have used the alias of "Nicholas Pratko." The defense lawyer who asked the question was trying to show how unreliable the prosecution's case was.

Pratko was a frequent caller to the state police barracks. A state police operator had said that she always put Pratko's calls straight through to state Police Commissioner Rocco Urella. Hunt, however, wrote a subsequent report, saying that when he testified that Sprague may have used the Pratko alias, he was talking about an allegation that he had investigated and found to be false.

In his report, Hunt said that the real user of the Nicholas Pratko alias was another state trooper, Metro Kardash, who had used that same alias to register an unmarked cop car seen prowling around the motor lodge. Kardash was subsequently court-martialed for illegal wiretapping. Hunt also said in his report that neither the defense lawyer nor anybody from the Inquirer ever asked him any follow-up questions about Nicholas Pratko, and he added, "needless to say, the entire situation surrounding Mr. Sprague has been taken completely out of context."

When he testified in court, Dick Sprague said that not only did he never engage in wiretapping at the George Washington Motor Lodge, but that during his lengthy career in the district attorney's office — where he prosecuted more than 10,000 criminal cases — he had "never wiretapped one single soul."

"I happen to be philosophically against it," Sprague told Beasley in court. "I think that [wiretapping] is a dirty business. I have always felt that way.... When government stoops to doing something illegitimately, that is as wrong as the crime they are trying to fight."

Beasley argued in court that the Inquirer knew that Sprague wasn't Pratko, but that the newspaper chose to go ahead and smear him anyhow. The Inquirer had in its possession a copy of a state attorney general's prosecution memorandum that stated that "Pratko is an assumed name used by Corporal Metro Kardash." A former state Justice Department official had also told Greg Walter that Pratko was the code name for Kardash.

On the witness stand in the Sprague libel case, Howard Shapiro, the Inquirer reporter who wrote the story after conferring with Greg Walter, said the article should have made it "clear… that Sgt. Hunt wasn't saying something he believed."

Shapiro also expressed regret about a subsequent story he wrote four days later that stated that Sgt. Hunt had also testified that Sprague had allegedly used the Pratko alias to register the unmarked cop car found abandoned at the motor lodge. Shapiro testified that he originally wrote in his follow-up story that Sgt. Hunt had merely linked Sprague's name to the alias used to register the cop car, but that the sentence was rewritten by an editor, and the result was, it was no longer accurate. Shapiro said he also originally wrote that the allegation against Sprague was "hearsay evidence," but that the phrase was edited out of the story.

• • •

"DID SPRAGUE QUASH HOMICIDE CASE AS FAVOR TO URELLA?" SUNDAY APRIL 1, 1973. "This story was written by Inquirer Staff Writer Kent Pollock following an extensive investigation by Inquirer Staff Writer Greg Walter and Pollock."

The lead of the story that ran on the front page: "First Assistant District Attorney Richard A. Sprague, whose name was linked last week to former State Police Commissioner Rocco P. Urella in a wiretapping controversy, once declined to prosecute Urella's son in a homicide case."

The story said that Sprague had "recently categorized his relationship to Urella as 'very close, exceedingly close.'" Sprague however, testified that his comments had been deliberately taken out of context by the Inquirer. Sprague said when he was talking about his close relationship with Urella, he was referring to the early 1970s, when Urella was state police commissioner and the two men had become friends. The Inquirer story falsely implied that the friendship had existed a decade earlier, in 1963, when Urella was a state police captain who had met Sprague the previous year at the prison riot.

That wasn't the only instance where the Inquirer tried to rewrite history. The official version of the Applegate homicide was that Applegate died after he was struck with one punch by Scalesa. The Inquirer story, however, implied that Urella Jr. might have been the one who struck Applegate. The primary witness the newspaper relied upon was Funk, Applegate's drunken roommate.

In the Inquirer story, Funk, referred to by the newspaper as a "former clergyman," said that before the "fatal assault," Urella Jr. and Applegate "might have gone in the bedroom" to look for liquor. "He [Funk] wasn't certain however," the story said.

Funk, however, wasn't a credible witness. According to Funk's testimony as well as others, Funk was so drunk the night of Applegate's death after he and Applegate drank a fifth and a pint of whiskey that Funk slurred his words and suffered memory lapses.

Funk also gave a deposition to Beasley that didn't do much to help Greg Walter. In the deposition, Funk said that when Walter came to interview him, he "flashed something," and Funk assumed the reporter was a detective. Funk also told Beasley that he never saw Urella Jr. strike anybody.

The Inquirer story downplayed Applegate's homosexual pass at Scalesa ("You're not leaving till I blow you"), saying instead that Applegate was merely accused of making "an improper suggestion." The Inquirer story also denied that Applegate was a homosexual, recasting the incident as a "fight that led to the beating death of a 48-year-old man."

Applegate was married and had a daughter, but he had also been arrested for performing sodomy on a man in 1953, and was sentenced to three years' probation. At the time of his death, Applegate was awaiting trial on another charge of soliciting to commit sodomy.

The Evening Bulletin originally reported both arrests when Applegate died in 1963. The Inquirer, however, reported in its 1973 story that a search of police records "did not turn up any evidence of Applegate's ever having been arrested on any charge." The police records of Applegate's two arrests would subsequently be discovered by the Inquirer after the 1973 story ran.

And Walter, according to the testimony of an old girlfriend, Carolyn Byrne, didn't harbor any illusions about the sexuality of Applegate's roommate of 14 years who had shared a one-bedroom apartment; Byrne said that Walter privately referred to Funk as "an old queen."

It was Beasley's contention at trial that Walter had fudged the facts because he identified with the bisexual Applegate, and was using the dead man as the vehicle for his revenge against Sprague.

The Inquirer story claimed that Applegate's children were "shocked" by the "allegations" about their father's homosexuality, and the story ended on this false note:

Meanwhile, John Applegate's family and his former roommate wonder why nobody was held accountable for his death.

John Applegate is now just a morgue number, along with thousands of others in the city's archives.

But the death — along with the apparently untrue accusation that he had a record as a homosexual — was an extremely personal tragedy to his family.

"After I read about this," his daughter recently told The Inquirer, "I called up the man who put the stone on my father's grave and I asked him to add one more line:

"Rest In Peace."

• • •

GREG WALTER WASN'T THROUGH DOING UNDERCOVER WORK. AFTER THE URELLA STORY ran, Walter outfitted his girlfriend with a wire and sent her over to see the wife of one of Sprague's assistant district attorneys, looking for more dirt on Sprague. The woman who was the target of the bug, reporter Kiki Olson, said things on tape, however, that were more damaging to Walter.

"It was intentional," Olson said on the tape. "The story was all wrong.... There are about 50 other people who will say that Greg did say that there was malice involved; Greg is talking all over the fucking town," Olson said. "Greg has been reporting all these months that he's going to do Sprague."

Walter's lawyer, Gregory M. Harvey, still doesn't think his former client got carried away while investigating Dick Sprague. "I'll tell you who went off the deep end," Harvey said in an interview. "It wasn't Greg. It was the Inquirer editorial board hammering away at Specter."

In what may be some kind of record, the Inquirer followed up its Sprague stories by running 32 consecutive editorials that ripped then-district attorney Specter for saying that Sprague had acted "entirely properly" in the Applegate case.

The editorials called for the release of all records in the original Applegate investigation, and the appointment of a special prosecutor. Most of the editorials ended the same way, asking, "What does Mr. Specter have to hide?" One of the headlines dubbed the Applegate case, "Mr. Specter's own Watergate."

• • •

JIM BEASLEY WAS THROUGH TREATING THE DEPOSITION WITNESS WITH KID GLOVES: "LET me ask you this, Mr. Walter. Have you ever been diagnosed during your psychiatric problems as being a pathological liar?"

Walter: "Oh, Jesus Christ, no."

Beasley: "I'm just asking you a question."

Walter: "Well, look, you have made me everything else. You want to make me a dope addict? Here, look at my arms."

Beasley: "Your answer was with a smile. Now, can I have a serious answer? Have you ever been diagnosed as a pathological liar?"

Walter: "Never."

Moments later, Greg Walter felt weak. "Mr. Beasley, I'm sorry, but I'm starting to feel an aura, which is an insulin reaction," he said. "It's very hard to think and talk, and I don't want to take a chance."

"When did you get this aura feeling?" Beasley asked. "After you consulted with your lawyer?"

Sam Klein stood up for his client. "Let the record note I noticed the witness take out a chocolate bar and start to eat. I also noticed his complexion change. In my untrained medical eye, I became concerned for his health."

"I'm afraid I can't continue," Walter said. "I can't think too well."

"Then we won't continue," Beasley said.

• • •

EPILOGUE: WALTER'S DEPOSITION WAS OVER, BUT *SPRAGUE V. WALTER* WOULD CONTINUE for 15 more years. The first trial took place in 1983 in Philadelphia Common Pleas Court, two years after Beasley deposed Walter. Walter had left the Inquirer by then, and was writing a freelance column for the Philadelphia Daily News. He also was recovering from a second open heart surgery, appearing briefly in court after Beasley subpoenaed him.

Sam Klein had talked about putting Walter on the stand because Klein believed that Walter would be a sympathetic witness. But when *Sprague v. Walter* came to trial, Walter's health had deteriorated so badly that neither side called him as a witness. "He looked like death eating a soda cracker," recalled Gene Roberts.

Beasley read large portions of Walter's deposition testimony into the record to prove his contention that the reporter had used the Inquirer to conduct a vendetta against Sprague. After deliberating 6½ hours, the jury agreed, awarding Sprague a $4.5 million verdict.

The Inquirer appealed. The state Supreme Court overturned the verdict in 1986, saying that Common Pleas Court Judge Charles A. Lord had erred when he prohibited Inquirer reporters from citing the state's Shield Law, which said that reporters did not have to reveal the identity of confidential sources.

The decision meant that Beasley would have to retry the case. And the retrial would turn on one of Beasley's most famous cross-examinations.

MARCH 1990

SUNDAY	MONDAY	TUESDAY	WEDNESDAY	THURSD
FIRST QUARTER 4	FULL MOON 11	LAST QUARTER 19	NEW MOON 26	
				1
4	5	6	7	8
11	12	13	14	15 ✗
18	19 ✗	20 ✗ SPRING BEGINS	21 ✗	22 ✗
25	26	27 ✗	28 ✗	29 ✗

◀◀◀ APRIL 1990 ▶▶▶

	MAY
S M T W T	
1 2 3	
6 7 8 9 10	
13 14 15 16 17	
20 21 22 23 24	
27 28 29 30 31	

TUESDAY	WEDNESDAY	THURSDAY	FRIDAY	SATURDA
3 ✗ PASSOVER	4 ✗	5 ✗	6 ✗ GOOD FRIDAY	7
10	11			

Chapter 13

❖

PINNING DOWN THE FROG

The calendar said it was March 15, 1990, but inside the courtroom it was the 1970s all over again. Jim Beasley had called Gene Roberts, the executive editor of the Philadelphia Inquirer, as a hostile witness, and he was dragging the reluctant editor line by line through the two-decade-old newspaper stories at issue in *Sprague v. Walter.*

The stories were so old they predated computers, and originally were written on copy books, three sheets of white, pink and yellow copy paper (with two sheets of carbon paper tucked in between) that were once fed into typewriters. Beasley asked about another relic.

"Do you remember Greg Walter?"

"Yes, I do," Roberts said.

Walter had left the Inquirer in 1977, and died of a heart attack in 1989, at age 55, but for Roberts, the dead reporter remained a liability. Beasley, bristling with raised eyebrows and heightened indignation, questioned the editor about his decision back in 1972 to hire a mentally unstable reporter with a drinking problem who had just been fired by the Philadelphia Evening Bulletin after he had been prosecuted for illegal wiretapping by Dick Sprague.

"Was he [Walter] hired with your approval?" Beasley asked incredulously.

"Yes, he was," Roberts said.

"Oh, by the way," Beasley asked in a voice dripping with sarcasm, "Do you want people to believe what you print in the Inquirer?"

"Yes, I would like for them to," Roberts said.

While Beasley continued his interrogation, Roberts remained trapped in a time warp.

"Here I am answering questions about things that happened 17 years ago," Roberts lamented on Day 5 of a cross-examination that would last an extraordinary 17 days.

It was the marathon match that would decide an epic libel case: James E. Beasley, 63, one of the country's top libel lawyers, versus Eugene L. Roberts Jr., 55, one of the country's top newspaper editors.

Unlike the deposition of Greg Walter, however, the cross-examination of Gene Roberts was conducted in front of a live audience. And Beasley knew how to play to a crowd.

• • •

GENE ROBERTS WAS FAMOUS FOR TRANSFORMING THE INQUIRER FROM A LOUSY newspaper into a great one. Under his direction, from 1972 to 1990, the Inquirer won 17 Pulitzer Prizes in 18 years. At the Inquirer, Roberts was surrounded by admiring colleagues, who, because of the boss's short, hunched-over appearance, jokingly referred to him as "The Frog." Underneath the good-old-boy from North Carolina exterior, however, Roberts was a cagey former U.S. Army counter-intelligence officer who talked slowly and chose his words carefully.

Facing a fearsome cross-examiner in Beasley, Roberts spoke even slower than usual in court and in general seemed to be moving in slow-motion. "Because Beasley was so rapid with his questions, the contrast was so noticeable," recalled the retired trial judge, Charles P. Mirarchi Jr., in an interview.

The results at times were comical. "There were several outbursts of laughter over his [Roberts'] responses," Judge Mirarchi said. "The jury tried to contain itself."

• • •

ON DAY 1 OF THE CROSS-EXAMINATION, BEASLEY HANDED ROBERTS A JURORS' PACKET OF exhibits and asked if he recognized an enclosed March 15, 1973, letter Sprague had sent him.

"Just a little more time, please," Roberts asked.

"Sure," said the impatient Beasley. "Take your time."

"I'm looking," Roberts said as he shuffled through the exhibits.

"Try looking at the top of the letter where dates usually are," Beasley suggested.

"I'm sorry," Roberts responded. "Would you repeat that?"

"Try looking at the top of the letter," Beasley said.

Roberts finally found the right letter and started to read it.

"I don't mean to interrupt you," Beasley said, as Roberts scanned the page. "You haven't read this letter in a long time?"

"I read through some letters in preparation for this, and I think I read through this letter," Roberts said.

"Well, if you need more time, you want to read it all, please take your time," Beasley said, playing to the jury. "Read as much as you want."

The courtroom was filled with awkward silence until Roberts finally said, "I'm simply waiting for your question."

Beasley apologized, adding, "OK, are we on the same frequency now, you and I?"

"I'm not sure," Roberts drawled.

•   •   •

"IT WAS KIND OF PAINFUL TO WATCH," RECALLED JAMES M. NAUGHTON, A FORMER NEW York Times White House correspondent and a top Inquirer editor under Roberts.

Gene Roberts was "such a truth-teller by instinct," Naughton said, but as a witness, he was handicapped by his "slow-talking style and his laborious precision.

"As a consequence, he may have looked evasive. In essence, it was a matter of Beasley using Roberts' own traits of care and caution and slow talking to defeat him in the eyes of the jurors and the judge."

Naughton also didn't care much for Beasley's courtroom persona.

"He [Beasley] was histrionic and clever and for the most part angry," Naughton said. "He sort of stoked his anger in the courtroom as if he was demanding justice when it was just an act."

"Gene was more uncomfortable looking than I'd ever seen him," said former Inquirer reporter Kent Pollock, who sat through every day of the 10-week trial. "There was nothing he could do once Beasley had him in his talons."

Pollock, who was also cross-examined by Beasley for four days during the trial, said that Beasley's forte was his ability to "take the truth and screw you with it.

"I remember being pissed off" watching the cross-examination of Roberts, Pollock said. "Remember, Gene was my boss. It was like he was attacking Daddy."

•   •   •

CALLING GENE ROBERTS AS A HOSTILE WITNESS IN THE SPRAGUE CASE WAS A SIGNATURE move out of the Beasley playbook. Beasley loved to call the defendant as the first or second witness in the plaintiff's case, when the element of surprise was on Beasley's side, and the witness was unprepared. But Beasley had another reason for calling Gene Roberts.

In 1988, just two years before the second Sprague trial, Beasley had tried another libel case against the Inquirer on behalf of former Philadelphia District Attorney F. Emmett Fitzpatrick. And Beasley had suffered a bitter defeat when he was denied the opportunity to cross-examine an Inquirer reporter who was the key witness in the case. It was a mistake Beasley wouldn't repeat.

Fitzpatrick had filed suit over a 1974 story by Inquirer reporter Tony Lame —

"D.A. Gets Ex-Client Off Light" — that accused Fitzpatrick of a conflict of interest. The story said that the district attorney had recommended probation for Joseph Nardello, a mobster who was a former private client of Fitzpatrick's, and was in court as a convicted criminal awaiting sentencing on a fifth felony. Beasley claimed in the suit that Fitzpatrick had never made any recommendation to the judge regarding Nardello, but had merely said that he would not object to a sentence of probation.

When the Fitzpatrick case went to trial, Beasley gave the Inquirer defense team an opening by reading from reporter Lame's deposition. Technically, that meant that Lame had testified in the case. It also meant that if the Inquirer decided not to call Lame as a witness, then Beasley was not entitled to the usual legal remedy, which was to ask a judge to instruct the jury to draw an adverse inference, said William Lytton, the Inquirer's chief trial counsel during the Fitzpatrick case. The Inquirer's defense team subsequently rested their case.

"Beasley was caught by surprise," Roberts recalled. "Beasley's shtick was to carve up the witnesses on the other side of the case." But in the Fitzpatrick case, Beasley never got the chance to cross-examine Lame. The jury then decided after 4½ hours of deliberations that the Inquirer had not libeled Fitzpatrick.

"It was clear Beasley was waiting to pounce on him [Lame] and try and make him look bad in front of the jury," Lytton wrote in an e-mail. "I don't think Beasley could even bring himself to talk to me after that. He did not like losing. Neither did I."

So when they retried the Sprague case, "Beasley changed his tactics," Roberts said. "He put me on as his witness. It was shrewd on his part."

•   •   •

AT THE PLAINTIFF'S TABLE, DICK SPRAGUE AND JIM BEASLEY WERE A FORMIDABLE TEAM. As far as Gene Roberts was concerned, the Inquirer was up against "two skilled courtroom actors."

By the time of the second Sprague trial in 1990, Sprague and Beasley had been in the trenches together for a decade battling the Inquirer. The two men had grown close. They represented each other professionally. They ate dinner together; they played tennis together.

Watching Sprague and Beasley collaborate, it was hard to believe that they had once been bitter enemies.

"They became like meat loaf and mashed potatoes," recalled Philadelphia District Attorney Lynne Abraham. "That's what happens in life when your worst adversary becomes your best friend."

Sprague and Beasley were on opposite sides of a 1975 state Supreme Court disciplinary hearing involving conflict-of-interest charges raised by Sprague against District Attorney Fitzpatrick. Sprague was first assistant district attorney when he accused his new boss Fitzpatrick of lying about his role in the sentencing of former mobster Nardello. When Sprague went public with his charges that the district attorney had done his old mob client a favor, Fitzpatrick promptly fired Sprague.

At the disciplinary hearing that grew out of Sprague's charges, Sprague took the witness stand as Fitzpatrick's chief accuser. And Beasley, representing Fitzpatrick, cross-examined Sprague in front of a standing-room-only crowd of lawyers who flocked to see the spectacle. "A heated, searing interchange," the Inquirer reported. The three-day face-off was, in the eyes of most witnesses, a draw.

"It was the most incredible thing to watch these two titans," recalled Kathleen L. Daerr-Bannon, a lawyer who worked for Beasley at the time. "One would jab and then the other, and nobody gained any ground. It was an absolute stalemate."

In retrospect, Daerr-Bannon wasn't surprised that the two men became best friends. "Strength respects strength," she said.

The state Supreme Court hearing, however, ended as a total victory for Beasley. Fitzpatrick was acquitted of all charges. And City Solicitor Sheldon L. Albert, a former Beasley law partner, approved an $80,537 bill that Beasley submitted to the city as the cost of defending Fitzpatrick.

Now, Sprague and Beasley were on the same side, but they had a big mountain to climb. Dick Sprague was a public figure in his own libel case, rather than a private citizen. That meant that Beasley not only had to prove that what the Inquirer had printed about Sprague was false, but also that the newspaper had printed it with actual malice, meaning the editors knew it was false when they ran it, or they acted with reckless disregard for the truth.

It's a high legal standard set by the U.S. Supreme Court in a 1964 landmark case, *New York Times v. Sullivan*, to protect the rights of a free press to criticize public officials. Some say it's an impossibly high legal standard, because to prove actual malice, you have to get inside the heads of the defendants. Some lawyers won't even take a libel case involving a public figure, because it's so hard to prove actual malice. But Beasley and Sprague loved a challenge.

· · ·

ON THE FIRST DAY OF CROSS-EXAMINATION, BEASLEY ASKED ROBERTS WHAT HE DID AFTER he received a letter from Dick Sprague charging that Greg Walter was going around town saying he was out to get Sprague.

"I took action," Roberts said. "The action was to ask our attorneys to check out fully the letter from Mr. Sprague and all the allegations that someone was out to smear and destroy him. And I picked the lawyers rather than the reporters to make sure that the investigation was insulated from the staff."

Beasley had Sprague's warning letter blown up four feet high and posted on an easel in the courtroom. He pointed to the exhibit while he questioned Roberts.

"Here you had repeated denials from Mr. Sprague about the truth of the article," Beasley said. He reminded Roberts that Sprague had filed his libel suit on April 19, 1973. "Isn't that true?," Beasley asked.

"Well, Mr. Sprague's credibility was not high with me at that time because I had had these allegations checked out," Roberts said, explaining that his lawyers had told him that they investigated Sprague's allegations and found them to be untrue.

Roberts had just made a big mistake. From the witness stand, the editor had turned his lawyers into private investigators. He had also divulged the substance of private conversations with his lawyers, which amounted to a voluntary waiver of the attorney-client privilege. That meant Beasley could pursue putting Roberts' lawyers on the witness stand to refute their own client.

• • •

ON DAY 2 OF THE CROSS-EXAMINATION, BEASLEY TURNED TO A BLOW-UP EXHIBIT OF Sprague's letter to Roberts, and its charges that Walter was conducting a vendetta against Sprague.

Beasley: "This was very serious information that you were getting, was it not?"
Roberts: "Yes."
Beasley: "And if it were true, then that story would have never been printed, would it?"
Roberts: "That is correct."

Beasley honed in on the time frame for the lawyers' investigation: "And how long did it take these people to do the investigation?"

"I don't recall at this point, but a period of two, three weeks to a month," Roberts said.

"I guess I'm a little confused," Beasley began. He pointed out that Sprague's letter was written on March 28, 1973; the main Inquirer article about Sprague allegedly fixing a murder case was published four days later, on April 1, 1973.

Beasley asked about the lawyers' investigation that had supposedly taken between two weeks to a month to complete, according to Roberts, and was so thorough that it included a trip to the bar that Walter hung out at.

Beasley: "When did it [the investigation] occur, Mr. Roberts?"

Roberts: "It occurred repeatedly that they [the lawyers] went out and out and out checking and double-checking over a period of time. And they gave me a preliminary report very early."

Beasley tried again to pin Roberts down on some specific dates, and this time, he got the editor to agree to an improbable timetable.

Beasley: "All right. So you had this letter from Mr. Sprague on the 28th and by the 31st, according to what you just told this jury, that investigation had been completed and the lawyers were talking?"

Roberts: "All of those people would have been contacted, yes, before the story ran."

Beasley: "Is it your testimony, Mr. Roberts, that all of the people that were identified in Mr. Sprague's letter, as well as checking with the bar, was done in those three days and the lawyers met with you face to face?"

Roberts: "Yes."

• • •

WHEN BEASLEY TALKED ABOUT CASES THAT HE SHOULD HAVE LOST, HE COULD HAVE easily been talking about the Sprague case. At Sprague's request, Beasley had taken it over from another top Philadelphia lawyer, the late Edwin P. Rome, who supposedly had deemed it a loser.

"Everybody was convinced this case was a loser," agreed Roberts. "And if we had not done the stories about the Supreme Court, it would have been a loser."

The Inquirer for years had been aggressively reporting about judicial misconduct in Pennsylvania, running numerous exposés. A 1978 series, "The Supreme Disgrace," found the state Supreme Court to be "a disgrace of maladministration, a swamp of self-protective secrecy." A 1983 series, "Above the Law," exposed ethical lapses by several state Supreme Court judges. A 1986 series, "Disorder in the Court," won a Pulitzer Prize for investigating the state's trial court, and discovering "a system that often delivers anything but justice."

As a result of those stories, the Inquirer racked up journalism awards, but was not too popular with Pennsylvania judges.

"At the time we ran the Supreme Court stories, the thrust of [Inquirer attorney] Sam (Klein)'s remarks was, as a citizen, I have to say, you're doing the right thing by running this series," Roberts recalled. But according to Roberts, Klein, who died in 2002, also told him, "And as a lawyer that is gonna have to defend you in future cases, you're gonna create enormous problems for yourself."

Another factor that benefited Sprague and hurt the Inquirer was the changing legal climate on libel. "For several years, nobody really thought it [the Sprague case] would come to trial," because they expected it would be thrown out of court, Roberts said. "It wasn't just me thinking that, it was also the lawyers."

For years, the media had been the beneficiary as judges tossed out libel suits on motions for summary judgment. But in a 1979 libel case, *Hutchinson v. Proxmire*, Supreme Court Chief Justice Warren Burger questioned in a footnote "the propriety of dealing with such complex issues by summary judgment."

That case involved a research psychologist, Ronald Hutchinson, who was given a $500,000 federal grant to study why monkeys clenched their jaws. A disgusted U.S. Senator William Proxmire gave Hutchinson his "Golden Fleece" award for wasteful spending, prompting Hutchinson to sue the senator for libel. The case was thrown out on summary judgment, but the U.S. Supreme Court reversed the ruling and held for Hutchinson. But the court found that since Proxmire's statements were not made with actual malice, they weren't libelous.

After Burger's footnote, the pendulum in libel cases filed in Pennsylvania, where many judges were upset with the Inquirer, swung toward plaintiffs, Roberts said. That meant that instead of having their cases thrown out on summary judgment, plaintiffs like Dick Sprague would have their day in court.

· · ·

ON DAY THREE OF CROSS-EXAMINATION, BEASLEY TRIED TO PIN DOWN ROBERTS ON which lawyers he had met with regarding the investigation of the Sprague letter that charged that Walter was out to get him.

"Give me the names of the lawyers at the meeting," Beasley asked. "Was that Dave Marion and Sam Klein?"

Beasley had good reasons for suggesting those two lawyers.

Roberts fell right into the trap. "And Sam Klein," he agreed.

Beasley: "Was anybody else at that meeting?"

Roberts: "As I said, at 17 years later, the sequence of the meetings blur, but at least one of the meetings, there were discussions with Harold Kohn."

Beasley expressed irritation with Roberts.

"What I'm trying to find out from you is, in view of the serious charges that Mr. Sprague was making against Greg Walter and the Inquirer, what you did to verify or point out that those charges were false," Beasley said. "That's what I'm trying to do."

"Yes," the folksy Roberts replied. "And I think we milked that cow yesterday and we are milking it again today. I think we've gone over that."

Beasley asked the editor whether Sam Klein had written any memoranda about the investigation of Greg Walter. There weren't any memoranda, Roberts said, so Beasley asked to see the judge in chambers.

"I find it strange that somebody as thorough as Mr. Klein is would not have prepared some memoranda," Beasley told the judge in chambers. "Now I think I'm entitled to know whether Mr. Klein, as Mr. Roberts said, interviewed these people."

Judge Mirarchi agreed: "Mr. Roberts didn't invoke any attorney-client privilege in his testimony when he kept referring to the delegation of the authority to the attorneys. Now, under the circumstances, the only person who can invoke the attorney-client privilege is the client." If the client elected not to invoke the privilege, the judge said, then the attorney would have to respond to Beasley's questions.

This was the same Judge Mirarchi that the Inquirer had criticized in a 1983 story on nepotism in the courts for hiring eight relatives on his staff. ("Do we only want orphans working for the courts?" Mirarchi had responded at the time.)

Mirarchi was the seventh judge in the case after five other judges had recused themselves, four at the request of the Inquirer. Before the Sprague trial began, Judge Mirarchi had summoned lawyers for both sides and also offered to recuse himself if either side objected, but nobody took him up on it.

The editors at the Inquirer would regret that decision, especially after Judge Mirarchi ruled to exclude 13 of 17 witnesses that the newspaper wanted to call in its defense. The Inquirer also sought to introduce a report by the state attorney general, Israel Packel, who had questioned Sprague's role in the investigation of the Applegate homicide because of Sprague's friendship with Rocco Urella Sr., but the judge excluded the Packel report as well.

Back in chambers, defense attorney Klein attempted to avoid becoming a witness in the case. Klein told the judge that in the seven years since the Sprague case was first tried in 1983, Beasley had never indicated that he was going to try to question the Inquirer's lawyers.

"Now in the middle of trial, after four weeks of the trial, he's seeking to elicit, in effect, testimony from counsel for PNI [Philadelphia Newspapers Inc.], and I think it's improper and I'm not going to do it," Klein told the judge. "He's trying to inject counsel into a factual issue in the trial."

Judge Mirarchi corrected Klein about who had injected the Inquirer lawyers into a factual issue. "Your client did," the judge said, meaning Roberts. "The objection is overruled."

· · ·

ON DAY 4 OF THE CROSS-EXAMINATION, THE JUDGE IN CHAMBERS COMPLAINED ABOUT Roberts being evasive. "And this witness has been able to artfully dodge every question fielded of him, and the record is replete that he answers it in the most broad form," the judge told lawyers on both sides of the case.

Back in open court, Beasley banged away at the Inquirer's use of anonymous sources from the U.S. Justice Department to claim that Sprague had been "in constant touch" with Urella during the illegal wiretapping conducted by state police at the George Washington Motor Lodge.

Beasley: "So you have people who don't have the guts to have their name published in the newspaper telling you information that can't be checked because you refused to tell me or the jury who they are?"

Levy: "Objection."

Judge Mirarchi: "Sustained."

"Well, we don't have any way of determining whether those people even exist," Beasley asked Roberts. "They could be the figment of the imagination of the reporter, couldn't they?"

"It's conceivable," Roberts replied, "But again, I know the names of the sources here and they were in a position to know."

•   •   •

ON DAY 5, BEASLEY PRESSED ROBERTS ABOUT WALTER'S CONFLICT OF INTEREST AS HE attempted to write about Sprague.

Beasley: "But you knew at the time that he [Walter] was assigned this task that he was then being prosecuted and by this time had been found guilty of wiretapping. You knew that, didn't you?"

Roberts: "Yes."

Beasley; "And you didn't think that Mr. Walter might have created a bias, and you and Mr. Walter and Kent Pollock were going to use the Inquirer to get back at Mr. Sprague for prosecuting him?"

Roberts: "Absolutely not."

Beasley: "And one of the most powerful weapons in this country, if it is abused, is the free press. Isn't that true?"

Roberts: "No, I would disagree with that."

•   •   •

AFTER HIS CAREER AT THE INQUIRER, ROBERTS WOULD GO ON TO BECOME MANAGING editor of the New York Times, in between stints as a professor of journalism at the University of Maryland.

When Roberts was asked about Beasley in 2006, he didn't harbor any grudges. "To me he was a lawyer you had to endure," Roberts said in an iinterview. "I didn't have any personal feelings about him."

Beasley, Roberts said, appeared to feel the same way. "He would follow me into the bathroom, and say, 'Nothing personal,'" after another bruising courtroom confrontation, Roberts recalled. But the truce was always temporary, "It would only last till we got back in the courtroom," Roberts said.

What Roberts remembered most vividly about Beasley were the gestures he used to play to the jury. Like the time Beasley asked Roberts if he had reviewed a reporter's notebook, something editors never do, and Roberts responded matter-of-factly, "I did not review any of the reporter's notes."

"A stricken look would cross his face," Roberts recalled. "And he'd almost clutch at his heart, as if this was the biggest ethical lapse of all time."

Sixteen years later, Roberts was still disgusted. Reporter's notebooks are for reporters to read, to jog their memories, Roberts said. And if an editor did attempt to read one, most are illegible anyhow. "That was part of his shtick," Roberts said of Beasley. "His whole appeal was to put on a play before a jury. I guess every good lawyer does."

Beasley's view was that Roberts brought most of his troubles on himself.

"He was a witness who was totally evasive," Beasley said in an interview. "He would not answer a question. We used so much jury time to get him to answer a question, and he would not do it. He was so wedded to his position that he became blind.

"It got to be a battle of wits, and he only came half-prepared."

• • •

ON DAY 7, INQUIRER LAWYERS MICHAEL L. LEVY AND SAM KLEIN TRIED AGAIN IN CHAMbers to avoid the spectacle of putting Klein on the witness stand. Klein had already indicated that his recollection about the investigation of Sprague's charges differed from Roberts.

"Will you please tell me how I argue that issue to the jury?" said Levy, who was the Inquirer's lead counsel. "How do I choose between my client and my partner?"

"Very simply," said a helpful Beasley. He advised Levy to tell the jury that when he made his opening statement that quoted Roberts's version of events, he had no idea it would subsequently be contradicted by Klein.

"And how do I close to a jury and say, believe Gene Roberts, don't believe Sam Klein?" Levy protested. "How do I argue that issue to the jury?"

Beasley was fresh out of sympathy. "How you argue that issue to the jury is your problem," he said. "That's not my fault. That problem was created by you, Mr. Levy, when you made the opening statement and you're not going to visit that sin on my client."

Judge Mirarchi: "The defendant's motion this morning to bar the use of the testimony of Samuel E. Klein, Esq., at trial and for a mistrial are denied."

Back in open court, the two combatants resumed fighting:

Beasley: "And you consider yourself and the rest of the people on North Broad Street the keeper of the public morals, and you were going to decide how you would publish this article to point out to the people what you said was a matter of public debate?"

Roberts: "No, sir. We considered ourselves newspaper people and one of the things newspaper people do is write about public officials and how they carry out the duties of their office."

• • •

"SAM [KLEIN] NAMED 10 JUDGES WHO HAD A TWO-DAY RULE," ROBERTS RECALLED, discussing informal guidelines for how long cross-examinations should last. A few of those judges, Roberts said, "might stretch it to three or four days, but there was no way anyone else was gonna let it go to 17.

"I was not an unbiased observer, but it seemed to me that he [Judge Mirarchi] was nursing his grudges on the nepotism story."

Roberts said he asked the Inquirer's defense team during the trial to push for removal of the judge, but Klein didn't think he had a chance, because of all the judges who were angry at the Inquirer. Roberts said Klein told him, "In any other jurisdiction in the world he would win, but that he would not win in either Philadelphia or ultimately the [state] Supreme Court."

Klein was also worried about further antagonizing the judge, especially if the Inquirer lost a public bid to replace him, Roberts said. The former Inquirer editor disagreed with the strategy. "I don't think he [Judge Mirarchi] could have been more antagonistic," Roberts said. "I don't see how he could have done any more damage."

Mirarchi said in an interview that Roberts was making excuses. "It's demeaning to me" and "completely false" to say he was out to get the Inquirer, Mirarchi said, especially after the judge offered to recuse himself at the beginning of the trial to both sides and he was turned down twice.

Mirarchi said he made the offer to both sides because the Inquirer wasn't the only party to have questioned his ethics. Back in 1983, Dick Sprague had accused Mirarchi of violating the code of judicial conduct. At the time, Sprague was special counsel to a state Judicial Inquiry and Review Board investigating alleged misconduct by state Supreme Court Justice Rolf R. Larsen, and Judge Mirarchi was chairman of the review board's hearing panel.

Sprague petitioned the state Supreme Court to remove Mirarchi from hearing testimony, charging that Mirarchi was guilty of the "grossest impropriety" because he allegedly had political connections with Larsen. Mirarchi disputed the allegations, and Sprague's petition was denied.

Mirarchi said that after he gave both sides in the Sprague case the opportunity to ask him to step aside, he called the trial right down the middle. Mirarchi, who sat on the bench for more than 30 years, said that Beasley's cross-examination of Roberts, done without notes, "was a masterpiece."

"I think that Jim was probably the best, the sharpest and the most enlightened attorney that I've come across," the judge said. As far as the cross-examination going 17 days, "I had no choice. He [Beasley] squeezed the juice out of every paragraph" in the old Inquirer stories. "He didn't repeat himself. I had no way of reigning him in."

The Inquirer's problems were "a result of their errors," Judge Mirarchi concluded. "They kept digging themselves in deeper and deeper. I just couldn't believe that they couldn't see that they were their own worst enemy."

Michael Levy, the Inquirer's lead defense lawyer, now working as an assistant U.S. Attorney, declined to discuss the case when contacted in 2006. "I got the shit kicked out of me," he told the American Lawyer back in 1991.

· · ·

ON DAY 8, BEASLEY TRIED TO GET ROBERTS TO DISCUSS WHAT BEASLEY THOUGHT WAS an absurd assertion printed in the Inquirer, namely that Donald Scalesa, "the son of a wealthy Washington D.C. physician," as the newspaper put it, had confessed to killing John Applegate to cover up for Rocco Urella Jr., the son of a state police captain.

Roberts, besides being a slow-talking witness, was also a contrarian prone to debate.

"I have my own theory that conflicts with your theory that I would be happy to state," Roberts said, before the judge interrupted.

"Mr. Roberts," the judge lectured, "in a trial a witness is called. The attorney puts a question to the witness. The witness responds to the question. The witness does not gratuitously offer remarks which tend to cloud the issue…. Do you understand that, Mr. Roberts?"

"Yes," Roberts said.

· · ·

"IF YOU COULD HAVE HEARD THIS MAN [ROBERTS] UP ON THE WITNESS STAND, YOU would have gotten up and slapped him yourself" — Marjorie Goldman, a juror in the Sprague trial, to Philadelphia magazine.

· · ·

ON DAY 9, BEASLEY PLAYED ONE OF THE SECRET TAPE-RECORDINGS MADE BY REPORTERS Greg Walter and Ken Pollock. On the tape, Donald Scalesa told the reporters, "I wouldn't want to be quoted on anything." "I'm not writing anything down," replied Walter, who assured Scalesa on the tape that their discussion was "all off the record."

But Walter had a microphone hidden in his briefcase and a tape recorder running in a nearby car. And when the story ran, Scalesa was quoted by name 17 times.

Beasley: "Is that how you folks work up at the Inquirer?"

Roberts: "That is not normal practice, but, as I said, at the time I told him they could do whatever was legal in the state in which they were operating, and it is my understanding it was legal in Maryland. . . ."

Beasley: "Do you condone your reporters lying to people?"

Roberts: "No."

On Day 10, Beasley asked Roberts if Walter had lied to Scalesa to get him to talk.

Roberts wouldn't call it lying: "It would mean he [Walter] would be trying to get him [Scalesa] to talk, which is a police technique that he was using."

Beasley: "I thought Mr. Walter was a reporter?"

Roberts: "He was a reporter."

Beasley: "Are you saying that your reporters develop a technique of lying to people?"

Roberts: "No, but most — at that period most of their training came from police-like courses on that type of interviewing."

Beasley: "I see. So Mr. Walter attended courses at some journalistic convention where they taught him how to lie?"

Roberts: "No. He would have talked to police investigators and was conducting investigations in a common police technique."

• • •

FORMER INQUIRER REPORTER KENT POLLOCK, NOW A JOURNALISM PROFESSOR AT SIERRA College in Rocklin, Calif., defended the Inquirer in an interview by saying that the cops during the Rizzo era were real "cowboys."

"It was just so unbelievable to me how cavalier these guys were about . . . taking money from hookers and druggies," Pollock said. A year into his investigation of the Philadelphia police force, Pollock said, about 30 cops had either been fired or sent to jail.

But Pollock conceded that the cops weren't the only cowboys out on the streets of Philadelphia. The investigative reporters were also pretty wild. Or as Pollock put it, "What were we doing running around with a bug and a briefcase?"

• • •

ON DAY 13, THE JUDGE REPEATEDLY WARNED ROBERTS ABOUT STICKING TO THE SUBJECT. "Mr. Roberts, would you just confine yourself to the question," the judge said. But Roberts didn't take the hint.

Beasley asked Roberts about a 1963 Bulletin story about the death of John Applegate:

Beasley. "Did you find this article accurate then?"

Roberts: "I found it very revealing in many respects."

Beasley: "You didn't find anything inaccurate in it, did you?"

Roberts: "I found it incomplete, but revealing insofar as it went."

Beasley: "My question, Mr. Roberts, please, I thought we had gone over this article.... Would it be fair to say that you found no inaccuracies in the article?"

Roberts: "Insofar as it went, but I found things incomplete and mystifying."

• • •

ON DAY 17, BEASLEY ASKED ROBERTS IF HE WAS STICKING TO HIS STORY THAT HE HAD had his lawyers investigate Sprague's charges that Walter was out to get him. Beasley read to Roberts his earlier testimony that the newspaper's lawyers had investigated Sprague's charges and found them to be without merit before the Inquirer published its stories. Then he asked, "Is that the testimony given on the 20th?"

"Yes."

"And was it true then?"

"Yes."

"And is it true now?"

"Yes."

Beasley asked if the billing records for the Inquirer's defense firm showed that the lawyers had gone to each of the witness' addresses.

"I don't know," Roberts said.

"Well, don't you think it would be important to determine whether they spent 15 minutes at the Inquirer or five or six hours checking these stories out?"

The newspaper's lawyer objected, but the judge overruled him.

Beasley: "You don't know?"

Roberts: "No, I don't know."

Beasley: "That's all."

After 17 days on the witness stand, it was finally over.

"Mr. Roberts, I think you may step down," the judge said.

"I'm delighted, Your Honor," Roberts replied.

• • •

"IN MY OPINION, GENE ROBERTS WAS DESTROYED IN FRONT OF THAT JURY," DICK Sprague said in an interview. Roberts ran into trouble as a witness "because he thinks he's smarter than everybody else," Sprague said. When you're the executive editor of the Inquirer, "everybody kowtows and bows to you, and that's what came over to the jury. That's why they hated him."

Former Inquirer editor Jim Naughton recalled testifying in another libel case, and being told by a defense lawyer that he had been a much better witness than Gene Roberts.

"Before I could feel puffed up about it," Naughton recalled, the defense lawyer added, "But that's like saying you see way better than Ray Charles."

• • •

THE STAGE WAS SET FOR BEASLEY TO CALL THE TWO LAWYERS — DAVID MARION AND Sam Klein — whom Roberts contended had conducted an investigation into

Sprague's charges that Walter was out to get him. Roberts had said the investigation was done before the Inquirer ran its stories about Sprague.

Marion, however, told Beasley that he only got involved in the case *after* Sprague's libel suit had been filed, which was after all the Inquirer stories about Sprague had been published.

"I have no recollection of that letter," Marion said.

Next up was Sam Klein. Beasley asked if Roberts had showed Klein a copy of Sprague's letter prior to publication.

"Not to me, no," Klein said.

Beasley asked Klein if Roberts ever met with him before the Inquirer story on the Applegate homicide was published on April 1, 1973.

"Not with me, Mr. Beasley."

"That's all."

Levy recalled Klein as a witness, and on cross-examination, Beasley asked if he had heard Roberts say that Klein had investigated the charges that Walter was out to get Sprague. Klein testified that he had indeed made such an investigation, but only *after* the story was published.

"My recollection just differs from his," Klein said of Roberts. Klein told Beasley he was just breaking in at his law firm 17 years earlier, and did not confer with high-level clients like the executive editor of the Inquirer.

"In 1973, I was practicing law for roughly six months," Klein said. "I didn't have those kinds of conversations with Gene Roberts directly in March of 1973."

• • •

ROBERTS, IN AN INTERVIEW, SAID HE REGRETTED NOT FOLLOWING HIS LAWYERS' ADVICE to sit in court every day and watch the trial. Roberts also regretted not checking out his law firm's billing records before Beasley confronted him.

"In the end, and I guess the thing I most regret is by not giving it all the time, I let Beasley catch me in things I should have known," Roberts said. The billing sheets showed that the only lawyer Roberts had talked with before the Sprague story was printed was Harold Kohn, because Klein was new and Marion hadn't even been hired yet.

"I should have known that," Roberts said.

• • •

AFTER SERVING AS A PROSECUTOR, DICK SPRAGUE WENT ON TO HAVE A FAR MORE lucrative career in private practice. He became one of the country's most successful lawyers, with Forbes magazine estimating his 1988 income at $1.6 million.

Sprague also was appointed as chief counsel to the U.S. House of Representatives

Select Committee on Assassinations. His national reputation was such that he could call on famed criminal defense attorney F. Lee Bailey as a character witness at his libel trial.

So Sprague didn't have any economic damages, as the Inquirer's lawyers were quick to point out. The Inquirer's lawyers also questioned whether Sprague's reputation had really been damaged, as Beasley had claimed, if Sprague could still land such a prestigious appointment as chief counsel to the House Committee on Assassinations.

So to prove the Inquirer stories had damaged Sprague's reputation, Beasley called Sprague as a witness.

"Did you read that article that Sunday morning?" Beasley asked.

"Yes, I read the article," Sprague said.

"And how did you feel?"

"It is today, 17 years later, and I can still feel the anger, the fury, the hurt, the feeling that newspapers can't get away with that sort of thing," Sprague told the jury. "They cannot feel invincible. They cannot feel that they're God. They cannot feel that they can destroy someone's reputation."

Sprague, who was on the witness stand for 11 days, concluded that the newspaper had done "an ugly, dirty thing and that somebody had to teach them a lesson.

"I also recognized that there's no way that you can undo the smear," Sprague said. "The printed word will always be there. If somebody wanted to look up something about me, they would see those articles and those headlines."

"It really made it impossible to ultimately go on in public life because it could always be used to tarnish me if I decided to run for public office," Sprague told the jury. "It's a blemish that once it's on you, how do you remove it?"

• • •

"I WOULD SUSPECT WITH [A] REASONABLE DEGREE OF ACCURACY THAT YOUR VERDICT tomorrow will be heard around the world," Beasley told the jury during his day-long summation of the trial that had lasted 10 weeks and filled 50 volumes of testimony.

Beasley talked to the jury about the media's responsibility to print the truth. When the Inquirer "abandons that responsibility and uses the newspaper for its own purpose, then people like Roberts, Pollock, Greg Walter . . . must be taught a lesson."

Beasley then revived the ghost of Greg Walter. He reviewed Walter's performance as an investigative reporter for the Bulletin, setting up hookers to bribe cops, getting arrested for illegal wiretapping and getting fired by the Bulletin.

"Boy, they're great references, aren't they?" Beasley told the jury. "The Bulletin fired him. They wouldn't tolerate that. That didn't bother the Inquirer."

Beasley discussed Walter's state of mind, the "twist" in his personality, and the vindictiveness that made him want "to punish anybody" that the reporter suspected was out to get him. Beasley read to the jury the account from Walter's psychiatric records of how a drunken Walter had picked up a hooker who turned out to be a transvestite.

"Patient describes himself as having been a 'psychiatric case' for most of his life," said Beasley as he read more of Walter's psychiatric records. "Mr. Walter talks about his ability to con people.... He states his best defense is his use of the language. He can literally tear somebody apart within seconds."

Beasley read to the jury the testimony of Walter's former girlfriend, Carolyn Byrne, about Walter's daily drinking binges, to the point of blacking out. He also recounted Byrne's testimony about what Walter had told her about the Applegate story: "What he indicated to me [was] that he could twist a story in such a way that the story would come out the way he wanted people to believe about Mr. Sprague."

In closing, Beasley talked about Sprague's "mental anguish, the pain that he has beared these 17 years, carrying this cross that was so unjustified, that was so vindictive on the part of the Inquirer." Beasley asked the jury to "remove a stain that would be forever on his tombstone."

• • •

THE JURY, AFTER DELIBERATING ONLY TWO HOURS, FOUND THAT THE INQUIRER HAD libeled Sprague with actual malice, and they came back with a whopping $34 million verdict that included $2.5 million in compensatory damages and $31.5 million in punitive damages.

"Members of the jury, I want to thank you from the bottom of my heart," Sprague said. "I felt I was fighting a battle for a good free press and an honest press, which is important for all of us."

In a 1993 opinion upholding the verdict, Judge Mirarchi concluded that Sprague had "enjoyed an unimpeachable reputation" before the Inquirer published its stories. In his opinion, the judge noted "similarities between Greg Walter and John Applegate: their problems with alcohol, Walter's own homosexual tendencies and Applegate's homosexual lifestyle." The judge described Walter as "a man with a disturbed mind" and speculated that in death Applegate "could serve as a catalyst for the fulfillment of Walter's vendetta."

It was a vendetta aided by Roberts' "willingness to ignore the warning signs and disregard the truth," the judge wrote in his opinion. Roberts' explanation was that he had merely forgotten which lawyers he had talked to 17 years earlier. The judge, however, took a harsher view, finding that Roberts had "made an attempt at duplicity" when he claimed to have his lawyers check out the allegations that

Walter was out to get Sprague.

"Gene Roberts was in a bind created by his attempt to deceive the jury and the Court," the judge wrote in his opinion. The judge also said that Roberts didn't tell the truth when he claimed that he had checked and rechecked every word, sentence and paragraph of the story that accused Sprague of fixing a murder case.

"These defamatory articles painted Sprague's reputation with a black brush, which is resistant to all erasable solvents," the judge wrote.

• • •

"WE WERE JUST OUT-LAWYERED," SAID FORMER INQUIRER REPORTER KENT POLLOCK IN a 2007 interview. Pollock said he still doesn't believe that the Inquirer libeled Sprague. The paper was raising a legitimate question about the conduct of a public official, Pollock said, namely whether Sprague should have recused himself from the Applegate homicide investigation because it involved the son of a friend.

But Pollock, Greg Walter's reporting partner, also blamed himself for not being more aware of Walter's personal problems.

"I didn't know how bad off he was," Pollock said. "He was pretty good at hiding his tracks.... I should have known he was a drunk, for God's sakes. I probably should have known that he went to Center City and picked up transvestites, for Christ's sakes."

• • •

THE WAR BETWEEN SPRAGUE AND THE INQUIRER HAD A TROUBLING LEGACY FOR ASSAS-sination buffs. In upholding the $34-million verdict, Judge Mirarchi noted that in 1977, four years after Sprague filed his 1973 lawsuit against the Inquirer, the newspaper admitted that an Inquirer editor had mailed editorials about Sprague's alleged mishandling of the Applegate case to the U.S. House of Representatives Select Committee on Assassinations.

Sprague had just been appointed chief counsel of the committee, charged with investigating the murders of John F. Kennedy and Martin Luther King Jr., specifically to determine whether both men died as the result of conspiracies. But after the committee received the Inquirer editorials, the New York Times published its own story about the Applegate controversy. The House committee then issued a "no confidence" vote in Sprague, and he was forced to resign, Judge Mirarchi wrote. In his opinion, the judge ripped the Inquirer for its "outrageous conduct," saying the people at the newspaper had demonstrated an "inability to comprehend the gravity of their acts."

One of Sprague's staff investigators on the house committee was Gaeton Fonzi, ironically a former editor at Philadelphia magazine, and the co-author of Greg

Walter's first big exposé back in 1967 about crooked Inquirer reporter Harry Karafin. Even Greg Walter's old reporting partner lamented that Sprague never got a chance to investigate JFK's death. In his 1993 book, *The Last Investigation*, Fonzi wrote, "There was absolutely no doubt in my mind when I heard of Sprague's appointment that the Kennedy assassination would finally get what it needed: a no-holds-barred honest investigation."

Famed criminal defense lawyer F. Lee Bailey asserted in an interview that if the government had turned Sprague loose, "I think they might have cracked the case." Bailey, a character witness for Sprague at both *Sprague v. Walter* trials, said that "Congress was feeding the press" because they were "scared to death" that Sprague might discover that an FBI or CIA agent was involved in the assassinations.

Back in 1977, when he was appointed chief counsel of the congressional committee, Sprague was fresh from his triumphs in unraveling the contract murders of Jock Yablonski, his wife and daughter. Sprague had spent five years unraveling the conspiracy behind the murder plot of the reform leader of the United Mine Workers. He had doggedly obtained the convictions of three paid assassins and four coconspirators, before he finally convicted union president Tony Boyle in 1974 for ordering the killings.

In taking the job of chief counsel of the House Select Committee on Assassinations, Sprague had proposed pursuing JFK's death as if it was a homicide investigation. And one of the government agencies Sprague wanted to investigate was the CIA and its connections with Lee Harvey Oswald.

Sprague had assembled a staff of 170 lawyers, investigators and researchers to conduct separate investigations of the murders of JFK and King. The Philadelphia prosecutor with the almost perfect record of murder convictions had high hopes of solving two of the most famous crimes of the century.

Was Sprague up to the task? F. Lee Bailey thought so. "Dick is the greatest lawyer alive," Bailey said. But Sprague was undone by a manufactured media controversy over the closed murder case of a drunken clerk named John Applegate.

• • •

THE INQUIRER KEPT APPEALING THE SPRAGUE VERDICT. THE PENNSYLVANIA SUPERIOR COURT IN 1994 reduced the $34 million jury award to $24 million, still a state record for a libel case. A year later, a panel of three Superior Court judges affirmed the decision in Sprague's favor. In 1996, the state Supreme Court refused to hear the Inquirer's last appeal in Pennsylvania.

The newspaper's only recourse was to seek a review from the U.S. Supreme Court. Eight days before a filing deadline with the Supreme Court, however, the Inquirer finally settled the Sprague case for a confidential sum. The newspaper also printed a public apology. The war was over. It had taken Dick Sprague 23 years to clear his name.

District Attorney Lynne Abraham had watched the Sprague case with interest since the 1970s when she was a "baby district attorney" working with Sprague. She credited the late Sam Klein with finally settling the case.

"Sam was finally able to get their attention," Abraham said of the Inquirer's bosses. "To say, 'Yo, cut your loses. This has gone on for a quarter of a century. Pay the guy off, and get over it.... Pay it off and get rid of it,' and they listened to him."

But not everybody thought it was a good idea. Gene Roberts, who retired as Inquirer executive editor three months after the Sprague verdict, said he never wanted to settle the Sprague case; he favored appealing it all the way to the Supreme Court. Would the Inquirer have won from the nation's highest court what it couldn't win from a Philadelphia jury? "I think there was a significant chance of that," Roberts said.

But to Roberts' chagrin, the lawyers for the Inquirer's parent company, Knight-Ridder, settled the case for a confidential amount. "To this day, I don't know what the settlement was," Roberts said. "I never wanted to know. I felt it would just piss me off."

• • •

THE FINAL $24 MILLION AWARD IN THE SPRAGUE CASE RANKED AS THE THIRD HIGHEST libel award in the country, according to a 2007 list, "Top Ten Final Awards in Media Libel, Privacy, and Related Cases," compiled by the Media Law Resource Center in New York City. The report, however, quoting a 2002 Washington Times story, also estimated the confidential settlement in the Sprague case as a "reported $20 million," which would would make it the highest ever known libel settlement in the nation.

Chapter 14

❖

LAST DAYS OF DISCO

JIM BEASLEY WAS TRYING TO GET THE JUDGE'S ATTENTION WHEN HE FILED EXHIBIT P-1, an X-rated color photo of a cannon shaped like a phallus that shot confetti into the air.

The phallus was found in the basement of the former headquarters of the Episcopal Diocese of Pennsylvania. The once grand "Episcopal Church House" in Center City, Philadelphia, had fallen far from grace. But help was on the way. Beasley, an Episcopalian by birth, bought the 19th-century Gothic revival castle on July 15, 1986, for $950,000, and he was planning to rehab it into a law office.

Beasley had climbed to the top of his profession, and he wanted to build a cathedral suitable for a legend of the law. But first, he had go to court to evict the building's current tenants. Barry and Wayne Geftman operated a disco on the second floor, and a gay dance club in the basement, where they kept the phallus.

In a petition for an injunction filed in Philadelphia's Common Pleas Court, Beasley cast himself as the sheriff in the white hat and the Geftmans as the forces of Sodom and Gomorrah. Beasley charged the Geftmans with using the former Church House "in a manner which is immoral, improper and objectionable," and he asked the judge to evict the Geftmans within 30 days.

"The renovation of this structure," Beasley said in his lawsuit, "will remove a clear and present danger to public health and safety, which has existed for many years," and "will restore this landmark building to productive, economic and social use."

The Rev. Ozi W. Whitaker, the former Episcopal bishop of Pennsylvania, used to have an office on the second floor of the five-story brick and limestone structure at 12th and Walnut Streets. But that was before the Geftmans hung silver disco balls in the second-story chapel with the stained-glass windows and 20-foot ceilings.

That wasn't the only crime committed at the former Church House. At an Oct. 29, 1986, hearing before Judge Alfred J. DiBona, Beasley called private investigator Bruce Brodie to the witness stand to testify how he paid $10 on a recent Saturday night to infiltrate the disco known as the Second Story.

"Did you visit the men's room?" Beasley asked.

"Yes, sir," Brodie said.

"And what did you notice in the men's room?"

"On one occasion, there were two men in the stall and another man leaning over the top of the stall looking in," Brodie said. "And from within the stall I heard sniffing noises. And as one of the men came out of the stall, he was wiping his nose."

Brodie testified that although a posted sign said the legal occupancy was only 220, the disco was packed with between 650 and 700 patrons. "The room in which the dancing took place was literally wall-to-wall people," Brodie said. "It was difficult to move in that room at all.

"There were two large speakers in the corners of the room where the dancing took place. And when the music was played, the bass was extremely loud, and it would make the floor shake."

Next, Beasley called David Brusha, a part-time janitor, who testified about his visit to the gay dance club known as the Catacombs, which catered to people under 21. At 8 in the morning, Brusha said, he saw 60 revelers still partying in the basement painted pitch-black and lined with couches.

"I've seen one girl and the rest were men, all men," Brusha said.

"And was there anything striking about these men that you saw?" Beasley asked.

"There was a couple with no clothes on," Brusha said.

"And what were they doing?" Beasley asked.

"Walking around with no clothes on," Brusha said. "So we left right after I seen that."

The club displayed posters of naked men, Brusha said, and the floors were littered with empty plastic baggies and marijuana roaches.

"Is there any other object in the game room… that caught your attention?" Beasley asked, referring to Exhibit P-1.

"Yeah, there is," Brusha said sheepishly. "I don't know how to say it in court."

"Say it," Beasley commanded.

"There is a penis that stands about three-feet tall and about that round," Brusha said, gesturing to show the width.

"You say it's round, like the trunk of a tree?" Beasley asked.

"Yes."

"…And you estimate that as being three-feet tall?" Beasley asked.

"Somewhere around there."

· · ·

THE EPISCOPAL DIOCESE OF PENNSYLVANIA BUILT THE CHURCH HOUSE IN 1894 FOR THE then costly sum of $155,000, according to a journal published by the diocese's 110th Convention of that same year. The diocese's original plans for the first floor called for building a fireproof library, and building and renting out two stores on the same floor to pay the interest on the entire building's $60,000 mortgage.

The second floor was to be the location of "a chapel and assembly room," according to the journal. The third floor was supposed to maintain a large room for the Woman's Auxiliary; and the fourth floor, rooms for a "Church Club."

The diocese, however, stayed only 27 years, selling the building in 1921 to the Philadelphia Chamber of Commerce for $325,000. Workers removed a pipe organ from the second-story chapel. Steeplejacks evicted eight stone statues of the saints posted like sentinels on the building's roof. Each of the statues was eight feet high and weighed two tons. The statues, however, which included Saints Peter, Paul and Patrick, did not make it safely down from the roof.

"Some of the statues had cracked partly through" by the time they touched the ground, the Philadelphia Record reported in March 1921. "The sights of parts of arms and legs and faces stacked against the base of the building attracted the attention of hundreds of passers-by."

The building reopened on Oct. 5, 1921. For more than two hours, some 2,000 businessmen passed through the assembly room to attend an official house-warming. The Chamber of Commerce ran its operations out of the former Church House for the next two decades, using the fourth floor as a reading room for city businessmen. The building was purchased in 1946 by Jefferson Medical College, which sold it in 1975 to Pierre Uniforms Inc.

The disco era in Philadelphia began when brothers Barry and Wayne Geftman arrived looking for a new location for a big city disco, after they ran the successful Music Box in Atlantic City. The Geftmans were ahead of their time, opening the Second Story in Philadelphia in December 1976, eight months before Studio 54 in New York.

The brothers, who rented space from Pierre Uniforms, thought the Church House was the perfect location for a disco. "When the 'chapel' became available, that settled it," Barry Geftman told the Philadelphia Inquirer in 1979. "It was acoustically perfect, it had terrific visual potential."

The Second Story was a private club that opened at 9:30 p.m. and closed at 3 a.m., an hour after city bars. Once the Second Story reached what was deemed to be full capacity, people stood in line outside the club, waiting for others to leave so they could take their place on the dance floor.

"The line waiting itself became a nightlife event," the Inquirer reported, "with people bringing their own liquor, socializing, flirting and sometimes dancing on the sidewalk."

Celebrities who frequented the Second Story included Sylvester Stallone, Smokin' Joe Frazier and then-District Attorney Ed Rendell. Musicians Boz Scaggs and Teddy Pendergrass also stopped by, as did dancer Ben Vereen. The bearded, clean-cut Barry Geftman was in charge of lights and décor; his brother, Wayne, with the long hair and punk wardrobe, was the disc jockey and sound-system guru. Every night, disco dancers gyrated in the former chapel that featured a baptismal font filled with popcorn, and stained-glass windows that depicted Jesus as the King of Kings and Mary as the Queen of Heaven.

The Second Story had a bar just off the disco floor and a circular metal staircase that led upstairs to two so-called "quiet rooms." The first quiet room was a lounge with a bar and open arches that overlooked the dance floor; the second quiet room was ringed with platform couches.

"These were the days when everybody was smoking grass and popping different kinds of pills," recalled Michael DiPaolo, a former Second Story patron who negotiated the deal for Beasley to buy the Church House.

"It was the age of *Saturday Night Fever*, and there were gorgeous women there," DiPaolo said. "The word was, if you couldn't get laid there, you couldn't get laid." The quiet rooms were in big demand. "There used to be group sex in there."

"I represented Jim," DiPaolo said. "I found the building . . . and negotiated the purchase. He fell in love with the building. How could you not?"

Much of the building's recent construction, however, was shoddy. When the disco owners hung speakers, "They just made holes" in the chapel ceiling, DiPaolo said. "They were Philistines. They had no appreciation for the architecture."

Beasley assigned two of his firm's brightest young lawyers, Tom Kline and Shanin Specter, son of U.S. Senator Arlen Specter, to the legal battle to evict the Geftmans. It was the first time that Kline and Specter had worked together.

"We were counsel to James Beasley," Kline recalled. "Jim said, 'I want you fellows to get those people out of there.'"

Beasley had Kline tour the building with a video camera. When the case went to court, Kline was sworn in as a witness and played his video for the judge marked as Exhibit P-13.

The video began with a tour of the first floor, showing extensive water damage, exposed wiring and water leaks in the ceiling. Then Kline descended into the basement. "And we are now going through one of the entrances down into the

Catacombs," Kline told the judge. "That's some of the trash that's left in the area…There was a very foul odor."

The camera focused on the star of the video, Exhibit P-1. "That's the phallus that Your Honor heard described," Kline told the judge.

"Did you take that out of a closet to bring that out and photograph it?" defense lawyer Leonard J. Bucki demanded.

"Yes," Kline said.

"It was visible," Beasley interrupted. "If you walked in the room, you could see it."

"Excuse me, Mr. Beasley," Bucki said. "You are not a witness."

"Gentleman, please," the judge said. "Mr. Kline, this was in a closet?"

"No, sir," Kline replied. "It was in a back room. The room was clearly open and it was a room that looked to me that would be visited by patrons…. There was no light in that back room so we moved it out."

The video panned the windows in the Second Story disco as Kline pointed out to the judge how they were "all boarded up."

"Could you get out a window in case of an emergency?" Beasley asked.

"There is no way," Kline said. "And that pretty much ends the tape."

• • •

THE SECOND STORY OPERATED UNDER A LIQUOR LICENSE ORIGINALLY GRANTED IN 1937 to the Jefferson Republican Club of the City of Philadelphia's 17th Ward. The disco had been grandfathered in under the club's 1934 charter. Beasley read aloud the original charter that said the Jefferson Republican Club existed to provide a meeting place where members "can read and discuss topics concerning the Constitution and laws of the United States, the economic and social welfare of the city and state, and the peace and prosperity of our country.

"In short," Beasley said, the goal of the supposedly nonprofit club was "to promote the welfare and happiness of its members and to make them better citizens of the United States." Beasley then asked Second Story owner Wayne Geftman if the disco was upholding the traditions of the Jefferson Republican Club.

"We would certainly conform within the guidelines of the charter," Geftman said.

"Do you and the members of the club… read and discuss topics concerning the Constitution and the laws of the United States?" Beasley asked Geftman.

"I generally don't. Possibly they do," Geftman replied from the witness stand. "I'm not sure what they talk about."

"The economic and social welfare of the city and state, do you discuss that?" Beasley sarcastically asked.

"That's generally not my topic of discussion when I'm in the club," Geftman said.

"…And how much did you pay for that phallus?" Beasley demanded.

"For what?" a startled Geftman asked.

"That object that you have in the basement, why is that there?" Beasley asked.

"That's a confetti cannon," Geftman said. "As a matter of fact, we paid $900 . . . . That was bought from a rock and roll band."

"What's the purpose of that?" Beasley demanded.

"It's a special effects prop that is not uncommon in discotheques," Geftman said.

In his closing argument, Beasley told the judge that since the Geftmans opened in 1976, they had operated "without any valid permits, without any licenses and without a certificate of occupancy."

Beasley argued that the club not only threatened public morals but was also a potential death trap. He alluded to a recent nightclub fire in Lexington, Ky., "where hundreds of people burned to death in a club under circumstances that exist in this club.

"Can you imagine what it would be like to get 650 or 700 people out of those doorways?" Beasley asked the judge. "Do you know how many people would ever make it to the exit? And the same is true of the Catacombs."

The disco had no working fire alarms and plenty of construction work that did not meet building codes, Beasley told the judge. "These people aren't interested in anything other than making money and at the sacrifice of what may be literally hundreds of human lives."

• • •

On Nov. 17, 1986, Judge DiBona refused to grant Beasley's petition seeking to evict the Geftmans, but the judge did issue an order for the Second Story and Catacombs to cease operations until they brought all existing violations into compliance.

When the Geftmans ignored the order, Beasley filed an appeal, and this time he told cocounsel Tom Kline to file the photo of the phallus as Exhibit 1-A.

"Not only has the property been wasted, but a dangerous threat to public safety . . . continues to exist," Beasley wrote in his appeal. Beasley charged that the Geftmans had "maliciously abused the property" and allowed flooding from large wet bars on the second floor to damage a first-floor art gallery. The floods included not only water, but also streams of "Coca Cola and orange juice from the ceiling," Beasley wrote.

Beasley padlocked the building to keep the Geftmans out, but somebody sawed through the locks. The judge filed a second cease-and-desist order nine days after his original order, but the Geftmans continued to operate both the Second Story and the Catacombs.

The Geftmans also applied for an occupancy permit, arguing that they had addressed all violations cited by the city. On Feb. 6, 1987, Judge DiBona decided to lift his previous cease-and-desist order, and allow the Geftmans to continue operating until the city ruled on their request for a certificate of occupancy.

On Aug. 12, 1987, the city notified the Geftmans that it had turned down their request for a certificate of occupancy because the Second Story and Catacombs still did not meet building and fire codes. Beasley kept up the pressure, filing a petition two days later for a temporary restraining order that charged the Geftmans with operating "establishments [that] were dens of immoral and illegal activities."

As they continued to battle in court, the Geftmans had only a few months remaining on their lease. They were operating under the third and final three-year extension of an original three-year lease signed on April 13, 1976, with Pierre Uniforms, the building's previous owner.

The original lease called for the Geftmans to rent the second floor of the old Church House for $9,000 a year. After all of the three-year extensions were exercised, the lease was finally set to expire on April 13, 1988, and the Geftmans knew they had no chance of getting a new lease from Beasley. So the disco owners made a practical decision. "They simply stayed open until their lease was up," recalled Shanin Specter.

On April 16, 1988, the Inquirer ran a story entitled, "The Second Story Club Is Closing."

"The city's most prestigious survivor of the disco era bites the dust tomorrow when the Second Story Club, 1127 Walnut St., throws its last party," the Inquirer wrote.

"The nightlife scene is wavering and fluctuating," Wayne Geftman told the Inquirer, as he attempted to spray deodorizer over his cadaver of a disco. "We are putting all of our equipment into storage until we can see some definite trend, whether it will be back to rock and roll or on to something else, something new."

At the old Church House, the disco era was finally over. And now it was time for Beasley to build his dream law office.

• • •

IN THE SUMMER OF 1986, BEFORE HE BOUGHT THE CHURCH HOUSE, BEASLEY TOOK A trip with girlfriend Nicole Chabat to Egypt, to see the pyramids.

"He and I were both interested in ancient Egypt," Chabat said. "It probably was one of the greatest trips I had ever taken in my life. He read a great deal about it before, and after we talked about the mind-set of the pharaohs, and what those people would create."

When they came back to Philadelphia, Beasley took Chabat on a tour of the Church House.

"We went through the building, and it was wrecked, totally trashed," Chabat recalled. The structure of the building "was not damaged, but it was sleazy" inside and the crumbling basement was infested with termites. Beasley, however, insisted, "I'm buying it."

"Well," Chabat told Beasley, "you have bought your pyramid."

When the building subsequently flooded inside, Chabat described it as the "coup de grace." Beasley, however, was energized. "He was a street fighter," Chabat said. "That's what was driving him, he loved to fight. When he was furious, he became so calm."

After the Geftmans finally left in 1988, a fireplace mantle in the former bishop's office disappeared, and the list of suspects was short. Beasley saddled up like the sheriff, and with DiPaolo riding along as deputy, he drove out to confront Wayne Geftman at his Main Line home. Beasley rang the bell, and when Geftman came to the door, Beasley announced, "The fireplace mantle is gone. I want it back there tomorrow."

He left without giving Geftman a chance to reply, DiPaolo said. The mantle was back the next day.

• • •

"IT WAS LIKE WE WERE DOING A CATHEDRAL," RECALLED S. NEIL SCHLOSSER, PROJECT architect for the renovation of the Church House. "It was a tremendous opportunity for us . . . maybe our best job."

In 1986, Schlosser and Karl Krumholz, both of SRK Architects of Philadelphia, began drawing up plans for the renovations. The biggest problem with the exterior was that much of the original first-floor facade had been destroyed to create ugly storefronts for an art gallery, a print shop and a boutique. The architects decided to rip out the existing storefronts, and recreate a historic limestone front.

The building's original front was also heavily stained, so the architects hired a crew to spray-wash it. "We just drenched the whole façade for days," Schlosser said.

The architects had a new slate roof installed and all the windows replaced. The new stained-glass windows on the first floor featured a trio of maidens depicting charity, justice and patience, and another trio of maidens representing music, painting and architecture.

In the new law library on the second floor, Beasley ordered leaded stained-glass windows featuring the crests of eight different law schools.

"He was very involved," Schlosser said. Beasley would call the architects and say, "I have something to review with you; be here in five minutes." Then he would just hang up the phone. "I wouldn't say he was a nice guy," Schlosser said, "but he was a character."

Electrical contractor Joe Brassell Sr. was hired in 1991 to rewire the building, after a demolition crew went in and "ripped it down just about to the bare walls,"

Brassell said. He worked on the building for a year, installing a new 13,000 volt electrical system, along with cables for phones and computers.

Brassell showed up at the old Church House at 6:30 every morning and found Beasley already inside, roaming. "He beat us in," Brassell said. "He was a hustler. If he was on a case, you didn't go near him."

Beasley wasn't the type to pat you on the back after a job, Brassell said. "But if you didn't get any comments from him," you knew you were in good shape. "Silence was good."

Chabat recalled visiting Beasley at the Church House while it was under construction, just three blocks down from Beasley's old law office, at 21 S. 12th St. At the time, the neighborhood on the east side of Market Street was in such bad shape that Beasley's female employees were afraid to walk the three blocks from the old office to the new.

"He was the project manager," Chabat said. "He was there every day, he was working on plans and designs." It was a huge commitment, but Beasley "had this capacity, he could take on so much intellectually and switch gears immediately," she said. "It was his pyramid, and he went at it with a vengeance."

Beasley was particularly interested in the design of his new office on the second floor, where the bishop had once been.

"I showed him some images and he got really excited," said architect Karl Krumholz. Beasley didn't want people to feel intimidated when they walked into his new office, Krumholz said, "but he did want them to be impressed."

The architects designed coffered ceilings, featuring a two-way grid of exposed cherry beams and hand-painted tapestries. They also picked out cherry paneling, Victorian candle chandeliers, and oak parquet floors. The architects hired artist Michael Webb to paint a frieze of nature scenes bordering the ceiling, featuring trees and open sky.

Another big project was the law library, to be created out of the former chapel that had once been a disco. "It was a complete wreck," Krumholz recalled. The architects found a historic Victorian wallpaper reproduction of a starry night that became part of another coffered ceiling. The architects custom-designed carpets and found some historic-looking reference tables and "some amazing Gothic revival chairs," Krumholz said.

Schlosser and Krumholz picked out wallpaper, paneling, cabinets and furniture for all five refurbished floors. When all the construction and furnishing was finally done, Schlosser said, the total cost of the project came in at "close to $5 million."

The Pennsylvania Historical and Museum Commission in 1992 awarded the former Episcopal Church House a Historic Preservation Commendation for Outstanding Achievement. The project also gave Beasley's architects tremendous credibility with other city lawyers.

"You finished Beasley's office and didn't get sued?" many lawyers asked Krumholz. "That," the architect said, "was the best recommendation."

· · ·

AFTER BEASLEY MOVED INTO HIS NEW LAW CASTLE, SOME EMPLOYEES DETECTED A CHANGE in the boss.

"He just became distant," said Shanin Specter, who had worked for Beasley for 10 years. "I think everybody felt that Jim was a father figure to all of us. And we all wanted a pat on the back, and he just didn't have it in him."

"I think what ultimately happened here was a lack of professional recognition, and a lack of an ability for me and Shanin to control our own destiny," said Tom Kline, who worked for Beasley for 15 years. Beasley continued to run the firm as a "benevolent dictator," Kline said, with "no clear successorship plan."

"He didn't want to give up any of the control," Kline said. "Jim still wanted to be in control."

So on Jan. 2, 1995, Kline and Specter were ready to make a move. The two lawyers had been secretly planning for months to launch their own firm. They had already rented office space at 1525 Locust St., but they hadn't gotten around to telling their old boss yet that they were leaving.

The way Kline explains it, it was a practical decision over money. "We know how the Beasley firm worked," Kline said. "Jim owed us money on the money we earned," Kline said, referring to the annual discretionary bonuses that Beasley passed out to employees every December. To heavy hitters at the firm such as Kline, those discretionary bonuses often amounted to $1 million or more.

"We wanted to get fair treatment, and you're not going to get fair treatment when you tell your boss 'I am going to leave in three months from now, and you can give me whatever discretionary bonus you want,'" Kline said. So Kline and Specter waited until the discretionary bonuses were passed out before they told the boss the bad news.

When Kline and Specter finally went in to see Beasley, it was Kline who did the talking. He was understandably nervous.

"Jim's office was so long that between the door and his desk, you would change your mind three times about what you were going to say," Kline said. "Anybody who has made that walk knows that feeling."

Kline told Beasley he and Specter were leaving, and Beasley simply said, "OK." The boss was "cool and distant in demeanor," Kline recalled. Beasley asked a few more questions, including when they were leaving (the answer was immediately). And then Kline and Specter walked out the door.

Beasley, however, had a secretary call Kline at his new office later that afternoon and request that Kline return for a meeting with Beasley the next morning. When Kline showed up in Beasley's office, the boss was overheard yelling, "How the fuck could you do this to me?"

"I understand how Shanin could do it, but I don't understand how you could," Beasley told Kline. "You know you are the executor of my will, and you were like a son to me. And I rarely lose a night's sleep and I haven't slept."

Kline argued that he could continue to be the executor of Beasley's will. "I can still be, there's no reason why I can't be," Kline said. "We're just going to be working in different places." But Beasley said no and shook his head.

Kline & Specter were now competitors. And Beasley treated them as such.

"You know, you had it pretty good here," Beasley told Kline. "I doubt you are going to do as well on your own."

As Kline was leaving Beasley's office for the last time, he felt "really, really angry."

"He wasn't wishing me well by any means, and I wanted him to," Kline said. Beasley was "really like a father to me," Kline said, and he wanted to leave with Beasley's blessing. But it was not to be.

When Kline got back to his new law office, he recalled Specter telling him, "You know it's Jim's way of playing mind games with you. It's understandable."

When the reporter from the Legal Intelligencer called to get Beasley's reaction to the departure of Kline and Specter, Beasley said, "It's no surprise," adding, "It happens all across town every January."

A month later, three more of Beasley's lawyers — James E. Colleran; his son, Francis T. Colleran; and Daniel L. Thistle — all left to start their own law firms. A year later, another Beasley lawyer, Nancy H. Fullam, did the same thing.

• • •

BEASLEY COMMISSIONED ARTIST MICHAEL WEBB IN 1997 TO PAINT A FIVE-STORY-HIGH mural on the back of the Beasley Building. "Beasley hired me to do something historical about Philadelphia," Webb said. The artist painted foundry workers casting outdoor sculptures on display in Philadelphia. The sculptures represented in the mural include the head and feet from the Billy Penn statue atop City Hall. Webb also painted a seated woman and child — "Wisdom Instructing Youth" — taken from a 1908 sculptural tribute to slain President William McKinley, posted on the south side of City Hall.

"It just sort of evolved into a family mural with all his kids in it and his grandkids," said Webb, who also tossed in a couple of pet dogs and some pigeons.

The late Philadelphia Mayor Richardson Dilworth appears in the mural talking with Mike DiPaolo. One of Beasley's young lawyers, Slade McLaughlin, was immortalized holding a chisel in hand; Beasley's file clerk, Charles Lee, was painted carrying a shovel. Webb added Jim Beasley Jr., now working at the firm as a lawyer, and his sister, Kim, a secretary. When Webb wanted to paint a "distinguished older man" into the mural, Beth Ann Robinson, Beasley's office administrator, suggested the boss.

"He never wanted to be in the mural," Webb said. The artist painted Beasley and his daughter, Pam, reviewing architectural plans from a balcony; Beasley appears to be glowering. It was an attitude that Webb became familiar with when Kim Beasley asked the artist to include in the mural a photo of her late, beloved mutt, Harold. Webb was painting black spots on the white dog at 6:30 a.m. when he noticed Beasley standing behind him, with a disgusted look on his face.

"Who told you to put that dog in the mural?" Beasley demanded. Webb said the culprit was Beasley's daughter. "I hate that goddamn dog," Beasley said.

When Beasley ran into Kim, he asked, "What's your goddamn dog doing on the side of my building?" But then he let it go. "I figured if he really was mad," his daughter said, "he would have had Harold painted over."

The artist said he did not know of another privately commissioned mural of its size in Philadelphia, where most outdoor artwork is the province of the city's Mural Arts Program.

"Part of the mission was to lift the neighborhood," Webb said. "He [Beasley] told me this was just a gift to the neighborhood."

At the time the artist was painting his mural, "the neighborhood was pretty bad," Webb said. When he showed up at 4 a.m. to begin painting, his audience included hookers, drug dealers and crack heads. "They were a bawdy, noisy bunch," Webb said. "It was the end of their workday, and they were pretty crazy."

"The neighborhood pretty much went down," recalled DiPaolo. "That's why we got it [the old Church House] at such a low price."

But a few years after Beasley opened his refurbished law office, "other people started coming in and buying on the block," DiPaolo said. A city realtor bought and rehabbed three buildings across the street from Beasley's law office. Other investors who followed Beasley's lead included DiPaolo, who bought two more buildings on the block. The neighborhood became revitalized, and the hookers and druggies moved on.

It took a while, but Sheriff Beasley had cleaned up Dodge.

Chapter 15

❖

FLYING COWBOY

IT WAS AN OLD WORLD WAR II FIGHTER PLANE THAT HADN'T FLOWN IN YEARS, sitting in a crop duster's barn. Its battle colors had been painted over, the body was all banged up and corroded, and the engine was shot. But it was still a genuine P-51 Mustang, one of the famous fighter escorts that protected Allied bombardiers in the skies over Germany and Japan. And when Jim Beasley saw it, he fell in love.

The year was 1978, and the 52-year-old Beasley was flying his family out to a lawyers' conference in San Diego. He was in the air when Jim Jr., then only 11, talked his dad into taking a detour 500 miles out of the way.

They stopped off in Harlingen, Tex., to see a group of warbird pilots known as the Confederate Air Force, later renamed the more politically correct Commemorative Air Force. Jim Jr., who had glued together models of the P-51, told his father it was "the coolest plane ever made."

His father agreed. This was Beasley's second chance to buy a Mustang. Just two years earlier, Beasley and son had seen a P-51 for sale at the airport in Cape May, N.J., for $75,000. "Dad, you got to get it," Jim Jr. had pleaded, but his father resisted. Now in Texas, another Mustang was for sale, this time for $140,000, a price tag that included a spare engine. And this time, Beasley couldn't say no.

Ironically, the Mustang had been registered with the FAA as "N51JB," with the initials representing the last two owners of the plane, both of whom had the initials JB. As far as Jim Jr. was concerned, it was an omen; a third JB had to buy it.

The plane that Beasley christened the "Bald Eagle" weighed 7,000 pounds and had a 37-foot wingspan. It came with an extra super-charged, 12-cylinder,

1,695-horsepower Rolls Royce engine that enabled the Mustang to fly up to 450 miles an hour.

"The most beautiful airplane ever built," Beasley rhapsodized to a reporter. "The P-51 is just a delight to fly."

"And there's nothing like the noise of a Mustang," Beasley said in another interview, trying to describe the sound a reporter once likened to a "clattering machine gun."

"Once you hear a Mustang — *one time* — you'll recognize it any other time that you hear that noise," Beasley said.

Flying a warbird was an expensive hobby. After Beasley spent $140,000 on the Mustang and an extra engine, it cost him an additional $100,000 to overhaul the plane. But the Mustang became a valuable collector's item. The magazine Air Show World reported in 2002 that of the nearly 15,000 original Mustangs built by North American Aviation, "just over 150 are still flying." Beasley's Bald Eagle was originally built in 1944 for $54,000, but by 2000, it was worth about $1 million.

By then, the cost of flying the Mustang had also skyrocketed, to $2,500 an hour. The price of parts, if you could find them, was even more prohibitive, with a new prop running about $60,000.

But when it came to flying the Mustang, Beasley didn't care about money. "Airplanes," he told a reporter, "are just machines that convert money into noise."

Beasley hired painter Dan Caldarale to restore the Mustang to its former glory. Caldarale, a fellow warbird pilot, painted the Bald Eagle blue and silver, with a yellow nose and yellow wingtips. He also painted eight black Nazi swastikas under the cockpit, to commemorate the Bald Eagle's authenticated kills during World War II.

The Mustang changed Beasley's life. Before he bought it, he was just another workaholic lawyer. But then he started flying the Mustang on weekends in air shows all over the country. He also would sneak out of the office on weekdays for a rendezvous in the sky with Caldarale, so the two pilots could practice formation flying.

Beasley was never happier than when he traded his lawyer's suit for a khaki flight suit and a baseball cap. He had a luxurious law office in Center City, and a country estate in Villanova, but his favorite hangout was his no-frills hangar at the Northeast Philadelphia Airport.

"Dad didn't have a hobby until he bought the Mustang," said Jim Jr., who also learned how to fly the P-51.

But it was more than just a hobby; flying warbirds was a passion that Beasley could only fully share with his son and fellow warbird pilots. Outside the courtroom, the place where Beasley felt most alive was in the cramped and roaring cockpit of the Bald Eagle.

• • •

A REPORTER ONCE ASKED JIM BEASLEY WHY HE LOVED TO FLY. "I HAVE AN EXTREMELY heavy trial schedule," Beasley said in a 1990 interview with Business Philadelphia magazine. "And nothing on earth relaxes me or relieves the pressure like flying. Anyone who has flown lazy rolls through summer clouds and seen the beauty of the green earth below must come down refreshed. The shame of it is having to come down at all."

"At 64, Beasley still slips into his flight suit like a knife into its sheath," Business Philadelphia reporter Shawn Hart wrote in 1990. "Though of average height, he looks imposing — hell, he's dashing — in the khaki coveralls covered with patches of the planes he flies: the T-6 Navy trainer, the P-51 Mustang, the Six of Diamonds formation-flying team emblem."

Beasley's romance with flying began when he was a kid down on the farm in Mississippi, and he saw crop dusters swooping low over cotton fields. As a teenager, he washed crop duster planes for an entire month in exchange for a single 30-minute flying lesson. He was only 14 when he first went up in a Piper Cub. He became so adept at flying the Piper that when a crop duster took him up, the duster sat in back, taking a nip from a hip flask, while young Jimmie flew the plane.

As a young man driving a Greyhound bus in highway traffic, Beasley day-dreamed about flying. When he became a successful lawyer, he finally had the time and resources to pursue his passion.

He acquired his own air force. His modern fleet included a single-engine Cessna, a twin-engine Aerostar, and, later, a Cheyenne prop jet. His warbird collection included two T-6 Navy trainers used during World War II, two T-33 jet trainers, two P-51 Mustangs, a MiG-15 jet fighter used during the Korean War, and a 1930s biplane known as a Great Lakes Trainer that featured an open cockpit.

Taking off in a P-51 wasn't for the fainthearted. The Mustang had a propeller that blew intense heat from 100-octane fumes. The pilot had to weave back and forth as he taxied down the runway, to see around the Mustang's high nose. It did-n't get any easier once the plane was in the air.

"It is hot and cramped," Philadelphia Inquirer reporter Michael Ruane wrote of his 1988 flight in the Bald Eagle. "The seats are hard. The noise is deafening. And at 300 m.p.h., on its short, rigid wings, the fighter seems to pound through the air like a powerboat.

"Its maneuvers can pound those inside, too, producing the sensation of a plum-meting elevator at one moment, and that of a trash compactor the next," Ruane wrote.

"It's a fierce animal," Beasley told Ruane, "a killing machine . . . designed for death and destruction."

· · ·

BEASLEY HAD NO PEERS AT HIS LAW FIRM, AND ONLY A FEW CLOSE FRIENDS AMONG THE MEMBERS of the Philadelphia bar. He was a mystery to most judges and lawyers in town, including the lawyers who worked for him.

But one group of men knew him best, and could call on him any time. They were his pilot buddies, and to them Beasley was just one of the guys. And that's how they treated him. Like the time Beasley was in a New Jersey diner and he got upset when Dan Caldarale grabbed the check first. Caldarale refused to back down, staring his multimillionaire pal in the eye and snarling, "Fuck you, Beasley."

"He loved it," Caldarale recalled. Beasley was just a "street guy" anyway, Caldarale said, and "since he got off the street, nobody talked to him that way."

The lawyers who worked for Beasley and waited outside his office door knew that they weren't going to get the boss's attention until he was off the phone with his flying buddies. As Jim Jr. said of his father, "He would hang up on a [state] Supreme Court justice, but not on Dan."

The members of the Six of Diamonds flight team used to address each other with lines like, "Hey, you peckerhead, get over here." Beasley loved the camaraderie. "The only people who knew him were the people who flew with him," said Joe Scogna, a trauma neurosurgeon and fellow warbird pilot.

The relationship between Beasley and his fellow pilots was built on trust. When you flew World War II airplanes at 200 miles per hour, with just a few feet between wingtips, you had to trust your fellow pilots.

"There's a cardinal rule that you never forget when you're in formation and you're flying wing," Beasley once said in an interview. "You never ever take your eyes off the lead. Never ever."

When you fly formation, "you have a box of air around you," explained Dan Dameo, another member of the Six of Diamonds. "You can go up three feet, you can go down three feet. You can go left three feet and you can go right three feet."

That's about it. Do it wrong just once, and everybody may wind up dead. But done right, it was exhilarating.

"You got the adrenaline pumping," Dameo said. "When you come down, your armpits are wet, your back is wet, because it's hard work. . . . It's better than sex 'cause it lasts longer."

· · ·

BEASLEY'S LOVE OF THE MUSTANG WAS NOT UNIVERSALLY SHARED BY FAMILY MEMBERS. He took cousin Walter Woodworth on a flight from Philadelphia to San Diego, but Woodworth hated it. "You're up in the air 15 minutes, you got a migraine headache because of that damn engine."

Helen Beasley flew many times with her husband in his Cessna and Aerostar, but didn't like the Mustang. "I was frightened," she said. "He started doing loops in the Bald Eagle. I just kept saying 'Oh, oh, and oh,' and I never went up again."

His daughter, Pam, however, loved it. "We were doing loop-to-loops over Manhattan," she said, and she got a chance "to see Manhattan upside down."

Beasley's flying buddies have their own stories.

"The Mustang, that was a harrowing experience," said Mike DiPaolo, a friend and business associate whom Beasley taught to fly. "He loved to scare the shit out of people."

The front seat in the Mustang cockpit was relatively roomy, compared to the cramped passenger seat in back. With a helmet on, a passenger soon discovered that because of the narrow Plexiglas cockpit walls, he could only move his head a few inches to either side. When the G-forces kicked in, a passenger could have his helmet bounced hockey-style off the Plexiglas. On one Mustang flight with Beasley, Joe Scogna banged his head so hard, he blacked out.

But people used to line up to fly in the Bald Eagle. "They couldn't wait to get in that plane," DiPaolo recalled. "But when they got out, a lot of them said, 'I'm never gonna do this again.'"

Beasley would take off and do some lazy figure 8's and barrel rolls before going into a tumbling free fall that made the horizon spin. "It was only 10 or 12 seconds, but it's an eternity when you're falling, and the sensations are incredible," DiPaolo said.

When Beasley pulled out of the dive, he would turn to his white-knuckled passenger and say, "That was really neat, wasn't it?"

And when he landed, he would tap his passenger on the knee and say, "Well, we cheated death again."

DiPaolo remembered one city judge who went up in the Mustang with Beasley and came down looking green. For Beasley, an expert in the art of intimidation, that meant "he always had the edge on that judge psychologically," DiPaolo said, because "he had brought him to the brink of wanting to die."

Some attorneys at the Beasley law firm viewed it as a hazing ritual, taking a ride with the boss in his Mustang. "It's cruel and unusual punishment," recalled Gerald F. Kaplan, a former doctor and lawyer who worked for Beasley.

Beasley would load an unsuspecting rookie attorney in the back of his Mustang and then fly 450 miles an hour upside down before executing some thrilling dives and barrel rolls.

"It's like going on a roller coaster times four," Kaplan complained about his

Mustang ride. "I was nauseated and dizzy for a whole day. . . . The whole point was to make you sick."

James J. McHugh was just breaking in as a Beasley associate in 1994 when the boss invited him up for a ride in his T-6 trainer. The 6-foot-2 McHugh was sitting in the office of Beasley's hangar when Beasley threw a pilot's jacket at him that was three sizes too small. The sleeves went to the elbow and the jacket didn't cover McHugh's navel. He looked ridiculous. Next, Beasley threw a parachute at McHugh and told him if they got in trouble and had to jump out of the plane, the best thing to do was to aim for the wingtips. While McHugh was pondering that advice, and trying to figure out how to put on a parachute, Beasley threw one last thing at him, one of those little bags they give you on the airlines, in case you have to puke.

Beasley and McHugh took off in the T-6, climbed up in the sky and leveled off. That's when McHugh discovered they weren't alone. He looked to his left and was shocked to see Dan Caldarale in another T-6, roaring up to within 20 feet of Beasley's plane.

"Boom, Dan is right near us," McHugh recalled. "Boom, we're right in formation."

Caldarale was leading the tandem. Over the radio, McHugh heard Beasley say, "OK, are you ready?" The two T-6s then executed a loop and a roll.

"Are you OK?" Beasley asked over the radio. "I guess so," McHugh replied. "I wasn't really ready for that." Beasley told McHugh to keep his eyes on the horizon, because it would stabilize his equilibrium. Then Beasley promptly followed Caldarale into another loop and roll.

"By this time, my stomach is getting a little queasy, and that horizon thing didn't help at all," McHugh said. He turned around in his seat, and, craning his neck, saw the two planes switching positions. Now, Beasley was in the lead, and Caldarale was behind on the wing, and once again, he looked too close. The two planes then went into another loop and roll. McHugh, craning his neck to keep Caldarale in his sights, got a glimpse of the other T-6 roaring off in the opposite direction. "It's too tight," he heard Caldarale say over the radio.

By this time, McHugh wasn't feeling too well. "I don't think we should do any-more of that," McHugh told Beasley over the radio. "Oh, Dan," Beasley said over the radio. "He's too sick. I've got to go back."

· · ·

DAN CALDARALE HAD HIS OWN HANGAR IN SOUTHAMPTON, N.J., AT THE RED LION Airport, where he painted vintage warbirds. His usual routine was to go out for an early morning stroll around his six-acre property. When he'd come back, he'd often find a phone message from Beasley: "Get the hell out of bed. Wake up, you lazy bastard!"

When Caldarale called back, Beasley would suggest they cut work to go flying. It took Beasley about 40 minutes to drive to the Northeast Philly airport from his Center City law office. When he got to his hangar, he'd give Caldarale another ring to let him know he was about to take off in his T-6.

Caldarale jumped in his own T-6 Trainer. "I'd take off and meet him in the air," he said. They'd rendezvous at 2,000 feet above Caldarale's air strip, or over the Ben Franklin Bridge, and then they'd fly down to the Pinelands in Jersey, a nature preserve, to practice formation work. Caldarale would take the lead position and Beasley would fly wing; then they'd switch.

The two pilots flew between 30 and 60 minutes at a time, practicing breaks and loops. They'd communicate on the radio and with hand gestures, sometimes obscene. "We flew so much together, we trusted each other," Caldarale said. "It's a beautiful thing."

They'd come down, often, without saying a word to each other, and head back to work. Caldarale had airplanes to paint; Beasley, cases to try.

Caldarale loved the T-6. "It's so responsive," he said. "It's just a dream to fly. When you move that stick, it's even lighter on the controls than a [Piper] Cub. It's like driving a Buick Skylark or getting into a Mustang or a Corvette."

The T-6 had a large canopy that provided great visibility and could be left open on a warm summer day, like a convertible in the sky, only this convertible had 650 horses. On takeoff, when the engine started, every piece of the aluminum plane shuddered as exhaust and cold air blew through the canopy. For a passenger, being up in the air in a T-6 was like flying a canoe in the sky. But in the hands of an expert pilot like Beasley or his son, Jim Jr., the takeoffs and landings in a T-6 were softer than any commercial plane.

The primary use of a T-6 was as a training plane for World War II pilots. "Every fighter pilot in this country flew a T-6," Caldarale said. "We would be at air shows and these old guys would come around."

It was Dan Caldarale who got Beasley into the Six of Diamonds flight team that Caldarale had been a member of for a dozen years. The team featured four to six pilots flying T-6s in a signature diamond formation. Beasley began flying with the team in the late 1980s. Caldarale also got Jim Jr. on the Six of Diamonds, as well as his friend, Ed Shipley.

The team practiced together for hours and then sat through multiple briefings at air shows, all for 10 minutes of choreographed flying. "It's really a challenge to do it right in front of thousands of people," Caldarale said.

And while they were doing all that flying, Beasley and Caldarale became best friends. Caldarale was a dapper, wiry guy with swept-back salt-and-pepper hair who was a couple inches taller and a dozen years younger than Beasley.

Beasley was usually the one to call Caldarale; the painter felt uncomfortable the other way around. "I figured, he's so busy, this guy's so important," Caldarale said. Then he realized, "Geez, he enjoys talking to me."

Beasley was always needling Caldarale about something, especially an old, beat-up Cessna of Caldarale's painted an ugly shade of brown. "It looked like a piece of shit," Caldarale admitted. "He wanted to know if I flew for UPS."

"He came off as being gruff and he could give you a look that could melt your brain. But the more I got to know him, I could see that he was all heart."

Beasley got a kick out of sneaking Caldarale into his world. Caldarale used to dress up in his "lawyer suit" and accompany Beasley to a trial, to watch Beasley tear apart some expert witness. Most people in the courtroom mistook the painter for another high-powered lawyer. Caldarale also accompanied Beasley to formal dinners. "One of the greatest things is, people would kiss my ass," Caldarale said, laughing. "'Oh,' they'd say, 'you're with Mr. Beasley.'"

Beasley, however, didn't have much patience for formal occasions, and after he gave a speech, he would usually whisper to Caldarale, "Let's get the fuck out of here," and they'd go to a bar for a nightcap.

On Oct. 7, 1999, Caldarale accompanied Beasley to a founder's recognition dinner in Beasley's honor at Temple University eight months after the university's trustees had announced that they were naming the university's law school after Beasley. Caldarale wore his lawyer's suit and got a kick out of the ROTC guys in dress uniforms opening the limo doors and asking, "How are you, Mr. Caldarale?" He was also greeted as a VIP by the dean of the law school and the president of the university.

Caldarale had no idea that the dinner that night was in Beasley's honor until Beasley stood up and gave a speech. When Caldarale asked Beasley about it afterwards, he shrugged. "I gave them a little bit of money, and they put my name on the building."

• • •

THEY CALLED IT THE "IN-TRAIL LOOP," A STUNT THAT BEASLEY DREAMED UP IN A BAR one night with his fellow Six of Diamonds pilots.

"Well, we all drank a few cocktails," recalled Dan Caldarale. "We call that the whiskey brief. Everything sounds like a good idea, and the next day reality sets in, but we do it anyhow."

"Jim has this rosy look on his face after his second or third glass of wine," Dan Dameo said. And he declared, "We've got to spice up the show a bit."

They decided to give Beasley's stunt a try. Four T-6 pilots took off and flew right

Opposite: Jimmie Beasley, about nine years old, in knickers with his kid sister, Peggy, on the streets of West Philadelphia, where they lived in a one-bedroom apartment during the Depression.

Top right: Jim Beasley's parents, Jim Sr. and Margaret, with their infant son.

Bottom right: Jim Beasley's grandfather, James E. Beasley, the former mayor and sheriff of Ora, Miss.

Previous page: This sketch of Jim Beasley in front of the stained glass windows of his law office was done by artist Ted Xaras in preparation for a 2001 portrait.

UNITED STATES NAVY

Identification Card

BEASLEY, James E.

James E. Beasley

Name

Signature

Color Hair AUBURN Eyes BROWN

Weight 140 Birth 7-2-26

Void after INDEFINITE

N. Nav. 516   Validating Officer

Above: Beasley (left) as a motorcycle cop in West Palm Beach, Fla.

Opposite: Jimmie Beasley the teenage submarine sailor during World War II.

Left: Beasley's Navy ID.

Top: Philadelphia Judge Theodore Reimel explains legal procedures to Temple University law school students visiting his Common Pleas courtroom. In this October 1953 photo, Jim Beasley is in the middle of the second row looking serious.

Opposite bottom: A portrait of young Jim Beasley the college student.

Below: The Six of Diamonds flight team goes for ride in the early 1990s' in a Mustang convertible after performing at the Oshkosh Air Show. Sitting behind Beasley are fellow pilots Dan Dameo, Bill Dodds and Rick Yersak. Seated next to Beasley is Dan Caldarale.

Jim Beasley Sr. and Jim Jr. in their P-51 Mustangs.
The shot was taken when the two warbird pilots were
on their way to a 1991 airshow in Oshkosh, Wis.

Top: Jim and his wife, Helen, in the late 1950s.

Middle: The Beasley family circa early 1970s. In between their parents, from left to right, are Kim, Jim Jr. and Pam.

Bottom: Beasley (left) and his favorite flying buddy, Dan Caldarale, standing in front of Caldarale's T-6.

Above: Jim Beasley in Florida, on the dock next to his fishing boat, with grandson Jimmy in 2003.

Left: Beasley and son in a 2001 portrait shot in Beasley's private office.

Cardoni

Above left: Jim Beasley's T-6 on the deck of the U.S.S. Carl Vinson in September 1995 on the occasion of the 50th anniversary of Pearl Harbor.

Above right: Beasley in the mid 1980s in the cockpit of his P-51 Mustang, the Bald Eagle.

Opposite: Beasley trailing smoke from his T-6 as he flies over Pennsylvania in 2002.

Cardoni

Top: The head of a cape buffalo bagged by Jim Beasley during a 1967 safari in the Serengeti Plain.

Above: Beasley's collection of silk designer ties, which were often conversation pieces for Philadelphia jurors.

Opposite: Jim Beasley, in suspenders, flanked by Jim Jr. and Slade McLaughlin, pose in Beasley's law library for a front-page photo in the Jan. 28, 2002 edition of the Philadelphia Inquirer. Beasley had just filed a wrongful death lawsuit against Osama bin Laden, al-Qaeda and the Taliban.

Above: Jim and Helen Beasley pose for a photographer in 2003.

Next page: Jim Beasley in shirtsleeves working in his office in 2001. His gold tie is covered with monkeys.

behind the other, about 30 yards apart, "in trail," or blowing white smoke. Each pilot had his eyes locked on the plane in front of him. It was hard to judge distances between planes until Caldarale got the idea of painting two grease marks on each windshield to show where the next pilot's wingspan would fit into from a distance of 30 yards. (The grease marks were later replaced by two pieces of black tape.)

The lead pilot would say over the VHF radio, "Push over now," and all four planes would go into a dive to get their speed up to 200 miles an hour so they could pull a loop. "Pull now," the lead would say, and all four pilots would begin the loop. They'd be flying straight towards the ground when the lead pilot would say, "Rolling left now" and everybody would pull a quarter-roll, to fly away from the crowd. The four planes would line up wing to wing and then pull another quarter-roll to fly back toward the crowd in their trademark diamond-shaped formation, trailing white smoke.

The tricky part was in the loops when the planes flew upside down, and the pilots were unable to see each other, so it was a totally blind maneuver. The in-trail loop had a short but popular run at air shows. "It was so hairy and so wild, we stopped doing it while we were all still alive," Caldarale said.

Another signature move for the Six of Diamonds flight team was the "squirrel cage loop" where all four planes followed each other in a loop, trailing white smoke. The "bomb burst" featured four T-6 pilots flying in tight formation before they peeled off in different directions. Another stunt was to have three planes use their white smoke trails to create heart shapes or clover shapes in the sky that a trailing T-6 pilot would then blast through. The "roll-around" featured three pi-lots flying slowly in a tight formation, with the landing gear down, while one pilot flew at full speed pulling big loops around the formation.

"It requires a lot of practice," Caldarale said. "We'd go out every weekend and fly two dozen loops till I was half crazy. We looped our asses off."

• • •

Joe Scogna, trauma neurosurgeon, recalled his fellow doctors warning him about the most dangerous medical malpractice lawyer in town, some lunatic named Beasley.

"Don't ever go up against him," Scogna remembers the doctors saying. "If he ever gets you on the stand, hell, he'll cut your balls off and stuff 'em right down your throat."

But Scogna and Beasley had something in common: a love of flying. Scogna grew up around the Warminster Naval Air Station, and if he had passed the vision test, he would have become a military pilot in a minute, and never given a thought to medical school.

Scogna, the son of a janitor, became a successful neurosurgeon, but he never lost the urge to fly. He took lessons as a pilot and then bought a P-51 Mustang, even though he didn't know how to fly it. One day, Scogna was at the Cape May Airport when he saw Beasley and Caldarale hopping out of their T-6s.

The doctor walked over and introduced himself. Beasley was standing on the wing of his airplane. "He jumped down and shook my hand," Scogna recalled. "From that moment on, I really liked the guy."

Beasley took Scogna up in the T-6, and when he became proficient, Beasley taught him how to fly the Mustang.

"It was an unlikely friendship; he's a malpractice lawyer and I'm a doctor," Scogna said. "He wasn't what your typical high-powered medical malpractice lawyer would be. Some of those guys are irritating and self-centered and obnoxious. This guy was not like that. He was soft-spoken, he was a real gentleman. He wasn't puffed up.

"I never saw him talk down to anybody," Scogna said. Beasley would occasionally ask Scogna's opinion about a potential malpractice case. "He had absolute integrity," Scogna said. "If I said you've got no case, he would drop it."

Whenever Scogna called Beasley's law office, he was put right through. The doctor asked Beasley if he had a minute, and Beasley replied, "For you, Joe, I've got all the time in the world."

"He was almost like a father figure to me," Scogna said. When word got around that Scogna was hanging with Beasley, "I got some hostile reactions from doctors that I was friends with.

"You don't know the guy," Scogna would say, but some doctors stopped talking to him.

But when Scogna went out for a drink, he preferred the company of his favorite medical malpractice lawyer. "He's a helluva lot smarter," Scogna said, "and he could talk about anything."

On weekends, Scogna dropped by Beasley's hangar at the Northeast Philly airport, where Beasley hung out with his son, talking airplanes. Other pilot buddies would stop by.

"He looked like any other dirtball in a ball cap and a single-piece green flight suit," Scogna said of Beasley. Another regular was Bud Nadler, a maintenance man who swore all the time. Nobody remembered how Bud joined the club. "He just liked airplanes, and he sort of wandered in one day and became part of the fraternity," Scogna said. "He was like a mascot."

In contrast to Beasley's elegant law office, his airplane hangar "was like a slum," Scogna said. "You'd sit on a stuffed parachute. It was real bare and a little smelly."

When they weren't hanging out at Beasley's hangar, the warbird pilots were flying off to air shows in places such as Oshkosh, Wis., and Geneseo, N.Y.

"It was really a guy thing, like when you were in college and all the guys go out for a beer or steaks on the grill," Scogna said. "It was just fun; there's a collegiality about it that I never had with anything else. I guess it's the kind of feeling you get on a football team."

Scogna got hooked on formation flying. "I felt more of a sense of accomplishment doing that well than doing brain surgery."

At the air shows, Beasley and his flying buddies ran into a lot of plane nuts and old pilots. "The veterans you would see with tears in their eyes," Scogna recalled. Once, at the Dover Air Show, "I had a guy who was in a wheelchair come up to me; he had flown Mustangs in World War II." Scogna asked the old pilot when was the last time he'd sat in a Mustang, and the guy said it'd been half a century, but that he couldn't fly anymore because he was paralyzed from the waist down.

So Scogna and his fellow pilots picked the guy up and hoisted him into the Mustang cockpit. "He was bawling," Scogna recalled. "It was a privilege; I felt honored by these people."

At the air shows, after the flying was done, Beasley's pilot buddies, ranging in age between 40 and 70, would all go out to dinner. "We'd stuff six or eight guys in a car like college kids," Scogna said, "all in our flight suits smelling like who knows what."

· · ·

"DAD TAUGHT ME HOW TO FLY," JIM JR. SAID. "INITIALLY, I WASN'T ALL THAT SERIOUS about it. I did it because Dad wanted me to do it."

Jim Jr. soloed in a Cessna at 16. Two years later, he gave the T-6 a try. He was in his second year of college and trying to live down his reputation with his father as "the 18-year-old asshole with the bong in his hand."

They would meet at 6 a.m. at the Northeast Philly airport in the dead of winter. "It was freezing," Jim Jr. recalled. He sat in front of the T-6 trainer while his father sat in back and barked orders.

"It's really hard to learn to fly in," Jim Jr. said of the T-6. "It's a tail-dragger, you can't really see over the nose." The gyroscopic effect of the propeller can pull the plane to the left, so the pilot has to compensate by using the right rudder to keep it straight. Jim Jr. also worried about wrecking his father's expensive plane.

"He was in some ways desperate to share this cool thing with me," Jim Jr. said. But as a teenager, Jim Jr. was caught between a desire to please his father and a desire to be independent. "That created a very volatile environment between the two of us."

"What the hell's wrong with you?" Beasley would snap. "What the hell are you doing? Pay attention!"

One morning at 6, father and son were out on Runway 24 at the Northeast

Philly airport, practicing takeoffs and landings, and it wasn't going well. Jim Jr. wasn't comfortable flying on a windy day, and on several practice landings, he bounced the plane.

"Pull over," his father barked. He climbed out of the back seat and walked across the wing of the plane. In those days, Beasley had a silver moustache. He had on his flight jacket, gloves, and a baseball cap. He stood on the wing, turned back toward his son, and gave him a one-word command: "Go," he said. And then Beasley hopped off the wing and walked away.

"What the fuck?" Jim Jr. yelled, but his father was firm. "Just go," he said.

Jim Jr. radioed the tower for permission to take off, which was granted. So while Jim Jr. soloed for the first time, his father watched from the ground.

"I was nervous," Jim Jr. said. "I didn't think I was ready." But that day he did three takeoffs and three landings, with a minimum of bouncing.

When he touched down for the last time, Jim Jr. found his father surrounded by airport security officers. The tower had noticed Beasley standing by the runway, and had dispatched several big yellow security vans. The officers yelled at Beasley to get off the runway, but he stood his ground.

"How the hell else am I supposed to solo my kid?" Beasley said.

· · ·

"HE ALWAYS RODE JIMMY," JOE SCOGNA SAID. "HE EXPECTED SO MUCH OF HIM."

Scogna recalled one year when Beasley flew his Mustang back early from the Geneseo Air Show in upstate New York. The weather was turning bad, and Beasley kept calling Jim Jr. to find out if he had taken off in time to miss the storm. "He was really worried," Scogna said. "The weather was coming in real quickly."

Beasley always had Jim Jr. call him every time he flew solo, so the father would know that the son had landed safely.

"I told that goddamn kid," Beasley muttered as he paced the ground and tapped the cell phone, with no answer. Then, Scogna watched as Beasley heard the familiar overhead roar of a Mustang.

"Here comes Jimmy rolling that Mustang around in a tight turn and his father looked up," Scogna recalled, and "that tough old bird" had tears in his eyes, tears of relief. But he kept muttering "that goddamn kid."

· · ·

DAN CALDARALE WAS OUT ON A BOAT FISHING ONE DAY WHEN BEASLEY STARTED BITCHING about "that goddamn kid." Caldarale cut Beasley off by telling him he was "just a dumb shit."

"Since you brought it up, it's time to lighten the fuck up," Caldarale yelled at

Beasley. "Jimmy lifts weights like you; he flies like you. He went to goddamn medical school like you wanted him to . . . and he also went to law school. What the fuck else do you want?"

Beasley mulled it over. "I guess you're right," he said.

• • •

BEASLEY WAS FLYING A BORROWED RUSSIAN MIG-15 OVER RENO ON AUG. 24, 1989, engaging in a practice dogfight with F-4 Phantoms from the Nevada Air Guard. When the dogfight was over, Beasley tried to land his Russian fighter jet, but the air brakes failed. After descending from an altitude of at least 15,000 feet, the MiG-15 was traveling more than 100 miles an hour when it skidded over the landing strip and crashed into a ravine overlooking a crowded highway.

The Reno Gazette-Journal reported the accident in its Aug. 25, 1989, edition, saying "no one was injured and the plane suffered only a few dents and a flat tire." But Beasley, who declined comment to the newspaper, had suffered compression fractures in two vertebrae.

Most men injured that badly would have checked themselves into a hospital. Beasley, however, insisted on taking a red-eye commercial flight back to Philadelphia.

"He broke his back; the injury was severe," recalled girlfriend Nicole Chabat. But Jim Beasley, ace medical malpractice lawyer, had a lifelong fear of hospitals. It was his nightmare that he would end up at the mercy of some doctor he had nailed in a malpractice case.

"He was petrified the doctors he sued would get even, so he would never go to the hospital," Chabat said. When Beasley arrived in Philadelphia, "he couldn't move," Chabat said. "He must have been in unbelievable pain. He was taking huge amounts of painkillers."

A large hematoma developed on Beasley's back. His face was gray, but he still refused to seek medical attention. A panicked Chabat called Beasley's flying buddy, Joe Scogna, also a trauma neurosurgeon, and Scogna made an emergency call to Beasley.

"He was in a lot of pain," Scogna said. "People cry with that kind of pain." Beasley, however, was stoic, but Scogna told him that his life was in danger, and then he talked Beasley into going to Bryn Mawr Hospital. When the doctor on call heard who was in the emergency room, Scogna recalled, he said, "Give him to somebody else, I'm not treating him."

Beasley's medical problems went beyond his broken back. He had taken so many Percocets that his intestines stopped working. He had developed an ileus, or paralysis of the bowels. But, before his trip to the hospital, that didn't prevent Beasley from taking his son out for a spicy last supper, a burrito at a Mexican restaurant.

But when you try to eat with an ileus, it only makes you nauseous. So, when Beasley arrived at Bryn Mawr Hospital, they had to run a tube down his nose to drain his stomach. Gerald F. Kaplan, an associate at Beasley's law firm, and also a doctor, stopped by to see how the boss was doing.

"He was lying in a hospital, helpless," Kaplan recalled. "He's pale and he's ashen, and he looked 30 years older. He was a mess, and he was feeling as bad as a human being can feel."

Kaplan clasped Beasley's hand. "Jim, it's Gerry Kaplan." He took a cool washcloth and sponged off Beasley's face, neck and back. Kaplan explained to Beasley the condition he had, the ileus, and told him, "You're gonna be OK."

Then, as he was leaving, Kaplan felt so bad for Beasley that he impulsively kissed the boss on the forehead. Beasley recoiled, and Kaplan knew he had made a mistake. "He didn't have room in his armor for another human being," Kaplan said. "He cringed from it and withdrew. It kind of gave me a chill. I had stepped over the line."

Beasley stayed in the hospital for a week, but then his paranoia took over. "It was clear the minute he started regaining his facilities, he was not going to hang around the hospital because they were going to kill him," Chabat said. When she came to visit him, Beasley told her, "That's it, help me get dressed.... I'm signing myself out. Here's the release; I'm gone."

Beasley had to wear a back brace for months, even in the courtroom. He recovered from the stress fractures, but there was one lasting repercussion.

"He lost a couple of inches" in height, Chabat said. "He did shrink."

Then Beasley started wearing cowboy boots.

"That could be why he made it a habit to wear those cowboy boots," Chabat said. "That cowboy thing came out of nowhere. He certainly wasn't a cowboy before."

• • •

WITHOUT WARNING, BEASLEY THE PILOT WOULD SOMETIMES MORPH BACK TO BEASLEY the lawyer. And for the people around him, there was hell to pay.

On July 10, 1992, Beasley, Jim Jr. and Ed Shipley were scheduled to fly with the Six of Diamonds in the Armed Forces Air Show at the Scranton-Wilkes-Barre International Airport. Airport officials had asked Beasley to bring along his MiG-15 jet. But the day of the air show, it rained, and the crowd was small.

Beasley asked an airport official where they wanted him to park the MiG, and according to Shipley, the official responded, "Ahh, we don't need it, you can just go home."

Beasley, acting "just as pleasant as can be," Shipley said, reminded the airport official that the air show sponsors had agreed to an oral contract to pay Beasley

$3,000 for the MiG to appear, plus $1,000 to cover fuel costs. Just pay my fuel expenses, Beasley said.

But the airport official didn't agree. "The guy just dusts Jim off," Shipley recalled, saying, "I feel bad for you, but that's show biz, a lot of shows get rained out." The official said he couldn't afford to pay Beasley his expense money, and when Beasley pressed him further, the official said, "I really can't help you with that."

Beasley showed the official several air show posters that advertised his MiG, but the official had heard enough. "Hey, look," he told Beasley, "if you've got a problem with that, *sue me.*"

"Thank you very much," Beasley said, and then he walked out the door without saying another word. When Shipley caught up with him, Beasley just had "this glow on his face, this peaceful look of almost like Christmas Day," Shipley recalled. "I'm the last person in the world that you ever want to say that to," Beasley told Shipley.

A month later, Beasley filed a lawsuit against six members of the Airport Bi-County Board of Commissioners, as well as both Lackawanna and Luzerne Counties. He also had liens placed on each of the commissioners' houses. When one commissioner tried to take out a mortgage, he was denied because of Beasley's lien. Beasley also generated more than $50,000 in legal bills for the defendants.

In a deposition, Wyrewood A. Gowell, assistant airport director and business manager, testified that Dan Dameo had warned him that stiffing Beasley wasn't a good idea.

"Dan said unequivocally that, 'No, no, Jim is in bad humor. He's got a divorce, he's got heart problems; he's not feeling well,'" Gowell testified. He ruefully repeated the last warning he got from Dameo: "You know Jim, he's a pisser."

"They finally got to the point where they were desperate to get out of it," recalled Shipley, a witness in the case. "He [Beasley] was like a cat that had a mouse under his paw."

In his lawsuit, Beasley had asked for $3,000 plus interest. Two years later, in 1994, an arbitrator awarded Beasley $2,500, but Beasley filed an appeal in 1995, upping his request to $4,000. They still owe me money, he told his flying buddies. The case was finally settled in 1999 for $3,000.

• • •

BEASLEY'S CAREER AS AN AIR SHOW PILOT EFFECTIVELY ENDED ON AUG. 10, 1992, WHEN he had his triple coronary-bypass operation. Air show pilots are required to have a class two commercial pilot's license because they're paid for performing. Beasley had the commercial pilot's license, but because of his heart condition, he was downgraded to a class three medical certificate. The only way the 66-year-old

Beasley could retain his commercial pilot's license was to undergo a painful cardiac catheterization, but he was unwilling to go through with it.

It was a tough time for Beasley. "I saw him right after the heart surgery," Nicole Chabat said. Beasley had suffered a postoperative hemorrhage at the Cleveland Clinic Hospital and had to be taken back to the operating room, where, according to medical records, doctors had to cauterize and suture his chest cavity to control the bleeding.

"The surgery was done improperly, and he almost bled to death," Chabat said. Somebody had even written "malpractice lawyer" on the top of Beasley's medical chart, but it didn't spare Beasley. The heart surgery confirmed Beasley's paranoia regarding the medical profession. "All his life," Chabat said, "he was afraid that somebody would get even."

When Chabat saw Beasley after the surgery, he was white-faced and moving gingerly. "They nearly killed me," Chabat recalled Beasley telling her.

By that time, Beasley's romance with Chabat was on hiatus. "We were just friends, not close friends," Chabat said. "We had dinner three months after the surgery, and he still looked awful. I was shocked by his appearance. He was kind of like a beat-up warrior, and he knew at this stage his life was going in the wrong direction."

But Beasley's ex-wife Helen said that Beasley may have contributed to his own troubles. Helen, who stayed with Beasley during the surgery, said that he was taking aspirin right up until the operation, which may have contributed to the bleeding.

Despite his health problems, however, Beasley continued to fly with his son on weekends. They had different styles. The father was an aggressive and instinctual pilot, much the way he acted in the courtroom. The son was more cautious and technical in nature, and depended on advance planning.

While Beasley left the air shows behind, his son got more heavily involved. Jim Jr. and Ed Shipley began flying with U.S. Air Force pilots in 1996, and a year later, they helped found the Heritage Flight to commemorate the 50th anniversary of the U.S. Air Force. Jim Jr. was designated by the U.S. Air Force Air Combat Command as one of only a dozen civilian warbird pilots in the country authorized to fly the Heritage Flight with Air Force fighter jet pilots.

The Heritage Flight featured vintage warbirds such as the P-51 Mustang and the F-86 Sabre, which flew in the Korean War, alongside modern fighters such as the F-16 Viper, the F-15 Eagle, and the F-22 Raptor.

"Even people inoculated against nostalgia react emotionally when they see the old airplanes with the modern fighters, and more so when they know some of the civilians flying the warbirds," the magazine Air Show World noted in 2002.

Other founding civilian pilots on the Heritage Flight included former astronauts Bill Anders and Frank Borman, and Chuck Yeager, the test pilot who broke the sound barrier. When the Heritage Flight formed in 1996, Jim Jr., at 29, was the team's youngest civilian pilot.

The Heritage Flight performed at 100 air shows in 2002, attended by nine million spectators. On Memorial Day 2006, Jim Jr. led the Heritage Flight into New York City, flying lead in the Bald Eagle. He was flanked by an F-15 Eagle, an F-16 Viper and an A-10 Warthog, as they flew up the East River, past the George Washington Bridge. Then Jim Jr. led the team down the Hudson River, past Yankee Stadium, Manhattan and the Statue of Liberty.

That wasn't all the formation flying that Jim Jr. was involved in. When the Six of Diamonds broke up in the 1990s, Jim Jr. and Shipley kept flying their Mustangs as members of the Four Horsemen, which also included Dan Caldarale. The pilots even talked about having Beasley share one team position on the right wing with Jim Jr.

The Four Horsemen gave Beasley a black team flight jacket, which he proudly wore, but he never flew with the team. They also invited Beasley to every air show as a spectator, but once you've been a player, it's hard to take a seat in the stands.

"He would always come up with a reason why he couldn't make it, or he'd pick a fight with me and he wouldn't go," Jim Jr. ruefully recalled. "We got to the point where we were doing stuff that nobody else in the world was doing, and it was kind of frustrating not to be able to share it."

Beasley continued to fly formation on weekends with his son and other members of the Four Horsemen. He told his buddies he didn't miss the air shows. "I'd much rather go to the airport and fly for as long as I want than go to the air show and hang out all day and fly for 20 minutes," he would say. When he did fly formation, however, he sometimes found it a challenge to keep up with younger pilots.

On one formation flight in 1998, Jim Jr. was leading three T-6s. He was performing some gentle turns when he heard his 72-year-old father bark into the radio that he wasn't calling out the maneuvers before he flew them.

Jim Jr. got irritated and snapped back over the radio, "Just follow me. I can't hold your hand forever." It was a comment he regretted as soon as he made it.

Once, Jim Beasley had taught his son how to fly, but then he was eclipsed by him. For both men, it was a painful moment.

Chapter 16

❖❖❖

THE PENIS CASE

T HE PLAINTIFF IN THE MEDICAL MALPRACTICE CASE, A SUBURBAN DISTRICT JUSTICE listed fictitiously in court records as "John Doe," claimed that after he underwent an adult circumcision, the skin on his penis was so tight, he was unable to achieve a normal erection. Proving truth was stranger than fiction, the name of the urologist accused of allegedly slashing too much foreskin was Dr. David M. Raezer.

On Aug. 31, 1993, jurors in Philadelphia's Common Pleas Court were having no trouble staying awake for the case of *Doe v. Raezer*, especially after Jim Beasley called his star witness.

"Jane Doe," who had filed a claim for lost consortium, took the stand to testify about her unsatisfying love life. The plump middle-aged woman was feeling nauseous and had tears in her eyes.

"I know based on your past conversations that it's going to be very difficult for you," Beasley said, eyeing the witness.

"Yes," Jane Doe replied.

"It won't take long," Beasley said. "I'm going to ask you a few questions. I want you, if you can and will, to give the jury a description of the sex life that you had with your husband, OK? Are you a little nervous?"

"Yes," said Jane Doe, who was so pale she looked as if she was about to pass out.

"I want you to just relax," Beasley said. "I put water up there if you want to stop and have some water."

While Jane Doe took a drink, Beasley changed the subject.

Q. "How long have you and your husband been married?"

A. "Thirty-five years."

Q. "And when did the marriage occur?"

A. "…1958."

Q. "And at that time, how old were you?"

A. "Sixteen."

Q. And your husband was how old?"

A. "Twenty-one."

Up on the witness stand, Jane Doe started to loosen up, as if it were just she and Beasley sitting around his office, talking. Beasley asked a few more questions about when her two children were born, before returning to the main topic.

"What was your sex life like?" Beasley asked.

"It was great," Mrs. Doe blurted. "It was very good. It always has been good."

"Did you consider sex as part of that marriage?"

"The sexual act was — the culmination of our lovemaking," she said. "It was my way of committing myself to my husband; that's very important to me."

Beasley asked Mrs. Doe what her sex life was like after her husband's circumcision.

"We couldn't have any sex," she stammered. "He didn't have anything. There was nothing there. It was —"

"Why don't you take some water and relax a minute, all right?" Beasley said.

After another drink, Mrs. Doe returned to the subject of her husband's anatomy. "It looks as if his testicles and his penis was all one, and it was just like a tiny projection at the top of his testicles," she said. "I didn't know what it was supposed to look like."

Jane Doe blushed. "John's the only man that I ever knew," she said. "Anyway, there was no sex now."

· · ·

IN HIS OPENING STATEMENT TO THE JURY, BEASLEY HAD DELICATELY BROACHED THE TOPIC of the Does' sex life.

"As I mentioned to you during the voir dire, this is going to be a very, very difficult case for the Does," Beasley said. "It involves the most intimate aspects of their lives. It's not something that I would feel comfortable talking to you about if we were to meet as casual strangers," he said. "Nor would it be something that you would care to discuss with someone who was not a most intimate and close friend."

"But our justice system does not allow any other forum except this forum for someone to express their complaints about the manner in which they were treated by a physician," Beasley said. "So, therefore, notwithstanding how difficult it is for the Does, you will have an opportunity, as strangers to these people, to share with them the most intimate details of their life."

John Doe was suing Dr. Raezer for negligence, pain and suffering; the district justice also claimed he was never fully informed about the risks of surgery. Beasley told the jury that Dr. Raezer was guilty of removing too much foreskin. After the surgery, the remaining skin was so tight, there was "no allowance for projection of the penis," Beasley said, making sexual intercourse impossible.

Beasley used diagrams to explain to the jury the anatomy of the penis. "What causes an erection," he began, "is this area, which is called the corpora cavernosa —"

"Your Honor," interrupted defense lawyer James C. Stroud. "Excuse me. Could we see you at sidebar?"

The judge asked both lawyers to meet him in chambers.

"Your Honor," Stroud began. "I believe that Mr. Beasley was going into a description of the erectile function of the male penis, talking about differences in erections. And I don't believe that there's going to be any evidence in this case with regard to that, and I think that it would be improper for him to instruct the jury in an area where there will be no evidence."

The judge looked at the plaintiff's lawyer. "Mr. Beasley?"

"Your Honor," Beasley said. "First of all, this whole case revolves around an erection…. Mr. Doe must have discussed an erection 50 times in his deposition, but I am not restricted to what I have to say concerning these things…. I have a right to tell the jury what my evidence is."

The judge overruled the objection, and the trial resumed; Beasley finished his anatomy lesson. When the defense lawyer stood to make his opening statement, he countered with the fat defense.

"We are not here to mock him in any way, but Mr. Doe, as you can see, is a big fellow," Stroud said. "The evidence will show that he weighed approximately 280 pounds or more at the time of this surgery. Because of that, the circumcision, which was performed correctly, had a problem in the healing process."

Stroud denied that Dr. Raezer removed too much foreskin. He contended that after the surgery, John Doe's erection was restrained by too much fat and scar tissue.

"I think the testimony will show that his belly came down so low and his legs were such that it was actually crowding the area of his penis and his scrotum so that when the circumcision was beginning to heal, the scar tissue that formed stretched and was causing the problem," Stroud said.

The scar tissue "prevented [the penis] from being as long as it was, according to Mr. Doe, before the surgery," Stroud said.

• • •

BEASLEY ASKED JANE DOE WHAT HAPPENED AFTER DR. RAEZER TRIED TO CORRECT THE problem with the original circumcision by performing a second procedure on

Nov. 11, 1987, known as a "V-Y plasty. The procedure involved cutting a V-shaped incision to extend the skin, but resulted in a gain of only about an inch.

"Now after the Nov. 11ᵗʰ surgery," Beasley asked, "was there any significant difference . . . ?"

"It was very minimal," Mrs. Doe said. "There was just one — one position where he could — there was just one position where we could even try to have sex. It was hard. There was hardly anything there to penetrate, and he would bleed. He would get an erection, it would bleed and it was just terrible."

While he questioned Jane Doe, Beasley glanced over at the plaintiff's table and saw Justice Doe, a large, balding, middle-aged man, stand up, and with his head bowed, march right out of the courtroom.

John Doe subsequently said that he could not bear seeing the pain on his wife's face while she testified about such an intimate subject. The jurors seemed surprised as they watched the justice leave. Beasley, however, carried on as if nothing had happened.

Before the circumcision, Beasley asked, "Were you and your husband capable of having sex in more than one position?"

"Oh, of course," Mrs. Doe said.

"Were you restricted to any one position?"

"No," Mrs. Doe said.

"Could you have it in any position that you felt like at the moment?"

"Yes," she said.

"You just told the folks on the jury that after the second surgery there was only one position . . . that you can have sex," Beasley said. "Would you mind telling us what that is?"

Mrs. Doe struggled to keep her composure. "It's on the edge of the bed," she said. "I can't describe."

"When you say 'the edge of the bed,' was it any particular portion of the bed?" Beasley asked.

"Yeah, the corner of the bed. He just —"

The only position that worked was when Mrs. Doe laid on the edge of the bed with her legs apart, while the justice had to stand.

"And was there any penetration?," Beasley asked.

"Very minimal," a blushing and stammering Mrs. Doe said. "He can't — because there's just —"

"How does that make you feel?" Beasley asked.

"I feel very frustrated," Mrs. Doe said. "I feel very sorry for him because I know it hurts him."

"Have you said anything to him about that?"

"About not — about what, not being satisfied?"

"Yes."

"I don't have to," Jane Doe said. "We've been married for 35 years and I wouldn't say that to him anyway. He knows."

"Has you or your husband's desire to have sex been diminished in any way because of this?" Beasley asked.

"It's not — it's not very satisfactory," Jane Doe said. "Our sex isn't satisfactory at all. What penis he has, has hair all around it. I don't know what else to answer you."

On cross-examination, the defense lawyer made the mistake of asking Jane Doe if her husband wore a condom during sex.

"The condom wouldn't stay on," she said. "That was part of the problem, too."

"So he would put a condom on, but it wouldn't stay on?" the defense lawyer asked, setting himself up for another hit.

"No," Mrs. Doe said, "because there was nothing to stay on to."

• • •

MEN IN THE COURTROOM WINCED AS JUSTICE DOE TESTIFIED ABOUT THE INTIMATE details of his painful procedure.

"Did there come an occasion during your visits to Dr. Raezer that you complained about the length of your penis?" Beasley said.

"Yes," John Doe said.

Beasley asked the plaintiff to tell the jury the particulars of that complaint.

"I expressed that prior to the operation, I had approximately 6½ inches of penis" when erect, the witness said.

"Now, I am asking you, after the surgery, did you give him [the urologist] any type of measurement as to the length of your penis when erect?" Beasley asked.

The witness held up one hand. "I had indicated that it came to the middle of the third finger, measuring from the bottom up, which was slightly over two inches," John Doe said.

"What was the condition that you had that eventually led you to see Dr. Raezer?" Beasley asked.

"When I urinated, the urine wouldn't completely leave me," the justice said. "Sometimes I would go to the bathroom and close up and go about my business and find that urine would leak out to the amount that it would be on my pants and [be] very embarrassing, especially if I had gone to the bathroom at a restaurant or in public."

That's how Justice Doe ended up in the office of Dr. Raezer. The urologist suggested an adult circumcision. The justice asked how painful it would be. According to the justice, the doctor said that at most, the pain would only last a week. "He said, 'You will be in discomfort, but it's really a simple procedure. Don't worry about it,' " the justice quoted the doctor as saying.

The district justice testified that he had to wait two months after the circumcision of July 1987 before he was finally given permission by his urologist to have sex again.

"Were you able to penetrate your wife?" Beasley asked.

"No," the justice said.

"Did you make an effort?"

"Yes."

The justice told Beasley he became so frustrated that prior to his second operation in November 1987, he angrily asked Dr. Raezer, "What the hell did you do to me?" The justice described how after the second procedure, the V-Y plasty, done without antibiotics, he suffered an infection and had to take a 40-minute Epsom salts bath as hot as he could stand, four times a day.

"Did you follow those instructions?" Beasley asked.

"To the tune of over a hundred pounds of Epsom salts," the judge said.

But the second surgery left even more scar tissue. The testicles had attached to the back of the head of his penis, so there was hair on the shaft. The result of both operations was, "I couldn't have penetration," the justice said. "The closeness of our sexual contact isn't as it was before. It's quite hampered and diminished."

"Can you tell me whether it goes to the heart of your manliness?" Beasley asked.

"Yes," the justice said. "Well, it's one of the functions a man enjoys through life, and it's just not there — it's just not there."

On cross-examination, defense attorney Stroud asked the district justice how often he and his wife had sex prior to the circumcision. Twice a week, the justice said. Stroud asked whether two months after the operation, the justice was able to obtain an erection.

"The erection that I obtained was inside me and not coming out," the justice said. "It didn't come out far enough to make penetration."

· · ·

"JIM LOVED THIS CASE," RECALLED GERALD F. KAPLAN, M.D., A FORMER SURGEON AND lawyer who was Beasley's cocounsel in *Doe v. Raezer*. "It's about penises, it's about sex. I worked the file for three years. He didn't even see the fucking file until two weeks before trial."

The case had sex appeal, but Kaplan had a difficult time finding a urologist who would back the plaintiff's story and testify against a fellow urologist in court. Kaplan finally talked his old urology professor into being an expert witness. Dr.

Nicholas Varano was a retired clinical professor of urology at Jefferson University Medical Hospital. He testified from a set of facts cobbled together from old medical textbooks from the 1930s that the doctor had stored in his garage.

Just before the trial, however, Dr. Varano had a stroke and was not well enough to appear in court. Kaplan had to take a deposition from the doctor, so he spent two days prepping him.

At the deposition, Dr. Varano suffered from slurred speech, but Beasley and Kaplan knew a transcript would not record hesitations or garbled words. For much of the deposition, Dr. Varano read slowly from medical records and reports.

"Jim had a horrifically bad expert; the guy was a very bad witness because of his age," recalled defense lawyer Stroud, who was at the deposition. "I think they were afraid he would be horribly incapacitated and they couldn't get anyone else."

But it didn't end up hurting Beasley's case. At trial, Beasley put Kaplan on the stand, and Beasley asked the questions from the deposition, and he had Kaplan read Dr. Varano's answers into the record. Dr. Varano had testified that before the circumcision, John Doe suffered from inflammation of the head of the penis; he also had scar tissue on a tight, contracting foreskin caused by diabetes.

In the case of inflammation brought about by diabetes, a circumcision is a dangerous procedure, Dr. Varano testified, because the inflamed skin is wrinkled, and, "You usually remove too much skin."

Dr. Varano testified that according to a pathology report, Dr. Raezer removed two inches of inflamed skin. "Two inches is two inches," Dr. Varano said. "But it's wrinkled skin, so he's taking off a little bit more than two inches."

When he finished reading Dr. Varano's testimony into the record, Kaplan breathed a sigh of relief. "The slickest lawyer move," he said, "was obtaining trial testimony from a professional witness that couldn't speak a sentence."

· · ·

DAVID M. RAEZER, M.D., WAS A 1964 GRADUATE OF HARVARD UNIVERSITY AND A 1968 graduate of the University of Pennsylvania School of Medicine. One morning, just before court, the doctor introduced his family to the jury. The family included a son who was a student at Harvard Medical School, and a thin, chic wife, who arrived at the last minute, looking as if she had just stepped off Fifth Avenue.

"Your timing is impeccable," the doctor told his wife.

When he took the stand, Dr. Raezer testified that Justice Doe was difficult to examine "because of the patient's weight."

"The driving force of the problem is the fat pushing out on the penis," the doctor explained. Fat can also contribute to psychological problems, the doctor testified. "As the amount of fat increases, one's perception of their penis decreases."

When Beasley cross-examined Dr. Raezer, he asked his opinion of a medical textbook, *Campbell's Urology*.

"Well, I think it's considered the gold standard of the textbooks of urology," the doctor replied. "There aren't many."

Beasley read aloud from the gold standard: "One of the most distressing problems we see is a patient who complains that the surgeon has removed too much skin.... The circumcision should be done precisely, and whatever procedure is to be carried out, the incisions should first be marked with the skin lying undistorted to the shaft."

"Do you understand," Beasley said to the doctor, "that in this case your testimony to this jury is that you eyeballed the area that you were going to cut?"

"Yes," the doctor said.

"And the gold standard says that it's important that the area should be marked on the undistorted shaft?" Beasley said. "Now why do you think that they put that in this text?"

"I think they're trying to address that to people who have done many — less circumcisions than I have," the doctor smugly replied.

"So, this gold standard text applies to everyone else but you, is that what you're telling this jury?" Beasley said.

The doctor responded with a rambling answer that ended with, "Putting a mark on the skin is certainly a help, if you feel you need it."

"Well, you didn't feel you needed it here, you just eyeballed it," Beasley said. "Is that correct?"

"Let me just say 'just eyeballed it' is a derogatory term, which I don't like," said the doctor, who appeared agitated. "Because all you do is when you put a pen on it is just eyeball it. You don't do it any different with a pen than you do with your scissors." So, "just eyeballing it" with a pen or a scissors makes "absolutely no difference," the doctor declared, his voice rising.

"I want you to calm down," Beasley told the defendant.

•   •   •

JIM BEASLEY WAS ALWAYS SUSPICIOUS OF LAWYERS WHO WERE ALSO DOCTORS, BECAUSE he thought they would be too sympathetic to doctor-defendants.

That's why Beasley had his doubts about Gerald F. Kaplan, M.D. And he was right. Thirteen years after the trial of *Doe v. Raezer*, Kaplan still felt sorry for Dr. Raezer. "I felt sorry for all my defendants," said Kaplan, who worked for Beasley for seven years before being fired in 1994. "I know I'm gonna put together a little theater act that's gonna make them look bad."

A trial, Kaplan shrugged, boils down to staging "a play with no dress rehearsal" for the benefit of a dozen people that you'd run into "at a bus stop." And doctors usually play right into it.

"Doctors," Kaplan said, shaking his head, "they're not well-grounded people. They're always looking over their shoulders. Every doctor fits that pattern. They've bought into a super-smart, superhuman image of themselves, but inside they know the truth, and they always worry about being found out.

"They can't transpose to the other side of the desk," Kaplan said. "They never understand what it's like to be a patient, or what it's like to be a human being."

If doctors could admit to a mistake, a jury might forgive them. But by denying their weaknesses, and their humanity, Kaplan said, they play right into the hands of smart trial lawyers like Beasley.

• • •

BEASLEY READ THE PROCEDURE FOR A CIRCUMCISION FROM A MEDICAL TEXTBOOK AND deliberately mispronounced the medical term "bleeders vulgarated." It was a common tactic of Beasley's, meant to offend, and Dr. Raezer bit.

"You kill the medical language, you really do," Dr. Raezer said. "If you would like me to read it, I would be happy to."

"Would you be kind enough to do that?" replied Beasley. The doctor read the explanation of the procedure to the jury. Beasley then asked Dr. Raezer about his consultation with the patient before surgery: "Now, at this initial meeting, what risk did you tell Mr. Doe that he might have to accept?"

"I explained to the judge that he would have the risk of infection and bleeding; I explained to him that he has diabetes," the doctor said. "And I told him also — he was overweight, as you know, I had mentioned to you earlier — that I specifically avoided what I consider sort of an argumentative or inflammatory term, 'obesity,' and I told him — he had the risk of complications on that basis."

Beasley asked when the doctor brought up the weight issue.

"When I was examining him," the doctor said. "As I mentioned to you, when I examined him, one had to be impressed because as I sat like this to examine him, I literally could not see his penis because of the fat."

"And I assume that in your career as a urological surgeon, you have operated on men's penises who have been overweight?" Beasley asked.

"Yes, but may I explain?" the doctor said, before proceeding to take another swipe at the plaintiff. "The judge did represent extraordinary amounts of fat."

Over at the plaintiff's table, Jane Doe felt that the defense had gone too far. "Just because we're fat, that doesn't mean we can't enjoy each other?" she would say in a subsequent interview.

Beasley read excerpts from a deposition Dr. Raezer had made in the case, but the doctor complained that the transcript contained an "overwhelming" number of errors, too many for him to correct. When Beasley asked the doctor to give some examples of those errors, the doctor complained that he was quoted repeatedly in the transcript as saying "yeah."

"You don't say yeah?" Beasley asked incredulously.

""No," the doctor replied. "I say 'Yes.' We come from a different background, Mr. Beasley."

For Beasley, the former Temple University graduate, this was a gift. "I didn't go to Harvard, if that's what you are saying," Beasley said, playing to the jurors, most of whom didn't go to Harvard either.

"No," the doctor said.

"I didn't go to Harvard," Beasley repeated, in case anyone missed the point. "Apologize to you for that, Dr. Raezer."

Beasley went over one exchange in the deposition transcript between a lawyer and Dr. Raezer:

Q. "So the suture line was incorporated in the area of fixture, is that right?"

A. "Yeah," the doctor was quoted as responding.

"If I change the 'yeah' to a Harvard 'yes,' would you agree with it?" Beasley asked.

"Yes," Dr. Raezer replied, "with the stipulation that it's a fixation, not a fixture," the doctor said, correcting the medical terminology.

When Dr. Raezer brought up the fat issue again, Beasley asked, "Well, you didn't refuse to operate on this man because he was either diabetic or obese, did you?"

"No, but I specifically told him, and I am glad you are bringing the attention of everybody to that, that, you know, that he was diabetic and he was obese and he could expect additional problems based upon that," Dr. Raezer said.

The doctor was testifying about the justice's "fat and all that was driving distally" on the penis when Judge Thomas B. Rutter wearily asked, "Mr. Beasley, do I perceive we're moving on to another aspect of your examination?"

"Well, do you mean if we're leaving the penis, no sir," Beasley replied. "But we're going to another subject —"

"With respect, I am reminded of James Thurber, who had a favorite niece, to whom he gave a book on penguins," Judge Rutter said from the bench. The judge said that Thurber once asked his niece, "'Janey, how did you like the book on penguins?' and she said, 'It told me more about penguins than I wanted to know.'

"I rather suspect that the jury and I are learning more about [penises] than we ever thought we really needed to know," the judge said before declaring a recess.

Despite the judge's objections, Beasley wasn't ready to give up questioning Dr. Raezer until he made one last point. After the recess, Beasley kept firing questions at Dr. Raezer until he answered one with a "yeah." Beasley turned to the court reporter. "Would you please read back the last answer?"

The reporter read the transcript, and Beasley turned to Dr. Raezer. "I thought you said you never use the word 'yeah?' "

"I apologize," the doctor said. "I may have on that one occasion. Thank you for correcting me."

• • •

JIM WOULD GET PEOPLE TO SAY AND DO STUPID THINGS," MARVELED JUDGE RUTTER. As for Dr. Raezer, "He didn't realize that his throat had been cut until he went to shake his head and it fell off."

For years after the trial of *Doe v. Raezer*, defense lawyer Stroud said he has cautioned associates about the dangers of arrogant answers on the witness stand. The classic example he used was Dr. Raezer's testimony, or as Stroud put it, I went to Harvard and you went to Temple.

"David Raezer's a very fine surgeon, but he's a difficult guy, very opinionated," Stroud said.

• • •

ON REBUTTAL, BEASLEY BROUGHT BACK JUSTICE DOE AND ASKED IF HE HEARD DR. Raezer's testimony.

"Yes," the justice said.

"Did you hear his testimony that he discussed with you your diabetic condition and what might occur as a result of that at the time of the surgery?"

"Yes."

"Did any such conversation occur?"

"No," the justice said.

• • •

JOHN DOE HAD BEEN A DISTRICT JUSTICE FOR 25 YEARS, AND WAS USED TO WATCHING lawyers in court. But he was amazed by Beasley.

"His every movement was significant," the district justice recalled a dozen years after the trial. Beasley had a dry throat during the trial and brought some hard candies into the courtroom. "Everybody was watching him unwrap his piece of candy," the justice said. "I said to myself, he really knows how to get people's attention."

The justice said that Beasley told him to stick close to his wife during the trial. "I want you to put your arm around her during any part of the testimony that hurts," the justice recalled Beasley telling him. He followed Beasley's advice.

"It was like watching a concert," the justice marveled.

"Every movement in court had a purpose," agreed cocounsel Gerald F. Kaplan, who recalled one courtroom incident that proved the point.

Beasley's usual practice during a trial was to stay in the courtroom and work through lunch. If he had a couple of Goldenberg's Peanut Chews for a snack, Beasley would leave the wrappers out on the table, so the jury could see them.

Kaplan made the mistake of grabbing the candy wrappers off Beasley's desk and throwing them away. That's when Beasley told Kaplan, "When I want you to move something from the fucking desk, I'll tell you."

· · ·

TERRANCE R. MALLOY, M.D., WAS A YALE GRADUATE, AND CHAIRMAN OF THE DEPARTment of Urology at Pennsylvania Hospital. He was also the author of 140 publications, the team urologist for the Philadelphia Flyers, and a well-known expert witness. That's why the defense in *Doe v. Raezer* paid Dr. Malloy $350 an hour for his expert testimony.

On cross-examination, Beasley asked how much time Dr. Malloy had spent reading records in the case. Between 3½ and 4 hours, the doctor replied.

Beasley went through a list of all the medical and legal records in the case, including the complaint, three lengthy depositions and the office records from two doctors and two hospitals, and then he incredulously asked, "And you did all of that in three or four hours?"

"That's my best estimate," the doctor replied. "It might have been longer, it might have been shorter."

Beasley began quizzing the doctor on the medical records, going line by line through Dr. Raezer's difficult penmanship:

"And the next [word]?"

"I can't tell," Dr. Malloy said.

". . . The next word after 1960?"

"I can't make out that word," the doctor said.

"This word here," Beasley said. "What does that mean?"

"I said it looks like D.Z.," the doctor said. "It might be for diagnosis."

"Are you guessing?" Beasley asked.

"No," the doctor said. "I'm just saying any time you read somebody else's handwriting, you're making an impression of what they're saying."

"Your impression, that is," Beasley said. "And what's the last thing on that line?"

"It's just a scratch mark," the doctor said.

"Dr. Malloy," Beasley said, "how much of the $350 an hour was used up when you first tried to interpret these office records?... Did you get on the telephone with Dr. Raezer and say to him, 'I can't read these office records, and if I'm going to give an opinion concerning the care that you rendered Mr. Doe, I would like to know what you have down here.' Did you do that?"

"No, I didn't do that, because that would have been totally inappropriate, and you know that," Dr. Malloy angrily responded. "You look at the records and you render an independent judgment based on what you find.... So I resent the implication I'm going to be calling up a doctor and get coached through his defense. I don't do that...."

"You're assuming that if you called the doctor on the phone that you would allow him to coach you," Beasley argued. "That he could persuade you to say something that you didn't believe was true, a man with your self-professed integrity?"

"No, but it's someone like yourself [who] would be making connotations of that, that Dr. Raezer and I had somehow collaborated on his defense," Dr. Malloy responded.

Beasley asked Dr. Malloy about the scarring on Justice Doe's penis. But Dr. Malloy didn't seem too concerned with the aftereffects of the surgery; he implied that the justice's diabetic condition was to blame for his problems.

"The length of the penis in diabetics can change the longer they have the diabetes," Dr. Malloy testified. "That's one of the number one cause[s] of impotence in men."

Beasley erupted: "Is there anything in the records that says his diabetes is — he's now become impotent because of his diabetes, like you tried to tell this jury a minute ago?"

"I'm not trying to tell the jury anything, I'm just answering your questions," the doctor replied.

Beasley asked the doctor to point out where it said in the medical records that the judge's "dysfunctional problems with sex was because of diabetes?"

"It's not in those records, as I recall," the doctor replied.

Next, Beasley questioned the doctor about the second surgical procedure done on the judge, the V-Y plasty. The doctor said the procedure to lengthen the penis was done on the bottom of John Doe's organ; then changed his mind when Beasley confronted him with evidence that the procedure was done on top. Dr. Malloy tried to reconcile the difference on the witness stand by saying that according to the operation notes, two procedures were done, on both the top and bottom of Doe's penis.

"I see," Beasley said. "Tell me, where do you say that in your report.... Where do you describe the two V-Y plasties, one on the bottom and one on the top of the penis?"

"I didn't," Dr. Malloy said.

"The fact of the matter is and the truth of it is you didn't bother reading these records, the hospital records or his office records and you are willing to come into court and say anything you had to say in order to tell the jury that Dr. Raezer practiced good care," Beasley said.

That set off Dr. Malloy. "That's a lie," he fumed. "You don't sit there and characterize me as a liar. I told you I came in here after reviewing those records in good faith, and my integrity means a lot to me.... So don't sit there and tell me I'm a liar."

• • •

"HE WAS A VERY ARROGANT HAUGHTY FELLOW," SAID JUDGE RUTTER OF DR. MALLOY. "He never saw a urologist who made a mistake."

• • •

WHEN BEASLEY GAVE HIS CLOSING, HE TALKED ABOUT THE ARROGANCE OF DR. RAEZER, and the damage he had inflicted on the Does and their marriage. Beasley asked the jury to "send a message" to the arrogant doctor.

Defense lawyer Stroud objected. "It was an inappropriate comment by Mr. Beasley, and it should not be considered for any purpose whatsoever."

The judge, however, overruled the objection. "It would seem to me to be surely aggressive, but within the bounds of advocacy, and I will not say anything for the jury."

• • •

DURING THE TRIAL, BEASLEY HAD PRESENTED NO EVIDENCE OF LOST EARNINGS, OR future medical bills. The only damages the Does were seeking were for the damage done to their marriage, particularly their sex life. So when the jury announced their verdict, John and Jane Doe were struck speechless

The jury found that Justice Doe had not been advised of the "material facts, risks and complications" of the circumcision, and that Dr. Raezer's performance was below the standards of care for a urologist. The unanimous verdict: $1.5 million in damages for the justice and $750,000 for his wife.

The defendants appealed, however, and a trial motions judge decided the verdict was excessive, because the Does "have resumed regular sexual relations, albeit somewhat reduced in pleasure." So a year after the 1993 verdict, the trial motions judge reduced the award to $300,000 for John Doe and $250,000 for Jane Doe.

Beasley appealed, and the Superior Court of Pennsylvania decided in 1995 that the trial motions judge had made a mistake. In the Superior Court opinion, Judge William F. Cercone found the conclusion of the trial motions judge to be "a gross understatement of the evidence presented at trial."

The Superior Court opinion said that the botched circumcision had "imposed a dreadful and traumatic impact on the life of the family of Mr. and Mrs. John

Doe" and that the jury's verdict was "an eminently fair result." So the Superior Court reinstated the original verdict. The removal of two inches of Judge Doe's foreskin ultimately cost Dr. Raezer's insurance company $2.25 million.

· · ·

FOOTNOTE: *Incidentally, the damages for loss of consortium awarded to Mrs. Doe were for a claim that did not exist when Jim Beasley began practicing law in Pennsylvania. In a personal-injury case today, the spouse of an injured plaintiff may bring an accompanying, derivative claim for loss of consortium, or the loss of the injured spouse's companionship, affection, or support. However, under former Pennsylvania law, a wife was basically viewed as chattel; so that, while a husband could file a claim for loss of consortium, a wife could not.*

This was the law of Pennsylvania until 1974, when the Pennsylvania Supreme Court, in the case of Hopkins v. Blanco, *abolished it, and extended the same rights to the wife as to the husband. The plaintiff's attorney in* Hopkins, *who secured this right for the wife in that case, as well as for all Pennsylvania spouses in subsequent cases, was Jim Beasley.*

✦

Chapter 17

THE CONTENDER

DON KING, THE BIGGEST BOXING PROMOTER ON THE PLANET, WAS SEATED AT THE HEAD of his 30-foot conference table. His famous electric hair was standing straight up. He was dressed casually, in a Hawaiian shirt and Bermuda shorts, but since he was Don King, he also sported a diamond-studded titanium necklace and a diamond-crusted watch, and he was chewing on a fat, unlit 14-inch Cuban cigar.

It was June 9, 1997, and King was scheduled for another afternoon of legal sparring in his private office in Deerfield Beach, Fla., filled with huge, overstuffed leather chairs and a giant, framed replica of the U.S. Constitution.

King was involved in so many lawsuits and ongoing investigations that he spent more time with lawyers than boxers. The man who had beaten federal indictments for tax evasion and insurance fraud had long ago accepted endless litigation as part of the price of doing business.

King conferred briefly with two lawyers, in preparation for the day's match, a deposition he had to give in a federal case filed against him by some lawyer from Philadelphia. King didn't seem too concerned, even though a friend in the room, James J. Binns, another Philadelphia lawyer who represented the World Boxing Association (WBA), had warned King that he was about to go up against the dean of the Philadelphia bar.

Jim Beasley had flown down to Florida in his P-51 Mustang. He strolled into King's office dressed casually, in frayed jeans, a leather vest and cowboy boots. He sat down at King's conference table, and, without any introductions, proceeded to ask Binns about documents in the case that a federal judge had asked King and the WBA to produce, documents that Binns tried to explain didn't really exist.

King's conference table was filled with four lawyers, a boxer, and a boxing manager, not to mention Don King himself, but Beasley spoke only to Jimmy Binns, as if the two Philadelphia lawyers named Jim were the only two guys in the room. Nina M. Gussack, King's defense lawyer, tried to butt in, explaining that some of the documents that Beasley had requested were outside the scope of the judge's expedited order for discovery, but Beasley didn't pay any attention.

"Are you with me?" Gussack asked, but Beasley didn't respond. "Jimmy," Beasley said to Binns, continuing their private chat, "you say you don't have that?"

King, not used to being ignored, sat there silently, taking it in. When Beasley finally turned his attention to the defendant, he didn't introduce himself or waste any time on pleasantries.

"Will you give us your name, please?" Beasley began.

"I'm Donald King," said the man with the big cigar.

· · ·

A WEEK EARLIER, IN U.S. DISTRICT COURT IN PHILADELPHIA, BEASLEY HAD STOOD BEFORE Judge Norma L. Shapiro to outline his case against Don King. Beasley charged that King had conspired to manipulate the ratings of the WBA to twice deprive Beasley's client, a not-so-famous boxer named Orlin "Night Train" Norris, of a heavyweight title fight, and a chance to earn millions.

"It is our position that Don King, in conjunction with the WBA, controls the ratings," Beasley told the judge. "And we can show this factually, without any dispute, showing the way that those ratings were manipulated. Therefore, Norris has been injured."

Beasley was a novice in the treacherous world of professional boxing. He had taken the case as a favor to Scott Woodworth, Norris's manager, and the son of Beasley's favorite cousin, Walter Woodworth. So Beasley was going after the reigning godfather of the fight game, a wily ex-con the feds had tried to bring down but couldn't.

Back in his younger days when he was a gambler, Don King had served nearly four years in prison for killing a man who owed him $600. Compared to manslaughter, manipulating the WBA rankings was hardly a crime, but King had hired several lawyers to say he had nothing to do with what happened to Norris.

Before the case was over, however, Beasley would not only use the courts to bend Don King to his will, but also the entire World Boxing Association.

Beasley's associate, Michael Smerconish, took the floor, introducing two color flow charts to show Judge Shapiro how the WBA heavyweight fighter ratings had been tampered with. The charts showed that during a 14-month period from February 1996 to March 1997, Orlin Norris had taken "a tumble" in the ratings, despite winning four straight fights.

Norris' real problem was outside the ring, Smerconish said, when he signed Scott Woodworth as his manager and dropped Don King as his promoter. There was a price to pay for disrespecting the Don.

In February 1996, Norris was the No. 2 ranked heavyweight contender in the WBA. According to WBA rules, if the No. 1 spot became vacant, Norris should have moved up and been given a title bout, Smerconish said. But on two occasions during the next 14 months, while Norris was still ranked No. 2, the No. 1 spot became vacant, but Norris never moved up, and he never got that title fight.

Instead, while going 4-0 in the ring, Norris actually *dropped* in the WBA rankings, falling from the No. 2 contender in February 1996 to the No. 6 contender by March 1997.

Five of the seven fighters who passed Norris in the WBA ratings during this 14-month period didn't even have to climb in the ring. They included Evander Holyfield, who'd been inactive for five months, and "Iron Mike" Tyson, who'd been in jail for three years. Other fighters who leaped over Norris included Tony Tucker, a fighter Norris had beaten the previous year.

And what did Holyfield, Tyson and Tucker have in common? Their promoter was Don King. It was all part of a conspiracy, Beasley and Smerconish contended in their complaint, "in furtherance of Don King's personal vendetta" against Woodworth and Norris pursued for King's "own financial gain."

To show how serious they were, Beasley and Smerconish asked Judge Shapiro for a temporary restraining order to halt next month's scheduled heavyweight title bout rematch in Las Vegas between Mike Tyson and Evander Holyfield.

Smerconish contended it should have been Norris in the ring with Tyson during the previous title fight, not Holyfield. And that the WBA should not be allowed to stage another heavyweight title fight without first giving Norris his shot at the crown.

Night Train Norris was no big deal to Don King, but the Tyson-Holyfield rematch certainly was. Holyfield was the upset winner of the first fight with Tyson. The rematch was scheduled to earn a $45 million payday for Holyfield and $30 million for Tyson, Binns told the judge. Binns, who represented the WBA, looked over at Beasley. "I can remember when it used to take Mr. Beasley the first four months of the year to make $40 million," Binns cracked.

But the big winner of Holyfield-Tyson II was already clear — Don King. King owned the exclusive rights, both foreign and domestic, to promote and broadcast the fight, and those rights were worth about $100 million, Binns told the judge. And Beasley was asking the judge to stop a fight that was going to put $100 million in Don King's pocket.

The judge wasn't much of a boxing fan. "People watch boxing to be entertained and to get some kind of emotional satisfaction about seeing some people hurt other people," she said dismissively.

Judge Shapiro was ready to rule. She denied a motion by King's lawyers to dismiss Norris' suit. She also postponed a ruling on Beasley's request for a temporary restraining order to stop the Tyson-Holyfield rematch until a second hearing could be held later in the month. So as the lawyers filed out of Judge Shapiro's courtroom, Beasley's challenge to Don King's boxing empire was still alive.

• • •

BEASLEY'S DEPOSITION OF DON KING WAS "GREAT THEATER," RECALLED ATTORNEY JAMES J. Binns, because it featured "a dogged pursuer" stalking "a great evader." But Binns, a former boxer himself, was not as impressed with Beasley's client. Night Train Norris was a "dogmeat fighter," Binns said, who had padded his record with several bouts against unranked fighters. And Binns the lawyer thought even less of Norris' legal case.

Don King had signed an affidavit saying he had never spoken to anybody in the WBA about dropping Norris in the rankings. So as far as King, Binns and the WBA were concerned, Beasley's allegations about King orchestrating a conspiracy against Night Train Norris remained unproven. But that didn't matter to Judge Shapiro, who gave Beasley another hearing to argue for a halt to the Tyson-Holyfield rematch.

"Jim Beasley had this capacity to make chicken salad out of chicken shit," Binns marveled. "Beasley could work miracles, and this was one miracle that he worked, second only to the loaves and fishes."

Binns was a colorful character himself; a flashy dresser who appeared in a couple of *Rocky* movies. He showed up at the King deposition wearing a lime Versace suit, with yellow socks and glasses. Binns, however, conceded he was upstaged by Beasley's ability to rankle King and his lawyers.

During a break at King's deposition, Nina M. Gussack, King's defense lawyer, complained to Binns that it was time for Beasley to "stop making nice" with Binns and "start making nice" with Don King.

Binns gave Gussack some advice. "I don't know how well you know Jim Beasley," Binns said, "but he doesn't give a fuck about you or your client."

Gussack just sat there, Binns recalled, "looking like I hit her in the forehead with a two-by-four."

• • •

"DO YOU KNOW SCOTT WOODWORTH?" BEASLEY BEGAN.

"Yes," King said.

Woodworth, who had worked for King until he filed his lawsuit, was seated at King's conference table, next to Night Train Norris.

Beasley's lawsuit charged that King had conspired to cheat Norris out of a heavyweight title fight against Iron Mike Tyson. And that King had pressured Norris to take a lesser bout, with Oliver McCall, a lower-ranked opponent Norris had already beaten.

"On or about April the 20th, 1996," Beasley began, "do you recall making a statement to Scott Woodworth to the effect that if Orlin Norris did not agree to fight Oliver McCall for the sum of $75,000, that they [Woodworth and Norris] 'could go about [their] business and in a couple of months we'll see where Orlin Norris is in the ratings. It might take a month or two, but he will disappear.' Do you recall making that statement?"

"No," King said.

"…Did you and Scott enter into any type of contract with Orlin Norris to fight McCall?" Beasley asked. The contract between Norris and McCall was one of the documents Beasley had requested the defense to produce, documents the defense lawyers said did not exist.

"Not to my knowledge," King replied. "…He [Woodworth] would say Orlin would fight anyone. So I said, 'OK, let's do this'…. So let him fight this guy, let him fight that guy…."

"Do I understand you're telling me there was a contract then?" Beasley asked.

"I don't know about no contract," King said.

Beasley was pulling one of his favorite courtroom maneuvers, leading a witness down a path of no return. And King was playing right along.

"Did Scott or Norris send you a signed contract agreeing to fight McCall?" Beasley asked.

"Not to my knowledge," King said. Without the contract, King seemed safe; it was just one man's word against another.

"Was there ever any arrangements made with any boxing association for McCall and Norris to fight?" Beasley asked.

"No," King said.

Beasley asked King about Dana Jamison, King's vice president of boxing operations: "Well, with this Jamison, would she have anything to do with arranging with the boxing authorities to do it?"

"No," King said.

King had just issued five denials about whether there had ever been a contract for Norris to fight McCall. Now the boxing promoter sat and watched as Scott Woodworth, a former paralegal for Beasley, slid a folder across the conference table to his "Uncle Jim."

Beasley flipped through the documents and told the court reporter, "Mark these please" as exhibits. Then he handed the documents to King. "Let me show you what's been marked as P-2, and tell me whose signature is on that page and what it refers to."

King's mouth opened, his eyes widened, and his long Cohiba cigar dangled precariously on his lower lip. "This is a signature of Dana Jamison," King said.

"What does that letter represent to you?" Beasley asked.

"This letter represents to me that she is sending a contract to Orlin Norris to get signed for a proposed fight."

"And this proposed fight was supposed to take place May 18, 1996, according to this letter?" Beasley asked.

King's defense lawyer interjected, asking to see the documents.

"It's a proposed fight," King repeated. He seemed stunned by the contract's sudden appearance. Then King put it all together and shot Woodworth a look that Woodworth described as a "rattlesnake smile."

Yes, there were only three original copies of the proposed contract for the McCall-Norris fight that would substantiate the allegations against King. And all three contracts were once kept under lock and key in King's office.

But Woodworth had had the good sense before he made his allegations public, to catch a red-eye flight to Florida, use his company key to slip into Don King's office, search the files and make a copy of that contract before it could disappear.

Beasley asked King about Frank Warren, a European promoter who represented Norris. "Do you remember telling Scott on that same call to get rid of Frank Warren, and we can do something with Norris?"

"No," King said.

Do you deny saying that to Woodworth? Beasley asked.

"I would have to say that I don't recall it, and so I couldn't put a reference to the — you know, denying this or denying that in a conversation with Scott," said an irritated King. "It's according to whether Scott was sober or whether he was drunk. And so you have to be able to deal with what Scott you're dealing with."

"Whether he was drunk or sober, I'm asking you, did you not have a conversation , , , ," Beasley began, before King cut him off. "I'm telling you —" King snarled, but Beasley cut him off again.

"Let me finish my question," Beasley barked, reasserting control. "Whether Scott was drunk or sober I'm asking you —" he said, before pausing in mid-sentence.

Beasley, an old tennis player, always enjoyed turning an opponent's volley against him. "Well," Beasley said, eyeballing King, "Let me ask you, were *you* drunk or sober during that conversation?"

"No," said a startled King, who suddenly recalled something about his conversation with Woodworth, a conversation King had previously not been able to remember. "He woke me up."

Beasley pressed the advantage: "Now, do you remember telling Scott Woodworth, whether Scott was drunk or sober, to get rid of Frank Warren, and we can do something with Norris?"

"No, I don't," King said.

"Are you denying that statement?"

"Well, I just answered you," King said. "I said no, I don't. And that statement goes for — whatever it is. No, I don't."

"Let me ask you, you don't remember saying it?"

"I don't remember saying it," King said.

"But my question is, do you deny it?"

"I don't remember saying it," King said. "So there is nothing to deny."

"You can't say whether it occurred or not?"

"I wouldn't recall saying — I'm answering hypotheses," King said. "I don't remember it, so I can't go any further than that."

· · ·

BEASLEY WAS TRYING TO SHOW THAT THE WBA IGNORED ITS OWN RULES WHEN IT WAS convenient: "And do they have a rule in [the] WBA that if you're inactive for more than six months, they can drop you out of the ratings?"

"I believe so," King said.

"How long was Mike Tyson in jail?" Beasley asked.

"Mike Tyson was in jail, I believe, three years," King said.

". . . Would it be fair to say that… he had been inactive for three years?" Beasley asked.

"Yes," King said.

"When he got out of jail, what was his rating?"

"His rating was No. 1," King said.

Meanwhile, Norris, who had won four straight fights in less than a year, had dropped in the ratings, from the No. 2 challenger to the No. 6 challenger.

"Do you know why?" Beasley asked.

"No," King said.

"Did you have anything to do with that?"

"No," King said.

"Are you saying that you had nothing to do with that?" Beasley asked.

"I'm not the WBA ratings," King said indignantly.

"I didn't ask you that question," Beasley said. "I'm asking you whether you had anything to do with it?"

"I told you no," King shot back. "But you keep asking me the same thing over and over. I told you no."

"You never talked to anybody at the WBA that persuaded those folks that Norris ought to drop off in the ratings?"

"No," King said.

Beasley switched subjects, inquiring about King's reputation for buying expensive dinners for WBA officials. If King wouldn't admit to controlling the WBA ratings, Beasley aimed to expose King's cozy relationship with WBA officials.

"Well, occasionally I help out in any way I can with the conventions of the organizations or the drug preventive programs," King said modestly.

"Will you translate your contributions to the dinners into dollars, please?" Beasley asked.

"…I can't give you an approximation," King protested. "Whatever the dinner costs, that's what I pay for."

"More than $100?" Beasley suggested.

"Mr. Beasley," King said, "you can't get a dinner for $100."

"Well, I'm a light eater," Beasley said. "More than $10,000?"

"Whatever the dinner costs, whatever it is, I pay for it," King said.

Beasley asked about a $100,000 dinner, and King didn't even blink. "Whatever the dinner costs, Mr. Beasley."

When Beasley raised the price tag to a $200,000 dinner, King's lawyer objected, saying that King had already answered the question.

Beasley seemed annoyed that a bit player at the table had spoken out of turn. "Will you please just stop making your speaking objections?" Beasley said, before telling King's lawyer to "just be quiet."

But King's lawyer continued to object as Beasley raised the price for dinner even higher. "Well, have you contributed $300,000 to the WBA?" Beasley asked, before throwing King a bone. "You're noted for your generosity."

King stared at Beasley. "I like you," he said. "No."

• • •

BEASLEY'S ATTEMPT TO STOP THE HOLYFIELD-TYSON REMATCH WAS REARGUED ON JUNE 16, 1997, less than two weeks before the big fight. Judge Shapiro's courtroom in the Federal Courthouse was crowded with legal combatants, including Don King, and lawyers representing three fighters — Tyson, Holyfield, and another challenger, Michael Moorer — as well as Showtime and Viacom. All the lawyers and parties in the case were referred to Chief U.S. Magistrate Judge James R. Melinson for mediation.

"While I always maintain the strictest confidentiality regarding mediations, the Norris case is the sole exception," Judge Melinson said in an interview. "Everything was made public by the parties themselves. . . . Hence, there never was any confidentiality."

Judge Melinson's style was to isolate the warring parties at different locations, like suspects in a criminal case, and question them separately. He also refused to let anybody out until a deal had been struck to give Norris his title bout. None of the defendants cared about Night Train Norris, but hanging over all of their heads was the fate of the Holyfield-Tyson rematch.

Judge Melinson set up the plaintiffs and the various defendants — King, the WBA, Showtime and Viacom — in separate rooms on four floors of the Federal Courthouse. The judge also found extra rooms for lawyers intervening on behalf of Mike Tyson and Evander Holyfield, as well as Michael Moorer, who wanted a rematch with Holyfield, if he got past Tyson.

The judge picked former jury rooms with no windows, rooms that were in such bad condition that they were no longer in use. Some, like the room Don King found himself stuck in for a day, had uncontrollable ceiling air conditioners going full blast. When the judge made the first of eight visits to King's room, he found that somebody had stuffed paper towels into the air vents, trying to warm the room to summer temperatures.

"They were all celebrities, and they were all used to their entourages, and the comforts and conveniences," Judge Melinson recalled. The judge said his philosophy with celebrities was, "If you don't treat them like celebrities, they finally come around and get real."

No one but King and his lawyer were permitted in that freezing cold jury room for the entire day. No cell phones were allowed, and nobody in any of the rooms had any idea where anybody else was, or what was going on.

King, dressed in a gray suit and dripping with jewelry, had been ignored for hours when the judge visited him for the first time. The boxing promoter was happy to see the judge, and even attempted to flatter him, prompting the judge to warn King's lawyer to rein in his client. The judge then left the room, leaving King to ponder his predicament for a few more hours.

In trying to force a settlement, Judge Melinson had a wonderful ally in Jim Beasley. "Jim's so self-confident," Judge Melinson recalled. "He always says he's gonna win. People who don't know him are really fearful of him." And whether they were in public or private, the judge said, Beasley "never deviated from the party line."

"I don't want to settle; why do I want to settle?" the judge quoted Beasley. "I'm gonna win."

"Jim," Judge Melinson told him. "It's just me. You don't have to be saying that."

For the judge, engaging in shuttle diplomacy, Beasley's posturing was useful bait. "It enables me in the caucuses with the defendants to say, 'You've got Jim Beasley on the other side. You've got to think about what you were doing.'

"The key to the whole settlement was Jim Beasley," Melinson said. "They knew they were up against a determined lawyer who was not going to back down, and they didn't want to see the light of day with discovery, where other things would come out. It put more pressure on them."

With mediation, judges often deal with reluctant types like King who have the power to do something, but don't want to do it for "reasons of the flood gates," Judge Melinson said. The reasoning was, if King did this for Norris, he might have to do it for others.

"I kind of convinced him this is unique, this is Jim Beasley," Judge Melinson recalled. "It took all day. I was running from room to room. At the end of the day, a certain boredom and ennui sets in."

King also got tired of being held hostage. "He was very cordial, he had a very winning personality, and he was very determined to get his own way," the judge said, "But eventually he became a realist."

As for Norris, Judge Melinson thought the boxer had a lot of heart, but he doubted his physical abilities. "He looks too small," the judge recalled thinking to himself. But the boxer was "very fortunate" to have a relative of Beasley's as his manager, the judge said, because "there was no case without Jim Beasley."

· · ·

THE LAWYERS IN THE CASE, AS WELL AS THEIR CLIENTS, WERE FINALLY LET OUT OF THEIR cages and summoned to Judge Shapiro's courtroom. When Judge Shapiro mentioned that, in her view, the parties had had ample time to settle the dispute, Binns interjected, "If by that you mean, Judge, that we were deprived of lunch, and communications with the outside, and behind a closed door, yes, we had sufficient time to consider everything Judge Melinson suggested."

"This is the agreement," Judge Melinson announced to Judge Shapiro: "Norris shall fight the winner of the [Franz] Botha- [Lee] Gilbert fight within six months of that fight. The winner cannot risk the WBA-NA [North America] title until he fights Norris; the winner cannot fight for the world championship WBA until he fights Norris. The purse for Norris is $50,000. Norris present promoter waives all rights in this matter. The fight will be promoted by Don King Promotions."

In return for the guarantee of a title fight for Norris, Beasley agreed to withdraw his challenge to the Holyfield-Tyson rematch in Las Vegas.

Don King told Judge Shapiro there were still a few details to be taken care of. "Your Honor, I can assure that they will fight, but the WBA has to make the decree that says that the fight will take place. So we have Mr. Norris' agreement to fight, what he's going to fight for, I have to negotiate a purse for Mr. Botha."

When the judge asked how much it would cost to get Botha, one of the WBA's top contenders, to fight Norris, King replied the purse had to be negotiated but, "Mr. Botha is not an unreasonable man."

• • •

BOTHA TURNED OUT TO BE UNREASONABLE. KING'S BID FOR BOTHA TO FIGHT NORRIS went as high as $450,000, but Botha turned it down, demanding $1 million. When the Holyfield-Tyson rematch went off as scheduled (Holyfield won again), and Don King failed to come up with an opponent for Norris, Beasley went back to court to file a motion to enforce the original settlement.

This time, instead of proposing that the judge shut down the next title fight, Beasley raised the stakes, asking the judge to shut down the entire WBA and put Don King out of business.

On Sept. 30, 1997, Judge Shapiro issued a Rule to Show Cause why the court should not "enjoin the WBA from sanctioning or sponsoring any boxing matches, and Don King from promoting any boxing matches after Dec. 21, 1997," because the previous agreement to arrange a title bout for Norris had not been complied with. The court also found that King had "negligently or intentionally misrepresented his ability to convince Botha to fight Norris."

On Oct. 15, 1997, Judge Shapiro, whom Binns dubbed "the czarina of boxing," held yet another hearing. All parties agreed that the WBA would canvas the top 12-ranked fighters in the heavyweight division, to see who would be available to fight Norris in the next five weeks before Dec. 21, 1997.

The only fighter the WBA could round up to take on the 5-foot-11 Norris was the lowest-ranked heavyweight contender, Henry Akinwande, a 6-foot-7 left-hander from Nigeria. The judge's order not only mandated a match between Norris and Akinwande by Dec. 21, 1997; it also mandated a title bout between the winner of the Akinwande-Norris fight and heavyweight champ Evander Holyfield by no later than June 28, 1998.

So if he got past Akinwande, Norris would finally get a heavyweight title fight. The Akinwande-Norris bout was scheduled for Dec. 13, 1997, at the Pompano Beach Amphitheater in Pompano Beach, Fla.

"It's not only a victory for Norris — it's a victory for boxing," Beasley told the Legal Intelligencer about his upset win over Don King. "The order is probably going to do more to clean up boxing than anything that's been tried so far."

Beasley said he hoped the judge's order would show other fighters the value of going to court. King "may be able to control boxing," Beasley told the newspaper, "but he can't control the courts."

. . .

THE BATTLE SHIFTED FROM THE COURTS TO THE BOXING RING. ALL THE LAWYERS IN THE case flew down to Pompano Beach to watch the fight, and they all ended up staying at the same hotel. Norris, a former cruiserweight champ who had to bulk up to crash the heavyweight division, was one win away from a heavyweight title fight. All he had to do was get past Henry Akinwande, the 12th-ranked heavyweight contender.

Jimmy Binns watched the fight with Jim Beasley. Just before the bell sounded for Round 1, Binns leaned over and told Beasley, "Here's where the rubber meets the road."

The stands were filled with cops and lawyers. Since Don King was under yet another federal investigation, the place was also teeming with FBI agents, many of whom were ringside.

After all the legal sparring Beasley went through to get Norris a chance in the ring, the actual fight was a letdown. Akinwande, using what one ringside commentator said were "spearing left jabs," scored a unanimous 12-round decision over Norris.

Binns, a former welterweight, compared the 6-foot-7 Akinwande to a "fighting giraffe," and said that Norris did little more than absorb punches. "The whole fight was a yawn," Binns said. All three boxing judges awarded every round to Akinwande. "The kid lost every round on every card," Binns said of Night Train Norris. "That's hard to do. He lost 36 rounds."

An embarrassed Beasley told Binns he had never been so disappointed in a sporting event. "It was a very devastating loss," Woodworth agreed. "Had we won that fight, they'd still be talking about it."

Akinwande took over the No. 1 heavyweight ranking after the fight, earning a title bout against heavyweight champ Holyfield, but the match had to be called off after Akinwande flunked his physical, testing positive for hepatitis. As for Night Train Norris, he wound up with nothing, and so did his lawyer.

The night Norris lost the fight in Pompano Beach, several lawyers in the case, including Binns and Beasley, went out for a steak dinner, then filtered back to their hotel. Beasley was walking through the lobby with Smerconish and Jim Beasley Jr. when he spotted Don King, another hotel guest.

"Hey, Beasley," King yelled from across the lobby. King strutted over and grabbed Beasley's outstretched hand with his two oversized mitts. "You," King said with a big smile on his face, "are one *fightin' motherfucker*."

Chapter 18

❖

THE KILLER HIPPIE

FEDERAL EXPRESS WAS MAKING AN INTERNATIONAL DELIVERY TO AN OLD STONE millhouse in the South of France. The man who answered the door was husky and middle-aged, with a weathered face and a wispy white goatee. He signed the delivery slip by scrawling only one word, "Einhorn."

Ira Einhorn was Philadelphia's most notorious fugitive killer, a former hippie guru who, after 16 years on the lam, was now living the life of a country squire in a rural region of France known for its fine brandies and cognacs. But when he opened his FedEx envelope on Jan. 2, 1998, Einhorn discovered that Jim Beasley was still after him.

Beasley was inviting Einhorn to return voluntarily to his hometown of Philadelphia, to stand trial in a wrongful death suit brought by the family of his murder victim, Helen "Holly" Maddux. Beasley filed the suit to prevent Einhorn from cashing in on a book or movie deal about his grisly murder of Maddux, and subsequent life on the run.

Einhorn had jumped bail and fled to Europe in 1981, rather than stand trial in Philadelphia on charges that he bashed in the skull of his former girlfriend, and then stashed her corpse in a steamer trunk.

There was no chance that Einhorn would ever willingly leave France, where a panel of judges had just refused America's attempt to extradite him, and where Einhorn had a team of lawyers to defend him, as well as his own support group. Einhorn was having too grand a time living with his wealthy new Swedish wife at their provincial estate known as Maison de Guitry, where he went skinny-dipping every day in a couple of streams by his house, and where he ate fresh pomegranates and strawberries plucked from his back yard.

But that didn't stop Beasley from trying:

"Dec. 30, 1997

"VIA FEDERAL EXPRESS

"Ira Einhorn

"Maison de Guitry

"Champagne-Mouton

"France 16350

"Re: *Estate of Helen Maddux v. Ira Einhorn*

"Dear Mr. Einhorn:

"Enclosed is a copy of the order which states that a Case Management Conference for the above-referenced matter will be held on January 14, 1998, in Philadelphia, Pennsylvania. You are invited to attend. Please call me when you expect to arrive and if necessary, I will ask the Court to continue the Case Management Conference to a date that suits your schedule.

"Very truly yours, James E. Beasley"

Maybe the audacity of Beasley's letter got to the equally audacious Einhorn. Six days later, the killer sent back a cheeky, autographed reply:

"Moulin de Guitry

"16350 Champagne-Mouton

"France

"Jan. 8, 1998

"Dear James E. Beasley,

"My present judicial status does not permit travel. The situation, according to my lawyers, will probably not be resolved before the end of the year 1998, if then. Thus it is impossible to give you a date. I hope this does not inconvenience you.

"Very truly yours, Ira Einhorn"

• • •

BEFORE HE BECAME AN INTERNATIONAL EMBARRASSMENT, IRA EINHORN WAS PHILADELphia's most famous counterculture icon; a bearded, pony-tailed, dashiki-wearing free spirit who didn't bother bathing, and didn't always wear pants when he answered the door.

Einhorn was a New Age intellectual who read widely and could pontificate on any subject, whether it was quantum physics, UFOs, or the beneficial effects of LSD. He organized a "Be-In" in Fairmount Park, and taught a popular free course in "psychedelics" at his alma mater, the University of Pennsylvania.

When Philadelphia held the first Earth Day in 1970, an event televised around the globe, Einhorn walked on stage as master of ceremonies along with the cast of the Broadway musical *Hair*, and then he joined them in singing, "Let the Sun Shine In."

Einhorn attracted even more attention when he ran for Philadelphia mayor in 1971 under the campaign slogan of "Let Them Eat Organic Cookies."

Since his last name in German meant one horn, Einhorn dubbed himself the Unicorn, and during the Age of Aquarius, he seemed to know everybody who mattered. His cosmic pals included radicals Abbie Hoffman and Jerry Rubin, beat poet Allen Ginsberg, and *Star Trek* creator Gene Roddenberry.

The Unicorn had mesmerizing blue eyes and was a legendary schmoozer who could talk a corporate executive out of his discretionary funds just as easily as he could seduce a liberated woman out of her bell-bottoms. Establishment types saw Einhorn as a spokesman for the counterculture, a group they wanted to woo, so they hired him to give speeches, mediate labor disputes, and set up neighborhood development corporations.

The suits loved Einhorn because he was such a forward thinker. Decades before the Internet, Einhorn developed a pioneering information-sharing network for more than 350 business executives, government officials and media members in 20 countries.

Every week, Einhorn would bundle together esoteric gleanings such as newly declassified U.S. government documents on UFOs and papers on Russian mind-control experiments. Then he would dispatch the gleanings, along with his own musings, to an influential list of contacts that included author Alvin *Future Shock* Toffler, Seagram's heir Charles Bronfman, and Stewart Brand, publisher of the *Whole Earth Catalog*. The network didn't cost the Unicorn a dime: all copying and mailing costs were picked up by Einhorn's corporate sponsors at Pennsylvania Bell.

Reporters in Philadelphia treated Einhorn as a celebrity, referring to him as "the city's oldest hippie," "town guru" and resident "hippie philosopher." The cops used Einhorn to mediate protests; local ministers saw him as an apostle of peace and nonviolence. So in Philadelphia, the Unicorn functioned as a one-man bridge between the establishment and the counterculture.

The Unicorn's favorite hangout was La Terrasse, a French restaurant on the Penn campus, where corporate executives were so anxious to pick his brain that Einhorn ate lunch there every day without ever picking up a check. It was there on Oct. 7, 1972, that Einhorn met Holly Maddux, a 5-foot-7 blonde, 110-pound former cheerleader and straight-A student from Tyler, Texas, who had the physique and grace of a ballerina.

Friends and family wondered what the ethereal Holly saw in the unkempt Einhorn, who at 5-foot-10 and 230 pounds, resembled a fuzzy bowling ball. But the small-town girl from East Texas who came East to study at Bryn Mawr College had never met anybody like the Unicorn. Holly Maddux, her siblings said, was also naïve, and had never encountered evil before.

And underneath his image as a fun-loving pacifist and tree hugger, Ira Einhorn was a serial abuser of women. As revealed in Steven Levy's *The Unicorn's Secret*, Einhorn choked one girlfriend until she passed out. And then he wrote in his journal, "Violence always marks the end of a relationship." He throttled another girlfriend and broke a Coke bottle over her head. And then he wrote in his journal, "To kill what you love when you can't have it seems so natural."

Maddux lived with Einhorn for five years in an on-and-off relationship marked by mental and physical abuse. Then she made the fatal mistake of running away and moving in with a new boyfriend. Einhorn lured Maddux back to his apartment by threatening to throw all her belongings out on the street. He also talked her into going out on one last date.

On Sept. 10, 1977, the couple saw *Star Wars* with some friends, and then Holly Maddux was never seen again alive. When a city detective visited Einhorn, he said that Maddux had simply gone out to the local food co-op for some tofu and sprouts and never came back.

Holly Maddux's parents, however, knew that Einhorn was abusive and had threatened their daughter with violence. The Madduxes also were upset with the attitude of local authorities, who treated their daughter's disappearance as a missing-persons case. The Madduxes suspected foul play. So four months after their daughter disappeared, Fred and Elizabeth Maddux hired two former FBI agents to investigate.

The former FBI agents interviewed two onetime neighbors who had lived below Einhorn's apartment and had complained to the landlord about a sickening odor, and a thick, sticky brown stain on their ceiling. When roofers went upstairs to investigate the source of the leak, Einhorn wouldn't let them inspect a locked closet near his bedroom. One of the former neighbors also told the agents he had heard a "blood-curdling scream" as well as "several sharp thuds" the night Holly Maddux was last seen alive.

The agents also found two sisters, who said that a few days after Maddux disappeared, Einhorn had asked them to help him dump a steamer trunk into the Schuylkill River. Einhorn claimed the trunk was filled with secret documents, but the sisters were suspicious, so they refused.

The former FBI agents finally brought the evidence they had gathered in a year-long investigation to police. On March 28, 1979, the cops showed up at Einhorn's apartment with a search warrant. They broke open Einhorn's locked closet and found Maddux's corpse in a steamer trunk buried under four inches of Styrofoam packing, old newspapers and plastic dry-cleaning bags. Holly Maddux's jaw was broken, her skull fractured at least 10 times. After 18 months of decomposition, the body weighed only 37 pounds.

"'Hippie Guru' Held in Trunk Murder" was the banner headline on the front page of the Philadelphia Daily News. But the resourceful Einhorn told everybody it was the CIA or the KGB that killed Holly Maddux, and planted her body in his steamer trunk to frame him. They did it, the Unicorn said, because he simply knew too much about government mind-control programs and what he claimed was a worldwide conspiracy to cover up the existence of UFOs. Besides, Einhorn told his friends, would anybody as intelligent as the Unicorn be dumb enough to kill somebody and then stash the body in his own apartment?

In the era of Watergate, when conspiracy theories were rampant, Einhorn was able to peddle his cockamamie story to many of the city's influential types. Enough backers came forward to enable Einhorn to hire former Philadelphia District Attorney Arlen Specter, a future U.S. Senator, as his lawyer. Specter promptly got Einhorn's bail reduced from $100,000 to a paltry $40,000. Barbara Bronfman, the socialite wife of Seagram's heir Charles Bronfman, put up the bail deposit of $4,000. The Bronfmans were subscribers to Einhorn's information network, and shared the Unicorn's interest in the paranormal.

But the future senator and the socialite weren't the Unicorn's only supporters. At Einhorn's bail hearing, a parade of Philadelphia's elite took turns extolling Einhorn's virtues, insisting that he wasn't a flight risk. A man of "excellent" character, said a corporate attorney. "The highest level of integrity," said an Ivy League lecturer. "A man of nonviolence," added an Episcopalian minister. So many "upper-crust professionals" showed up to testify on Einhorn's behalf, the newspapers said, that the judge didn't have time to hear them all, so he simply asked all of Ira's supporters to stand.

Einhorn left them all hanging. On Jan. 14, 1981, two weeks before his murder trial was supposed to start, the Unicorn fled the country. The Philadelphia Inquirer reported that Ira's pals weren't the least bit surprised. Einhorn had even told a reporter, Greg Walter of Philadelphia magazine, in a tape-recorded interview, "I'm not about to spend my life in jail. It's as simple as that."

"The only ones caught unprepared by Einhorn's disappearance," the Inquirer reported in 1984, "were the legal system that allowed him to run free after posting $40,000 bail and the host of agencies that have been trying to find him ever since."

A Philadelphia jury convicted Einhorn in absentia of first-degree murder in 1993, and sentenced him to life in prison. He remained at large, successfully eluding

Interpol, the FBI, and investigators from the Philadelphia district attorney's office.

Then, on June 13, 1997, Einhorn was sleeping in the nude inside his French cottage when he was arrested by a dozen gendarmes brandishing high-powered weapons. For the first time in 16 years, the world knew where the fugitive killer was hiding, and what he looked like. The old hippie had gone gray, whacked his ponytail, trimmed his beard, and lost some weight.

• • •

ON NOV. 18, 1997, A FEDERAL EXPRESS DELIVERY ARRIVED AT THE MAISON D'ARRET DE Gradignan Jail in Bordeaux, where Einhorn was a guest.

According to the terms of a U.S. international treaty with France, Beasley's civil complaint against Einhorn had to be translated into French and served on Einhorn.

"I sent it FedEx," Beasley told the Philadelphia Daily News. "He signed for it."

In the complaint, Beasley described Einhorn as "a vicious animal" whose "conduct was so malicious, outrageous, atrocious and so extreme in degree as to go beyond all possible bounds of decency and to be utterly intolerable in a civilized community."

"I think he envisioned him [Einhorn] as an animal who needed to be caged," James J. McHugh Jr., then a Beasley associate, said. "It was almost as if he was prosecuting him."

Beasley also sent Einhorn 43 interrogatories, asking him to admit or deny in writing specific allegations that he murdered Maddux, as well as physically and mentally abused her.

Although Einhorn signed for the papers, he did not reply to the interrogatories. Back in Philadelphia, Judge Sandra Mazer Moss entered a default judgment in the case, meaning that since there was no legal dispute, Beasley's claims against Einhorn would be admitted in court as facts.

"Even though he was in France, all he had to do was get a piece of paper and write 'denied' and fax that in," Beasley told the Philadelphia Inquirer. "He had an opportunity to respond to everything I sent to him. He was kept fully aware by me."

Beasley said he intended to try the case whether Einhorn showed up or not. "I don't want him to make a mockery out of this family's loss."

• • •

EINHORN'S WEALTHY NEW WIFE HIRED A TEAM OF LAWYERS TO DEFEND HIM. The lawyers creatively argued that the Unicorn was not some fugitive murderer, but a political prisoner who was the victim of a barbaric American human-rights atrocity. Since Einhorn didn't attend his in absentia trial in Philadelphia, his lawyers pointed out, he didn't have an opportunity to defend himself. Einhorn's lawyers also noted that the European Convention on Human Rights opposed in-absentia trials. Einhorn, speaking in his own defense, rambled on in English for 15 minutes about *Star Trek*, and how he was framed by the CIA. Maybe it made more sense when an interpreter translated it into French.

On Dec. 4, 1997, a three-judge French appeals panel decided that France did not recognize Einhorn's in-absentia conviction, and after six months in a French jail, the Unicorn was a free man. Photographers snapped pictures of the gap-toothed Einhorn kissing his wife outside the courthouse; then the Einhorns drove back to their country estate to celebrate.

Back in Philadelphia, District Attorney Lynne Abraham began work on a new attempt to extradite Einhorn. Pennsylvania's General Assembly passed a law that legislators freely admitted would benefit only one man, Ira Einhorn. The new law promised that if Einhorn ever did return to Pennsylvania, he could petition the courts for a new trial.

Meanwhile, Jim Beasley was still writing letters to the Unicorn.

• • •

"SEPTEMBER 2, 1998
"VIA FEDERAL EXPRESS
"Ira Einhorn
"Maison de Guitry
"Champagne-Mouton
"France 16350
"Re: *Estate of Helen Maddux v. Ira Einhorn*
"Dear Mr. Einhorn:
"As in the past, I am keeping you informed as to what is going on in your case — a case, as you know, where you are a central player. I am going to a pre-trial conference on October 26th at 9:45 a.m., in Courtroom 253, City Hall in Philadelphia, Pennsylvania.

"Do you have a travel agent who can make arrangements for your transportation here? If you want, I will try to make the necessary arrangements. Just let me know.

"Very truly yours, James E. Beasley"

• • •

BEASLEY WROTE ABOUT 20 LETTERS TO EINHORN, ALL SENT BY FEDERAL EXPRESS. MOST of the letters were signed for by Einhorn, or Annika Flodin, the Swedish woman he married while on the lam. The letters were always about the same subject, the *Estate of Helen Maddux v. Ira Einhorn*, the civil case Beasley had filed on behalf of Holly Maddux's brother, John, and sisters Meg, Buffy and Mary.

The Maddux siblings carried a heavy burden. Their older sister had been brutally murdered more than 20 years ago, but her killer was still on an extended European holiday.

Holly's siblings blamed Einhorn not only for the death of their sister, but also for hastening the death of their parents. Fred Maddux, who always referred to Einhorn as the "king of the pig people," blamed himself for not saving his daughter, and he committed suicide in 1988; his wife, Elizabeth, passed away two years later.

"My parents died thinking that Ira had beaten them," Elisabeth "Buffy" Maddux Hall told a reporter. "Well, I want to go put some roses on my parents' graves and tell them, 'We got the bastard.' "

Holly's three sisters flew to Philadelphia on the Labor Day weekend of 1997 from their respective homes in Texas, Seattle and Massachusetts. The Maddux sisters planned to interview a trio of Philadelphia lawyers, in hopes of talking one of them into pursuing a civil case against Einhorn. The first lawyer they spoke with, however, said no, and the next two said they would have to think it over.

"We didn't have a clue" about what was involved in chasing Einhorn in the civil courts, Buffy Maddux Hall said in an interview for this book. All the Maddux family knew was that Einhorn had taken advantage of his newfound media celebrity to shop a proposal for a book and movie deal.

"We were very discouraged" about the chances of stopping him, Hall said. The three Philadelphia lawyers that the Maddux sisters talked to all gave them the "pat on the head, sorry for your troubles" treatment, Hall said. They wouldn't say why they weren't interested in the case, but Hall said, "I'm sure it was cost-prohibitive."

Then, well after lunch, the Maddux sisters got a phone call from a friend who was still trying to recruit a Philadelphia lawyer. The friend said that Jim Beasley, who had been flying his Mustang that morning, was on his way to his office and would meet the Maddux sisters in one hour.

"He was quite the cowboy," recalled Hall, a retired nurse and former quarter horse breeder from Ft. Worth, Texas. "He came in with the belt and the boots and the jeans." Hall recalled thinking, "You were born in the wrong century."

Sit down, let's talk, Beasley told the Maddux sisters. Tell me what you want to do. Hall was struck by how much the "ramrod-straight" Beasley reminded her of her father, a former 82nd Airborne paratrooper at Normandy, who "could talk to anybody."

"Daddy would have loved this guy," Hall remembered thinking to herself. "They would have gotten along like a house on fire. They were just the same kind of straight-shooting, no-bullshit, force-of-nature kind of guys."

Jim McHugh sat in on the meeting with the Maddux sisters. "It was an emotional situation," McHugh recalled. The sisters described Holly as "the free spirit" of the family who was never replaced. At one point, Mary Maddux, the youngest sister, looked as if she was about to cry when Beasley reassured her with a pat on the arm. "He really was as soft as I can ever remember," McHugh said.

What happened next was why they called Beasley the people's lawyer. He didn't have to talk it over with anybody; he didn't have to think about it for one more minute.

Beasley told the Maddux sisters he was "personally offended" by Einhorn's crime, and the stain it had left on Philadelphia. He would take the case, he said, and handle it personally. "We can't pay you," Hall cautioned. Don't worry about that, Beasley said.

We're going after that SOB, Beasley said, and we're going to spend whatever it takes to make sure "this monster" doesn't profit from the murder of your sister. With any luck, he told the Maddux sisters, we'll get that chateau in France. Over the weekend, Beasley's lawyers began drafting a civil complaint against Ira Einhorn.

"It still blows me away that anybody that big in the legal community would bother," Hall said in an interview for this book. She wondered if the meeting with Beasley had been arranged in heaven. "We think it's Daddy that lined up the appointment. We walked away from that meeting completely relieved because we knew we were in good hands."

"Our whole family adored Mr. Beasley," added Margaret "Meg" Maddux Wakeman, a high school nurse from Seattle. "You could just tell that this man respected everything about human rights in the Constitution. And the fact that our sister's human rights were trampled on did not sit right with him."

Whenever he wrote Einhorn, Beasley always copied all four of Holly's siblings. The family looked forward to Beasley's letters. "I was laughing my ass off," Wakeman said. "It helped take the edge off the pain."

• • •

"MARCH 19, 1999

"VIA FEDERAL EXPRESS

"Ira Einhorn

"Maison de Guitry

"Champagne-Mouton

"France 16350

"Re: *Estate of Helen Maddux v. Ira Einhorn*

"Dear Mr. Einhorn:

"Enclosed is a copy of the Notice of a Trial Scheduling Conference which I received from the Court. As you can see the conference is on April 20, 1999 at 10:00 a.m. here in Philadelphia.

"Your attendance would be appreciated.

"Very truly yours,
James E. Beasley"

• • •

"APRIL 20, 1999
"VIA FEDERAL EXPRESS
"Ira Einhorn
"Maison de Guitry
"Champagne-Mouton
"France 16350
"Re: *Estate of Helen Maddux v. Ira Einhorn*
Dear Mr. Einhorn:

"I missed you at the Trial Management Conference, which was held today before Judge Sandra Mazer Moss.

"For your immediate information and to assist you in preparing for the upcoming trial, I am enclosing a copy of the Trial Management Order which was entered today. First, your case is scheduled to start trial at 9:30 a.m. on July l2, 1999. The jury selection for the July 12 trial date is July 9. . . . If you have any questions concerning the Order, please feel free to have a lawyer of your selection contact me, or you may contact me yourself, and I will help you in any way I can.

"I hope to see you on July 9, 1999.

"Very truly yours, James E. Beasley"

• • •

"JUNE 30, 1999
"VIA FEDERAL EXPRESS
"Ira Einhorn
"Maison de Guitry
"Champagne-Mouton
"France 16350
"Re: *Estate of Helen Maddux v. Ira Einhorn*
"Dear Mr. Einhorn:

"Well as you know, the trial is rapidly approaching and we are to pick a jury on July 9, 1999. . . . If you have any exhibits that you feel are relevant to your defense, if you will let me know what they are we will make arrangements to have them marked as defense exhibits.

"Of course, it goes without saying, if you have any questions do not hesitate to call or write. Hope to see you on the 9th, or the day that we select the jury.

"Very truly yours, James E. Beasley"

• • •

BACK IN PHILADELPHIA, JIM MCHUGH KEPT TRACK OF ALL THE FEDEX DELIVERY SLIPS to Einhorn, to document that Beasley had kept him notified of every stage of the legal process.

"We were surprised that knowing that the case was going forward against them, that they had the audacity to continue signing for" Beasley's letters, McHugh said, as if it didn't mean anything, "as if they were delivering chocolates."

The correspondence between Beasley and the Unicorn also made an impression on the judge in the case.

"I think he was a complete sociopath," Judge Sandra Mazer Moss said of Einhorn. "He was matching wits with him [Beasley]. He wasn't afraid to sign for that stuff. He didn't care."

When the case went to trial on July 26, 1999, the defense table in Judge Moss's courtroom was empty. Einhorn didn't show, and he didn't send a lawyer, so the trial went on without objections or interruptions. The media, however, was well represented, so the Maddux family seized the opportunity to lob a few bombs at Einhorn.

"This is a preemptive strike to prevent him from exploiting murdering my sister," Buffy Maddux Hall told the Inquirer. "We've been hearing rumors that he's shopping his story around. We hear that his wife, Annika Flodin, is writing their love story. There is no way in hell he is going to profit from murdering my sister."

"We want to show you the suffering and pain for punitive damages," Beasley told the jury in his opening statement, as he pointed to a large color 30-by-40-inch blowup of Maddux's battered, mummified skull. "You must know what Holly went through."

"We can legally attach any earnings of Einhorn or his wife. If he can spend it, we want it."

Beasley had the steamer trunk that served as Holly Maddux's coffin brought into the courtroom and placed directly in front of the jury box. He asked former Philadelphia Detective Michael J. Chitwood, now the police chief of Portland, Maine, to take the stand. Chitwood took the jury back 20 years, when he first knocked on Einhorn's door with a search warrant. Chitwood recalled that Einhorn wore a bathrobe when he came to the door.

Chitwood told the jury that he used a crowbar to crack open a padlocked closet, after Einhorn told him he didn't have the key. Then Chitwood discovered a padlocked trunk and pried it open. "I saw a hand," he told the jury. "It was mummified. I saw a blue flannel shirt. I went down to the elbow, then I stopped searching."

The wrinkled, leathery hand looked as if the victim had been trying to claw her way out of the trunk, Chitwood said. "She may have been placed in there alive."

Chitwood told the jury he turned to Einhorn and said, "Looks like we found Holly."

"You found what you found," the former detective quoted Einhorn as saying.

Beasley asked Chitwood to come down off the witness stand and open the trunk. What was it like, Beasley asked, to see the trunk again. "After all these years," Chitwood said, "there's still that faint smell of decomposition."

The dusty, battered trunk sat in the courtroom all day while Beasley tried the case. It was the first time the Maddux siblings had ever seen it. "I was 15 when they found her," said Mary Maddux, a photographer, musician and artist from Stockbridge, Mass., in an interview for this book. "And so the fact that she was basically buried alive was not something that was told to me."

Einhorn wasn't in the courtroom to give an alibi, so Beasley played a videotape of an ABC News 20/20 show from 1998, when Connie Chung had obtained an exclusive interview with the Unicorn. On the tape, Chung asked Einhorn who killed Holly Maddux. "As far as I can tell, one of the large intelligence agencies" did it, Einhorn replied.

Beasley presented an actuarial report to the jury that assessed Maddux's lost earning capacity as a result of her premature death. Holly Maddux was only 30 years old when she was murdered. She was the 1965 salutatorian from John Tyler High School in Tyler, Texas, out of a class of 426 students, a straight-A student voted "Most Likely to Succeed." Her SAT scores were 722 Verbal, 624 Math.

 She attended language and art classes at Tyler Junior College in 1966, then transferred to Bryn Mawr College, where she graduated in 1971, majoring in languages. She was an artist, dancer, and seamstress, and also held a brown belt in judo. Holly Maddux had aspirations of developing her own clothing line. If she had lived a normal life and retired at age 70, the actuary said, she would have earned $4.2 million in salary and fringe benefits.

Beasley entered as an exhibit a 30-by- 40-inch black-and-white blowup of a photo of Maddux as a smiling high school cheerleader, doing a split. Other blowup exhibits were gruesome photos of the corpse as it lay in the steamer trunk, covered with Styrofoam packing, as well as close-ups of the mummified hand and skull.

Beasley told the jury how Einhorn had struck Holly Maddux so many times that he had literally crushed her skull. Can you imagine, Beasley asked, the pain that Holy Maddux felt with the first blow? But that wasn't enough for Einhorn, Beasley said. He had to hit her again and again and again.

Beasley told the jury he wanted them to see how small the trunk was, and how Einhorn had to "distort the body" to stuff it into the trunk. Beasley talked about how "this man bludgeoned this woman to death," and then he covered the body with Styrofoam and even went to the extent of putting three air fresheners in the trunk, because he knew the body would putrefy.

"Within 10 feet of his bed lay the coffin of Holly Maddux," Beasley told the jury. "What type of individual can spend 18 months within 10 feet of a corpse that he put in a trunk?" Beasley told the jury that Maddux was still alive when Einhorn put her in the trunk, and that her last breath was taken there.

"Her mummified hand was reaching up, to push the lid, or perhaps she was reaching up to God for help," Beasley told the jury. "And that moment, that must have been when death grabbed her. That must have been the moment that God took her."

He also pointed out to the jury that by keeping the body imprisoned in his apartment, Einhorn had also stolen from the victim "any dignity of a decent burial."

Because Einhorn had chosen not to dispute any of Beasley's allegations, the jury did not have to determine guilt or innocence; all they had to do was assess damages. Beasley asked the jury to return a verdict "so substantial that it has meaning and gets attention around the world. You are going to announce to the world what you think of Ira Einhorn."

"He has mocked American justice," Beasley said. "He took my requests for admissions and this complaint and he laughed, and he and his wife enjoyed a glass of wine."

"You can feel Holly Maddux in this courtroom," Beasley said. "She is no longer silent. She has had an opportunity to let you look at her life and the horror of her death."

• • •

AFTER LESS THAN TWO HOURS OF DELIBERATIONS, THE JURY CAME BACK WITH A VERDICT that made the Maddux siblings gasp. It was the largest jury verdict ever handed down in Philadelphia: $155 million in compensatory damages, and $752 million in punitive damages, for a total of $907 million.

"This verdict will be a shot heard around the world," Buffy Maddux Hall told the Inquirer. "It's a psychological blow to Ira. I hope it hurts."

The jurors appeared shaken as they left the courtroom. "It was very emotional," jury foreman Don Wilent told the Philadelphia Daily News. "I just wanted to make sure I did the right thing. My conscience's good. I can answer to God."

"Several [jurors] were crying," Buffy Maddux Hall told the Daily News. "Everyone shook our hands and hugged us. One of the jurors said there wasn't enough money in the world to give us."

The judge also hugged the Maddux siblings.

Reporters reached Einhorn at his home in Champagne-Mouton, but he declined comment. On a syndicated radio show in Washington, however, Einhorn said, "I'm not really interested in making money out of someone else's misery."

Einhorn told the interviewer he would continue to fight extradition to the United States. "I was a superstar in Philadelphia with incredibly good press. Overnight, I was turned into a demon." He vowed to stay in France and avoid his home country, where there's been "a witch-hunt that's been going on for 20 years against me.

"I would also like to write a book," Einhorn conceded on the radio show recorded before the verdict was announced. "That would be a very difficult thing to do because I can't publish the book because of the civil suit that's under way right now." Once again, Einhorn declared that he was framed. "I'm innocent of the crime as charged. I will declare that until my dying breath."

Einhorn's "dying breath" quote was replayed on Michael Smerconish's radio show that afternoon. The in-studio guest, Jim Beasley, couldn't believe it.

"It's just an incredible thing to say," Beasley told Smerconish. "Innocent people don't flee to foreign countries."

Smerconish asked Beasley what had attracted Maddux to Einhorn in the first place.

"I think she found him intellectually attractive," Beasley told Smerconish. "He certainly wasn't physically attractive. After he abused her, that attraction lost its charm."

Smerconish asked Beasley if Einhorn had any assets to go after.

"Strangely enough, a man who's supposed to be this bright has never worked a day in his life," Beasley said, adding, "I doubt very much if he has any assets."

In the next morning's Inquirer, Norris E. Gelman, the lawyer who defended Einhorn during his 1993 in-absentia murder trial, complained that the $907 million verdict was excessive. "More than the gross national product of many countries," the lawyer griped. "Even if he [Einhorn] were to get a job and make $50,000 a year, he would pay this off in 18,000 years. You figure the math out."

Beasley was interviewed that same morning on NBC's *Today* show. "The size of the award was somewhat surprising," Beasley admitted. "But I said upon reflection, it could just as easily be justified."

The *Today* Show wasn't the only national media outlet pursuing the Unicorn. Russ Baker wrote a lengthy profile of Einhorn for Esquire's December 1999 issue, which featured a nude photo of actress Sharon Stone on the cover and, inside, a nude photo of Ira Einhorn skinny-dipping in a stream near his French country retreat.

Author Baker was at a fine French restaurant when he recorded Einhorn's reaction to the Philadelphia verdict. A friend had treated Einhorn to an evening of champagne and foie gras and strawberries in cognac. After his belly was full, Einhorn scoffed at the jury award:

Ira thinks it's the funniest thing he's ever heard, great material for after-dinner mischief. "I guess I'll call Mom to ask her to lend me a billion," he says, laughing. Then, in French, he pronounces it crazy: "C'est fou."

"It's obscene," Annika says.

Ira and Annika clink glasses. "To a billion dollars!" Ira cackles. He shows all of his teeth and wails with laughter, a great, heartfelt fuck-you belly-laugh.

As far as Philadelphia District Attorney Lynne Abraham was concerned, the verdict wasn't high enough.

"Given the arrogance of Einhorn and the fact that he literally stood naked in the pages of Esquire and thumbed his nose at everybody, especially the Maddux family, I thought that the harshest verdict possible in the civil court was the best verdict, so it could have been 10 trillion for all I cared," Abraham said in an interview for this book.

"It was well deserved after what he put that family through for 25 years," said Abraham, who referred to Einhorn as a "condescending, self-aggrandizing publicity-seeking individual" who "deserved to get really whacked."

Beasley made sure the judgment against Einhorn was filed in compliance with international law, so it would be applicable around the world, Abraham said. The district attorney described Beasley as "Philadelphia's version of the king of torts," and said she was proud of him for taking on the civil case against Einhorn. Beasley did the case pro bono, and it cost him more than $20,000 in expenses.

"Everybody needs to tilt at windmills," Abraham said, before looking around her office for a favorite statue. "Where's my Don Quixote that I got in Spain?"

• • •

THE MADDUX FAMILY HAD TO WAIT UNTIL 2001 FOR ALL THE APPEALS IN FRANCE TO BE exhausted, before Einhorn could finally be extradited to the United States. Before it was over, District Attorney Abraham would have to buttonhole President Clinton at a political fund-raiser, and convince him to personally intervene with French Prime Minister Lionel Jospin.

When Einhorn found out the French prime minister had finally signed the extradition order, he took a kitchen knife and, in front of reporters, sliced his throat. It was a bloody, but not life-threatening wound. His wife termed it a "political act."

On July 26, 2001, after 20 years of freedom, Einhorn was sitting in solitary confinement in a Pennsylvania jail cell when he received a first-class, certified letter from James E. Beasley:

"Ira Einhorn
"Number ES6859
"C/o Graterford Prison
"Graterford, PA 19426
"Re: *Estate of Helen Maddux v. Ira Einhorn*
"Dear Mr. Einhorn:
"Welcome home.

"Enclosed please find Interrogatories in aid of execution of the judgment of $923,732,217.46 against you (verdict plus interest). Please be advised that you are entitled to thirty days to respond to these questions which must be accompanied by the attached verification.

"Please advise your present counsel of these documents.

"Very truly yours, James E. Beasley"

• • •

ALTHOUGH HE NEVER GOT THAT BOOK OR MOVIE DEAL, IRA EINHORN DID GET A NEW murder trial, and a chance to testify in his defense. Once again, he rambled on about conspiracies involving intelligence agencies. On Oct. 17, 2002, after 2½ hours of deliberations, a Philadelphia jury convicted Einhorn of the first-degree murder of Holly Maddux.

Einhorn now serves a life sentence at the State Correctional Institute in Houtzdale, Pa., where he resides in a 12-foot-by-7-foot concrete cell. He wears a brown prison uniform and works as a janitor on his cell block for a salary that varies between 19 and 42 cents an hour.

The Maddux family spent two decades chasing Einhorn across two continents, and, according to Buffy Maddux Hall, not many people were sympathetic to their plight. Besides the Philadelphia district attorney's office, Hall said, only Jim Beasley took notice of Holly as a person.

"There was such validation for us because for the first time Holly was as important to somebody outside of the family as she was to us," Hall said. "That was a huge thing for me. And Beasley did it on such a huge scale and he made it personal. That's something I'll never forget, and I could have never have thanked him enough for, the validation that Holly was worth this effort."

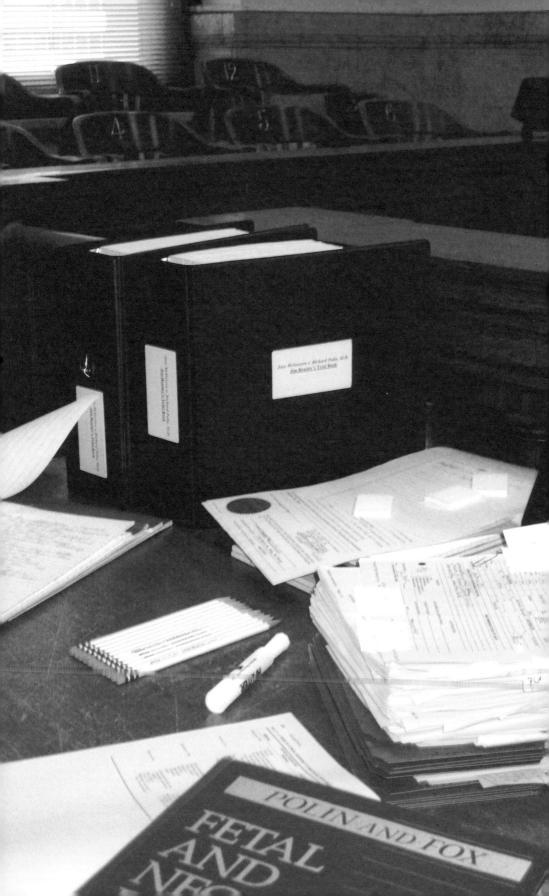

Chapter 19

❖

"GET ME THE BOOK!"

THE DEFENSE LAWYER WAS LOBBING SOFTBALL QUESTIONS TO HIS LEADOFF WITNESS.

"Doctor," the defense lawyer said, "have you received any awards or honors in your career?"

"Yes, several," the witness replied.

Dr. Richard A. Polin was a professor of pediatrics and a neonatologist, a specialist in the diagnosis and treatment of disorders in newborns. The tall and thin doctor with the glasses and receding hairline told the jury about three awards he had received for being the "outstanding faculty person" at two different hospitals in Pennsylvania and New York.

"In addition, Temple University about two or three years ago recognized me as the outstanding alumnus from my medical school class at that time," Dr. Polin said proudly. "And I'm also listed in *The Best Doctors in America.*"

It was April 10, 2000. On the fourth floor of Philadelphia's elaborate Victorian City Hall, Courtroom 480 was packed for the medical malpractice case known as *McGovern v. Weil et al.*

A team of ten defense lawyers was presenting a half-dozen doctors accused of malpractice, especially the two lead defendants, as brilliant and caring physicians. And over at the battle-scarred plaintiff's table, where a stone-faced Jim Beasley sat with two youthful sidekicks, the goal was to expose those same doctors as being arrogant and negligent.

Behind an iron gate, Courtroom 480 was a long, narrow curiosity from the 19th century, furnished in dark oak and Italian marble. The Hon. Myrna Field sat on the bench, flanked by dark oil portraits of two late jurists. The two defense tables were so crowded that some of the doctors on trial had to sit in back of the court-room, with their lawyers, on two rows of wooden chairs set aside for spectators. A prominent marble wall clock gave the courtroom a sense of timelessness, with its hands permanently frozen at 12:21.

Up on the witness stand, dressed in an expensive suit, Dr. Polin explained how *The Best Doctors in America* is compiled. "It's listed by specialty, and there are only three neonatalists I can say in the whole state . . . recognized as being part of *The Best Doctors in America*," Dr. Polin said. "One is myself," the 54-year-old doctor said. "And one is my other codefendant, Dr. Fox."

At the plaintiff's table, located right next to the jury box, Beasley studied the witness while he fiddled absentmindedly with his pencils. Beasley had a dozen sharpened No. 2 pencils aligned in perfect military formation, with the tips all pointing in the same direction, right next to a stack of legal pads covered with notes. As nearby jurors watched with curiosity, Beasley slowly rolled the pencils back and forth under his fingers while he listened to Dr. Polin describe his awards and honors.

If Beasley was going to win this case for his clients, the parents of a severely disabled child, he would not only have to outwit two of the country's top doctors, he would also have to deflate them.

At 73, Beasley still commanded attention with his trim body, shock of white hair, and high-beam glare that made men flinch. He was dressed in full battle uni-form: a blue lawyer's suit bought off the rack sometime during the Reagan administration, a splashy yellow silk designer tie, and cowboy boots. Pinned to his lapel was a set of silver "QB" pilot's wings, the emblem of the Quiet Birdmen, a self-described "ancient and secret order" of pilots founded in 1921 whose mem-bers had included Charles Lindbergh. Dangling from Beasley's wrist was a gold bracelet from Warbirds of America, a group of vintage military-plane enthusiasts whose motto was "Keep 'Em Flying."

"Doctor, you have a number of national societies," the defense lawyer said. "Would you tell the ladies and gentlemen of the jury which ones you consider important or prestigious perhaps?"

"Yeah, I belong to several national and international societies, but three of them are very selective of who gets into the society," Dr. Polin said. "One is called the Society of Pediatric Research. This is a society that recognizes your publications, your scientific publications and achievements."

The defense lawyer asked about additional highlights in Dr. Polin's 19-page curriculum vitae, which listed a half-dozen textbooks he had edited, and more than 90 scholarly papers.

"I'm constantly being asked to write reviews," the doctor said. "I have been the editor of a number of books which are widely used throughout the country and in fact the world." The books included *Fetal and Neonatal Physiology,* a two-volume textbook of 2,500 pages. "I don't know if we have a copy," the doctor said.

"Doctor," said the helpful defense lawyer, brandishing the bulky textbooks. "I have the two volumes here."

"And if you look at that, it's Polin and Fox," Dr. Polin said proudly. "Dr. Fox and I are the editors of that book, and it is the recognized standard in its field throughout the world.

"I have also published a book called *Pediatric Secrets,* which is a question-and-answer book which is used widely throughout this country by practitioners and medical students and interns and residents."

The defense lawyer asked about the doctor's move in 1998 from Children's Hospital of Philadelphia (CHOP) to Columbia Presbyterian Medical Center in New York City.

"It was a promotion," Dr. Polin said. "At Columbia, I'm chief of the division of neonatology." The doctor, who was commuting to trial daily on Amtrak's Metroliner, should have left it at that, but he added a comment sure to offend local jurors: "And for me it was professional satisfaction, moving from Philadelphia up to New York City."

When Beasley stood to question the doctor about his credentials, he sounded like the bumbling detective Peter Falk used to play in *Columbo.*

"I just have a few questions and maybe you can help me 'cause I'm not quite sure, me not being in the field," Beasley began apologetically. He asked Dr. Polin whether he was the sole author of all 95 original academic papers listed on his resume.

"No, I wrote them with many other academians," the doctor explained. Beasley asked about one of the coauthors. "Now there's a guy named Lou," Beasley began, but the doctor corrected him. "It's a woman," Dr. Polin said, referring to Dr. Stacey Lieu.

To the jury, Beasley must have seemed overmatched against the rich, sophisticated doctor from the Big Apple. But Beasley was setting a trap.

He asked Dr. Polin what happened back in 1991 when the doctor served as acting director of the division of neonatology at CHOP. Dr. Polin had formally applied to become permanent director and was interviewed by a hospital committee, along with several other candidates.

"And I assume that, since you were on the staff at CHOP from 1979, that most of the committee members would be familiar with you?" Beasley asked.

"Yes," Dr. Polin said warily. "Although some of the committee members were new... so they may not know me as well."

"They would certainly know how long you had been there?" Beasley asked.

"They knew how long I was at CHOP," the doctor agreed as he watched Beasley, waiting for the other shoe to drop.

"And after a deliberative process," Beasley asked, pausing for effect, "this committee *passed over you?*"

Beasley and Dr. Polin locked eyes for a moment. The committee's deliberations were supposed to be kept secret, so Dr. Polin had to wonder who on the committee had leaked the embarrassing news to his adversary. And, as he pondered his answer, and how this was going over in the courtroom, the doctor's face slowly turned bright red.

"That's correct," he finally stammered.

Beasley looked over at the jurors and flashed a knowing smile. "Thank you very much for helping me with that," he said and then he sat down.

. . .

"DOCTOR, DO YOU REMEMBER JOEY MCGOVERN?" THE DEFENSE LAWYER ASKED.

"I do not," the doctor said.

So the defense lawyer used medical records to tell the patient's story. Joseph Daniel McGovern was born June 6, 1992, at Pennsylvania Hospital, 11 weeks premature. He was delivered by cesarean section, because his mother had high blood pressure and diabetes. The infant's airway collapsed, and doctors had to insert a ventilator tube in his throat.

Joey was diagnosed with respiratory distress syndrome [RDS]. He was in such bad shape that doctors at Pennsylvania Hospital decided to ship him to the neonatal unit at CHOP for more tests. The diagnosis on the transport slip said "severe tracheal obstruction." Dr. Polin was the attending physician at CHOP who accepted Joey's transfer.

"Joey was incredibly ill," the doctor said, reading from notes. Although he could not remember the patient, Dr. Polin professed confidence in the treatment he had prescribed. "Yeah, I have treated hundreds of children in my medical lifetime over the last 25 years who have had a disease probably identical or very similar to Joey McGovern's," the doctor told the jury.

The defense lawyer asked Dr. Polin to step down from the witness stand and use some courtroom diagrams to explain Joey's condition to the jury. "I will give you my mike," the defense lawyer offered, but Dr. Polin said it wasn't necessary. "I have a loud voice, and I don't think there will be a problem for anybody to hear me speak."

Joey arrived at CHOP in shock, with low blood pressure. He suffered from spells where his left lung would collapse, and his right lung would hyper-inflate, Dr. Polin told the jury. Joey was on 100 percent oxygen, steroids and morphine. The infant was also given drugs to dilate his lungs and paralyze his body, so he wouldn't suffer another collapsed airway. But despite all the drugs and a ventilator, Joey still wasn't getting enough oxygen.

Also, because Joey wasn't able to exhale properly, the level of carbon dioxide in his blood rose to dangerous levels. The only solution was to remove the ventilator tube, put a mask over Joey's face and use a hand pump to force oxygen into his lungs, and then a suction machine to clear them out.

When doctors partially inserted an oxygen tube, however, they noticed that Joey's breathing problems continued. But when the tube was lowered farther down the trachea, bypassing some sort of obstruction, Joey's breathing returned to normal.

•   •   •

SUSAN MCGOVERN HAD HAD NO TROUBLE RECALLING HER SON'S HOSPITAL STAY WHEN Beasley put her on the witness stand a week earlier, during his presentation of the plaintiff's case. Joey's mother was a former hotel chambermaid, supermarket cashier and sandwich-maker who had to give up working to become Joey's full-time caretaker.

McGovern told Beasley how powerless she felt during Joey's ordeal. She wasn't allowed to ride in the ambulance that took Joey from Pennsylvania Hospital to CHOP. She wasn't allowed in the intensive care unit to see her son whenever Doctors Polin and Fox made the rounds. She also never got a chance to talk to either of the doctors supervising her son's care. All she could do was watch her son struggle to breathe.

"I — my — right now, my nerves are bad," McGovern stammered. "Just to see my son hooked up like that did — it just takes a toll on you."

Joey spent six months in intensive care at CHOP, then four months in a rehab hospital. When the McGoverns brought their 10-month-old son home, they had to hire overnight nurses. They also fell behind on the electric bill because Joey was on the ventilator 24 hours a day, and needed to stay cool with nonstop air-conditioning. By the time the case went to trial, Joey's medical bills had already reached $1.4 million, or, over the course of his young life, about $3,000 a week.

Whenever McGovern took her son to the doctor, it was a production. She told the jury how she and a nurse had to bring along a portable ventilator, oxygen tanks, a diaper bag full of medical equipment and a portable suction machine in case Joey's lungs clogged up again. "It was very hard," she said.

Joey was still having spells where he would stop breathing. Then, when Joey was almost 3 years old, a pediatrician ran a CAT scan and discovered that Joey had a condition known as a vascular ring. That's a birth defect when an artery from the aorta loops around the trachea and esophagus. A vascular ring can press down on the trachea, cutting off oxygen.

A heart surgeon operated to correct the defect, and a brain surgeon placed a shunt in Joey's head to drain fluid on the brain. Joey's breathing problems disappeared. He went off the ventilator, and he didn't have to go back to the hospital.

That raised the question of why doctors at CHOP had never previously run a CAT scan on Joey. Three different doctors at CHOP had suggested in writing that Joey be given a CAT scan, along with other tests, to discover the source of his breathing obstruction.

If the doctors at CHOP had given Joey a CAT scan after he was first admitted, they would have discovered the vascular ring almost three years earlier, and spared Joey McGovern brain damage. The fluid that drained from Joey's brain could have also been a result of the high level of carbon dioxide in the infant's blood. But Dr. Polin didn't approve the repeated request for a CAT scan, a questionable decision considering the scan was routine and inexpensive.

Although his health improved, Joey struggled with his disability. Doctors told his parents that Joey was "borderline retarded."

"Joey is very limited," his mother told Beasley on the witness stand. "I mean, Joey can't play sports, he can't be involved in any kind of team thing, because of the shunt in his head. I mean, if he, you know, just runs a little bit, you can hear him breathing hard. A little bit of exertion takes a lot out of him."

Beasley asked McGovern about the day Joey's sister bought him some Pokemon cards, and Joey went outside to show the cards to the neighborhood kids.

"Joey thought he'd fit in, and he took his binder of Pokemon cards out and the kids took most of them," McGovern said. She told Beasley how the kids teased her son, calling him *baby, retard* and *weirdo*. She began to stutter and look faint.

"Do you want some water?" Beasley asked. "Take your time. You OK? Hang in there." Beasley switched to simple yes or no questions:

"When Joey had the trach in for that 2½ year period, could he talk?"

"No."

"Could he cry?"

"No."

After a break, McGovern, a diabetic on an insulin pump, let out a gasp and collapsed in the back of the courtroom. "She went down so hard I thought she was dead," recalled Slade McLaughlin, one of Beasley's cocounsels.

The team of doctors that McGovern was suing immediately began working to revive her. The doctors lay McGovern across four chairs, and one doctor bent over the patient, tapping her chest. Meanwhile, court employees ushered the jury out of the courtroom, along with McGovern's children. A doctor was getting ready to start CPR when McGovern choked and began breathing again.

. . .

JOSEPH MCGOVERN, JOEY'S FATHER, TOOK THE STAND TO TESTIFY ABOUT HOW HE HAD used up all his vacation and sick time as a postal clerk on the night shift to stay with his son at the hospital. "It was tough," Joseph McGovern said. "He [Joey] would be paralyzed a lot of the times. They'd have to put drops in his eyes because he couldn't even lubricate his eyes. He had tubes everywhere."

Joey's father explained how every day his son, now almost 8, needed help to pull on his sweat pants, tie his shoes and even go to the bathroom. Joey's father talked about how discouraging it was to try to play catch with his son.

"I try to encourage him, but deep down it really hurts that he's not able to do them things," he said. "And I played ball all my life. I ran track. I like to lift weights . . . . You know, it's hard knowing that he probably will never be able to run like I do or lift weights or do stuff like that."

Beasley called Joey McGovern to the witness stand. The boy with the short dark hair, chubby cheeks and prominent front teeth looked sheepish.

"Joey, can you spell your last name?" Beasley asked.

Joey looked to his father for help, then shrugged his shoulders. "You have to look to Mr. Beasley," the judge told Joey. "And if you don't know, you can say you don't know."

"I don't know," Joey said.

Beasley asked Joey gently about the Pokemon cards: "Did you trade them?"

"Yeah."

"And what kind of cards did you get back?"

"I don't know. Like, with dirt on them."

Beasley asked about the neighborhood kids. "What names do they call you?"

"A dummy and idiot and retard."

"And how does that make you feel?"

"Sad," Joey said.

Over at the defense tables, Elaine M. Ross, one of the lawyers representing Drs. Polin and Fox, had a lump in her throat because Joey was such a "heartbreaking witness." While Beasley had Joey trying to write his ABCs on a tablet, the defense lawyers passed notes to each other. "Look at the jury," one note said. "We're dead."

. . .

BEASLEY'S EXPERT WITNESS WAS DR. GEORGE J. PECKHAM, A FORMER CHIEF OF PEDIATRIC services at CHOP who had originally hired both Drs. Polin and Fox to join his staff. Dr. Peckham had personally examined Joey as an infant. Dr. Peckham also had written a note in Joey's medical records saying that he agreed with a resident doctor's diagnosis that a CAT scan was needed, as well as other tests, to determine the cause of the "obstruction or external compression of the airway."

Beasley asked Dr. Peckham why he was testifying against his former colleagues. Dr. Peckham said he didn't want to at first. "I looked at the medical record," he said, "And I was quite frankly shocked because there was an obvious diagnosis there, and there seemed to be almost an aversion of trying to get to the diagnosis.

"I had to consider the concept of testifying against your own colleagues, which is horrible, versus the outcome, the damage that was done to this little boy, and I agreed to go ahead."

Dr. Peckham wrote a report concluding that the failure of Joey's doctors "to diagnose and treat the vascular ring increased the risks that this child would sustain the injuries from which he presently suffers."

But Beasley ran into trouble when he tried to get the doctor to testify about specifics of Joey's case, such as elevated carbon-dioxide levels in Joey's blood.

"Objection," the defense lawyer shouted.

"I think I have to call you back on this one," Judge Field said, as she summoned the lawyers to a conference in chambers. "I'm sorry. Come in."

Beasley was stewing as he trooped into the judge's chambers with all the defense lawyers. He asked the judge if she was purposefully prohibiting Dr. Peckham from discussing topics previously covered by Beasley's other witnesses. "Yes," the judge said.

Beasley complained that by not allowing Dr. Peckham to testify in support of other doctors in the case, the judge was allowing him only one witness on most medical matters in dispute. Beasley also argued that Dr. Peckham deserved more latitude to answer questions because he was not only an expert witness, but also one of Joey's treating physicians.

"Your Honor," Beasley argued, "what you're doing is you're not allowing me to develop for the jury the basis of his opinion if I'm only —"

The judge interrupted Beasley: "Then you're saying they're brain-dead and don't remember anything, that's what you're saying," the judge said of the jury.

"I'm not saying they're brain-dead," Beasley replied, but the judge complained that the testimony in Beasley's case had become too repetitive. "I'm trying very hard," the judge began, but this time Beasley cut her off. "I'm suggesting that you're trying very hard to keep evidence out," he shot back.

The judge and lawyers filed back into the courtroom. Beasley asked Dr. Peckham whether the doctors on trial had erred by not taking an X ray of their infant patient after he had inadvertently yanked an endotracheal tube out of his throat. A defense lawyer objected, and the judge sustained the objection. That was it for Beasley, who asked if he could put something on the record. The judge said yes, so in front of the jury, Beasley ripped into her:

"Your Honor, I don't know whether it's a problem you have with me. I'm certainly not the most personable lawyer in the city, but you're giving the jury the clear, unmistakable idea that this child is not entitled to a verdict," Beasley lectured. "You have sustained objections for reasons that boggle my mind, and I don't feel that this child would get a level playing field with you as the judge."

"You have said that several times, sir, and I find it offensive," the judge replied. "You're not my friend coming in here, nor was anybody else in this room. . . . You're accusing me of being biased and there is no other word for it, and I think that's very unfair and unprofessional, and on a personal basis, I take offense."

The acrimony between the judge and Beasley reached its peak when the defense presented its case. The judge called Beasley into her chambers for a conference. "He baits her," recalled one of the defense lawyers in the room, and "she lets him have it." Unfortunately for the judge, Beasley had left his microphone on, some thought deliberately.

"She's screaming at him and it's reverberating in the courtroom," the defense lawyer said. Beasley was yelling back at the judge. Then, the court crier burst into chambers and told the judge that the jurors were hearing everything.

Judge Field was so shocked "she was near tears," the defense lawyer said. The defense lawyers immediately moved for a mistrial, but the judge denied it.

• • •

DR. PECKHAM, BEASLEY'S EXPERT WITNESS, BLAMED JOEY'S INJURIES ON HIS DOCTORS, for failing to make an obvious diagnosis.

"When I was in first year medical school, they taught us you will only find what's wrong with the patient if you look for it," Dr. Peckham told Beasley. "No disease comes with a label. It doesn't pop out at you. You have to look for it."

When it was his turn on the witness stand, however, Dr. Polin blamed Joey's problems on other factors. Joey's lung disease was common among premature babies, as well as babies with diabetic mothers, Dr. Polin testified. Joey was also probably born with a "congenital malformation of the brain," the doctor told the jury. Dr. Polin also didn't think that the high levels of carbon dioxide in Joey's blood could cause brain damage.

Dr. Polin also testified that he had reason to doubt whether Joey had a vascular ring at birth because an echocardiogram showed an "aortic arch" on the infant's left side, where he had a blockage. The doctor said it was his experience that vascular rings only cause obstructions of the airway when located on the right side of the body.

"So when I'm asked what caused Joey's problems, it's a composite, it's all those things that went on," Dr. Polin explained to the jury. "If I had my choice, I would want every baby to survive and be normal."

"Thank you," the defense lawyer said. "I have no further questions, Doctor."

• • •

Jim Beasley rose to cross-examine Dr. Polin. He stood directly in front of the witness and leaned one cowboy boot on the plaintiff's table. "Was a vascular ring right there from birth?" Beasley asked.

"That's correct," the doctor said.

Beasley asked if the doctors had performed a CAT scan on June 29, 1992, shortly after Joey's arrival at CHOP, would it have shown a vascular ring? "I'm not sure that it would have shown a vascular ring, or read as a vascular ring," the doctor said.

"But there's only one way of finding out," Beasley said. "That would be to do the CAT scan at that time, which was recommended by a resident?"

"That's correct," Dr. Polin said.

Beasley asked if the medical staff had run a CAT scan on July 5, 1992, as recommended by Dr. Peckham, would it have shown the vascular ring? Dr. Polin replied that he thought Dr. Peckham had requested another type of test.

"Let's just see what Dr. Peckham recommended," Beasley said. "Before we get to Dr. Peckham… do you agree with an old Chinese proverb, 'He who asks a question may be a fool for five minutes, but he who does not ask a question remains a fool forever?' Do you agree with that?"

The doctor looked puzzled. "In general, I agree with that."

"Why do you say in general?" Beasley asked. "Do you agree with it?"

Dr. Polin seemed trapped. "I haven't thought about it very much. But there could be some exceptions to that rule, but as a philosophical statement, I agree with it."

"Is that a philosophical statement that you made in some of your writings?" Beasley asked.

"That particular quote?" the doctor said. "I don't remember using that particular quote in my writings."

"I see," Beasley said. "What's the next exhibit?… I'm going to show you plaintiff's exhibit P-110 and ask if you recognize the author of that preface…. Do you recognize the first one?"

"The first one is Richard A. Polin, M.D.," the startled doctor said. Beasley read the preface to *Pediatric Secrets*: "Never should the spirit of inquiry be discouraged or curiosity repressed." He asked the doctor to read the rest of the quote. "For according to a Chinese proverb," the doctor dutifully read, "he who asks a question may be a fool for five minutes, but he who does not ask a question remains a fool forever."

Dr. Polin tried to recoup. "I might add that that preface was written by my coeditor of this book, Dr. Mark Ditmar," Dr. Polin said. "It was not written by me. I'm one of the two co-editors on that book."

"I see," Beasley said, staring down the doctor. "When your co-editor Dr. Ditmar wrote that preface and you reviewed it, did you say to Dr. Ditmar this book is being written for residents, medical students and anybody else who is interested in neonatology, and I don't want that sentence in there?"

"No," the doctor said, "I did not say that."

"As a matter of fact, you don't even recall this child, do you?" Beasley reminded the doctor.

"I don't recall Joey McGovern, that's correct," the doctor said.

Beasley asked the doctor about his statement that Joey could not have a vascular ring because Joey's echocardiograms showed an aortic arch on the left side of the infant's body. The doctor maintained that only a vascular ring on the right side could cause obstruction of the airway. Beasley, however, offered as an exhibit a page of several medical illustrations of vascular malfunctions on the left side of the body that had caused obstructed airways.

Beasley asked the doctor if the illustrations were anatomically correct. The doctor looked them over and said he wasn't sure. He didn't seem familiar with the book that the illustrations were taken from, so Beasley asked if the doctor recognized the book title, *Pediatric Secrets*.

"I do," the chagrined doctor said. "It was edited by me."

Beasley hammered away at Dr. Polin, asking if the book was authoritative, and whether it was accurate enough for medical students and residents to rely on. Yes, the book was authoritative, Dr. Polin said; yes, it was reliable. Beasley took the doctor through the text of the illustrations that stated what side of the body the vascular rings were located on.

"I apologize," the doctor said. "It shows — the middle one does show a left aortic arch and the far right one also shows — it appears to be a left aortic arch."

Beasley asked about a note a resident physician had written Dr. Polin on July 13, 1992, recommending a CAT scan for Joey to rule out anatomic or vascular abnormalities, such as a vascular ring. Beasley read from Dr. Polin's pretrial deposition, saying if the recommendation had come from an attending physician, Dr. Polin would have discussed it with the attending physician. But residents, Dr. Polin had responded during his deposition, "write all kinds of crazy things on the chart that I don't have responsibility for."

Now, on the witness stand, Dr. Polin tried to repair the damage. "People in training sometimes can't distinguish between important observations or erroneous observations or observations which are ridiculous," he told Beasley.

Beasley stayed on the attack: "When you refused to accept the recommendation of three qualified physicians, were you not putting this child at tremendous risk for future disability?"

"No," the doctor said.

"Isn't the fact of the matter . . . that the child did suffer permanent disability because of your refusal to do a CAT scan on a recommendation of three other physicians?"

"That's untrue."

"And if a CAT scan had been done and a vascular ring was indeed the cause . . . and it was relieved, that child would be home in a couple of days?"

"That is also untrue, sir."

"[Joey] would have not stayed in the hospital 10 months and then thereafter undergone a tracheostomy and then 2½ years on a ventilator?"

"That's untrue."

· · ·

MCGOVERN V. WEIL WAS THE FIRST BIG CASE FOR ELAINE M. ROSS, ONE OF THE DEFENSE lawyers representing Drs. Polin and Fox. It was highly complex and went on for three weeks. Ross found it a challenge to be in the courtroom every day, because the routine wore her down mentally and physically. Some mornings she could barely keep her eyes open. Then she would look over at Beasley and see a guy well past retirement age who seemed to be getting more energetic as the case wore on.

Ross watched as Beasley showed up early many mornings with a new bone to pick with the judge. In chambers, Beasley objected to the judge's facial expressions, her open "disdain" for the plaintiff's lawyer, and her "bad rulings," which Beasley griped were "cutting the heart out of my case."

Beasley didn't win any of the arguments, of course, but he did succeed in setting the agenda and keeping the judge and the opposing lawyers on the defensive. Ross also marveled at Beasley's stamina, referring to him as the "Energizer bunny."

At lunch time, the judge, jury and most of the lawyers would file out of the courtroom. But Beasley stayed behind, poring over documents while munching pretzels and Goldenberg's Peanut Chews.

Ross decided to fraternize with the enemy. She had heard so much about Beasley before trial that she was expecting some stiff and lofty character like Atticus Finch in *To Kill a Mockingbird*. But Beasley smiled at jurors, said a cheerful good morning to the doctors he was suing, and flirted openly with the court reporter half his age.

Ross worried that jurors saw Beasley as "a lovable old man, like somebody's grandpa." But Ross saw a wily adversary who knew how to manipulate the system and was doing his best to "dice up my clients."

"Do you really like being in a courtroom day after day?" Ross asked Beasley. "Are you enjoying this?"

"You know, if I wasn't in this courtroom, I would be in another one," Beasley told Ross. "This is what I love to do."

Beasley asked Ross what she was doing over at the defense table. "You would be wonderful representing these poor injured children," he said.

Ross kidded Beasley, telling him she had gone over "to the dark side." Then the judge walked through the double doors, and court was back in session. Beasley and Ross went back to their respective tables, which bumped right up against each other.

• • •

"DOCTOR," ASKED ELAINE ROSS. "IN YOUR PRACTICE AS A PEDIATRICIAN AND NEONA-tologist, have you received any special awards?"

"Yes," the witness replied. Dr. William W. Fox was a senior physician at CHOP and medical director of the Newborn ICU, where Joey had been a patient in 1992. The 59-year-old Dr. Fox, who wore a navy blue blazer and khaki pants, appeared relaxed and confident as he talked about the highlights of his 19-page curriculum vitae.

"In about 1979 there was a book that came out called *The Best Doctors in America* and I was in that book," Dr. Fox told the jury. "There were only 30 neonatol-ogists throughout the United States that were in that first edition." The doctor said he was also mentioned in another book, *The Best Doctors in the Northeast*.

"And this past year, I was named to the teaching honor roll at Children's Hospi-tal," he said, after the resident physicians voted to select the hospital's best teachers.

"From looking at your CV, I note that you have approximately 250 publica-tions," Ross said. It was closer to 300, the doctor corrected her.

"Doctor," Ross said, "in addition to the journals and the abstracts, have you published any books?

"Yes," Dr. Fox said. He talked about how proud he was of the textbook he had coedited with Dr. Polin, *Fetal and Neonatal Physiology*.

"I think it is considered one of the landmark texts in the field," Dr. Fox said, as he turned toward the judge. "I was just in [a] conference in Austria and people over in Russia and in Asia and even, Your Honor, South America, people all over the world are using this textbook."

• • •

WHEN BEASLEY STOOD TO CROSS-EXAMINE THE WITNESS, HE MADE SHORT WORK OF ALL OF DR. Fox's awards and credentials. Beasley asked the doctor if he ever bought a copy of *The Best Doctors in America.*

"Yes," the doctor said.

"How much did it cost?" Beasley barked.

Dr. Fox seemed taken aback. "I think it was $30."

"And how much was *The Best Doctors in the Northeast*?" Beasley demanded.

The doctor seemed puzzled. "I think it was $100," he said.

Just because the doctor was written up in both books, Beasley said, did that mean he was incapable of being negligent?

"I don't understand the relationship," the doctor said.

"Well," Beasley said, "I'm trying to figure out why you feel that being in *The Best Doctors in America*, whether it gives you some type of immunity from being negligent?"

Dr. Fox mulled it over. "I suppose it doesn't make me immune from being negligent," he said.

Over at the defense table, George L. Young Jr. was feeling sorry for Dr. Fox. "He'd bore in on you on cross-examination," Young said of Beasley. "He had those heart-of-darkness eyes."

Next, Beasley asked the doctor about a noisy, rasping breathing condition known as stridor: "If the child has an endotracheal tube in place, you don't have stridor?"

"You can," Dr. Fox said.

Beasley whipped out Dr. Fox's pretrial deposition and read from it:

" 'Would a patient who is intubated have stridor?' Your answer: 'No.' " Beasley stared at the doctor: "Now, which do you want the jury to believe?"

"Objection, Your Honor," Ross said.

A second defense lawyer rose to object and demanded that Beasley read the doctor's entire answer in the pre-trial deposition. "Well, if there's something omitted from the deposition, he's entitled —" the judge began, but Beasley took charge of the courtroom, cutting off the judge.

"There's nothing omitted from the deposition," Beasley told the judge. "I read the entire question and answer." Beasley then turned to Dr. Fox: "Now, which is it that you want the jury to accept? Yes, a child intubated can have stridor, or if he's intubated, he can't have stridor? Which is it?"

Dr. Fox gave a long technical answer, saying that generally, patients with a breathing tube stuck in their throats can't make rasping sounds, because the tube would keep the airway open. But if, in an unusual situation, the tip of the tube was as high as it could go, but right around the vocal chords, then stridor was possible.

Beasley stayed on the offensive. "Was there any reason why you couldn't have given that explanation" when first asked the question? "Objection, Your Honor," the defense lawyer said, but the judge overruled it. "You may answer the question," the judge said.

"The answer is I'm not a lawyer, I'm a physician," the frustrated doctor blurted. "If I'm in a court of law, and we're going through single words at a time, and very specific definitions, then I have to be a lot more careful." But while the doctor raised his volume, Beasley kept asking his rapid-fire questions in the same tone of voice.

"Is there anything legal about the question . . . if I ask you if a patient intubated would have stridor? Is there anything legal about that?"

The doctor tried to remain calm. "I think we're in a legal situation here, and I have to be very, very specific about the answers I give," Dr. Fox said. He said he was not as specific when he was teaching medical students. "We try to talk about the most common situation. In here, we're taking single words in a sentence and trying to define them very specifically. That's what I'm doing in my answer now."

Beasley: "Weren't you in a legal situation when your deposition was taken?"

Dr. Fox: "I haven't been in these legal situations very often, so I don't know."

Beasley refused to let it go: "No. Weren't you in a legal situation when your deposition was taken on Jan. 6, 1999?"

"I suppose so," the weary doctor finally conceded.

Over at the defense table, the lawyers realized that they were taking another pounding. Drs. Polin and Fox were both smart, accomplished people who weren't used to being interrogated by somebody like Beasley, or being told that they might have screwed up. On the witness stand, the two doctors came across as arrogant, and Beasley was making them look foolish as well. And it was about to get worse.

Beasley raised the topic of elevated carbon-dioxide levels, known as hypercarbia. Both Dr. Polin and Dr. Fox had testified that elevated carbon-dioxide levels in Joey's blood could not have caused brain damage. (A normal carbon-dioxide level was between 30 and 40; Joey's was above 100.)

Dr. Fox stuck with his position: "I would say that the levels seen in this baby are not associated with brain damage."

Beasley asked Dr. Fox if he was familiar with another medical text, *Neurology of the Newborn*, written by Dr. Joseph J. Volpe. "Yes," said Dr. Fox.

"Is it an authoritative text?" Beasley asked.

Dr. Fox was dismissive: "It is a good text. I wouldn't call it authoritative."

Beasley read an excerpt from Dr. Volpe's book. "Hypercarbia results in impairment of cerebral vascular autoregulation," Beasley read, referring to involuntary blood flow in the brain. "The infant then becomes especially vulnerable to *ischemic* cerebral injury," Beasley read, referring to brain damage caused by a lack of oxygen. "Do you agree with that statement?"

While the doctor's lawyers hastily flipped through the book, trying to find the passage Beasley was quoting, Dr. Fox hesitated: "I don't think I am qualified to comment on that statement."

Beasley was right on top of the witness. He turned back to the plaintiff's table, where cocounsels Slade McLaughlin and Jim Beasley Jr. were stationed, and in a loud, commanding voice he yelled, "Get me the book!"

Jim Jr. reached under his desk and pulled out two bulky volumes of *Fetal and Neonatal Physiology*. Because of Beasley's high volume, everybody in the court was staring at him, waiting to see what would happen next.

"I see," Beasley said, flipping through one of the textbooks. "Are you the same Fox that edited this book?"

"Yes, I did," Dr. Fox said.

"On page 2176, 'Acute elevations of carbon dioxide, however, may depress cerebral metabolism,'" Beasley said. "Is that true?"

"I don't think I am qualified to comment on this issue," Dr. Fox said.

Beasley kept reading: "'Most importantly, hypercarbia abolishes the autoregulatory response because of marked vasodilation [dilated blood vessels], and this disturbance may add to the risk of *ischemic* brain injury.'"

"Now that is out of your book," Beasley told the doctor. "Are you saying you are not qualified to pass on that?"

To the two cocounsels at the plaintiff's table, it was like a bomb going off in the courtroom, and with it, the doctor's credibility went up in smoke. On the witness stand, Dr. Fox backpedaled, trying to explain that the book was a two-volume set, 2,800 pages in length, with about 200 authors, and that he was only one of two editors, and not an expert on every topic. But the looks on the faces of the jurors told the defense lawyers everything they needed to know.

• • •

THE NEXT MORNING, FRIDAY, APRIL 14TH, BEASLEY APPEARED IN COURT AND TOLD THE judge the case had been settled. The jurors clapped; the defense lawyers felt they had dodged a bullet because terms of the settlement were confidential. "We didn't get a big verdict in the paper," Elaine Ross said.

The judge told Beasley that the jurors wanted to meet with him after the trial. So Beasley walked into the jury room, trailed by his two young cocounsels. The jurors, most of whom were African Americans, gave Beasley a standing ovation. Slade McLaughlin felt chills up his spine. He looked over at Beasley, saw him smile sheepishly and say, "Thank you."

"Oh, Mr. Beasley," several jurors gushed, "You were great!" They asked for his business card, so Beasley took out a stack and passed them around

Babies & Children's
Hospital of New York
Founded in 1887

Richard A. Polin, MD   May 2, 2000
Director. Division of Neonatology
Columbia University College of Physicians & Surgeons

Mr. Peter Liacouris
President,
Temple University
Office of the President
1801 North Broad Street
Philadelphia, Pennsylvania 19122

Dear President Liacouris:

4959 Broadway. BHS 115
New York. NY 10032
212.305.5827 Telephone
212.305.7086 Fax

     I am a graduate of both the College of Liberal Arts (1966) and the Temple University School of Medicine (1970). In the past, I have always tried to make contributions to Temple University because I felt that my education at Temple University was excellent.

     At this time, however, I must express my great dissatisfaction at naming the law school after Mr. Beasley. As you know, Mr. Beasley is a plaintiff attorney for malpractice cases with considerable expertise in that area. You may not be aware that Mr. Beasley has made much of his money by suing graduates of the Temple University School of Medicine, including myself. I recently spent three weeks at a trial in Philadelphia with Mr. Beasley and I was saddened by the tremendous dishonesty on the part of the plaintiff attorneys and experts.

     I realize that Temple University is benefiting by Mr. Beasley's donation, but I think it was poor judgement to name one of Temple's illustrious schools after him. Therefore, I must regretfully decline to contribute any more to Temple University.

                Sincerely,

                Richard A. Polin, M.D
                Professor of Pediatrics

RAP:fob

TEMPLE UNIVERSITY

PHILADELPHIA, PENNSYLVANIA 19122

THE PRESIDENT

June 30, 2000

Richard A. Polin, M.D.
Professor of Pediatrics
Babies and Children's Hospital of New York
3959 Broadway, BHS 115
New York, NY 10032

Dear Dr. Polin:

Thank you for your letter of May 2 on Jim Beasley. Knowing Mr. Beasley personally, and having witnessed and reviewed his professional work for thirty years, I have great respect and admiration for him. Comparing Beasley's life with Vanderbilt University's namesake, we're indeed lucky!

It's understandable that when you're being cross-examined by Jim Beasley and confronted with expert witnesses contradicting what **you** may believe to be the truth, it's hard to adopt a broader perspective. It's not unlike the reaction of persons unfairly criticized in the media, or in reacting to articles or books attacking their own cherished beliefs: for many such persons, the constitutional guarantees of the First Amendment appear indefensible and they demonize the critic.

My point is that you're entitled to your opinion and what you believe is the truth and on how you practice medicine and how you think law should be practiced and to what causes you choose to contribute. When, however, you seek to leverage your own views onto an institution that provided you with an excellent education, you appear to be over-reaching.

Again, thanks for sharing your thoughts and decision. I wish you well.

Sincerely,

Peter J. Liacouras

received
12-5-97

12481 PL

Attorneys for Defendant,
Marshall Jacobs, M.D.

No. 73447
Kreeman
tion No. 79048

092108
⑤

PA 19462

PHILADELPHIA COUNTY OF COMMON PLEAS
PETITION/MOTION COVER SHEET

A MINOR BY AND
HIS PARENTS KEVIN PECK
PECK AND KEVIN PECK AND
PECK, IN THEIR OWN RIGHT

v.

CHILDREN'S HOSPITAL OF PHILADELPHIA
and
MARSHALL JACOBS, M.D.
and
JOHN D. MURPHY, M.D.
and
SUSAN T. NICHOLSON, M.D.

: COURT OF COMMON PLEAS
: PHILADELPHIA COUNTY
:
:
:
:
: JULY TERM, 1994
:
: NO. 821
:
:
:
: TWELVE JURORS DEMANDED

ORDER

AND NOW, this ___28th___ day of ___November___, 1997, it
is hereby ORDERED that Defendant's Motion for Summary Judgment is
GRANTED and all Claims and Crossclaims against Defendant,
Marshall Jacobs, M.D., are dismissed.

BY THE COURT:

RECEIVED

DEC 0 2 1997

CIVIL ADMINISTRATION

[signature]

Chapter 20

❖❖❖

THE LOCKED CREDENZA

AT 8 A.M. ON A SATURDAY MORNING, JIM BEASLEY AND AN ASSOCIATE, SLADE McLaughlin, were pacing the fourth floor of The Beasley Building, waiting for an emergency locksmith to show up and crack open a locked credenza.

The credenza belonged to Thomas W. Smith, a Beasley associate at the center of a rapidly unfolding scandal. A day earlier, on Jan. 30, 1998, Smith was on vacation in Florida when his secretary notified McLaughlin that there might be trouble with a few of Smith's cases.

McLaughlin had been asked by Smith to cover for him, so he checked some court files and discovered that three of Smith's medical malpractice cases had been dismissed because of unopposed motions for summary judgment. Two of the cases involved catastrophic brain injuries to infants, and were potentially worth millions of dollars in damages. But now, because of Smith's inaction, all three cases had been thrown out of court without an argument or a hearing. And none of the plaintiffs knew a thing about it.

The locksmith arrived and picked the lock. Smith's credenza was jammed full with piles of unopened mail and stacks of unanswered legal motions. As he dug through the paperwork, McLaughlin felt sick to his stomach. "This is unfucking believable," he said to Beasley. "Look at this!"

Beasley's jaw muscles tensed, his eyes narrowed. "Where's he staying?" the boss demanded. "Get me the number."

Beasley dialed Smith in Florida. "Tom. Jim Beasley. What the fuck is going on? I'm in your office. What's happening with these summary judgments? You're not responding."

Beasley was silent as he listened to Smith try to explain himself. "You lost your mind?" Beasley erupted. "Bullshit, you're fired!"

Beasley slammed down the phone. He looked around Smith's office, at all the family photos and framed diplomas that Smith had left behind, as well as several suits and ties, and a pair of golf shoes. "Slade, I want you to take all this personal stuff and throw it on the goddamn street," Beasley fumed, and then he stormed out.

It was the start of the worst crisis of Beasley's career.

Beasley, Jim Jr. and McLaughlin spent the rest of the day organizing the paperwork from Smith's credenza. By nightfall, Beasley and son were on the phone, ordering all 15 of the firm's remaining lawyers to report to work early Sunday morning for emergency triage. The next day, Beasley's lawyers combed through Smith's files for more than 60 cases, to determine how many others were in jeopardy of dismissal.

The lawyers discovered that other cases handled by Smith had been dismissed due to unopposed summary judgment motions, unopposed preliminary objections, unopposed motions to preclude expert testimony, and unopposed motions for sanctions. Eleven medical malpractice cases had already been thrown out of court, and three more cases were in danger of imminent dismissal.

The lawyers found something else to worry about, a copy on Smith's desk of an article from the New England Journal of Medicine, "Assessment and Treatment of Suicidal Patients." Smith wasn't handling any cases involving suicide, so his colleagues wondered if Tom Smith planned to kill himself.

Beasley called all the clients in the 11 dismissed cases, and told them to come in immediately. When he met with clients, Beasley promised to do everything he could to get their cases reopened. But if he was unsuccessful, Beasley told them, "I want you to sue me for malpractice."

For Beasley, the stakes couldn't have been higher. He operated a sole proprietorship, and if he was simultaneously hit with a wave of malpractice cases, he faced the prospect of personal bankruptcy. He had malpractice insurance, but it covered negligent acts, not intentional ones. And nobody had enough insurance to cover all the claims that might result from the Tom Smith debacle.

In one weekend, Beasley's reputation, his fortune, and his whole life's work were suddenly all at risk. And soon, the press would be on the story.

Tom Smith was an unlikely villain; a big, jovial guy who played Santa Claus at office Christmas parties. Jurors liked Smith, so did fellow lawyers, even the ones who tried cases against him.

"I first met Tom Smith in the spring of 1994 when he was an adversary representing the Children's Hospital of Pittsburgh," Beasley stated in an affidavit. "I was favorably impressed with Mr. Smith's handling of the trial on behalf of his client, and I made inquiries about his abilities to a number of judges, each of whom favorably recommended Mr. Smith, who they said was an excellent trial lawyer."

The case Beasley tried against Smith settled for $250,000. A few months later, on June 20, 1994, Smith came to work for Beasley. By 1998, Smith had 20 years of experience as a trial lawyer, having tried some 200 cases.

Smith, however, also had a reputation for being disorganized, as well as having persistent money troubles. When Smith's house faced a sheriff's sale, Beasley bought it back and rented it to Smith. Beasley also leased a Cadillac for Smith to drive.

"I treated him like a son," Beasley griped to McLaughlin. "All I've done for that SOB, and he's gonna sell me down the river? It's unacceptable."

• • •

ON SUNDAY NIGHT, FEB. 1, 1998, SLADE MCLAUGHLIN RECEIVED A PHONE CALL FROM Tom Smith, who had just flown in from Florida. Smith asked McLaughlin to meet him at one of their usual hangouts, Pizzeria Uno.

Smith, at 54, was 15 years older than McLaughlin. The two men had worked together as defense lawyers at the Philadelphia firm of Griffith & Burr, where McLaughlin considered Smith a close personal friend and mentor. Then, both lawyers joined Beasley's firm within a week of each other.

They ate lunch together nearly every day. McLaughlin had always thought of Smith as a happy-go-lucky guy until the past year, when Smith's mother was afflicted with Lou Gehrig's disease and faced a slow, painful death. Smith's wife had also been hospitalized with a preliminary diagnosis of cancer. Smith told McLaughlin he was having difficulty sleeping at night and concentrating during the day.

When the two lawyers met at Pizzeria Uno, McLaughlin thought his old buddy looked ghastly. Smith's face was gaunt, his hands were trembling, and he spoke just above a whisper. He hadn't slept in days, and he said he was contemplating suicide. Smith tearfully told McLaughlin he was having a breakdown and that he had lost his mind.

McLaughlin talked Smith into seeing a psychiatrist. McLaughlin also returned all of Smith's personal belongings from his old office at The Beasley Building. He followed Smith home to continue their conversation. And before he left, McLaughlin made Smith promise that he wouldn't try to hurt himself.

Back at the office, McLaughlin and David A. Yanoff, another Beasley attorney, resumed plowing through Smith's abandoned paperwork, along with Jim Jr., who was supposed to be studying for his law boards.

"Slade, David Yanoff and I moved in here for a week, and did nothing but triage these cases," Jim Jr. recalled. "We had all the files, and we basically stayed up for a week."

The lawyers took turns napping on couches. Yanoff researched Pennsylvania case law and typed away at a brief that would attempt to reopen all of Smith's dismissed cases.

On Feb. 3, 1998, psychiatrist Wolfram Rieger examined Tom Smith and wrote a letter to a staff psychiatrist at Friends Hospital in Northeast Philadelphia, urging a prompt admission.

Smith, Rieger wrote, had a number of stressors in his life. His mother had died in December 1997, after a long illness; Smith also owed the I.R.S. "a large sum of money," Rieger wrote. "Since they attached his wages, he found himself with insufficient funds to carry on a normal lifestyle for someone of his stature and level of experience."

But while Smith was having a breakdown at work, "he was able to maintain the facade of a highly competent, capable professional, thus keeping his colleagues and his superiors completely in the dark," Rieger wrote. Now, however, Smith was struggling to accept reality.

"During today's psychiatric examination, I found Mr. Smith to be indeed clinically depressed to the point of being tearful," Rieger wrote. "He reported sleep disturbance and some appetite disturbance. He is quite pessimistic and hopeless and helpless…. Diagnostically, Mr. Smith presently has a major depression, superimposed on bereavement."

While Tom Smith checked into a psychiatric hospital, his former colleagues tried to come to terms with what he had done. Paul A. Lauricella admitted he was "apoplectic" the day he vented to Beasley about the toll the Tom Smith debacle was taking on the firm.

"Why?" Lauricella kept asking Beasley, as they walked to a settlement conference. "Why would he have done it? Doesn't it make you crazy to think that after everything you did for him, that he would do something so stupid? He could have handed the motions to me."

"Paul," said Beasley, placing a firm hand on Lauricella's shoulder, "if people stopped making mistakes, we would be out of business."

But despite Beasley's outer calm, the scandal was taking a toll. When Donoloy stopped by his son's house, Jim Jr. was shocked by his father's appearance.

"For the first time, he looked old," Jim Jr. said. "He looked very, very old. And he also looked like he was scared about what was going to happen."

· · ·

L. Stuart Ditzen was a veteran reporter at the Philadelphia Inquirer who covered the civil courts, and he had already received several tips about the Tom Smith scandal. "The defense bar was having a picnic" buzzing over it, Ditzen recalled. So Ditzen called Beasley and told him he planned to write a story about this extraordinary disaster that had befallen one of the city's preeminent plaintiff's lawyers.

Beasley responded with a threat. "I wouldn't take kindly to anybody interfering with my business," he warned Ditzen. But Ditzen didn't need Beasley's cooperation to write the story; it was already laid out in court files.

On Feb. 6, 1998, just six days after he broke into Smith's credenza, Beasley had filed a "Petition for Extraordinary Relief in the Nature of an Omnibus Petition to Open Judgments and Provide Further Relief." In the petition, Beasley and Yanoff charged that Smith had been "grossly derelict" and had engaged in "wholesale abandonment" of his clients "due to his recently discovered personal and psychiatric problems."

The one-inch-thick document featured a 29-page brief and 25 attachments, including supplemental affidavits from Beasley, McLaughlin and Tom Smith's secretary. In the petition, Beasley and Yanoff asked the court to simultaneously reopen all 11 dismissed cases, as well as to grant new scheduling orders for three other cases in danger of being dismissed.

Ditzen marveled at the quality of the document, and how fast it had been assembled. "I was very, very impressed," he said. "I still thought he was gonna get his ass kicked."

Defense lawyers stood in line to file opposing motions. Several questioned whether Smith had really had a breakdown. Other defense lawyers charged that Beasley himself had been negligent for not adequately monitoring Smith, whom they claimed had a well-known history of sloppy work habits.

Ditzen met with Inquirer editors to brief them about the story. I was in the Inquirer newsroom at the time, and saw several editors filing out of a conference room, after meeting with Ditzen. They all had smiles on their faces.

That's because the Tom Smith story was bullet-proof. It was told in court documents that carried a legal privilege allowing reporters to quote freely without the legal jeopardy of being sued for libel. The only thing Beasley could do was write threatening letters.

"You want to question me further with respect to the Thomas Smith matter, and I told you that I had said everything that was necessary to be said in the past correspondence," Beasley wrote Ditzen on May 1, 1998, in a letter copied to the Inquirer's in-house counsel. "It is quite obvious that you know precisely what my position has been, and I can see no valid reason in submitting to an interrogation by you.

"I believe you have an ulterior purpose," Beasley wrote. "I told you my feeling that your reporting on this litigation was for the singular purpose to punish me for my past litigation with your employer, Philadelphia Newspapers Inc., and Knight Ridder Inc."

Beasley argued that plenty of summary judgment motions and other petitions had been filed over the years without the Inquirer ever reporting on them. "I can only conclude, therefore, that your attitude that you are going to write this story about me, come hell or high water, is evidence of gross and intentional abuse of a privilege and not for any newsworthy purpose, but only to embarrass me and my clients."

Three days later, Beasley wrote another threatening letter to Ditzen, and again copied the Inquirer's in-house counsel. "It is the intent of The Inquirer to do what it can to destroy the credibility of myself and other members of this firm," Beasley charged. "I see this desire on the part of The Inquirer as the guiding light behind any story that you intend to print about an unfortunate event that has no public interest at all."

Ditzen, in an interview, dismissed Beasley's written threats as "baloney" and "just huffing and puffing."

"I viewed it then, and I view it now, as strictly posturing and intimidation, which were standard tools of his," Ditzen said. "He's vigorously posturing and attempting to intimidate, in this instance, from a position of weakness, and he knew it."

"I knew that we were on solid ground," Ditzen said. "This was a legitimate story and a fascinating story. He had gotten himself into an unimaginable mess, and he didn't want any publicity about it."

. . .

THE HEADLINE ON THE BOTTOM OF THE MONDAY, JUNE 15, 1998, FRONT PAGE WAS "Legal giant finds big trouble in his own firm."

The Inquirer, under Stu Ditzen's byline, reported that Tom Smith's breakdown posed "a huge potential legal malpractice problem for Beasley himself," variously described in the lengthy story as a "famed trial lawyer," "legal titan" and "white-haired litigator."

The front-page story on Beasley's legal problems ran 65 column inches. That was more than the combined 48 inches allotted for two front-page stories about "Operation Sunrise," a task force of federal, state and city law enforcement officials launching an unprecedented assault that morning on drug-and-crime-infested Philadelphia neighborhoods.

The space that the Inquirer devoted to the Beasley story was also nearly three times the 22 inches allotted to a front-page, self-described Washington Post "bombshell" revealing that independent counsel Kenneth Starr had been briefing reporters all along on a background basis about his investigation of President Clinton's affair with Monica Lewinsky.

Ditzen, in an interview, said the Inquirer at the time routinely ran in-depth project stories of that length, usually about complicated matters, and that the editors typically held those stories until they had sufficient space to run them. He also said it was unfair to compare project stories with breaking news stories.

For the Inquirer, however, the attraction was laying out its longtime nemesis in print. Or, as Ditzen explained in an interview, "Because he [Beasley] had engaged in combat with the newspaper he became more of a higher profile."

Beasley declined to be interviewed by the Inquirer. He was quoted as asserting in letters that the Inquirer was seeking to "punish" him for winning two libel verdicts against the newspaper, both in 1990, for a total of $40 million. Beasley was referring to the $34 million verdict in *Sprague v. Walter*, and a $6 million verdict in *McDermott v. Inquirer*, on behalf of a state Supreme Court justice that was subsequently overturned.

But Inquirer Editor Robert J. Rosenthal was quoted in the story as denying that Beasley had been treated unfairly. "We've reported this story because it is newsworthy," Rosenthal said. "And we have made every effort to be accurate, balanced and fair in describing a very unfortunate situation."

The Inquirer story reported that Beasley had argued that the dismissals of the 11 cases were caused by circumstances beyond his control, since Smith had deceived his boss as well as his clients.

"Some two dozen lawyers representing defendants in the lawsuits have responded with an oratorio of protest to Beasley's request to reopen the cases," the Inquirer story said. "Those lawyers and their clients, more than 20 doctors, six hospitals, a drug store chain, a pharmaceutical maker and a law firm, have won their cases by default without having to go to trial.

"Now, several of those lawyers argue in court pleadings that Beasley is the one who should be sued for professional malpractice — by his own clients — for failure to supervise his employee," the Inquirer story said.

The Inquirer quoted several defense lawyers who opposed Beasley's motion to reopen the cases: "'Mr. Beasley's focus on Mr. Smith's alleged mental illness is an apparent attempt to divert this court's attention from Mr. Beasley's independent responsibilities to his clients,'" wrote Allan H. Starr, whose firm, White & Williams, represents defendants in eight of the dismissed cases…. "'Mr. Beasley had a duty to supervise Mr. Smith to ensure that he completely performed his professional duties.'"

Another defense attorney, Andrew K. Worek, asked for a court order disqualifying Beasley from further representing any of the clients whose suits had been dismissed. Worek contended that Beasley had an "irreconcilable conflict of interest" if he continued to represent clients in the 11 dismissed cases because those clients all had "looming malpractice claims" against Beasley, the Inquirer reported.

The story noted that Beasley — "widely regarded as one of the best trial lawyers in America"— faced a crisis "unlike anything he had dealt with before in his 42-year career, and it has placed him uncharacteristically on the defensive."

And, the Inquirer informed its readers, Beasley's legal attempts to extricate himself from the mess seemed like a long shot. "In general, courts are reluctant to allow a lawsuit to be reopened after dismissal, particularly after a 30-day appeal period has lapsed, as it had in most of Smith's cases," the Inquirer said. "Beasley is asking that 11 cases be reopened in a single stroke."

· · ·

MAYBE STU DITZEN HAD BEEN TALKING TO TOO MANY DEFENSE LAWYERS. ON AUG. 11, 1998, Ditzen wrote another front-page story for the Inquirer: "11 suits handled by city lawyer reinstated." Judge John W. Herron decided that Tom Smith's "professional dereliction and deceit" constituted "a unique and compelling case" requiring that all of Smith's former cases be reopened. The Inquirer described the judge's decision as "highly unusual," but the judge sided with arguments made in Beasley's petition for extraordinary relief.

Beasley associate David A. Yanoff had cited several state cases that provided precedents for reinstating cases previously dismissed. Yanoff found that in Pennsylvania, cases may be reinstated for "proper cause" upon "a showing of mere oversight or neglect of a client's affairs, whether based on an attorney's error or his or her simple illness."

Yanoff also found several cases that met the standard for "extraordinary cause" for a judge to reinstate a dismissed case. One of those cases was *Estate of Gasbarini v. Medical Center of Beaver*, dismissed in 1979, after the plaintiff's lawyer, Franklin Rubin, failed to show up at a hearing regarding preliminary objections to his complaint. Rubin had a good reason for not showing; he'd been disbarred and hadn't bothered to tell his client.

The case was reinstated by the state Supreme Court. "Under these circumstances, it would be harsh, indeed, to hold that appellant's possible cause of action be lost forever because of the conduct of an attorney this court has deemed unfit for the practice of law in this Commonwealth," the court decided.

"Mr. Smith, like the attorney in *Gasbarini*, misled and deceived his clients, and on a far greater scale," Beasley and Yanoff had argued in their petition for extraordinary relief. "Moreover, although Mr. Smith had not been deemed unfit for the practice of law during the time period at issue herein, his unfitness, in retrospect, is distressingly clear." The brief said that Smith might face future disbarment. (His license to practice law was subsequently suspended.)

The Inquirer story reported that several defense lawyers had "argued in court papers that Beasley should be disqualified because his clients had potential malpractice claims against him for failure to supervise Smith."

Judge Herron, however, rejected that argument. The judge "ruled that there was no conflict of interest because Beasley and his clients shared the same goal: to get the dismissed cases back on track," the Inquirer reported. The judge also found that Beasley was a victim of Smith's deceit.

The judge, in a portion of his opinion not quoted by the Inquirer, wrote that "a critical aspect of Mr. Smith's dereliction was a pattern of deceit directed towards his colleagues as to the true status of the cases at issue in this petition, including the secreting away in a locked credenza pleadings and correspondence ordinarily placed in appropriate court files."

Herron also "held that Beasley had documented a pattern of lies and neglect by Smith," the Inquirer story said. The judge had cited the case of twin babies catastrophically brain-injured at birth, a case that had been dismissed in March 1997 because Smith did not reply to court motions. "Seven months after the dismissal, Smith met with the parents, who did not know their case had been lost, and discussed a possible $2.2 million settlement," the Inquirer story said.

Ditzen also tracked down Tom Smith, who, after his firing, spent "a brief period" at a psychiatric facility in Northeast Philadelphia. "I'm very pleased for the clients that they will get their day in court, and I think that with Beasley, they're in the best hands," Smith told the newspaper.

"This was a tragedy that should not have happened, but now it has been made right," Beasley told the Inquirer. "The clients will have their day in court. That's the important thing."

The judge agreed. In a Sept. 18, 1998, scheduling order, Judge Herron wrote that "although defendants suggest that it was an error to grant this petition because discovery at this juncture will reveal that at least some of the plaintiff's cases were without merit, the best method for making this determination is to place these cases back on track where they will prevail — or fail — on their merits either at trial or prior to trial."

Of the 11 reopened cases, seven would eventually be settled, including one involving the family of a brain-damaged baby awarded a record $55 million verdict. Four remaining cases were either rejected by Beasley, transferred to another law firm or voluntarily dismissed.

Ditzen said in an interview that he was amazed that Beasley managed to wiggle out of his predicament. "He was able to close the barn door after the horses were out and get them back in there," Ditzen said. "Not too many people get to do that in life."

• • •

"The most egregious part of what I did was misleading everybody," Tom Smith said in an interview.

"It was crazy," Smith said of his crash. "I was drinking heavily. I was an alcoholic," Smith said before correcting himself. "I am an alcoholic."

Smith was asked about arguments made by defense lawyers that Beasley had been negligent for not supervising him properly. "That's patently ridiculous," he replied. Smith said he caused his own problems, and the media attention made it worse.

When a scandal hits the press, "it takes on a life of its own," Smith said. "I'm sorry I put him [Beasley] through what I put him through. I'm a lot wiser now."

"I think he was hurt," Smith said of his former employer. "I was hurt too," he said, but he added, "I don't have a bad thing to say about Jim Beasley."

Smith said he gave up drinking, lost 50 pounds, and started attending church regularly. "I changed my life."

• • •

So Beasley had survived the Tom Smith scandal, but he was still ticked off by what he perceived as the Inquirer's exploitation of the situation. That's why he was so eager to take my case.

The two controversies went off almost simultaneously in the press. My boss, Robert J. Rosenthal, editor of the Inquirer, had ripped me in a story that ran July 13, 1998, in the Washington Post. Two days later, the Inquirer published Ditzen's front-page story about Beasley's legal problems with Tom Smith.

The first lawyer I talked to about my situation was Michael Smerconish. A few days later, Jim Beasley called me at work, and introduced himself over the phone. "To what do I owe this honor?," I asked. Beasley told me something I didn't know; Smerconish worked for him. And what's more, Beasley said, I might have a good case. Come see me, he said; let's talk about it.

Smerconish subsequently told me that Beasley had big-footed him. "I never was elbowed out of the way so fast for a file."

Three days after the Inquirer ran its second front page story about the Tom Smith scandal, announcing that all 11 lawsuits had been reinstated, Beasley filed my libel suit against the Inquirer.

And Rosenthal, the Inquirer editor who had justified the decision to run the lengthy front-page story about Beasley's legal troubles with Tom Smith, was now the lead defendant in *Cipriano v. Philadelphia Newspapers Inc.*

For Jim Beasley, as well as his client, it was payback time.

Chapter 21

❖❖❖

A FOOTBALL GAME
WITHOUT REFEREES

Rᴏʙᴇʀᴛ J. Rᴏsᴇɴᴛʜᴀʟ, ᴇᴅɪᴛᴏʀ ᴏꜰ ᴛʜᴇ Pʜɪʟᴀᴅᴇʟᴘʜɪᴀ Iɴǫᴜɪʀᴇʀ, sᴛᴏᴏᴅ ɪɴ ᴛʜᴇ ᴍᴀʀʙʟᴇ lobby of The Beasley Building, looking pale and fidgety in his trench coat. At his side were two grim-faced lawyers.

The trio of visitors was looking up at the Victorian candle chandeliers when Jim Beasley came scampering down the carpeted steps in cowboy boots. As Beasley's client, I was by his side, and watched as he glad-handed his guests, flashing his gunslinger's smile.

Beasley was jubilant because his latest libel case against the Inquirer had attracted national publicity. "Philadelphia Inquirer Sued by Own Reporter" was the headline in The New York Times. "A move so unusual that nobody could think of a precedent," was how media critic Howard Kurtz described it in the Washington Post.

We didn't know how much of a novelty it was until Beasley associate David A. Yanoff did some research and discovered that I was the *only* reporter in the history of American journalism to sue his own newspaper for libel.

Sept. 30, 1999, was the opening day of depositions in the case of *Cipriano v. Philadelphia Newspapers Inc.* Both sides went into pregame huddles. I had never been to a deposition before so I asked Beasley what it was like compared to a trial. Well, he said, there's no judge around to set the rules.

"So," I said, "it's like a baseball game without an umpire?"

"No," Beasley said, flashing that smile again. "It's more like a football game without referees."

We filed into Beasley's conference room, past an ominous display in the lobby, a five-foot-long scale model of the Titanic. Beasley and Rosenthal took seats on opposite sides of the table. The two combatants sized each other up while the court reporter set up shop.

It was an interesting matchup: Beasley vs. "Rosey," my old boss — two decades younger, and a newsroom legend for his ability to slip out of tight jams, whether in foreign combat zones or office politics.

Rosenthal raised his right hand and swore to tell the truth. And then my old boss said something I knew was a lie:

Beasley: "Whose idea was it to put Mr. Cipriano on the religion beat?"

Rosenthal: "I don't know."

Beasley: "That wasn't your idea?"

Rosenthal: "I don't know if it was my idea. I don't recall if I specifically thought that Ralph should be the religion writer."

• • •

SHORTLY AFTER HE WAS APPOINTED INQUIRER CITY EDITOR IN 1991, ROBERT J. ROSENTHAL personally recruited me to become the paper's religion writer. Rosenthal said he was looking for an independent thinker to liven up a dull beat. My boss, a secular Jew, said he chose me, a fallen Catholic, because we both shared the same skeptical view of organized religion. Rosenthal spoke disparagingly about the paper's long-time religion writer, a former seminarian who wrote deferentially about local religious leaders. "Nobody remembers a fucking story he ever wrote," Rosenthal said.

I was trying to satisfy my boss's demand for lively copy when I sought an interview with the Catholic archbishop of Philadelphia. Cardinal Anthony J. Bevilacqua had become the target of weekly demonstrations outside his office by members of his own flock after he decided to close about 20 inner-city churches and schools located in predominantly black and Latino neighborhoods.

I discovered that at the same time he was closing poor churches and schools, supposedly to save money, His Eminence was secretly building a multimedia conference center on the 12th floor of archdiocese headquarters. The center featured a custom-built 25-foot-long black cherry conference table with a dozen computers built into it, two big screen TVs, and a future satellite hookup for video-conferencing. Nobody would let me in to see the place or tell me how much it cost, though the conference table without the computers listed in a manufacturer's catalog for $58,000.

Before I could interview the cardinal, however, his public relations guru, Brian Tierney, launched a preemptive strike to get me kicked off the beat. Tierney and an associate, Jay Devine, met with my editors in the newsroom. The cardinal's men had marked up all the stories I had written about the archdiocese's downsizing efforts in green and yellow magic markers, to highlight the negative and positive comments. Tierney and Devine argued that by reporting on public controversy over the church and school closings, I was guilty of writing overwhelmingly negative coverage that was unfair to the cardinal.

The demonstrations were hard to ignore. They were held every Wednesday outside archdiocese headquarters and the adjacent cathedral for a year and a half, and were attended by nuns, Catholic school kids in uniform, and grandmothers carrying rosary beads. The protests included a Martin Luther-like posting of a list of grievances on the cathedral door, and a 10-day hunger strike by Frank Maimone, leader of the local chapter of the Catholic Worker.

Tierney's preemptive strike failed, and I got my interview with His Eminence. I asked the cardinal if his boss would approve of the multimedia conference center. I was thinking about the Pope. The cardinal, however, talked about somebody higher up.

"If Jesus Christ was alive today, He would have used all of the electronic media of today," the cardinal declared, with a couple of tape-recorders rolling. "Absolutely, no doubt about it. He would have, you know, updated everything. He would have used an automobile. He would have used a plane. . . . He would use television.… That's what I'm trying to do."

(Some of the cardinal's fellow Catholics would be outraged by his contention that Jesus was no longer alive, as well as his claims that Jesus would have flown on a plane and appeared on TV.)

While my story about the cardinal was being edited, Rosenthal took me aside and said he had decided to make a change on the religion beat. He insisted he wasn't caving in to pressure, but then he asked me to take another assignment.

I agreed to leave the beat in 1993, as long as they published my story about the cardinal, which, under Rosenthal's direction, had evolved into a "profile" of His Eminence. To balance the hard news, my editors told me to include flattering quotes and references to the cardinal — for supposedly revitalizing the office of archbishop — that were readily supplied by admirers such as Tierney. I did what I was told.

My watered-down story ran on the Sunday front page, under a huge photo of the cardinal kissing an elderly woman lying in a hospital bed. But the story still contained some punch. It began with a description of the secret multimedia conference center, and went on to detail the cardinal's history of big spending and multimillion-dollar budget deficits when he was bishop of Pittsburgh. One of my Catholic sources told me that when His Eminence read the story, they had to peel him off the ceiling.

I left the religion beat, and my life was peaceful for three years. Then, in 1996, the editor of the Inquirer Sunday magazine asked me to write another profile of Cardinal Bevilacqua, this time for the magazine. When I went out to do research, Catholic sources handed me folders of confidential archdiocese documents that told a fuller story about the cardinal's lavish spending in Philadelphia. The documents showed that at the same time he was closing poor churches and schools, His Eminence secretly spent $5 million to renovate and redecorate church offices, a mansion that was his private residence, and a seaside villa that served as his vacation home.

The records showed that the multimedia center I'd written about three years earlier had cost more than $500,000 and was so top secret it was constructed without building permits, in violation of city law. The records also showed that the cardinal had spent another $500,000 renovating and redecorating his seaside villa. I was also given interior photos of the 30-room mansion where the cardinal lived alone and had spent hundreds of thousands of dollars on fancy new furnishings that included Queen Ann chairs, brass chandeliers and pink brocade couches.

I also obtained records from a workers' compensation claim filed against the archdiocese by a veteran employee who was in close contact with the cardinal. In the claim, the employee, a devout Catholic, alleged that he had suffered "serious mental and physical distress" and was no longer able to work as a result of the cardinal's "rude and abusive treatment." The employee, who was fired after he suffered a heart attack, charged that much of his stress was caused by female companions who allegedly rode in the cardinal's limo and stayed overnight at the cardinal's mansion. The records showed the archdiocese had settled the claim by paying the employee $87,500.

My story was transferred from the magazine to the projects desk, where they edited long, investigative stories. My new editors were interested in the archdiocese's confidential financial records, but they told me to forget about the workers' compensation claim, saying I didn't have a prayer of getting it printed in the Inquirer. So I concentrated my efforts on getting the archdiocese's secret financial records published.

I went down to the Municipal Services Building one afternoon to pull some public records about recent construction at archdiocese headquarters. My request was denied. By the time I walked back to the newspaper, a 15-minute stroll, the phone at my desk was ringing.

It was Brian Tierney, to whom I had not spoken in three years. Tierney had just been tipped off about my snooping by a friendly city bureaucrat who was also a Catholic, and Tierney demanded to know what I was up to. He was angry that I was even thinking about writing about the cardinal again. Tierney told me I had no chance of getting the cardinal to sit for another tape-recorded interview, especially after the last disaster. This time around, Tierney said, nobody at the archdiocese would talk to me.

Tierney also told me flat-out that there had been a deal back in 1993 to get me off the religion beat, and that Rosenthal was the only editor left from the "negotiations." I got rid of you once, Tierney said, and I'll get rid of you again.

Tierney was launching another preemptive strike. He called two of my editors, including Rosenthal, to threaten them with a news blackout and a nasty public relations campaign that would ruin me and the newspaper, if they decided to run any story I wrote about the cardinal. But my bosses' biggest fear, one editor confided, was that the cardinal might stand up in the pulpit some Sunday morning and call for a boycott of "our lousy Protestant rag."

It was a fear that Beasley sought to expose in court.

· · ·

BEASLEY: "WAS THE INQUIRER CIRCULATION OR READERSHIP DECLINING DURING THIS period?"

Rosenthal: "Yes."

Beasley: "Weren't you fearful that Tierney and Bevilacqua would ban the Inquirer from the pulpit?"

Rosenthal: "No."

Beasley: "Did Bevilacqua threaten to do that?"

Rosenthal: "I have no idea."

Beasley: "You have no idea?"

Rosenthal: "I have no memory of that. Since then I've been told that happened."

· · ·

THE ARCHDIOCESE WAS OUT TO STOP MY STORY. JAY DEVINE, ONE OF TIERNEY'S ASSOCIates, spelled it out over the phone to one of my editors, who was taking notes. Devine told the editor he represented 1.4 million Catholics, and "we have a responsibility to make sure the newspaper doesn't tell them things we don't want them to know."

The editor Devine spoke to was Jonathan Neumann, a projects editor who was my advocate at the paper. Neumann, however, was outranked by Rosenthal, then the paper's third-highest editor, and Rosenthal balked at printing my story. Rather than argue with the facts, Rosenthal (as well as Tierney) said my story was unfair and anti-Catholic, even though all my sources and all the cardinal's on-the-record critics were Catholics.

· · ·

BEASLEY: "DO YOU REMEMBER THE CARDINAL THREATENING TO TELL ALL THE PARISHioners not to buy the Inquirer?"

Rosenthal: "I know — I believe I remember the cardinal saying that, but I don't know the time frame."

Beasley: "And do you know how many Catholics live in the Delaware Valley area?"
Rosenthal: "I believe the number usually is around 1.4 million."
Beasley: "And the Inquirer can't afford to lose 1.4 million readers, can it?"
Rosenthal: "It doesn't have — no, it can't."

• • •

BRIAN TIERNEY WAS ON THE ATTACK WHEN HE MET FACE TO FACE WITH INQUIRER editors in a series of three private meetings held at archdiocese headquarters. I was there for all the sessions, but was under orders from my bosses not to say anything, for fear of further antagonizing the archdiocese.

Tierney, according to a lengthy Editor & Publisher story on my case, was "a major player in Philadelphia." The ad division of his firm, Tierney Communications, claimed annual billings of $230 million, handling clients that included McDonald's and IBM. Tierney's firm, according to E&P, also "places a substantial amount of advertising in the Inquirer." So, the magazine said, "when Tierney talks, it's no wonder Inquirer executives listen."

The Inquirer, on the other hand, was losing readers at a rate faster than any major American newspaper of comparable size. The Inquirer's daily circulation had dropped from 511,000 in 1990 to 402,000 in early 1999, a 21 percent reduction; the Sunday paper over that same period had fallen from 996,000 to 802,000, a 19 percent decrease. In an effort to boost circulation, Maxwell E.P. King, the paper's editor, had proposed that Cardinal Bevilacqua write a weekly column for the Inquirer that could be hawked on Sundays, outside Catholic churches, but His Eminence declined the offer, saying he was too busy.

Tierney dominated the three meetings with Inquirer editors, making speeches for 20 minutes at a time. He attacked me as a biased reporter out to get the cardinal, and he accused the newspaper of being unfair and biased against the Catholic Church. My editors usually just sat there, like sinners enduring a fire-and-brimstone sermon. But at the last meeting, which was tape-recorded, Lois Wark, a feisty projects editor, decided to talk back.

It began when Tierney asserted that the church was just like any other business in town, such as the one run by Inquirer Publisher Bob Hall, so what was all the fuss over a little construction work? Wasn't it normal for a business to undertake a construction project?

"I don't think Bob Hall's mission is to help the poor and do good," Wark said. "Bob Hall's mission is to make money."

Tierney bristled. "I think we handle our mission pretty well, and I think we should get credit for it too," he said indignantly. "And since we do our mission so well, I don't think we should necessarily have to go through hour after hour of meetings about $10,000 ceilings and about allegations made by irresponsible members of the carpenters' union as if we were a part of organized crime."

(The carpenter's union, composed predominantly of Catholics, had picketed the archdiocese, claiming that church leaders had reneged on a promise to use only union labor on city construction projects.)

"I think it would be useful if we put a little context into this discussion," Wark said, "because you seem to be concerned that we're worried about nickel-and-dime issues here."

Wark talked about how the cardinal's lavish spending took place at a time when the archdiocese was in financial straits and had to ask for more money from working families, at a time when the archdiocese was closing churches and schools in poor neighborhoods. The church could do whatever it wanted with its money, Wark said, but when concern rose to the level of public controversy, the newspaper had an obligation to cover it.

Across the conference table, the trio of archdiocese public relations officials erupted. Jay Devine said the controversy had been raised by a "handful of people." Rather than investigate the archdiocese, Devine said, the newspaper should look at "Who are these people? What is their agenda?" Tierney argued that the vast majority of Catholics was solidly behind the cardinal.

"Now, the fact that out of 1.5 million people, I gotta tell you, God strike me dead, I've never heard any of these issues ever brought up, any concerns at all in my parish, [or] in any of other parishes that I've visited," Tierney blustered. "Never. The only guy we get is [protest leader] Frank Maimone . . . and a band of about seven guys who've gotten more press than the Beatles because of the Inquirer."

Tierney asserted that based on the mail and phone calls that the archdiocese received, the "satisfaction level" among local Catholics was "basically 99.5" percent.

"And not to be inflammatory, but I've got to be honest with you," Tierney said: His fellow Catholics had told him "hundreds of times in the last few years" that the Inquirer "is perceived to be anti-Catholic." Tierney assured the editors that he wasn't engaged in arm-twisting. "I'm just telling you what I hear from Catholics." Conflict between the archdiocese and the newspaper was inevitable, Tierney said, but Catholics "feel that stuff like this is a little unfair."

Wark was unimpressed. "Just about every group in the city feels the same way about the paper," she said. But Tierney pressed on with his summation.

"Let's be honest, there's a sense of hostility around the table, but I've got to tell you this," he said. "You guys will survive great and the Philadelphia Inquirer will be around. The church has been around for 2,000 years, and I think it'll survive and we don't have to have any relationship, really," Tierney said ominously. He warned that the church had "other ways to get the message out."

"What's the point?" Wark demanded.

"We want to work with you if we think you're being fair," Tierney said. "And if you're not, my advice to the church would be to just to not work with you and find other ways."

· · ·

AFTER TIERNEY'S THREATS, MY STORY ABOUT THE CARDINAL'S $5-MILLION SPENDING spree was gutted and reduced to a tale about a $500,000 multimedia conference center that had been built and then quietly mothballed by the archdiocese, kept under lock and key because it might have become a public embarrassment. There was no mention of the closed churches and schools, the context that would have made the story relevant.

The archdiocese should have been happy with how the battle turned out, but Jonathan Neumann told me they were enraged that anything I wrote was printed. So the archdiocese demanded that a critical three-page letter to the editor be printed in the Inquirer, in its entirety. In the letter, which was as long as the story I wrote, archdiocese officials tried to refute their own financial records, by falsely claiming that the multimedia center had not cost $500,000. They also made other accusations against me that Neumann concluded in a memo were "false and libelous."

"What the archdiocese is trying to do is once again bully the Inquirer," Neumann wrote Maxwell E.P. King, then editor of the Inquirer. Neumann warned King in the memo against "caving in" to Bevilacqua. The editors, however, came up with a compromise: they decided to print the archdiocese's letter in its entirety, along with an editor's note from King that defended me as an "objective and ethical" reporter.

The archdiocese responded by sending out a special mailing of the cardinal's monthly newsletter, "The Voice of Your Shepherd," to every church and every parishioner in the archdiocese. The newsletter ran a photo of the smiling cardinal in his ceremonial robes and bishop's cross, under the headline, "Where is the Inquirer's Judgment?"

In the bulletin, the cardinal railed against my story and attacked me by name, concluding: "Given the history of this reporter's attitude and posture towards the archdiocese, it is difficult to rule out intentional bias.... As your archbishop, I will not remain silent, allowing any reporter or news organization to unjustly malign the Catholic Church."

In a 2001 interview with Joe Nicholson of Editor & Publisher, Cardinal Bevilacqua praised Tierney as "a great help to us" in the church's campaign to censor the Inquirer.

"He stopped the story," the cardinal told E&P. "That was the important thing."

Bevilacqua subsequently petitioned the Pope to personally anoint Tierney a Knight of St. Gregory the Great — "the equivalent of saying he had jumped on a grenade for the Church," wrote Philadelphia magazine. The 1998 award that Tierney received from Pope John Paul II boosted his stock with Catholic leaders across the country. Tierney subsequently served in the 2000 presidential race as national head of Catholics for Bush.

•　•　•

AFTER THE BEATING I TOOK FROM THE CARDINAL, TIERNEY AND ROSENTHAL FOR SUPposedly being anti-Catholic, I rewrote and expanded my original story, and sold it to the National Catholic Reporter (NCR) of Kansas City, Mo. The independent news weekly, written and edited by lay Catholics, was famous for exposing the pedophilia epidemic among Catholic priests during the 1980s, decades before the mainstream media discovered the story.

In contrast to my bosses at the Inquirer, Tom Roberts, the editor of NCR, seemed eager to use all of the confidential archdiocese documents, including the workers' compensation claim filed by the veteran employee that contained the allegations about the cardinal's female companions. Roberts had a practical suggestion: Why not visit the woman identified as the cardinal's closest companion and see what she had to say? So I went to see her and she denied everything, said she was just a friend. The editors at NCR then decided to print the employee's allegations that he was personally abused by the cardinal, as well as the archdiocese's subsequent payment of $87,500, but they kept the allegations about female companions out of the story.

The headline on the NCR cover story of June 1998 was "Lavish spending in archdiocese skips inner city." The story fully detailed the cardinal's $5 million spending spree. It also made the connection the Inquirer had declined to make: that His Eminence was renovating and redecorating archdiocese offices, the cardinal's mansion and his seaside villa at the same time he was closing poor people's churches and schools.

(The story would subsequently win first prize for best investigative reporting from the Catholic Press Association of the United States and Canada, an organization of Catholic newspapers and magazines that included the Catholic Standard & Times, Cardinal Bevilacqua's own archdiocese newspaper.)

The week before the NCR story ran, Howard Kurtz of the Washington Post, who had obtained an advance copy of my story, called Rosenthal and left a message, asking for comment. Rosenthal was on a honeymoon of sorts. Just six months earlier, he had been promoted to editor of the newspaper, succeeding Max King.

Kurtz wanted to know why Rosenthal hadn't run my original story. His curiosity was piqued by a lively Philadelphia City Paper cover story by reporter Frank Lewis that went into the history of the "uneasy relationship" between the archdiocese and the Inquirer and my personal battles with the cardinal and Tierney. In the City Paper story, I called the cardinal "a Pharisee," and Tierney described me as "a low-grade infection that keeps coming back."

In the City Paper, I also told Lewis how reading the Bible and getting baptized in the Jordan River while on assignment for the Inquirer had changed my life. That had to upset my boss, who had chosen me for the religion beat because I was a skeptic. "Is 'Holier than thou' in the Bible?" Rosenthal yelled at me in the middle of the newsroom.

Before he called back Kurtz, Rosenthal met with Neumann for advice on how to handle the Washington Post interview. Neumann told me after the meeting that he advised Rosenthal to take "the high road," so I breathed a sigh of relief.

But when Kurtz's story ran June 13, 1998, on the front page of the Post's Saturday Style section, it was obvious that Rosenthal had chosen another route:

Crossed Agendas: Church vs. Reporter
By Howard Kurtz
Washington Post Staff Writer

Ralph Cipriano of the Philadelphia Inquirer has just produced a 10,000-word piece charging the local archdiocese with all manner of mismanagement and wasteful spending.

But it didn't run in the Inquirer.

"He came to us and said he couldn't get it printed in his own paper," said Tom Roberts, managing editor of the National Catholic Reporter, an independent weekly that is publishing the story next week.

This is the latest salvo in a battle between the city's biggest newspaper and a powerful religious institution, one that involves an unusually personal campaign against a single journalist. It is also the story of a strong-willed reporter whose passion has raised doubts among some of his own editors. Now the name-calling is bursting into public view, with a "Holy War" cover story in the Philadelphia City Paper and a growing buzz about why the Inquirer failed to publish Cipriano's findings.

At the center of the conflict is Cardinal Anthony Bevilacqua, who has been complaining to Inquirer editors for years about Cipriano's work. These complaints helped persuade the paper to remove Cipriano from the religion beat in 1993, and to spike much of an earlier version of the investigative report that he gave his editors.

"I wrote the story because I believed this guy was not above scrutiny," Cipriano said. "He was a sacred cow at my newspaper."

Inquirer Editor Robert Rosenthal is not standing by his man. "If you were an editor dealing with someone who has the kind of feelings Ralph admits to, how would you handle it?" he asked. Rosenthal said Cipriano "has a very strong personal view and an agenda.... There were things we didn't publish that Ralph wrote that we didn't think were truthful. He could never prove them."

· · ·

LIBEL CASES, BEASLEY HAD WARNED, WERE ALWAYS DIFFICULT TO WIN, ESPECIALLY WHEN they involved a public figure. A public figure in a libel case was usually a government official or a celebrity. But Beasley said a judge might just decide that I was also a public figure, because I was a newspaper reporter speaking out on a public controversy that I was involved in.

To win a libel case involving a public figure, you not only had to prove what they wrote about you wasn't true, you also had to prove malice, meaning they knew it wasn't true, but they went ahead and printed it anyhow, with reckless disregard for the truth.

So when Beasley questioned Rosenthal about the truthfulness of his remarks to the Washington Post, my lawyer was looking for evidence of malice. Rosenthal countered with a sudden memory loss:

Beasley: "Did you discuss what you would say to Kurtz with Neumann prior to the interview?"

Rosenthal: "I have no memory of that."

Beasley: "Did Neumann urge you to take the high road and embrace the critical City Paper story?"

Rosenthal: "I have no memory of that."

Beasley: ". . . Did you tell Neumann, quote, 'I guess I fucked up' regarding the Kurtz interview?"

Rosenthal: "I have no memory of that."

Beasley: "If you had said to Neumann, 'I fucked up' regarding the Kurtz interview, you think you would have remembered that?"

Rosenthal: "No."

· · ·

BEASLEY ASKED ROSENTHAL WHAT I WROTE THAT WAS UNTRUE, AND ROSENTHAL CLAIMED that "the basic premise" of my unpublished story was unfair to the church. Beasley tried to get some specifics in a long-winded debate that ended with this exchange:

Beasley: "You cannot point to any sentence or paragraph in any unpublished article where you can say this is untruthful, this is a lie, can you?"

Rosenthal: "I cannot."

Rosenthal, however, had a fallback position. It was stated in a letter of clarification that Rosenthal wrote to the editor of the Post, with the help of an Inquirer lawyer.

"I should not, however, have described as untruthful some of the material Mr. Cipriano wrote that we did not publish," Rosenthal wrote in the letter that ran in the Post six weeks after the original Kurtz story. "I should have said he told us things as he was reporting that he had not substantiated, and that we would not, of course, publish them until they were substantiated."

Beasley tried again to get some specifics, asking what I wrote that was unsubstantiated:

Beasley: "You cannot point to any portion of any of the unpublished articles Ralph submitted that he could not prove?"

Rosenthal: "That's true."

Beasley: "As a matter of fact, what really happened here, Mr. Rosenthal, is that when you read the City Paper story, you got pissed at Ralph. And that's what caused you to make the comment that you did to Kurtz —"

Rosenthal: "That's not true.… I felt that we had been betrayed."

Rosenthal was jumpy, leaning forward in his seat, and frequently cutting off Beasley in mid-question. Arthur Newbold, the Inquirer's defense lawyer, repeatedly tried to get his client to slow the pace. "Let the question come to a conclusion before you try and answer," an exasperated Newbold told Rosenthal.

But Beasley would lean forward across the table, glare at Rosenthal, and fire off another question. And Rosenthal was so eager to go toe-to-toe that he almost bolted out of his chair. My old boss, a wiry, former hockey player at the University of Vermont, could not resist an invitation to brawl. When words failed to restrain Rosenthal, Newbold put his hand on his client's shoulder and forcibly shoved him back into his seat.

Next, Beasley tried to get into what was going on in Rosenthal's head during the Kurtz interview: "What were you referring to when you said what Ralph wrote was untruthful?"

"When I was speaking to Howard Kurtz, I was specifically thinking about one thing," Rosenthal said. "What I was thinking about were allegations that Ralph had said about the Cardinal's sex life that we could not substantiate. That's what I was thinking about when I spoke to Howard Kurtz."

I could not believe my old boss was desperate enough to try this, since in my memory, I had never spoken to him about the subject. But my lawyer was elated. During a break, Beasley looked at me and smiled. "He's dead now."

• • •

BEASLEY: "MY QUESTION IS, DO YOU BELIEVE WHAT YOU SAID TO MR. KURTZ WAS DAMAGING to Mr. Cipriano's reputation as a reporter?"

Rosenthal: "I thought it might be, and I also thought part of it was true."

Beasley: "Whether it was true or not, did you consider it damaging to his reputation as a reporter?'

Rosenthal: "I thought it could be damaging, yes."

• • •

BEASLEY GLARED OVER HIS READING GLASSES AT ROSENTHAL. HIS VOICE RISING, BEASLEY demanded to know who at the Inquirer had told Rosenthal the accusations about Cardinal Bevilacqua's sex life. Did he hear it from me? From some editor? From another reporter?

"I have no memory of that specific conversation," Rosenthal said.

Beasley rolled his eyes. "What had not been substantiated about the cardinal's sex life?" he barked.

Rosenthal: "Any of the details?"

Beasley: "What were they, sir?"

Rosenthal spilled some rumors: the cardinal supposedly had a girlfriend, there was some "back of the car stuff" going on, and also talk of the cardinal "sneaking" the girlfriend "into his residence."

When Beasley asked what he meant by 'back of the car stuff," Rosenthal stammered, "Sex." And who told him those rumors? "I can't tell you who exactly," Rosenthal said.

Beasley turned his withering gaze on the Inquirer's defense lawyer.

"Let me just say something, Arthur," Beasley said. "I'm trying to be delicate about this, but if I don't get clearer answers, I'm going to file a motion, and all this is going to become a matter of public record. I really don't care if that happens. I don't think it's something that should be a matter of public record. Now if you want to force my hand on that, you're going to give me no choice but to do it."

"I have no wish to have this be in the public record either," Newbold said. "I think it's highly desirable not to." But Newbold complained that all Beasley was doing was asking Rosenthal the same questions over and over again. "All I want are straight answers," Beasley griped. "And I'm not getting them."

It was 4 p.m. and tempers were flaring, so Newbold asked to adjourn for the day. When the deposition resumed the next morning, Beasley and Newbold resumed their sparring over Beasley's right to question Rosenthal about his previous answers.

"All I can tell you is that in 30 years of practicing law I've never let a witness be cross-examined about what he said on an earlier deposition, going over the same material, and I'm not going to start today," Newbold declared.

"Mr. Newbold," Beasley declared. "Let me say that for 30 years you've been damn lucky we haven't had any depositions together or you wouldn't be getting away with it."

Beasley renewed his threat to file a motion that would reveal the sex allegations involving the cardinal. "Even if the Inquirer doesn't pick it up, the Legal Intelligencer will," Beasley said, referring to the Philadelphia Bar Association newspaper. "Now, I'm trying to avoid all of that, and I'm trying to do it out of courtesy to the Inquirer and to the cardinal. I have no purpose in any way embarrassing anyone, but if you're going to force the issue, then you leave me no choice."

Newbold decided to allow Beasley to continue his questioning. Beasley asked Rosenthal if it was proper for a reporter to follow a lead, such as the sex allegations about the cardinal. Yes, Rosenthal said. If there were two reliable sources, Beasley said, would the Inquirer print it? "It was something we definitely would have considered doing," Rosenthal said.

Beasley introduced a confidential report from Dr. Wolfram Rieger, who had conducted a comprehensive psychiatric examination of the veteran employee who had filed the workers' compensation claim against the archdiocese.

In the report, the psychiatrist, who had been hired by a lawyer for the claimant, described the employee as a "devout Catholic" respectful of the clergy and loyal to Bevilacqua's predecessor, the late Cardinal John Krol. Beasley began reading:

[The employee] was also severely troubled by the cardinal's frequent habit of meeting women on airplanes and inviting these women to spend time at the cardinal's mansion. . . . [The employee] was troubled by the fact that Cardinal Bevilacqua would frequently ride with women in the back of the cardinal's vehicle. Cardinal Krol (Bevilacqua's predecessor) had never allowed women to ride in the back of a vehicle with him.

. . . [The employee] was severely troubled by one woman who would follow Cardinal Bevilacqua to every function no matter if it was a local event or something in Downingtown, or Brooklyn, N.Y.

The woman, Mrs. X, would have closed-door meetings with Cardinal Bevilacqua after every function. [The employee] was troubled to see Cardinal Bevilacqua frequently massaging the back of Mrs. X, hugging her and showing undue affection to Mrs. X. [A relative of the employee] was also troubled to see Cardinal Bevilacqua meeting with Mrs. X on the property at night and also meeting with Mrs. X on the St. Joseph's College campus early in the morning.

"Is there any statement there that would deal with the cardinal's sex life?" Beasley asked.

"It would certainly raise questions about it," Rosenthal said.

"Next paragraph," Beasley said.

[The employee's relative] would frequently walk on St. Joseph's track for exercise and one day saw Cardinal Bevilacqua and Mrs. X meeting behind a building near the St. Joseph's track. Cardinal Bevilacqua had his arm around Mrs. X. [The employee's relative] found this very strange and immediately told [the employee] regarding the covert meeting between Mrs. X and Cardinal Bevilacqua.

Beasley asked Rosenthal if there were two sources for this information, the employee and his relative. Rosenthal agreed there were two sources. "Is there any intimation in there that there was sex between Mrs. X and the cardinal?" Beasley asked. "There's an intimation of fondness, certainly," Rosenthal said. Beasley resumed reading:

[The employee] was so troubled by Cardinal Bevilacqua's frequent meetings with Mrs. X that he spoke to various bishops, monsignors and priests regarding this conduct. Various monsignors and priests would jokingly refer to Mrs. X as Fatal Attraction and would jokingly ask [the employee] whether Fatal Attraction had shown up at the cardinal's latest destination.

Mrs. X drove a vehicle that had the license plate, 1AB-FAN. After three years of Mrs. X showing up at every appearance of the cardinal, Cardinal Bevilacqua informed [the employee] that the residence phone number had been changed and that [the employee] was forbidden to give out the phone number to anyone.

Beasley asked, "Again, is there any intimation in that paragraph of the cardinal having sex —"

"No," interrupted Rosenthal.

"With anyone?" said Beasley, finishing his question.

Beasley asked Rosenthal if it would be improper for a reporter under his supervision to check out this kind of a lead.

"No," Rosenthal said.

"As a matter of fact that would be part of his job?" Beasley asked.

"Yes, could be," Rosenthal replied.

"If the reporter following up on a lead interviewed Mrs. X, and she denied that there was any kind of intimate relationship between her and the cardinal, don't you believe that that reporter would have a right to say this is the end of the matter and we're not going to go into this thing further?"

"Yes," Rosenthal said.

"And that would be the honorable thing to do?"

"Yes," Rosenthal said.

· · ·

"Fatal Attraction" was an attractive middle-aged woman who came to the door with a puzzled look. A recent widow, she dressed modestly, and wasn't wearing one of those low-cut blouses that I had been told had scandalized the nuns working at the cardinal's mansion.

I identified myself as a reporter for National Catholic Reporter, and told her I was writing a story about the cardinal. I said her name had come up in the veteran employee's claim against the archdiocese. I handed her the relevant portions of the psychiatrist's report. She seemed shocked.

"Oh, my God," she said. "We were just the best of friends." She said she visited the cardinal's residence, as well as traveled to Rome to see the archbishop elevated to cardinal. "But my children and my [late] husband were along at all times, and I have the pictures to prove it."

The cardinal was just a warm, friendly guy, she said, who hugged her the way he did everybody else. She said she was concerned that the veteran employee who filed the claim had gone off the deep end. I asked about her license plate, 1AB-FAN. She laughed and said her favorite singer was Anita Baker.

Mrs. X said the real reason she became friends with Cardinal Bevilacqua was because he admired her so much for adopting three foster children. She said the cardinal also prayed over her sick niece.

"You know when they pray to God, it goes right to God," she told me with an ecstatic smile. "They're so much closer to God than we could ever be. They have an in."

Mrs. X had a male visitor waiting inside. I thanked her for her time and left wondering whether she was a mistress or just a spiritual groupie.

· · ·

Beasley was still grilling Rosenthal.

"Would you criticize a reporter for going to a workers' compensation file if there was evidence in there that may help them decide whether there's a story to it?"

"No," Rosenthal said.

"…And you don't have any information that Ralph did anything other than follow a lead?" he asked.

"Correct," Rosenthal said.

When it was over, I sat in Beasley's office, relieved but disgusted. I told Beasley

I was amazed that the whole case had boiled down to Rosenthal's hazy recollections about whatever was going on between the cardinal and Fatal Attraction.

Beasley smiled. Libel suits, he said, never make sense. When it comes to libel, logic goes out the window. Beasley had a gleam in his eye, as if he was about to let me in on one of the secrets of the legal universe.

"A libel suit," Beasley said, "always boils down to the groin."

• • •

WHEN BEASLEY DEPOSED JONATHAN NEUMANN ON JAN. 13, 2000, HE BEGAN BY ASKING whether Neumann had won any awards. Beasley wanted to establish that the credentials of Neumann, my direct supervisor, and the editor who read everything I wrote first, were superior to Rosenthal's.

So Neumann, a big, soft-spoken teddy bear of a guy, described some three dozen national awards he had won as a reporter and editor, including five Pulitzer Prizes and three Silver Gavel Awards, for best coverage of legal affairs in America.

"Do you have all these plaques in your home somewhere?" Beasley enthused. "Do you have a room large enough to hold them?"

"They will fit in a box in the attic," Neumann dead-panned.

With Neumann established as our star witness, Beasley read out loud Rosenthal's words in the Washington Post: Cipriano "has a very strong personal view and an agenda…. There were things we didn't publish that Ralph wrote that we didn't think were truthful. He could never prove them."

Beasley: "Is this a true statement?"

Neumann: "No, sir, it is not."

Beasley smiled, then asked his next question: "Did you ever find anything Ralph submitted for publication that was not truthful?"

Neumann: "No, I never did."

Beasley: "Was there anything that he ever submitted to you for your review as an editor that he could not prove, that he did not have adequate sources for?"

Neumann: "Ralph never showed me an article or a draft of an article that he could not prove."

Beasley asked Neumann if he had given any prior advice to Rosenthal about how to handle the interview with Kurtz. "Did you ever say anything to him about taking the high road?"

"Yes," Neumann said. "This is what I said to Bob, that you're the editor of a major national newspaper, and what is important is to maintain the dignity of the newspaper, to take the high road. That whatever personal battles you may have had with Ralph, or Ralph may have with you, however substantial or insubstantial they may be, they definitely do not belong in a national forum.

"If he's angry," Neumann continued, "he [Rosenthal] should deal with the person …behind closed doors. But taking the high road means if you've got a problem with somebody, you deal with the problem privately. When you're the editor of a major national newspaper, you don't air your dirty laundry in public like that."

And what was Rosenthal's response, Beasley wanted to know.

"He *agreed*," Neumann said.

Beasley asked Neumann about what happened after the Post story ran, and Neumann's repeated attempts to get Rosenthal to apologize. "Did you ever tell Rosey that he trashed Ralph's reputation?" Beasley asked.

"I never used those words," cautioned Neumann. "When I talked to Rosey on more than one occasion after he talked to Howie Kurtz, I said that what he said about Ralph wasn't true and Rosey acknowledged that. He acknowledged that he made a mistake, and I think you have to correct that. It's — we are talking about Ralph's reputation. It's very important. And Rosey said that he would."

Neumann, at Rosenthal's request, had even drafted a letter to the Post that said I was a "fine and honest reporter" and that Rosenthal had "full faith and trust" in me. But Rosenthal never sent the letter. More evidence of malice.

Beasley was so pleased with the witness that he had only one more question, namely whether Rosenthal had ever made any confession of sorts after the Washington Post interview:

Beasley: "Did he ever say to you, 'I guess I fucked up?'"

Neumann flashed a pained but knowing smile. "I think he did," he said.

Beasley grinned broadly. "That's all."

• • •

LAWYERS ON BOTH SIDES OF THE CASE WERE GETTING READY FOR TRIAL BY DRAWING UP lists of potential witnesses. It was a game of legal chicken, with plenty of posturing. The Inquirer put Cardinal Bevilacqua at the top of its witness list, along with several archdiocese public relations consultants and a bunch of Inquirer editors. I had always suspected those guys were on the same team. Not to be outdone, Beasley's witness list included the former employee who filed the workers' compensation claim against the cardinal, and Fatal Attraction.

Beasley wrote Arthur Newbold a letter on Dec. 18, 2000, saying he was about to make a big mistake. "Turning, for the moment, to your insistence on calling the cardinal as a witness," Beasley wrote. "As I have told you repeatedly in the past, the cardinal's testimony has absolutely no relevancy to any issue in this case…. Because you, through some legerdemain of reasoning, feel that the cardinal's testimony is somehow more helpful to The Inquirer than harmful to the cardinal's reputation, I am enclosing a rough draft of our counter-statement of the facts, so you can read what you have forced me to put on paper for the world to read."

Beasley said an Inquirer reporter might pick up the court filing, and if that reporter did his job as well as I used to, "the story would be greeted by banner headlines, capable of translation into Italian," so that they could read it at the Vatican.

"If your threat to call the Cardinal as a witness is meant to frighten me — don't let that threat rest comfortably in your head, for it does not," Beasley wrote. "The time to get this case settled is like the sand in an hourglass, and it's running out fast. Be kind to yourself. Very truly yours, James E. Beasley. P.S. And the cardinal."

I had been warned that Beasley was a gambler. David A. Yanoff had prepared a summary of the case, a 57-page Memorandum of Law that detailed all of the veteran archdiocese employee's allegations about the cardinal's female companions, and Yanoff was ready to file. It was Beasley's idea to ship a copy of that memorandum over to the Inquirer's editorial offices at 400 North Broad St. the day before the filing deadline, to give the editors a preview of what he was going to bomb them with in court.

Yanoff's memorandum went into the history of the case, describing how when I was on the religion beat, the archdiocese had tried to get rid of me. "Of course, for a seasoned reporter doing his job properly, this may not have been all that remarkable, as it is certainly not unusual that powerful institutions or figures in society attempt to influence and dictate favorable press coverage," Yanoff wrote.

"What is unusual, however — or should be, at least in the eyes of most ethical and hard-working journalists — is for a newspaper to in any way allow such attempts to be (or even to be perceived to be) the least bit successful," Yanoff wrote. "That is what happened at the Inquirer."

So when Howard Kurtz, the Washington Post media critic, called the Inquirer to ask Rosenthal why the Inquirer didn't run my archdiocese story, "there really was no defensible answer," Yanoff wrote. "To tell the truth would have been to admit to the very same sort of journalistic cowardice that has become such a hot topic of criticism directed at the mainstream press in this day of corporate domination of the media, as to give rise to beats like Mr. Kurtz's in the first place."

Beasley's gamble paid off. After more than two years of foot-dragging, alarm bells went off at the Inquirer. Newspaper lawyers tried frantically to get Beasley on the phone, but he had sent his memorandum just before flying off to Florida on vacation in his P-51 Mustang. An Inquirer lawyer called Yanoff and asked him to join in on a conference call, to jointly request that the judge in our case, the Honorable Mark I. Bernstein, extend the filing deadline.

The judge's law clerk took the conference call from the two lawyers. She heard the newspaper lawyer explain that both sides in the case urgently needed to speak to the judge, to request an extension of the filing deadline. The clerk put the phone down and went to look for the judge. When the clerk came back, she reported that Judge Bernstein had said he was too busy to come to the phone. The clerk, however, also said that the judge had told her to pass along some unsolicited advice to Mr. Beasley: Go ahead and file your papers.

· · ·

THE PAPERS WERE NEVER FILED. ON JAN. 3, 2001, THE INQUIRER RAN A NEWS STORY about the decision to settle my case. The financial part of the settlement remains confidential. The story included a public apology from Rosenthal: "I regret having made my comments to the Post," he was quoted as saying. "They were intemperate, and I apologize for them. . . . I regret my remarks and that we weren't able to resolve this in a way other than litigation, but I am happy we've been able to put this matter behind us."

The Inquirer's lawyers sought to seal the files in my case, but Beasley flatly refused. "We ain't sealing shit," he said.

Rosenthal didn't last the year. On Nov. 7, 2001, Howard Kurtz wrote a story in the Washington Post about a change of editors at the Inquirer. Publisher Bob Hall had fired Rosenthal, ostensibly because of disagreements over how to cover local news. The Post, however, quoting sources, attributed Rosenthal's firing to declining circulation, and one other problem.

"In an embarrassment earlier this year, the Inquirer paid several million dollars to settle a lawsuit against Rosenthal by former reporter Ralph Cipriano," Kurtz wrote. "Rosenthal apologized for having told The Washington Post in 1998 that Ralph Cipriano had written things 'that we didn't think were truthful.'"

Rosenthal made his only public comments on the case as he was leaving town in October 2002, to take a job as managing editor of the San Francisco Chronicle.

"If I had it to do all over again, I probably wouldn't have spoken to Howie Kurtz until I calmed down," Rosenthal told Jonathan Valania of Philadelphia Weekly. "I wish it hadn't happened, but it did. All I can say is you learn from your mistakes."

· · ·

JIM BEASLEY NEVER GOT A CHANCE TO CROSS-EXAMINE CARDINAL BEVILACQUA IN MY libel case, but the cardinal did have to answer some tough questions a few years later when he was repeatedly summoned to appear before a grand jury investigating sex abuse.

The subject matter that the grand jury was investigating was far more serious than any of the questions Beasley or I had ever raised about the Philadelphia archdiocese, but some issues remained the same — namely institutional secrecy and the arrogance of power.

On Sept. 21, 2005, the grand jury released a 418-page report that accused the retired 80-year-old archbishop and his predecessor, the late Cardinal Krol, of orchestrating a systematic cover-up that managed to shield from prosecution 63 Catholic priests who had sexually abused hundreds of children.

The two archbishops had "excused and enabled the abuse," the grand jury charged, by "burying the reports they did receive and covering up the conduct ... to outlast any statutes of limitation."

"What makes these allegations all the worse, the grand jurors believe, is that the abuses that Cardinal Bevilacqua and his aides allowed children to suffer — the molestations, the rapes, the lifelong shame and despair… were made possible by purposeful decisions, carefully implemented policies, and calculated indifference," the report said.

The sex abuse and subsequent cover-up was documented in 45,000 pages of secret documents once kept at archdiocese headquarters under lock and key. In response to the grand jury report, lawyers for the archdiocese resorted to a familiar playbook, attacking the messenger, and crying persecution. Archdiocese lawyers accused prosecutors and grand jurors of anti-Catholic bias, even though many of those prosecutors and grand jurors were themselves Catholics.

Archdiocese lawyers also labeled the grand jury report "a vile, mean-spirited diatribe" that seeks "to convict the Catholic Church and its leadership in the court of public opinion… based upon an unfair and inaccurate portrayal of facts."

Archdiocese lawyers further charged that the grand jury had attempted to "bully and intimidate" Bevilacqua, who was called to testify on 10 separate days, and faced "hostile and unnecessarily combative" interrogation from two and three prosecutors at a time.

Responded District Attorney Lynne Abraham: "Any persistence in the questioning of Cardinal Bevilacqua may have resulted in part from his evasiveness and claimed forgetfulness on the witness stand."

• • •

BRIAN TIERNEY WASN'T CONTENT WITH MERELY INFLUENCING THE INQUIRER'S NEWS coverage. He put together a group of local investors in 2006 to buy both the Inquirer and its sister paper, the Philadelphia Daily News, for $562 million. Tierney took over as CEO of the new ownership group, Philadelphia Media Holdings Co.; he subsequently also named himself publisher of the Inquirer.

Tierney recruited an old friend, Jay Devine, to help him with public relations. Devine, the man who once told Jonathan Neumann, "We have a responsibility to make sure the newspaper doesn't tell them things we don't want them to know," was now the official spokesman for both Philadelphia dailies.

Chapter 22

❖❖❖

THE LAST DISCIPLE

Jᴉᴍ Bᴇᴀꜱʟᴇʏ ᴡᴀꜱ ʜᴀᴠɪɴɢ ᴅɪɴɴᴇʀ ᴡɪᴛʜ ʜɪꜱ ꜱᴏɴ ᴀɴᴅ ꜰᴏʀᴍᴇʀ ᴡɪꜰᴇ, Hᴇʟᴇɴ, ᴀᴛ Frangelica's, a pasta and fish house on 12th Street, a block south of his law office. In between the Caesar salad and the fish special, Jim Jr. was trying to explain to his mother a birth defect known as a coarctation, or a narrowing of the aorta.

So Jim Jr. hoisted his empty Miller Lite bottle and turned it upside down. "See how it's fat and it gets narrow?" he told his mother. "That's similar to what a coarctation looks like."

In October 2000, Jim Jr., then 33, was helping his 74-year-old father prepare for the trial of *Gault v. Norwood*, a medical malpractice case involving a catastrophically injured infant. Both Beasleys were familiar with *Gault*, because it was one of the "Tom Smith cases" that had been dismissed and subsequently reopened by a judge's order.

Jim Jr. was the latest bright young lawyer to take on the challenge of backing up his father in the courtroom, a job known around The Beasley Firm as "baggin' for Mr. B." The son, who graduated from both medical school and law school at the University of Pennsylvania, had been working with his father for six years.

Beasley, drinking a glass of red wine, noticed how quickly his ex-wife picked up on the beer bottle analogy, so he told his son to bring the bottle with him to court. And that's how Jim Jr.'s empty Miller Lite bottle ended up as Exhibit P-51 in *Gault v. Norwood*.

• • •

Aꜰᴛᴇʀ ᴛʜᴇɪʀ ʙɪᴛᴛᴇʀ ꜱᴇᴠᴇɴ-ʏᴇᴀʀ ᴅɪᴠᴏʀᴄᴇ ᴡᴀʀ ᴇɴᴅᴇᴅ ɪɴ 1988, Jɪᴍ ᴀɴᴅ Hᴇʟᴇɴ Bᴇᴀꜱʟᴇʏ saw each other over the years at their children's weddings and at their grandchildren's christenings and birthday parties. The hostilities had mellowed, and the two were cordial.

By the early 1990s, Beasley's romance with longtime girlfriend Nicole Chabat was breaking up. His next steady was Heidi M. Peditto, a secretary 18 years his junior.

"I was told Beasley had a thing for blondes," Peditto said in a 2007 interview. She said she had also been warned by Beasley's receptionist, "He's going to try and intimidate you.

"He's looking at my resume," Peditto recalled of her initial job interview back in 1984. "He gave me the stare, and I just looked right at him. I sat there with my legs crossed, and my hands in my lap, and I looked him right in the eye."

"How's your typing?" she recalled Beasley asking her.

"I think it's pretty good," she said. "Some days, I can go pretty fast."

She got the job. Occasionally, when they worked late, the boss would make off-color remarks to his secretary, who was married to a doctor. "I think he did it just for shock value, to see how you would respond," Peditto said. "In other words, are you a wuss?"

Peditto worked for Beasley for a couple of years before she left in 1986, because, she said, her husband didn't want her to work any more. But in 1992, when she was in the process of getting a divorce, she came back.

The boss and secretary had known each other for years when Beasley asked her out to dinner. "Call me Jim," he said, but Peditto had a hard time referring to him as anything but "Mr. Beasley." Back at the office, Beasley told Peditto she was a lot smarter than some of the lawyers working for him. "You would have made one helluva trial lawyer," she remembered him saying. He also encouraged her to go to law school (she settled for becoming a paralegal), and he occasionally took her flying to air shows in his T-6 trainer.

Soon, Peditto was the only secretary allowed to use the firm's parking lot, usually reserved for lawyers and clients. When Jim Jr. raised the issue of favoritism, his father responded, "I don't care."

Beasley expanded Peditto's legal duties, asking her to draft letters for him. He sent back the drafts with compliments penciled in the margins. One day, when he particularly liked one letter, he crossed out Peditto's title of secretary, and wrote over it "legal assistant."

When Peditto turned 50 in 1994, Beasley arranged a surprise helicopter ride for the two of them to New York City, flying over the Statue of Liberty. Then he took her to see *Beauty and the Beast* on Broadway. Beasley brought in fresh flowers every day from his Villanova estate, and left them on Peditto's desk. He also brought in flowers for the receptionist, and his daughter, Kim, who worked at the firm as a secretary.

But Beasley could be "very jealous," Peditto said. He didn't like her talking to other men at the firm. And when she left the office before him to drive to his Villanova estate, he would time the drive and call her the moment she walked in the door. If she was late, he wanted to know why.

Employees at the firm cracked jokes about Mr. B's "sex-retary." But when Peditto became Beasley's legal assistant, she also functioned as his gatekeeper. She clashed with some lawyers on staff, most notably Jim Jr., who felt his father's open affair with an employee was a lapse in judgment.

"You'll never be your father," Peditto yelled at Jim Jr., in an argument that had everyone at the firm buzzing. "That's OK," he responded. "You'll never be my mother."

The relationship between Peditto and the boss ended, she said, about a year after Beasley proposed marriage, and she turned him down. "I knew if I ever married him, I would be stuck in the big house in Villanova," she said. She didn't want to be a suburban housewife again, so that was one reason why she quit in 1998.

People at the law firm, however, as well as Beasley's kids, disputed Peditto's story. Jim Jr. maintained it was his father who broke off the relationship because of Peditto's "constant attempts to compromise his relationships with his kids."

But Peditto said another reason she quit was because she didn't want to come between a father and a son. It was a difficult decision, she said, because she loved her job, and she loved the boss.

"Everyone has one love in their life and it wasn't my husband," Peditto said. "It was Jim.... I get goose bumps just talking about him."

• • •

Since his divorce war erupted in 1981, Beasley had dated younger women for two decades. His next girlfriend, however, was a shocker, especially to three of his kids: Pam, Jim Jr. and Kim. That's because Beasley was dating their mother, Helen.

And it was serious. Beasley seemed intent on winning back the wife who had walked out on him years before, because of his philandering. But this time around, it was Helen who was playing the field. She had another beau in Colorado. "I think he [Beasley] got a little worried that I was going to move out there," she recalled with a smile.

On New Year's Eve, Dec. 31, 1999, Helen was in Boston, planning to go out to dinner with her daughter, Pam, and Pam's husband, Steve. The doorbell rang, and it was Jim Beasley, dressed theatrically in a leather coat with a cape, a button-down shirt, neatly pressed jeans, cowboy boots and a wide-brimmed leather hat.

On a whim, Beasley had flown up to Boston in his recently purchased Piper Cheyenne II, a turboprop business aircraft. He told Helen he couldn't think of anybody else he would rather spend New Year's Eve with. She was touched. "I thought he was dashing."

Beasley wore a big smile that night out on the dance floor. And Helen, now a blonde, looked elated as she sipped champagne with her surprise date.

"Jim was my only love," she subsequently said. "I guess we never got over each other."

"I think he finally realized he might lose her for good," Pam said. Her father had also changed. "It was amazing," Pam said. "It was like, from that time on, he completely mellowed."

Beasley was planting more flowers than ever at his Villanova estate. "I think he really tried to have his house be an oasis, "Pam said. "He loved tulips…. He loved walking around the property and feeding fish in the pond."

• • •

WILLIAM I. NORWOOD JR. M.D., CHIEF OF CARDIOTHORACIC SURGERY AT CHILDREN'S Hospital of Philadelphia, was internationally known for the "Norwood Procedure," a pioneering reconstructive heart surgery technique credited with saving hundreds of infant lives.

On Nov. 3, 1992, Dr. Norwood was scheduled to operate on 3-month-old Stephen R. Gault, to repair a coarctation. The surgery called for making an incision between two infant ribs, and placing a clamp on Stephen's tiny aorta to repair it. But on the morning of the surgery, Dr. Norwood stunned Stephen's parents by announcing that he was also going to perform open-heart surgery. The doctor planned to cut open Stephen's chest to repair a second birth defect, known as a ventricular septal defect (VSD), a tiny hole in the membrane separating the two pumping chambers of the heart.

The Gaults were upset because their pediatric cardiologist, Dr. James C. Huhta, had told them he wanted to wait and see about the VSD, because it was so small it might close by itself. But the morning of the surgery, Karen Gault testified, Dr. Norwood said that baby Stephen was his patient now, that "he was the one with all the medical knowledge," and that it was his decision alone whether to perform bypass surgery on Stephen.

The Gaults claimed that Dr. Norwood ended a 10-minute conversation by grabbing his white smock and heading off for the operating room. The doctor didn't ask the Gaults to sign a consent form for bypass surgery, the parents testified, nor did he advise them of any potential risks.

"He just took him away from me," Karen Gault said in a deposition read in court by Beasley. "He was very emotional and he's very intimidating, Dr. Norwood."

For little Stephen, open-heart surgery was vastly more complicated and dangerous than simply repairing a coarctation. During open-heart surgery, Dr. Norwood had to stop the flow of blood through the infant's heart so he could see the VSD and repair it.

That meant that Dr. Norwood had to hook up Stephen to a heart-lung machine so that the infant's heart, about the size of a plum, could be shut down. Before that could happen, however, Dr. Norwood had to cool Stephen's body to a point where it could tolerate extreme conditions of no blood flow and no heart beat. To accomplish this, Dr. Norwood employed a controversial rapid cooling strategy.

Stephen was placed on a temperature-controlled blanket and ice bags were packed around his head. Dr. Norwood cut open Stephen's chest and connected the infant to a heart-lung bypass machine. The bypass machine ran Stephen's blood through a heat exchanger, rapidly cooling his blood to 15 degrees centigrade, or 59 degrees Fahrenheit. Once Stephen's body had also reached approximately 15 degrees centigrade — a cooling process that took just five minutes — the pump was turned off, and circulation came to a complete stop, as did Stephen's heart.

For the next 45 minutes, as Stephen's cold, lifeless 10-pound body lay on the operating table, Dr. Norwood worked on the infant, placing a patch on the tiny VSD, and repairing the aorta.

After the surgery, Stephen's heart was restarted, and his blood pressure returned to normal. The day after the surgery, however, when Stephen woke up, his legs began to jerk and his eyes rolled back in his head.

The infant was having a seizure. He stopped breathing and then he turned blue. Doctors said that Stephen had suffered catastrophic brain damage and bleeding, caused by a lack of oxygen. He was left a spastic, partially blind quadriplegic who could only say a few words and was so impaired he could not even be toilet-trained. To make matters worse, Stephen also developed cerebral palsy.

· · ·

"THE FIRST THING THAT I WANT TO TELL YOU," SAID CAROL L. VASSALO, REPRESENTING Dr. Norwood before the jury, "is that there was informed consent in this case. Now, can I point to a piece of paper, the paperwork that says this VSD repair [was] on a consent form? No, I cannot. I'm going to be honest with you about that. I cannot point to a piece of paper, a consent form, that says there's going to be a VSD repair. But that is not the end of the story.

"Because he's performed so many of these surgeries, he does have his methodology for explaining surgery to the parents of these children, and he will testify that he did go through all of these possibilities with Mr. and Mrs. Gault," Vassalo said of Dr. Norwood.

"In fact, they knew that there was going to be open-heart surgery on the morning of the surgery," Vassalo said of the Gaults. "They knew there was going to be an incision in Stephen's chest. They knew that there was going to be bypass surgery; and Dr. Norwood explained it all to them."

The Gaults' pediatric cardiologist, Dr. Huhta, had said that baby Stephen's VSD was "around 2 millimeters in diameter," Vassalo told the jury, but "that's not the size of the VSD that Dr. Norwood found in the surgery."

The VSD that Dr. Norwood operated on to correct "was actually four millimeters," Vassalo claimed. "On an 11-week old baby, a 4-millimeter VSD is significant. And it was not Dr. Norwood's view, at that point, that it should be left alone.

"He felt that it was a significant VSD, and he had Stephen's best interest at heart, or he would never have pursued this course of action."

"The unfortunate facts of life, ladies and gentlemen, are this: Children suffer brain injuries in open-heart surgery all the time," Vassalo told the jury. "Sometimes, it's not because of medical malpractice. It's just because this is really serious surgery. These are really little kids. It's really dangerous."

"We don't know what caused the injury," Vassalo said. "We are counting on you to be able to set the issues of sympathy aside, so that you can determine these issues that are very technical issues, kind of objectively."

• • •

At the trial of *Gault v. Norwood*, Judge Mark I. Bernstein wondered why Beasley kept ordering his son around the courtroom, asking him to get one thing after another for him. The judge finally asked court reporter Helene Christian what was going on. "Why is he treating Jim Jr. like a paralegal?" the judge asked. "Is this their relationship?

"Don't you get it?" Christian told the judge. "He's demonstrating by example the very special relationship between a father and a son. Jimmy would do anything for him."

As far as Christian was concerned, it was a subconscious appeal to the jury, to demonstrate what the Gaults had lost in the case. But if it was a deliberate strategy, Beasley didn't let his son in on it. "I wasn't aware of any plan," Jim Jr. said, "because he always yelled at me like that."

• • •

Beasley taught by example, his son said. Rather than giving lectures "he would have me come to court and watch him," Jim Jr. said. "He wouldn't sit down and say, 'Here's what you do.'" Instead he'd say, "Look, just fucking watch."

Slade McLaughlin, who worked on several cases with both Beasleys, described their relationship as "volatile."

"I saw the greatest of bonds between them, and I saw instances of great hatred between them," McLaughlin said. "They wouldn't talk to each other for weeks at a time for little picayune things. I always treaded lightly around them. They say blood is thicker than water."

"He adored Jimmy," longtime girlfriend Nicole Chabat said of Beasley's relationship with his son. And when they fought, she said, Beasley would become his son's "worst enemy."

"Jimmy just adored his dad, but his father was always looking for battles."

One perennial bone of contention between father and son was a daughter-in-law, the former Elizabeth "Liz" Pia. Jim Jr.'s wife was a fellow premed biology student whose parents were from the Philippines.

"We started out as friends and study buddies," Liz said. "He just had wonderful eyes, and he was telling me that he wanted to be a veterinarian in Africa." Her reaction: "Wow, that is so cool. For me it was love at first sight."

Liz was a quiet and shy but pretty bookworm. She was understandably nervous about meeting her boyfriend's father for the first time in 1987, when she had dinner at Beasley's Villanova home. It was already going to be a tense evening because Jim Jr. and his father had not spoken to each other for about a year.

Fortunately for Liz, Nicole Chabat was Beasley's date that night, and "she made things bubbly and light," Liz said. But Beasley was another story. "I was just very intimidated from the get-go," Liz said. "He was not a warm and welcoming guy."

Chabat said she instantly liked Liz because she understood what she had done for Jim Jr., who had struggled to accept his parents' divorce. "Jimmy was on a destructive path," Chabat said. "The day he met Elizabeth, Jimmy turned around. She was an incredibly positive influence in his life, and then she had to deal with his awful father."

On one early date, Liz and Jim Jr. were in the basement of Beasley's Villanova home, watching TV. Beasley went downstairs and issued a warning. "He said, 'No hanky-panky' in the sternest voice," Liz recalled. "Even when we were married, I was afraid to touch Jim because I remembered the words 'No hanky-panky.'"

"When you marry her, your kids will be ostracized" because of the mixed races, Beasley had warned his son. But the couple went ahead and in 1994 got married anyway.

"Was I the person he wanted his son to be with? No, I was made to feel I wasn't," Liz said. "I didn't come from the right socioeconomic background, or the right racial background. I wasn't tall, blonde and beautiful, from a wealthy, well-to-do family."

Beasley's concern stemmed from his own experience of being an Irish Protestant who married Gloria Fletcher, an Italian Catholic. That hadn't worked.

But Liz, the petite daughter of an electrician and a nurse, was also an honors student studying to become a doctor. And even her father-in-law eventually realized how smart she was. "It started to change when I did my residency," Liz said. "He started to have more respect for me."

Liz received an undergraduate scholarship for medical school from the Air Force and graduated summa cum laude from Temple University undergrad. Then she graduated in the top 10 percent of the class from Temple University School of Medicine. But Liz and Jim Jr. also wanted to raise a family. Liz gave birth in 1994 to the couple's first child, Ilissa.

Jim Jr. was working full-time at his father's law firm and preparing for the bar exam. He was also, with daily help from his mom, caring for his daughter when Liz began a demanding residency in obstetrics and gynecology. For a young family, it quickly became too much. Liz made the painful decision to give up the residency and was mad about it for a year. But she was surprised when Beasley stuck up for her, telling Jim Jr. she shouldn't have had to give up her residency. Beasley also took some pressure off Liz by paying off all her college and medical school loans.

Beasley took his daughter-in-law aside and expressed regret about their relationship. "The past is the past," he said. "You are my daughter-in-law and I love you."

After that, "He would hug and kiss me," Liz said. "He became very endearing with me. When we were in Florida and I was pregnant, and we were walking across the street, he would put his arm around me to protect me."

Liz gave birth to a son, Jimmy 3rd, in 1998. She was pregnant with a third child in 2003, but struggled with gestational diabetes. Two days before she was scheduled to deliver, Liz went to see her doctor because of decreased fetal movement. The baby the couple had already named Tommy was 38 weeks old. But when the nurse attempted to capture the baby's heartbeat on an ultrasound, Liz saw the baby's heart had stopped.

Beasley got the first call. Jim Jr. was in court that day and had his cell phone turned off, so Beasley called the judge's chambers to give his son the bad news. "Tommy's dead. Get back here now."

Jim Jr. raced to the law firm to grab his truck. His father met him in the parking lot, and, uncharacteristically, gave his son a big hug. Beasley knew what it was like to lose a child, and now his son had suffered a similar tragedy. Father and son raced to Liz's bedside at the hospital, where Jim Jr. continued to be amazed by his father's behavior. "He was wonderful with her."

Back at the office, people noticed a difference in the way Beasley treated his son. After Tommy's death, "I saw a real change in JEB," Slade McLaughlin said. Beasley's attitude became "'Let me cut Jimmy some slack,'" McLaughlin said. "I saw Mr. Beasley ease up on him after that."

• • •

BEASLEY CALLED STEPHEN P. GAULT, A CAR SALESMAN, AS A WITNESS. "MR. GAULT, I asked you to bring Stephen in this morning," Beasley said, referring to the son, now 8 years old. "I want you to step down and show the jury the bonding that exists between you and your son."

"Sure," said the elder Gault, who often spent nights lying on the floor of Stephen's room, to make sure his son didn't choke while he was sleeping. But before Gault could step off the witness stand, the defense attorney was on her feet.

"Objection, Your Honor," Vassalo said.

"The objection is sustained," said Judge Bernstein.

"May I see you at sidebar?" Beasley asked.

"Absolutely," the judge said.

In the sidebar conference, Beasley fought to give his case the emotional punch that would win the jury's sympathy. Beasley wanted young Stephen to sit in his father's lap, but the defense attorney and the judge were opposed. So Beasley tried to come up with another way to show the emotional rapport between father and son.

"One of the issues in this case is whether the child is going to be institutional-ized or stay at home," Beasley began. "There's a large difference in that."

"True," the judge said. The previous week, Beasley had brought an actuary in to testify that if young Stephen lived out his expected lifespan of 75.7 years, the present-value cost of caring for the boy at home was $41 million. If the parents would consent to put Stephen in an institution when he turned 22, then the cost of caring for him would drop dramatically, the actuary had testified, to $16 mil-lion. But the Gaults had no intention of doing that.

Karen Gault, a senior assistant buyer at Strawbridge & Clothier, had told the jury that she and her husband planned to take care of Stephen for the rest of his life. She explained how they had divvied up the parental chores. Karen Gault took her son to doctor's appointments, and made him do his stretching and the rest of his physical therapy. She also changed and bathed him. And when Stephen Gault came home from work, "My husband is the fun guy," Karen Gault told the jury.

When the father "walks into a room, this child hears his voice," Beasley told the judge. "He — the child — looks all around to try and find him, and he reaches out for him. He will hug his father all day long.

"Mr. Gault will sacrifice anything to stay with this child," Beasley said. "He has bonded so strong to him.... I think it's very critical to the believability, the credibility of Mr. Gault, when he says, 'I will never put this child away, even when he's old.' How else can I show that?"

"I don't know how you're going to show it, anyway," the judge said. "What is it you're asking your client to do?"

"I'm asking him to step down, sit in the chair, bring the wheelchair close to the chair, and you will see that child immediately reaches out for Mr. Gault and hugs him and pulls him over. And tries to kiss him on the ear."

"OK, OK," said the judge.

"Now, I can't describe that," Beasley said. "Mr. Gault can't describe it. There are some things in the world that words are not adequate to show."

"OK," the judge said. But the defense lawyer was upset.

"Your Honor, first of all, it's just a tactic to raise the passions… of the jury towards Mr. Gault and his son," Vassalo said. "This is not the first time this jury has seen Mr. Gault and his son interact. It is obvious to the jury, I am sure, that this boy has an attachment to his father. There's testimony from the mother that they would never institutionalize him. Obviously, how many more different ways can we establish that these parents… will not institutionalize this child?"

"Are you willing to stipulate to it?" Beasley asked.

"No, I'm not willing to stipulate to it," Vassallo said. The defense lawyer suggested that Beasley simply ask the father whether he would institutionalize the son. "To take the additional step to have him come down from the witness stand and display that kind of affection, I think, would be highly prejudicial and inflammatory, and I strongly urge the court to sustain my objection."

A second defense lawyer representing the hospital also objected, and the judge sustained the objection.

"I have no idea what it means to come down and show the affection and the bond between the plaintiff and child," said the judge, who then proposed his own solution. While Beasley wanted to bring the son to the father, the judge said it should be the other way around.

"If you would like to do a demonstration of placing the child in a specific location, and having your client step down and sit in proximity to see what the child does, I don't think that's objectionable," the judge told Beasley. "But that's very different from the question that you asked."

"Yes, Your Honor," Beasley replied, as he returned to the plaintiff's table. "Mr. Gault, would you step down, please, and sit in that chair."

Stephen Gault took a seat right in front of the jury, next to his son, who had been brought into the courtroom in his wheelchair. The boy wore braces on his legs; his head rolled from side to side, and his eyes wandered while he made grunting sounds. But when his father began talking to him, the boy lit up and smiled, stretching out his hands. As the jury watched, the boy began to hug and caress his father, petting his nose and face. It went on for nearly a minute.

"Thank you, Mr. Gault," Beasley said.

When Stephen Gault stood up to return to the witness stand, he was crying. And as they wheeled his son away, the boy was crying, too.

"That was like a knife to my heart," Judge Bernstein would subsequently say. And if that's what happened to such a "callous heart," the judge wondered, "how are these jurors feeling? You could sense his father is his whole life."

Over in the jury box, two jurors were crying. "It was very moving," said Angela

Couloumbis, a Philadelphia Inquirer reporter who, on a hunch, Beasley had decided to put on the jury. Couloumbis subsequently became the jury foreman. "He was the sweetest thing, just this beautiful kid, who had a very close relationship with this dad."

The court reporter was also choked up. "I wanted to cry," Helene Christian said. "This child was closer to his father than he was to his mother. It was just the magic between them."

• • •

DEBORAH M. FRIEDMAN WAS DIRECTOR OF PEDIATRIC CARDIOLOGY AT ST. LUKE'S Roosevelt Hospital in New York. She was also Beasley's expert witness who had reviewed the echocardiogram from Stephen's operation.

While Dr. Norwood had said that Stephen Jr.'s VSD was 4 millimeters in size, Dr. Friedman testified that the echocardiogram showed that Stephen's birth defect was only "3 millimeters in size," or, as Dr. Friedman put it, "certainly not an emergency."

"Now, based on what you've seen and told the jury, at that time, was there any medical reason to subject this child to deep hypothermic circulatory arrest to correct the defect that you've described?" Beasley asked.

"No, there was not," Dr. Friedman said. "This was a small [VSD]."

"Do you have an opinion, based on reasonable medical certainty, whether subjecting this child to the risk of deep hypothermic circulatory arrest was below the standard of reasonable medical care?"

"Yes, I do," Dr. Friedman said.

"Do you have an opinion, based upon reasonable medical certainty, whether that is a direct cause of this child's brain damage today?"

"Yes," said the doctor, who, after the judge overruled a defense objection, added, "I believe it was a direct cause of the brain damage."

Beasley's next expert was Dr. Daniel G. Adler, a pediatric neurologist who reviewed an electroencephalogram from Stephen's operation, the record of electrical activity in the brain. Dr. Adler testified that Stephen's body had been cooled so rapidly that the innermost regions of the brain remained at a warmer temperature. The uneven cooling of the brain was "the only explanation available to explain the injury to this child," Dr. Adler told Beasley.

"The only fact in the medical records that stands out is the fact that the baby was cooled fairly rapidly, over several minutes, and the operation was started in nine minutes," Dr. Adler testified.

"My knowledge as a pediatric neurologist, regarding the mechanism of brain injury and the effect of deep hypothermia, indicates that the amount of cooling was not satisfactory," Dr. Adler said. "And in my view, the only explanation for the baby's brain injury is the fact that this [inner] area of the brain was warmer than it needed to be. It wanted more oxygen than was being delivered."

· · ·

WHEN DR. NORWOOD TOOK THE WITNESS STAND, HE TOLD HIS DEFENSE LAWYER HE DID not recall the details of his conversation with the Gaults the morning of Stephen's operation. He told Vassalo, however, that he always discussed with parents the possibilities of "favorably influencing" the patient's medical history, as well as the risks of surgery. Dr. Norwood also insisted that his rapid cooling process "does not cause injury."

When Beasley cross-examined the doctor, he asked again about the conversation between Norwood and the Gaults on the morning of their son's operation. The doctor told Beasley that all he could recall was discussing his review of medical data regarding the infant's birth defects.

"That's your recollection of what occurred?" a disbelieving Beasley asked.

"Yes," Dr. Norwood said.

"Are you saying that what Mr. and Mrs. Gault said did not occur?"

"Objection, Your Honor," the defense lawyer said. "Overruled," the judge said.

"I'm not impugning their sincerity or veracity," Dr. Norwood said. "It is a little surprising to me, what their recollections are of what we had talked about that particular morning."

"Would that be a surprise to you, if shortly, within a few hours, their baby was brain damaged?" Beasley shot back. "Don't you think that would make a significant impression on them as to what they told you a couple of hours earlier?"

"Objection," the defense lawyer said. "The objection is sustained," the judge said.

"…Did you tell Mr. and Mrs. Gault that you were going to repair the VSD, and that you knew the medicine, they didn't, and you were going to make the decision as to what to do with their baby?"

"I would never say such a thing," Dr. Norwood said.

Beasley asked Dr. Norwood about a quotation from a medical textbook, *Cardiopulmonary Bypass Principles and Practice*: "A period of no less than 20 minutes should be used to cool the patient to a temperature of 20 degrees" centigrade, or 68 degrees Fahrenheit.

"Do you agree with that?" Beasley asked.

"…Absolutely not," Dr. Norwood said.

When Beasley asked Dr. Norwood about whether his rapid cooling strategy was responsible for Stephen's brain injuries, the doctor became visibly angry and loudly declared, "There is no evidence whatsoever that the rate of cooling causes brain injury; not a whit of evidence. …"

"That's all," Beasley said.

• • •

"A LOT OF PEOPLE," BEASLEY SAID, TAKE "OUR JURY SYSTEM" FOR GRANTED. "SO LET ME say, without further delay," he said, as he stared at the jury, "you are the most important people in the life of this child. There will never be anybody more important than each one of you."

Beasley quoted British philosopher G. K. Chesterton: "Our civilization has decided, and very justly decided, that determining the guilt or innocence of men is a thing too important to be trusted to trained men.

"When it wants a library catalogued, or a solar system discovered, or any trifle of that kind, it uses up the specialist," Beasley said, as he continued to quote Chesterton. "But when it wants something done that is serious, it collects 12 ordinary people, standing around. The same thing was done, if I remember right, by the founder of Christianity."

He may have been an agnostic in his private life, but when he stood in front of a jury, Beasley sounded like an evangelical preacher. He then denounced Dr. Norwood, the world-famous heart surgeon, for the sin of pride.

"It was around 11 o' clock on the morning of November the 3rd, when he sat in his office, picked up the file, looked at the file, and told the parents in a very arrogant way, 'I know what's best. I know the medicine and you don't,' " Beasley said.

He went through the devastating effects the brain damage had on Stephen Gault, pausing to dwell on the boy's partial blindness.

"His optic nerve is damaged," Beasley said. "You know the importance of the optic nerve. It's the window to the world. It's the window through which you see the changes from fall to winter to spring; the flowers, whatever it is that's out there that pleases our soul.... And when you please your soul, you wake up with a smile. Every day, you say, 'Thank God I'm alive.'

"You know something else?" Beasley told the jury. "Just think about this. In the last eight years, this child has missed, has not been able to appreciate 2,848 sunrises and sunsets. Does that have any value?"

Beasley reminded the jury that Stephen Gault had also missed Halloweens and Christmas mornings. And, if the boy lived out his expected life span, Beasley calculated, over the next 67 years, he would not see 24,455 more sunrises.

"And when God calls his parents, think about it, he will be alone," Beasley said. "And you know what the parents will say? 'When I'm gone, who is going to love my child? Who is going to cleanse his body, and who is going to comfort him, and hold him, and give him whatever security he needs? Is it a stranger?'

"So for 25 to 30 years, he's going to be alone, and alone, to him without his parents, is an enveloping emptiness," Beasley said. "He will be lost in this world."

Beasley closed his summation by telling jurors that "no matter how long you live, the name of Stephen Gault will be somewhere within your heart."

Dr. Norwood, Beasley told the jury, "will go about his business, his trade. Children's Hospital, we, and the rest of the world will go on as though Stephen Gault never existed.

"Only you can make sure that what he has in the future is secure," Beasley told the jury. "I've done everything that I can for this child. I want you to do everything that you can."

· · ·

KAREN GAULT GOT NERVOUS WHILE THE JURORS WERE SENDING OUT QUESTIONS TO THE judge. The defense had also upped their original settlement offer of $1 million, which Beasley had told the judge was ridiculous, to $7.5 million.

If the Gaults took the $7.5 million, Beasley's cut would be one-third, or $2.5 million. That would leave the Gaults with $5 million.

When the Gaults asked Beasley about the offer, he told them he was confident that the jury would come back with a good verdict. But the settlement offer was nothing to sneer at. If the $5 million was properly invested, Beasley told his clients, it should take care of a lifetime of medical costs for Stephen.

There was also the matter of expediency. Even if they won a big verdict, they would probably have to wait a few years for the inevitable appeals to be decided. But if the Gaults took the $7.5 million, they would get their money right away.

In the end, the Gaults decided to play it safe and take the $7.5 million. Moments after Beasley had agreed to the deal, the jury came back with a $55-million verdict, at the time the largest medical malpractice award in Pennsylvania history.

The jurors wondered why the Gaults showed no visible reaction when the verdict was read. The Gaults, however, as well as Beasley, had already decided that they had done the responsible thing by taking the guaranteed money for Stephen.

· · ·

AT HOME, JIM BEASLEY CONTINUED TO ACT LIKE A CHANGED MAN. "WELL, HE HAD mellowed," Helen said. He even tried to avoid arguments, telling his former wife, "You're the boss."

They were at Beasley's vacation home in Ft. Lauderdale, playing tennis on July 5, 2002, when Beasley told Helen he was going to drive down to City Hall to pick up a marriage license application. It was Beasley's way of proposing. OK, Helen said. So they drove down to City Hall together in their tennis whites.

Helen wore her mother's wedding ring because years ago she had had her first wedding band from Beasley made into a bracelet. But Beasley still had his original 1958 wedding band. "I kept it all these years," he told Helen.

When they returned to Philadelphia, the newly remarried couple celebrated with dinner at Le Bec-Fin, with Dick Sprague and his longtime companion, Edith Magaziner. The first time he was married to Helen, Beasley had never worn a wedding ring. But from the moment he married Helen the second time, he wore his wedding ring every day. He also made other changes Helen insisted on.

"I got tough," Helen said. "I stopped putting up with dalliances. I finally convinced him that there should only be two people in a marriage."

"Guys like us, we just have to fuck around," Beasley had once confided to flying buddy Ed Shipley. But this time, Beasley was finally able to cut out his philandering. Or, as his wife put it, "It took him 74 years to grow up."

Beasley's former girlfriends were stunned to hear he was back with Helen.

"She was the smartest one of us all," Nicole Chabat said. "I also think he got tired."

Beasley, however, told flying buddy Dan Caldarale, "Helen's good for me."

"They were the exact opposites," Caldarale marveled. When Caldarale and his wife double-dated with the Beasleys, Helen would saunter downstairs, all dressed up, and say, "Here I am." Beasley would be pacing and grumbling, "Let's get the fuck out of here."

But after a lifetime of being a warrior, and well into his 70s, Beasley had not only mellowed, he was also sentimental. "You have my heart," he wrote his wife in a card. "Keep it well. Love, Jim."

"Hi pretty girl, Hope you are able to get this message of love," Beasley wrote in an e-mail sent from the office. The subject of the e-mail was listed as "love," and in case his wife missed the point, it was signed, "Love, your husband, James E. Beasley."

• • •

There were even signs that Beasley might have been rethinking his lifelong hostility toward religion. When Mel Gibson came out with *Passion of the Christ*, Beasley wanted to see it. Helen, however, thought the movie might be too graphic, and she begged off. So Beasley went by himself.

It was around the time that Beasley and I had begun work on his book. When Beasley told me about watching the *Passion,* I was stunned. "What's an atheist like you doing at a movie like that?" I asked. But Beasley didn't laugh. He praised the movie, saying it was "a historically accurate portrayal of what that fellow went through."

Beasley's favorite cousin, Walter Woodworth, said in his last years Jim Beasley was searching. "He always questioned me about the Bible because he knew I was reading the Bible every night," said Woodworth, a born-again Christian. Beasley always ended those Sunday night phone conversations by saying, "I love you, Walter."

. . .

AFTER THEY REMARRIED, JIM AND HELEN BEASLEY OCCASIONALLY REVERTED TO PREVI-ous bad habits. "You guys, as soon as you get married, you started fighting again," Jim Jr. griped. "I wish you stayed living in sin."

Beasley was still restless. At his vacation home in Florida, he kept a 37-foot fishing boat. But by the third day of a vacation, he was always bored.

"He tried, but he was so fidgety he couldn't relax in Florida," Jim Jr. said. His parents would spend Christmas vacation in Florida, but Beasley brought so much work home with him, he was always on the computer or grabbing something off the fax machine.

"Will you please just go back to the office?" his wife finally said. "You might as well be there." So Beasley would fly back to Philadelphia alone.

"When you've been running at 100 miles an hour for 45 years, you can't just stop," Jim Jr. said.

Chapter 23

❖

TARGET: OSAMA

On NBC's Today show, host Matt Lauer was interviewing Jim Beasley Jr. about the "first of its kind lawsuit" he and his father had just filed against the world's most wanted terrorist.

It was Oct. 15, 2001, and the post 9/11 headline on the screen said, "America Strikes Back." Lauer, the talking head from the NBC studio in New York, posed a practical question: "How do you plan on serving Osama bin Laden?"

Jim Jr. was sitting in the lobby of his law office; the headline under the live camera feed from Philadelphia said, "James Beasley/ His client is suing Osama bin Laden."

"We don't know the address to his cave," Jim Jr. conceded on the air with a smile. "There are various direct or indirect ways of doing it. I don't want to get into the specifics. . . . It will get done though. Trust us."

• • •

The ad, which ran for six weeks on Al Jazeera TV, featured solemn flute music and the clacking sounds of an electric typewriter as it printed out a legal notice in Arabic:

"To: The Islamic Emirate of Afghanistan;

The Taliban;

Al Qaeda/Islamic Army;

Sheikh Usamah bin-Muhammad bin-Ladin a/k/a Osama bin Laden.

Notice Served by:

James E. Beasley Esquire."

Beasley was using Al Jazeera to formally notify bin Laden and the Taliban that he had filed suit against them in U.S. District Court in Manhattan, on behalf of the families of two 9/11 victims, George Smith and Tim Soulas.

The legal notice, approved by the federal judge in the case, said as of Nov. 15, 2001, the defendants had 20 days to file with the U.S. District Court and respond by mail to Beasley at his Philadelphia law office.

"If Defendants fail to do so, judgment by default may be taken against Defendants for relief demanded in the Complaints," the notice warned, "for wrongful death, assault, battery, and violations of international and U.S. laws."

In case the defendants didn't watch TV, Beasley also had legal notices published in two national newspapers in Pakistan, where bin Laden was believed to be hiding.

Beasley didn't know bin Laden's whereabouts, but he did locate the address of a former Taliban ambassador, Mullah Abdul Salam Zaeef. And then Beasley hired a Pakistani lawyer, Muhammad Hasnain Ibrahim Kazmi, to serve the ambassador with legal papers.

On Dec. 31, 2001, the Pakistani lawyer, escorted by armed guards, showed up at the ambassador's home in Islamabad, but the ambassador refused to see his visitor or accept the papers he was carrying. So the Pakistani lawyer notified Beasley by affidavit that he had "affixed copies of the legal papers" by nailing them to the ambassador's front door.

•   •   •

ON 9/11, LIKE MILLIONS OF AMERICANS, JIM JR. HAD WATCHED THE HORRIFIC VIDEO OF the World Trade Center collapsing, as well as the endless network file footage of Osama bin Laden. "We should sue the bastard," Jim Jr. told Slade McLaughlin.

That's just what they ended up doing.

A neighbor of Jim Jr.'s, Steve Soulas, had a brother killed in 9/11. Tim Soulas, 35, of Basking Ridge, N.J., was the director of foreign securities at Cantor Fitzgerald who worked on the 105th floor of the North Tower of the World Trade Center. He left behind five children and a pregnant wife.

The conventional approach to filing a wrongful death suit was to go after the airlines or the airports for damages, for failing to stop the terrorists from boarding the planes, or to sue American Airlines, the owner of the planes that crashed into the towers.

But Jim Jr. and McLaughlin had another idea. Why not go after the hundreds of millions of dollars in assets frozen by the United States government that formerly belonged to nations such as Afghanistan, nations that the United States had accused of sponsoring terrorists? Why not use those frozen assets to compensate 9/11 victims?

The first time Jim Jr. approached his father about suing bin Laden and the Taliban, Beasley's response was, "Are you insane?" But the son explained there was case law behind it.

Congress had amended the Foreign Sovereign Immunities Act (FSIA) in 1996 to allow American victims of terrorism to sue nations identified by the State Department as sponsors of terrorism. Three former U.S. hostages held in Iran had filed suit under FSIA, and shared a 1998 judgment of $68 million. One of the former hostages, Joseph Cicippio of Norristown, Pa., subsequently collected $30 million in frozen Iranian assets from the U.S. Treasury.

Beasley was converted. His firm sued on behalf of the Soulas family, and then the Smith family joined the lawsuit. George Smith, 38, of West Chester, Pa., was a senior business analyst for SunGard Systems who worked on the 97th floor of the South Tower of the World Trade Center. He was survived by a grandmother, a father and eight siblings.

Beasley and son were now on a mission to convict the 9/11 terrorists in court as well as the nations that had sponsored them. And if they pulled that off, then the only way to collect on behalf of their clients was to pry millions of dollars in frozen assets out of the grip of the U.S. government.

• • •

THE CASE OF *SMITH V. TALIBAN* WAS THE SUBJECT OF A FEB. 28, 2003, HEARING IN U.S. District Court in the Southern District of New York. Representing the plaintiffs were a trio of Philadelphia lawyers: James E. Beasley Sr., James E. Beasley Jr. and Slade H. McLaughlin.

Since Beasley Sr. filed *Smith v. Taliban*, however, a funny thing had happened to those frozen assets he was chasing. After 9/11, the U.S. government had seized $250 million in assets that had once belonged to bin Laden's collaborators, the former Taliban government of Afghanistan. Then in January 2002, the State Department announced it was turning over $221 million of those assets to the new Afghan government.

So Beasley had a problem. Since the Bush Administration believed at the time that Iraq had collaborated on 9/11, Beasley's solution was to add two new defendants to the case: Saddam Hussein and the Republic of Iraq.

Just 23 days before the *Smith v. Taliban* hearing, Secretary of State Colin Powell had testified before the United Nations Security Council about the existence of a "sinister nexus" between Iraq and the al Qaeda terrorist network that supposedly went back decades. The United States back in 1990 had frozen nearly $2 billion in Iraqi assets. So Beasley went through the U.S. State Department to formally notify Iraq's Ministry of Foreign Affairs about his new claim against Iraq in *Smith v. Taliban*.

None of the defendants, however, old or new, ever bothered to respond to Beasley's lawsuit, so they were all in default with Judge Harold Baer Jr. That meant that the proceedings would not be delayed by objections from defense attorneys, or cross-examinations.

So Beasley's strategy was simple: Put the family members of the victims on the stand and let them tell the judge what happened.

"May I proceed?" Beasley asked.

"Yes," the judge said.

"The plaintiff calls Katherine Soulas."

Katy Soulas, Tim's widow, was a petite blond nurse now raising six children on her own.

"Katy, would you tell the judge something about your background, where you were raised and your education?" Beasley asked.

"I was born in Bryn Mawr, Pennsylvania, and raised in Broomall, which is a suburb of Philadelphia," Katy Soulas said in her soft-spoken manner. "I attended Cardinal O'Hara High School with Tim. We started dating in high school. I went on to the University of Pennsylvania and he went to Drexel, which is across the street. And we were married the week after he graduated from school and started having babies 10 months later."

"And tell us . . . what type of individual he was," Beasley said.

"When we met in high school, he was the class clown," Katy Soulas said. "He was the funny one. I was the studious one involved in sports and NHS [National Honor Society]. And he was the guy who could get great grades without studying, and the life of every event that took place from the rugby field to the classroom."

Beasley showed his client a photo of a pee-wee football player with his coach.

"And this is your husband?"

"That's Tim, uh-huh."

"And that's little Timmy?"

"My son," she said. "Tim coached every sport for our children.... He coached each of our son's T-ball teams for Little League and was also coaching roller hockey, Pop Warner football, and he assisted coaching in ice hockey."

Tim Soulas loved sports, whether he was playing or coaching. After he got off work at the World Trade Center, he would change clothes in his truck and drive straight to the practice field.

"So, he was a coach through all the seasons?" Beasley asked.

"He was the jack-of-all-trades," his widow said. "He could throw a ball or skate or rollerblade or throw the football. He tried to be involved in every aspect of our children's lives."

"Katy, tell us something about Tim's work ethic, please," Beasley asked.

"Tim was the most honest broker in the world," Katy Soulas said. "If a client wanted a certain price, he would search for it, and if he couldn't get it, he would say, 'It's not going to happen. I can't get it there; this is where I can make it happen.'

"And for that, I have heard over and over again from countless of his clients that because of his honesty, they trusted him," Katy Soulas said. "He wasn't going to make up something that wasn't going to happen or tell somebody what they wanted to hear."

"Give us a little brief background of his work history," Beasley asked.

Tim Soulas, a former currency broker at the Philadelphia Stock Exchange, was always "brilliant at math, but [also] brilliant at probability and predicting where the markets were going to go," Katy Soulas said. So when Cantor Fitzgerald hired him in 1993, Tim Soulas became indispensable to clients and coworkers. His projected salary in 2001 was $1.2 million.

"Now, what was going to happen on 9/11?" Beasley asked, "so we put this in context."

On 9/11, Katy Soulas was three-months pregnant with the couple's sixth child. She had an ultrasound examination scheduled for 1 p.m., because doctors had found an eight-centimeter ovarian cyst and wanted to monitor it.

The night before the appointment, "I felt a lot of discomfort with the cyst, and Tim was very concerned about it and wanted to come with me to the ultrasound examination," Katy Soulas testified.

"What was the conversation between you and Tim, and what was it that led him to go to work?" Beasley asked.

From her perch on the witness stand, Katy Soulas gave Beasley and the judge an intimate account of her husband's last night. She spoke calmly and matter-of-factly and without tears, as if she didn't have any left.

"He took the boys on a bike ride after work, and then they sold Cub Scout popcorn and met their quota for the year for fundraising," Katy Soulas said. "And we went to bed, and he wanted to make love, and I said, 'Honey, I'm really uncomfortable. I can't. I'm worried about this cyst.'"

Katy Soulas recalled how she told her husband not to worry about the doctor's appointment, because she was going to be OK. "I really think you should go to work," she had said. "You've just had a long weekend." Tim Soulas had stretched the Labor Day weekend by taking Tuesday off.

Go to work, his wife had insisted. "If there's a problem, I'll call you from the doctor's office."

But Katy Soulas never made it to the doctor's.

"Let me go back to 9/11," Beasley said. "Share with the judge how you came to find out about the disaster that was then occurring."

Katy Soulas explained she was on the treadmill that morning, running four miles, when a neighbor burst into the house, crying and talking about a plane hitting the Twin Towers.

Katy tried to call her husband, but the line was busy. She told Beasley how she got hold of Tim's boss in London. "'I just talked to Tim,'" she remembered the boss saying. She then related to Beasley what Tim's boss had said: "'Everyone's leaving the building right now. I told him to get out. So they're hopefully on the staircase on their way out of the building. You're going to have to hold tight.'"

"And there I was," she said, staring at Beasley. "Helpless, holding tight.

"At 9:05, my phone rang," she testified. "And it was static, loud static. And then it went dead. And that happened again at 9:10 and then again at 9:40. And I know in my heart that was Tim trying to call me."

"How did you feel?" Beasley asked.

Katy Soulas told Beasley that as she watched TV, and saw the black smoke pouring out of the World Trade Center, she realized, "I don't think he's going to get out."

"And I — you know, I don't want to sound freaky religious, but I prayed to Mary that this must be what it was like for her to watch her son die on the cross," she testified. "I'm watching my husband die right now. And I was physically sick. I got sick to my stomach. You know, not just because I was pregnant, but — it was horrifying, to realize I was watching him die on TV."

"How did you handle the children the rest of the day?" Beasley asked.

"I called the school," she said. "Do the kids know anything about this?" she recalled asking a counselor. The counselor told Katy Soulas there were no TVs at school and no Internet access. The kids were safe, the counselor said; there was no reason to alarm them. But the counselor told Katy Soulas not to let her kids watch TV.

"And I said, 'OK,'" Katy Soulas testified. "And as we were on the phone, Tim's building collapsed, and I did, too."

"Have you had any help [from] support groups since 9/11?" Beasley asked.

Katy Soulas told Beasley about the candlelight vigil on 9/11, followed by a Mass the following night at St. James Roman Catholic Church, where they prayed for the victims and their families. Katy Soulas talked about the support group that the monsignor at her church had organized, because on 9/11 17 families in Basking Ridge had lost a family member.

"Would you share with the judge how you handle adult loneliness?"

Katy Soulas talked about the survivors-group meetings every Thursday night. "It was really my time to just cry for me and for my kids," she said. "It's an amazing sorority I belong to now of victims' families. That we have this understanding of each other, and of this horror, and how bad it really is for us and for our kids.

"And I've had to put myself on the back burner because I've got [six] little kids that really need to be — need to come to terms with this themselves," Katy Soulas said.

"This is a horrifying situation," she told Beasley. "And we really have to pull ourselves together. And in the beginning, we weren't together. And going to the support group, I found out, no one's together. Everyone's doing this. All of the 10-year-olds are talking about body parts and blood and gore, and they all want to kill anyone who has a turban on their head."

Beasley asked about the memorial service in Tim's honor at St. James, which attracted 1,200 people. And the grim discovery that came afterward.

"And was there any time that a portion of Tim was found?" Beasley asked.

The only body part rescue workers found, Katy Soulas testified, was a piece of a jawbone. The medical examiner called to say if she decided not to hold a funeral service, they would dispose of it.

"And it reminded me of when I put our dog to sleep that 'they'd dispose of it,'" she told Beasley. "And it was pouring salt in the wound when he was found, that they found a piece of him and they have more pieces that they're not sure who they are."

Katy Soulas testified that she told the medical examiner, "Tell me at the end when you're done with the identification process, and we'll bury what we have at the end.

"And at this point now, I regret doing that," she told Beasley, "because my kids realize we haven't had a funeral for Daddy, and that he is somewhere in New York City. At this point, I wish I had just gone ahead and buried the remains that we had."

"Did that happen?" Beasley asked.

"Not yet," she said.

"Just one or two more things, Katy," Beasley said. "I want to show you what has a marking, 80435. Would you show that to the judge and tell him what it is?"

"This is Tim's personal effects that were found," she said, holding up a plastic bag of evidence. The bag contained a charred piece of a key to a Lexus truck and the remains of a driver's license. "I was told by the police department that it had melted," she said. "What strikes me about that is the smell. It smells horrible."

Katy Soulas stared at Beasley and the judge.

"This is what I have left," she said. "I haven't recovered his wedding band or the watch he had on that day."

Beasley looked up at the judge.

"Does the court have any questions?"

"No," the judge said. "You are excused."

• • •

IN THE COURTROOM, JIM BEASLEY WAS USUALLY A ONE-MAN SHOW, BUT IN *SMITH V. TALIBAN*, he shared the spotlight with his son and Slade McLaughlin. Beasley gave the two young lawyers credit for landing the case, and then he got excited about it. As a World War II veteran from the Greatest Generation, Beasley was an America-first patriot who was gung-ho about the idea of striking back against the terrorists that had attacked his country. When the three plaintiff's lawyers divvied up the witnesses, Beasley was "very gracious," McLaughlin recalled.

"He gave both Jimmy and me lots of opportunities to do our thing," McLaughlin said. "He was there for advice, but never stepped on our toes. He was a class act all the way."

Beasley encouraged his son to handle the media, never one of his favorite chores. He showed up in court with a miniature American flag pinned to his chest. And from his seat at the plaintiff's table, he cheered on the young guys when it was their turn to question a witness.

"Steve, good morning," Jim Jr. said to the next witness.

"Good morning," Steve Soulas replied.

"Please tell us your relation to Tim Soulas," Jim Jr. asked.

"Tim was my younger brother."

"How much younger?"

"He was five years younger than me."

Jim Jr. asked about the day after 9/11, when Steve Soulas was at his brother's house, talking with a couple of Tim's friends. And Tim was still missing.

"Was there ever an attempt to see if you could find Tim?"

"We decided… we're going to New York City to find Timmy," Steve Soulas said. Their first stop was Jersey City, where Tim Soulas parked his truck every day, to commute to New York.

"We pulled into this parking garage," Steve Soulas said, and one of his brother's friends spotted Tim Soulas's Lexus truck.

"And we walked over and looked in… and there was his cell phone sitting on the console," Steve Soulas said. "We'd all been calling the cell phone the previous day and getting his voice mail and hoping to God he had his cell phone. He left it in the car. You know, that happens."

Besides a cell phone, Tim Soulas had also left behind shorts, sneakers, socks, and a coach's whistle.

"So we went into New York and walked through the streets," Steve Soulas testified. "We went to all the hospitals. . . . We had pictures of Tim. We were, you know, with a throng of people who were doing a similar type of thing. And then, at the end of the evening, we ended up at, I guess, the medical examiner's office. …Of course, we got no information."

Jim Jr. asked Steve Soulas if he was still "involved with Katy and her kids, trying to help them?"

"You know, I like to think so," Steve Soulas said with a sigh. He told Jim Jr. how he showed up every Wednesday night at his brother's house, "just to hang out, you know, have dinner, help with homework…. Whatever it takes."

"…Tim's death, did it personally affect you physically or mentally?" Jim Jr. asked.

"…In October of 2001, I started having these tremendous chest pains," Soulas said. A doctor told him, " 'You know, it's stress…. I'm going to prescribe something for you to relieve the burden that you're feeling. You have to work on relieving the stress.'

"I reached kind of a boiling point, and I decided to get some, you know, some consulting-style help," Steve Soulas testified. "And I walked into a psychoanalyst I was referred to, not knowing what to expect. And he has a picture on his floor — and he doesn't know why I'm there — and he has a picture on his floor of the cross at Ground Zero. And I thought, well, isn't this perfect? And he said, 'Why are you here?' And I said, 'Because of that.'

"And I've been seeing him, you know, weekly ever since, and it's helpful."

• • •

"Go get 'em, Tiger," Beasley said over at the plaintiff's table, as Slade McLaughlin stood to call the next witness. Raymond Anthony Smith was a big guy with dreadlocks who looked like the tight end on a football team.

"Ray, you were George's brother, correct?" McLaughlin asked.

"Yes," Ray Smith said. He explained how he and George were from a brood of 11 children with the same father, but that the family had split up. Ray was raised in Phoenixville, Pa., by his grandmother, and George lived in Philadelphia with his mother. And George had the tougher road.

"It was my understanding that their life was pretty rough," Ray Smith testified. "Their mother was running the streets. There were periods of time when they were out on the street begging for food. Roaches, rats infested their house. Just a real hard time."

"What were the circumstances that led your brother to go from Philadelphia to Phoenixville?" McLaughlin asked.

"His mother was killed one day by a stray bullet," Ray Smith said. "They just assumed she was out on one of her binges and she would be back either today or tomorrow, and they were left alone in the house with no electricity, no food. Just nothing. They were by themselves."

"So what happened as a result of that?"

"…The neighbors called my grandmother, Marion Thomas, who was living in Phoenixville, and said, 'Your grandchildren are begging for food and they're out on the street. If you don't come get them right now, we're going to call Children's Services.' "

That's how Ray Smith, then in sixth grade, ended up sharing a room with his older brother, George, then in eighth grade, for the next four years.

"He was my older brother. Someone I always looked up to," Ray Smith told McLaughlin. "I wanted to be like him. In Phoenixville, George was the man."

Ray Smith told McLaughlin how George, at 6-foot-4, made the Phoenixville High varsity basketball team four years in a row, and was the starting center in his junior and senior years. And how, after Ray didn't make the varsity basketball team as a freshman, George took Ray out on the court to show him some moves. Ray went on to become a three-year starter on the high school team.

McLaughlin asked about the events of 9/11: "How did you react to the news that your brother was there, and possibly lost?"

"In my head, I understood what they were saying: He was on the 97th floor, the plane hit under that. I understood that in my head," Ray Smith said. "But, in my heart, I thought that he could get out, because when we were younger, he was a guy that could do everything."

"…Did there come a time, Ray, when the family received news that some remains had been found of George?" McLaughlin said.

"Yes," Ray Smith said. "After the memorial service, in the next year, they found a leg bone, foot bone or something."

"And what was done with that bone?"

"It was brought back, it was cremated, and we had another service."

• • •

It wasn't hard to prove that Osama bin Laden was involved in 9/11. He was on videotape bragging about it:

"We calculated in advance the number of casualties from the enemy, who would be killed based on the position of the tower," bin Laden said on a translated tape that Beasley played in court. The tape was made during a visit bin Laden and his lieutenants made to an unidentified Saudi Arabian sheik at a guesthouse in Qandahar. On the tape, bin Laden sat cross-legged on the floor; at times he laughed and appeared gleeful.

"We calculated that the floors would be hit would be three or four floors," bin Laden said on the tape. "I was the most optimistic of all, due to my experience in this field. I was thinking that the fire from the gas in the plane would melt the iron structure of the building and collapse the area where the plane hit and all the floors above it only. This is all that we had hoped for."

"Allah be praised," said the sheik, who was listening to bin Laden, and subsequently kissed the terrorist mastermind on the forehead.

"We had notification since the previous Thursday that the event would take place that day," bin Laden said on the tape. "Immediately we heard the news that a plane had hit the World Trade Center.... After a little while, they announced that another plane had hit the World Trade Center. The brothers who heard the news were overjoyed by it."

Regarding the other defendants, Beasley had written in his legal briefs that "the Taliban provided safe housing and terrorist-training sites to Osama bin Laden and al Qaeda beginning in 1996. On Sept. 30, 2001, the Taliban spokesperson and ambassador to Pakistan, Mullah Abdul Salam Zaeef, described the relationship between the Taliban/Islamic emirate and bin Laden as follows:

"He [bin Laden] cannot move around freely. Wherever he goes, there are people assigned to him, and he cannot move without their permission. He's under the control of the Islamic Emirate of Afghanistan and only security people... know where he is," the ambassador was quoted as saying in Beasley's brief.

So as far as Beasley was concerned, bin Laden, al Qaeda and the Taliban were already guilty for 9/11. But it would be much harder to prove that Saddam Hussein and Iraq had been involved.

• • •

AMONG THE SPECTATORS AT THE *SMITH V. TALIBAN* HEARING WAS RICHARD D. HAILEY, an Indianapolis lawyer who in 1997 was elected as the first black president of the Association of Trial Lawyers of America.

Hailey was interested in Beasley's case because he was one of a consortium of eight lawyers who had filed a similar action under the Foreign Sovereign Immunities Act. The suit against the nations of Iran and Iraq was filed on behalf of 94 victims of 9/11. "This is a very specialized niche of law," Hailey said in an interview. "We had entered a forest for which there are no maps." And Beasley was a good trail guide, Hailey said. "He navigated that forest like he was in there 100 times."

Hailey, who had never met Beasley before, watched him in a hallway outside the courtroom, talking to his witnesses. "He was revved up like a racehorse," Hailey recalled. "But the minute he hit that courtroom, he was methodical.

"What I felt was, we were part of a historic event here," Hailey said. "We had lost more people [in 9/11] than Pearl Harbor. And here's this cowboy out of Philadelphia who's gonna dare to get ahead of the federal government in trying to provide a remedy for these people."

Hailey was impressed with how Beasley had scoured Washington, D.C., to gather intelligence on Iraq, much of it technical in nature, and was able to weave it into a convincing courtroom narrative.

At the time of the *Smith v. Taliban* hearing, in March 2003, the theory that

Saddam had aided and abetted al Qaeda in 9/11 was publicly subscribed to by President Bush and Vice President Cheney, as well as Secretary of State Powell and Secretary of Defense Donald Rumsfeld.

It was before the invasion of Iraq; the Bush Administration was keeping a tight lid on the flow of information, and the press was being cautious. Then, after the invasion, the political winds shifted. In September 2003, six months after the *Smith v. Taliban* hearing, President Bush told the Washington Post, "No, we've had no evidence that Saddam Hussein was involved with September the 11th." In July 2004, the report of the 9/11 Commission also flatly denied an Iraq-al Qaeda connection.

"We know that some of that information turned out to be a mixed bag," Hailey conceded about preinvasion intelligence on Iraq. At the *Smith v. Taliban* hearing, however, Beasley was working with the evidence available in early 2003, and he was characteristically tenacious.

"He's like a bulldog grabbing a bone," Hailey marveled. "You know, the guy has no quit in him."

• • •

ON MARCH 3, 2003, IN U.S. DISTRICT COURT, BEASLEY SWORE IN AS AN EXPERT WITNESS R. James Woolsey Jr., former director of the CIA from 1993-95 under President Clinton. Beasley wanted to use the professorial Woolsey to lay out the then-known connections between Iraq and al Qaeda. So Beasley asked Woolsey about a reported meeting in April 2001 in Prague between Mohammed Atta, the lead suicide bomber in 9/11, and an Iraqi intelligence official.

It wasn't a "reported meeting," Woolsey said, it happened.

"The Czech intelligence service on several occasions, and its superiors — the deputy foreign minister on one occasion, [the] interior minister on another — have all affirmed that there was a meeting between Atta in Prague and a man named Al-Ani, who was a senior Iraqi intelligence officer who was sometime after that declared *persona non grata* by the Czech government and expelled," Woolsey testified.

Beasley showed the former CIA director slides of satellite surveillance photos taken inside Iraq of an alleged terrorist training camp known as Salman Pak. The photos showed a jet sitting on the camp grounds. Intelligence reports had said that non-Iraqis in groups of four or five were training at Salman Pak, learning how to hijack an airplane with knives, but Iraqi officials had denied it. They had also denied that there was a plane at the camp.

"This is an image of Salman Pak that was taken in 2000, and it shows an airplane in this area," Beasley said. "In viewing this, sir, is this sufficient when you're looking at this to give a thought about whether training on this airline for hijack-ing would give material support to any attempt to terrorize the United States?"

"I think when you put the confirmed existence of the aircraft in the face of the Iraqi government official denials," along with statements from three other witnesses, Woolsey said, "it is quite probative, as far as I'm concerned, that there was training of terrorists, Islamist terrorists, from countries other than Iraq, religious fundamentalists, in how to hijack aircraft.

"The Iraqi government has subsequently said that if there was training going on, it was training on how to counter hijackings, which I think is ludicrous.

"What it strongly suggests to me is that in some fashion, there was a common purpose here of the Iraqi government training of terrorists, and those who conducted the Sept. 11 attack," Woolsey said.

"This is too much of a coincidence," Woolsey concluded. "If one suggests that there was no connection of any kind, I think it's far more likely than not that there was some, let's say, cross-fertilization of ideas, of personnel, or training, of planning, of something."

Beasley showed Woolsey a transcript of the current CIA director, George Tenet, testifying before the U.S. Senate. Beasley asked Woolsey his opinion of Tenet, and Woolsey replied that he had "a very high regard for his intellect and his probity."

Beasley had Woolsey read aloud a portion of Tenet's remarks to the Senate: "There's solid reporting of senior level contacts between Iraq and al Qaeda going back a decade," Tenet had testified. "Iraq has provided training to al Qaeda members in the areas of poisons and gases and making conventional bombs."

Beasley asked Woolsey about whether current evidence indicated that al Qaeda and Iraq were collaborators.

"…I believe it is definitely more likely than not that some degree of common effort in the sense of aiding or abetting the conspiracy was involved here between Iraq and the al Qaeda," Woolsey testified.

The former CIA director likened the Iraqi government and al Qaeda to "two Mafia families who hate each other, kill each other's members from time to time, insult each other, but are still capable of cooperating against what they consider to be a greater enemy — namely us.

"So I have never been persuaded by the view that since one, al Qaeda, has its roots in extremist Islam, and the other, Iraqi Baathists, have roots in secular ideology, that that means they could never work together," Woolsey said. "I think that view is wrong. I think they are quite capable of working together."

• • •

JIM BEASLEY JR. CALLED LAURIE MYLROIE, AUTHOR OF *STUDY OF REVENGE: SADDAM HUSSEIN'S UNFINISHED WAR AGAINST AMERICA*, published in 2000 by the American

Enterprise Institute.

"What was the basic premise of that book?" Jim Jr. asked.

"The argument was that the Gulf War never ended for Saddam Hussein," Mylroie said. "That, starting in February of 1993, he was working with Islamic militants to attack the United States, and that Iraqi intelligence had been behind the World Trade Center bombing; that Ramsey Yusef, the mastermind of that attack, was in fact an Iraqi intelligence agent."

Mylroie was a former associate professor at the U.S. Naval War College in Rhode Island who served as a 1992 campaign advisor on Iraq to President Bill Clinton. She had also worked as a consultant to ABC News during an investigation of the first terrorist attack on the World Trade Center.

"Speaking about Ramsey Yusef," Jim Jr. said, "what type of passport did he have?"

"Ramsey Yusef entered the United States on an Iraqi passport," Mylroie said. Jim Jr. asked about Abdul Rahman Yasin, another suspect allegedly involved in the first attack on the World Trade Center.

"Abdul Rahman Yasin is an indicted fugitive, and he is in Baghdad," the professor said.

"…And he's been indicted for, what was it, mixing the chemicals, or something," Jim Jr. asked.

"Yes, he's been indicted," the professor said. "The indictment suggests he mixed the chemicals. He has a chemical burn on his thigh. That's one of the distinguishing features in the wanted poster for him."

"Based upon your investigation of World Trade Center One [the first terrorist attack in1993]," Jim Jr. asked, "do you have an opinion as to whether Iraq has provided safe housing, such as a form of material support or resources, to this individual, Abdul Rahman Yasin, who was indicted in World Trade Center One?"

"Iraq has definitely provided safe haven to Yasin," the professor responded. "He had been there since he left the United States in early March 1993."

Jim Jr. asked the professor whether she believed Iraq collaborated with al Qaeda to provide "material support or resources to the individuals who ultimately caused the World Trade Center disaster?"

"Yes," the professor said. "Iraq, I believe, did provide support and resources for the Sept. 11 attack."

"Can you give us a description, if you will, of, say, how al Qaeda — and by that I mean Osama bin Laden and the other hijacker types – how they would work or coordinate this operation with a state such as Iraq —?"

"Well, I think that in many respects, al Qaeda acts as a front for Iraq intelligence," the professor said. "Al Qaeda provides the ideology, the foot soldiers and the cover. Increasingly, bin Laden is described as a symbol, the philosopher of it all, rather than the operational director. And that's my view. And Iraqi intelligence provides the direction, the training, and the expertise."

"…Based on your understanding of al Qaeda, do you believe they alone had the intelligence material or resources to conduct such a synchronized operation as that which we saw on Sept. 11?" Jim Jr. asked.

"No, I don't think they have that sophistication capability, and that it required the support of an intelligence agency of a terrorist state like Iraq, and I believe that it was Iraq," the professor said.

"…Finally, do you have an opinion as to whether the Sept. 11, 2001, attacks were done pursuant to and in furtherance of a common scheme between Iraq and al Qaeda towards America?" Jim Jr. asked.

"Yes," the professor said. "The United States is the declared enemy of both the Iraqi government and al Qaeda."

•   •   •

ON MARCH 20, 2003, JUST 17 DAYS AFTER THE LAST DAY OF TRIAL IN *SMITH V. TALIBAN*, the United States, Great Britain and their allies invaded Iraq. On the same day, President Bush issued an executive order under the International Emergency Economic Powers Act that confiscated all frozen funds in America held in the name of the government of Iraq.

In court, Beasley asked for an expedited decision from the judge, fearing that the Iraqi frozen assets might be used to finance the war, but the judge declined.

The invasion of Iraq ignited a national political debate. On one side, the Bush Administration and some Republicans claimed that Iraq had been a collaborator with al Qaeda on 9/11, while Democrats denied it. But in U.S. District Court, Judge Harold Baer Jr. had heard enough evidence to settle the issue as a matter of law.

"I conclude that plaintiffs have shown, albeit barely, 'by evidence satisfactory to the court' that Iraq provided material support to bin Laden and al Qaeda," the judge wrote on May 7, 2003. The judge based his decision on testimony provided by Beasley's expert witnesses, former CIA director Woolsey and Professor Mylroie.

The judge noted that "a very substantial portion of plaintiff's evidence is classically hearsay [and often multiple hearsay] and without meeting any exceptions is inadmissible for substantive purposes. … However, the opinion testimony of the plaintiffs' experts is sufficient to meet plaintiffs' burden that Iraq collaborated in or supported bin Laden/al Qaeda's terrorist acts of Sept. 11."

The judge, appointed by President Jimmy Carter, noted that under the Anti-Terrorism Act of 1991, victims of terrorism were allowed to collect triple damages. He then awarded the heirs of George Smith $1.1 million for lost earnings, and $1 million for pain and suffering, which, under triple damages, meant an additional $4.2 million for lost earnings and pain and suffering. The judge also granted damages for loss of solatium, or the mental anguish, bereavement and grief suffered by relatives of the victims. For this loss, the judge awarded an additional $4.7 million for the Smith family.

The judge wrote that the defendants were also liable to pay Tim Soulas' heirs $15.1 million for economic losses, and $3 million for pain and suffering. With triple damages, that amounted to an additional $36.2 million. For solatium damages, the judge awarded $39 million to the Soulas family.

The total damages Judge Baer awarded in the case amounted to a staggering $104 million. On July 28, 2003, the judge determined that Iraq's liability in the case for compensatory damages came to $63 million. At the time, the United States government had frozen $1.9 billion in Iraqi assets.

The judge also ruled that al Qaeda and the Taliban were liable for more than $40 million in damages, but that part of the award seemed moot. Bin Laden had no frozen assets in the United States, and the State Department had previously shipped $221 million of frozen assets belonging to the Taliban to the new Afghan government. So if Beasley was going to collect any money on behalf of his clients' judgment, he would have to go after the frozen Iraqi assets, as well as the U.S. government that was holding them.

· · ·

ON ABC'S GOOD MORNING AMERICA OF MAY 8, 2002, HOST CHARLES GIBSON TALKED about how "a legal precedent was set yesterday" in a federal case that may be a "significant victory" for the families of 9/11, but Gibson cautioned that "it might also be an empty one."

Gibson dwelled on the "over $100 million in damages," saying, "The two families involved, I suspect even, were shocked at the size of the award."

On camera from Philadelphia, however, Jim Beasley Jr. disagreed. "Considering what these terrorists did to America," he said, "there's a fairly reasonable relationship to what happened."

"This is a little bit more than compensation," Jim Jr. told Gibson. "This is an attempt to get information out there as to who was really behind this. And with a lot of work and diligence, we were able to show information that a lot of people were trying to hide."

Gibson noted that "the most interesting part to a lot of people" was that "the judge linked Saddam Hussein to 9/11," adding that the evidence of that was "much debated… (and) very controversial."

"It is controversial certainly in the press and the political circles," Jim Jr. said.

But he told Gibson that if he saw the evidence presented in court and heard the testimony of the expert witnesses, "it's not all that controversial.... It's pretty straightforward."

Gibson then asked the big question: "Is it possible that the families will never see any of this money because Iraqi money that exists in the United Sates is frozen, the assets, are they not?"

"That's a good question," Jim Jr. replied. When Gibson asked what The Beasley Firm was doing to collect the money for its clients, Jim Jr. said they were preparing "appropriate documents" for the Office of Foreign Assets Control, working their contacts in Washington, and putting in "a lot of late nights."

· · ·

THE $104-MILLION JUDGMENT AGAINST THE DEFENDANTS IN *SMITH V. TALIBAN* WAS recorded on May 21, 2003, in U.S. District Court in Manhattan. One day later, President Bush signed an executive order stating that lawsuits against Iraq were a threat to national security, and that all suits and judgments against Iraq were hereby voided. The president said he wanted to use those frozen Iraqi assets to rebuild Iraq.

Beasley was a registered Republican who broke with his party over the issue of tort reform and often voted for Democrats; his fellow lawyers described him as a live-and-let-live libertarian.

So far in *Smith v. Taliban*, Beasley had echoed the Bush Administration's line on Iraq. But Beasley's next move in the case would demonstrate how apolitical he was.

Beasley responded to the president's executive order by suing the U.S. Federal Reserve Bank in New York, where Iraq's frozen assets were being held, to seek a preliminary injunction to prevent the assets from being shipped abroad.

When Beasley had gone after the Taliban, bin Laden and Saddam in U.S. District Court, the defense table was empty and so were the galleries, except for the few lawyers who showed up to watch. But this time around, Beasley had targeted his own government, so the courtroom was crowded with legal adversaries. At a Sept. 3, 2003, hearing, Beasley was opposed by a deputy assistant attorney general, a U.S. attorney for the Southern District of New York, two assistant U.S. attorneys, and two lawyers for the Federal Reserve Bank.

At the hearing, Beasley let his son argue to a federal judge that President Bush had exceeded his constitutional authority in seeking to transfer the frozen assets to Iraq.

Jim Jr. cited a legal precedent: President Truman had issued an executive order in 1952 to seize the country's steel mills in an attempt to avert a threatened labor strike that would have disrupted the flow of supplies to American troops during the Korean War.

The steel mills responded by suing the president. In *Youngstown Sheet & Tube v. Sawyer*, the steel mills conceded that the government had the right to pass a new law to seize their properties. But the steel mills argued that under the Constitution, only Congress and not the president had the authority to make new laws. Truman's executive order, the steel mills argued, violated the constitutional doctrine of separation of powers. The U.S. Supreme Court agreed, ruling that President Truman's executive order was unconstitutional.

"You are suggesting that the March 20 executive order is the kind of order that the Supreme Court criticized in *Youngstown* as being beyond presidential power?" Judge Baer asked.

"Absolutely," Jim Jr. responded. It was also the clear intention of Congress, Jim Jr. argued, to use any frozen assets from terrorist-sponsoring nations to compensate the victims of terrorism. Congress had repeatedly stated this intention in laws such as the Foreign Sovereign Immunities Act, Jim Jr. said. He also argued that the transfer of frozen assets to Iraq would pose an undue hardship on his clients.

"It's clear that if these funds are transferred over to Iraq, there is no other source of funds for the plaintiffs to satisfy their judgment, no adequate remedy of law for plaintiffs once these funds are gone."

The judge disagreed about whether President Bush had exceeded his authority. "You ought to have put this in your memory bag," he told Jim Jr. "In foreign affairs, the president has a degree of discretion and freedom on statutory restrictions… that's clearly of this ilk."

Shannen W. Coffin, a deputy assistant attorney general for the U.S. Department of Justice, argued that the frozen Iraqi assets were urgently needed to rebuild Iraq.

"…The United States voluntarily decided to give you time to reach the merits of this case and kept the money in the account, despite very pressing needs in Iraq, Your Honor," Coffin told Judge Baer. "To date, everything in that [$1.9 billion] account, except for $63.9 million, has been removed, sent over to Iraq."

"Now we promised to hold that account until Sept. 10," which was a week away, Coffin said. "We are going to move that money out immediately."

Coffin also disputed Jim Jr.'s comparison of President Bush and the frozen assets of Iraq to President Truman's seizure of the steel mills. *Youngstown*, Coffin said, was a case "where the president by executive order alone tried to set aside a piece of domestic legislation." He was referring to the Taft-Hartley Act, which said that the most a president could do to avert a labor strike was to call for a mandatory 80-day cooling-off period.

Congress had passed a joint resolution in 2002 authorizing the president to use military force against Iraq, "so this is not the case where the president is acting on his own," Coffin told the judge.

The judge told both sides that it was time "to settle this once and for all so that there is nothing hanging over anybody's head. Either the money belongs to the plaintiffs or it belongs to the government." The judge asked the Justice Department lawyer to "give me a few more days to resolve this.

"I am conscious of the problems in Iraq, and I know this money is going to make all the difference, but I would like until the 15th of September," the judge said.

"I think we can agree to that," Coffin said.

• • •

ON SEPT. 11, 2003, THE SECOND ANNIVERSARY OF THE 9/11 ATTACKS, JUDGE BAER RULED that the families of the 9/11 victims could not have access to the frozen Iraqi assets because "the government contends that these funds, which might otherwise be used for compensation, are needed to rebuild Iraq."

In his decision, the judge sounded conflicted. "The need [in Iraq] is clear, nonetheless, one wonders whether American families who lost loved ones as a result of terrorism here and abroad ought not be compensated first," the judge wrote. "That said, compensation sought by plaintiffs, at least from this source, must be denied."

Beasley filed an expedited appeal with a panel of three judges at the Second Circuit Court of Appeals. At an emergency hearing in New York, Deputy Assistant Attorney General Coffin once again argued that the money was literally on the tarmac, ready to go to Iraq. And the Bush Administration wasn't going to allow that money to be hijacked by some trial lawyer from Philadelphia.

The panel of judges gave the plaintiffs 24 hours to file a brief and make oral arguments. Beasley, Jim Jr., Slade McLaughlin and David A. Yanoff filed their papers, and the next day took the train to New York to deliver their arguments. But the panel of judges ruled against them. And then the plane that the feds had been holding up was finally allowed to take off for Iraq, loaded with $63.9 million in cash.

For Beasley and his associates, it was a bitter loss. They had worked long hours and run up more than $200,000 in expenses to win a federal case that set a legal precedent. But when it came time to collect the judgment on behalf of their clients, the Philadelphia lawyers were trumped by their own government.

• • •

FOUR YEARS AFTER HE TESTIFIED AS AN EXPERT WITNESS IN *SMITH V. TALIBAN*, JIM Woolsey was working as a security consultant at Booz Allen, a defense contractor in McLean, Va. In an interview for this book, Woolsey said that the debate over whether al Qaeda and the Iraqi intelligence agency had a cooperative relationship had "gotten bogged down in the dispute about the war.

"One thing I think is quite clear: The Baathist regime under Saddam worked with a wide range of terrorist groups including al Qaeda," Woolsey said. He maintained that the Iraqis extended assistance to other terrorist groups over the years such as "providing training, safe haven, meeting places and passports."

He brought up the CIA as a comparison, saying his former agency had relationships with some 200 intelligence agencies around the world, but that "the number with which we would do operations together is very small, you could probably count them on one hand.

"Of course there was a relationship" between al Qaeda and the Iraqi intelligence agency, Woolsey insisted, but he added that what critics of the war were really saying was that they didn't believe that al Qaeda and Iraq had an "operational relationship."

Woolsey acknowledged that some of the matters he had testified about, such as Mohammed Atta's alleged meeting in Prague with an Iraqi intelligence official, were now in dispute. In 2004, CIA Director Tenet, responding in writing to a question from a U.S. senator, wrote, "Although we cannot rule it out, we are increasingly skeptical such a meeting occurred."

"I don't know who's right about that," Woolsey said about the alleged "Prague connection." At the time of the *Smith v. Taliban* hearing, Woolsey said, "I just called it the way I saw it."

Woolsey described Beasley as "a most impressive counsel," and added "it's a shame that there wasn't any recovery" for the plaintiffs. But as a former history major, Woolsey said he did not regret paying his own way to testify in the case. "I don't think adding to the historical record about something this important is ever a waste of time."

Professor Laurie Mylroie has not changed her mind since her testimony in *Smith v. Taliban*; she is still convinced that the Prague connection was real, and that Saddam and Iraq had provided material support and resources to al Qaeda for the 9/11 attack.

"The truth is very important — and that's what Beasley brought out," she wrote in an e-mail. "He won the case — which was his burden. He could not know that the Bush administration would then step in to protect Iraqi assets."

Mylroie also faulted the Bush Administration for "not ever really addressing the question of just what happened on 9/11; why the U.S. went to Iraq; and why, at this point, nearly 3,800 U.S. soldiers have died there."

Mylroie concluded that the Bush Administration's failure to come clean on 9/11 and Iraq stood in sharp contrast to the behavior of the lawyer who had fought single-mindedly on behalf of his clients. "Beasley showed himself to be a far bigger man than all the senior administration officials."

As far as Richard Hailey was concerned, Beasley's triumph was not diminished by new intelligence disclosures or the shifting winds of politics. Beasley was going with the best evidence available in 2003, as supported by administration officials from the president on down, Hailey said.

"Don't politicize what he did," Hailey said. "A half-dozen lawyers had claims pending against Iraq for 9/11 involvement. No one other than Beasley has been successful.

"He hit a home run," Hailey said, and he didn't use "a corked bat," so there was no need to put an asterisk beside the $104-million verdict. "He used the rules and the law and the evidence that was available at the time."

Hailey added that the *Smith v. Taliban* case brought under the auspices of the Foreign Sovereign Immunities Act may yet prove valuable to future victims of terrorism. Beasley's "use of the statute for an event like this becomes a template," Hailey said, "for bringing [future] cases of terrorism-related activities against nation states."

The Beasley
Firm

Attorneys At Law

1125 Walnut Street

Chapter 24

✦✦✦

"WHO'S RESPONSIBLE FOR THIS?"

J IM BEASLEY WANTED TO READ A PORTION OF A DEPOSITION TRANSCRIPT TO HIS EXPERT witness, but a defense lawyer objected, and so did the judge.

"I'm not going to allow you to read it to her, OK?" Judge Patricia A. McInerney told Beasley during a sidebar conference. "I'm not going to allow you to read it to her at this point under the guise of reading it into the record . . . . I'm going to sustain that objection."

"Please —" Beasley said, but the judge cut him off. "No, we're done," she said.

Back in open court, Beasley tried again to ask a question of his expert witness, Dr. Carolyn S. Crawford.

"My hypothetical question is, that Dr. [Linda] Baker testified that 'I was a member of the Institutional Service Board —,'" Beasley began, before describing the duties of the board, as detailed in Dr. Baker's deposition.

"That's not a hypothetical format," the judge interrupted, "you're not asking a hypothetical format."

Another lawyer might have taken a different tact at that point, but Beasley only dug his boot heels in deeper.

"…From a review of Dr. Baker's deposition," he began, but the judge interrupted him again. "Let me see counsel at sidebar," she commanded.

"Mr. Beasley," the judge said during the conference, "it is a ruse to pretend to be asking a hypothetical question by holding up the deposition and reading it in question-and-answer form, OK?"

"Your Honor," Beasley began, but the judge cut him off. "I know you know how to ask a hypothetical question, Mr. Beasley," she said. "I don't want you to argue with me in front of the jury. Just ask a proper hypothetical question."

Over at the plaintiff's table, Beasley's client, Mark F. MacDonald, himself a lawyer, cringed because he thought the judge was talking to Beasley "as if he was a bad child."

But over at the crowded defense table, some lawyers felt Beasley had it coming. "He brought it on himself," was how George L. Young Jr. saw it. "Intimidation was a large part of his game." But this time around, Young said, Beasley had run into a judge "who was not going to be intimidated."

On the morning of June 23, 2004, Beasley was representing the parents of a catastrophically injured child, and he was doing it in his usual uncompromising style, only this time it wasn't working. And what nobody in the courtroom knew was, this was Jim Beasley's last trial.

When Beasley stood to question the witness, it was clear that he had no intention of following the judge's instructions.

"Doctor," Beasley began, "in the preparation of this hypothetical question that I'm asking you, I'm going to try, from my memory, to give you the basis of that hypothetical question."

That was enough for Judge McInerney. "Let me see counsel at sidebar," she demanded. "Now."

The judge, who wasn't in kindergarten yet when Beasley won his first case, smirked and rolled her eyes to convey her disgust with the plaintiff's counsel.

"I do not want any more speeches," she lectured Beasley. "I do not want any more preludes to your questions, Mr. Beasley. Just ask the question. It's not from your memory. You don't need a big hypothetical question. Just ask the doctor, 'Assume these facts are true' and then ask her the question."

"Judge," Beasley replied, but that was the only word the court reporter recorded before the judge went off again.

"If you can't do it, then we'll take a recess and you can write out your question," the judge fumed. "But you are not going to give a speech to the jury, OK? We're going to take a short recess. Write out your question. No speeches to the jury."

• • •

MARK F. MACDONALD, A PHILADELPHIA LAWYER WHO SPECIALIZED IN DEFENSE WORK, had gone looking for a plaintiff's lawyer to represent his catastrophically injured daughter. He scheduled interviews with three of the city's top plaintiff's lawyers, and Beasley was second on the list. But "after I met with him," MacDonald recalled, "I didn't want to meet with anybody else."

Why did he go with Beasley? "It was a number of things," MacDonald said. Beasley had pored over the records MacDonald had sent him. And when McDonald stopped by his office, Beasley was already extremely knowledgeable about the case.

"He jumped on things right away," MacDonald said. "He was very charismatic, and I'm sitting there and I'm realizing that here's this legend who is obviously not resting on his laurels; he was already into the case. I said to myself, Erin couldn't have a better advocate."

Erin MacDonald, born Oct. 25, 2000, at Chestnut Hill Hospital, would not wake up to eat. Doctors had to rouse her by swabbing her forehead with an alcohol swab, which for an infant, was the equivalent of smelling salts. Erin would take a few sucks from her mother's breast, then go back to sleep. The still-sleepy baby and her mother, Ruth, were discharged from the hospital two days after birth.

The day of the discharge, Ruth MacDonald was changing her baby's diaper at home when Erin's chest began to heave and then she turned blue and purple. Erin was taken by ambulance to two hospitals that same day. At the second hospital, after several hours, they checked Erin's blood sugar and discovered she was profoundly hypoglycemic.

A day later, Erin was transferred to a third hospital, and when she arrived, she was having seizures and was diagnosed with brain damage. Doctors discovered her pancreas was overactive, pumping out large amounts of insulin. They removed the pancreas, but Erin was left with legal blindness, epilepsy and severe mental retardation.

Erin was an angelic-looking child, with fair skin, blonde hair and blue eyes. She was on an insulin pump, and her blood-sugar levels had to be checked every two hours during the day and every hour at night.

Ruth MacDonald had given up her own career as a lawyer to become Erin's primary caretaker, along with round-the-clock nursing assistance. In her first three years of life, Erin ran up $880,000 in medical bills. If she lived to 65, Beasley estimated, her total health-care costs would reach $24 million.

And in Beasley's estimation, it could have all been prevented. Beasley contended that during the first two days of Erin's life, if doctors had performed a simple test known as a heel stick — which only takes a few seconds and costs less than $10 — they would have discovered that Erin was hypoglycemic and spared her catastrophic injuries.

Beasley filed *MacDonald vs. Chestnut Hill Hospital* on behalf of Erin MacDonald and her parents. The suit listed as defendants four doctors, three hospitals, and a pediatric group.

When the case went to trial in June 2004, the defendants were represented by nine defense lawyers from five law firms. And over at the plaintiff's table, it was just Jim Beasley and his associate, Marsha F. Santangelo, M.D.

• • •

THE PLAINTIFF'S CASE, HOWEVER, GOT OFF TO A BAD START DURING JURY SELECTION. Beasley had his clients in court because he wanted prospective jurors to see Erin, but Judge McInerney took exception.

"Erin was tapping a book," MacDonald said. He and his wife were seated behind the plaintiff's table, near the jury box. The judge was on the bench and couldn't see who was making noise in her courtroom.

The judge came out and started yelling, "What's that noise, what's that noise?," Mark MacDonald recalled. It was the plaintiff, then 3½ years old. The judge told Beasley and Erin's parents that she would not tolerate distractions in her courtroom.

The MacDonalds had also brought Shaelyn, Erin's 5-year-old sister, to court. Beasley wanted jurors to see not only how handicapped Erin was, but also how her parents and older sister tended to her.

The judge, however, said that being in a courtroom all day would be too much for Erin, and that the baby's distant gaze and occasional grunts might distract jurors. The judge went so far as to accuse Beasley of abusing the child by putting her on permanent display, an accusation that enraged Beasley.

On Tuesday, June 15, 2004, Beasley told the judge he wanted to put something on the record. What happened next was true to one of Beasley's maxims, which he drilled into the young lawyers who worked for him, namely, "Never take any shit from anybody, and that includes a judge."

"You instructed me that my client, the baby, could not be in the courtroom during jury selection, and I was to put the child in an anteroom; that the plaintiff could stay there," Beasley began. "So the panel, as it now constitutes, have never seen the child, don't know anything about the child's condition," Beasley said. "And that's certainly a very pertinent observation for both the plaintiff and the defendants in this case. But that's been denied."

Beasley did not bother to hide his anger.

"I think that is not only a gross abuse of discretion on behalf of the court, but it is a clear violation of the child's right to be in the courtroom," Beasley lectured the judge. "But because I objected to the child's being absent from the courtroom, you accused me, in front of other lawyers and the court officers, of abusing the child with — the way you put it was 'reprehensible conduct'; that I was not acting with the responsibility as an attorney; that I was using the child," Beasley said.

"And that is such a grossly wrong statement. There's no substantive basis. Simply because I wanted the child in the courtroom, I was abusing her."

Beasley continued to berate the judge, raising his voice to a level that prompted the court reporter to switch to italics: "*Do you want the jury to see the child, and in the condition she is?*

"I have a serious problem with your accusation that I abused this child," Beasley said, while the judge sat in silence. "And for that reason alone, there's no way that this child is going to get a fair trial, because whatever it is I've done that's piqued your anger, you are taking it out on this child.

"And I can assure you," Beasley continued, "that if any one of these lawyers in this room, or yourself, had a baby in this condition, you would be as outraged as I am about the manner in which this case has been handled."

Beasley was frustrated because he said the judge had granted a dozen pretrial defense motions concerning admissibility of evidence; motions that Beasley claimed had knocked out much of his case. Beasley wanted the jury to consider the impact Erin's injuries had on her older sister; he also wanted to sue the emergency room nurses, but the judge granted defense motions eliminating those arguments from the case.

Beasley also accused the judge of not ruling on at least 14 pretrial motions of his own, which he said would force him to object, in the presence of the jury, to the testimony of at least 17 defense witnesses.

"I think that the only healthy remedy for this bad, bad situation is for you to recuse yourself or to grant a mistrial," Beasley told the judge. "Because I can see that no matter what I do in this case, I will not be able to present this child's case to a jury in a fair and unbiased fashion.

"That's just the beginning, Your Honor," he said as he finished his scolding. "And I again renew my motion, because this child will never get a fair trial in your courtroom because of me; not because of the child."

"Are you finished?" the judge said.

"Yes, ma'am," Beasley said.

"Your motion is denied," said the judge, who subsequently defended her actions.

"I've always said to you, Mr. Beasley, that your client is entitled to be here during the trial," the judge said. "But you have to deal with the fact that if the child didn't have any developmental issues, it's tough to have a child sit through a trial. It's just a tough thing to do, because they can't sit still. They're kids."

• • •

"Let me say initially, so this comes out very clear," Beasley said in his opening statement to the jury. "It is not my contention that any doctor in this case is incompetent. My contention simply is that their feet are made of clay, and, like all of us, all put our pants on one leg at a time. They can make mistakes. It's those mistakes in this case which we contend caused a catastrophic injury to this child."

Beasley outlined his theory of the case, that the hospital staff could have prevented Erin MacDonald's injuries if they had done the heel-stick test and discovered she was hypoglycemic.

"Hypoglycemia," Beasley told the jury, "if not treated promptly, will lead to severe and permanent brain damage."

Beasley talked about the high medical cost of caring for Erin. "One of the important considerations for the MacDonalds is this: *Who is going to take care of my baby when I'm gone?*"

"This is the MacDonalds," Beasley said, pointing out the plaintiffs. "This is Erin. As I said before, she doesn't eat, and she has a feeding tube and she has an insulin pump...."

"You've been very kind. I appreciate your listening to me," Beasley told the jury. "And I'll just say this. I know it's a sacrifice for some of you people to be here, and we appreciate it."

After he made his opening statement, Beasley had his clients remove Erin MacDonald from the courtroom, so she wouldn't disrupt the opening speeches of the defense lawyers.

Richard A. Kolb, representing Chestnut Hill Hospital, was the first of five defense lawyers to address the jury.

"Chestnut Hill's medical facility [is] up on Germantown Avenue, and it's a building," Kolb said. "And we all know that. But what is at issue in this case is the care and treatment that was rendered by the people who attended to Ruth MacDonald and Erin MacDonald following her birth.

"A number of them are here today, and I'm not going to embarrass them and ask them to stand up," Kolb said. But the defense lawyer proceeded to introduce five Chestnut Hill nurses sitting in the second row of spectators' seats.

"And it's important to know the people, because, ladies and gentlemen, they're all accused, in one way or another, of violating their professional responsibilities and causing harm to this little girl," Kolb said. "Because if you believe plaintiff's claim in this case, they all were wrong in their monitoring and evaluation of this child. They were all wrong."

Kolb argued that the evidence would show "very clearly that the nursing staff at Chestnut Hill Hospital rendered proper and appropriate and reasonable care to this young child."

Next up was George L. Young Jr., defending two pediatricians in the case. Young argued that what happened to Erin was nobody's fault, especially his clients'.

"You see, ladies and gentlemen, this unfortunate young girl was born with a very, very rare and very, very severe form of pancreatitis," Young said. "There was no indication at that time to perform any sort of heel stick. That baby was a normal baby who liked to sleep and what nursing mothers would call a fussy eater. . . . But these women were looking at her color, her tone, her weight. That's what you analyze. And everything about that was normal, ladies and gentlemen."

The symptoms of Erin's "rare congenital condition" only began to show after she was discharged from the hospital, Young argued.

Daniel J. Divis represented the emergency room doctor at Chestnut Hill Hospital. After Erin turned blue at home, she was brought back to Chestnut Hill Hospital, Divis told the jury, where she "was completely stable in the emergency room.

"Her color returned, her respirations returned and she was fine," the defense lawyer said. He added that he expected jurors to feel sympathetic toward Erin, but that they also had a duty to consider the evidence. "We're all on an equal playing field here in the courtroom," Divis reminded the jury.

Benjamin A. Post represented Abington Memorial Hospital and its doctors. Abington Memorial was the second hospital that Erin was brought to, and the place where her hypoglycemia was discovered.

"Ladies and gentlemen, our evidence will show that the doctor, the nurses at Abington, acted entirely appropriately in their care and treatment of Erin MacDonald," Post said. Erin's condition was so rare, Post told the jury, it afflicted only one out of 50,000 babies.

Abbe F. Fletman represented Children's Hospital of Philadelphia, the third hospital that treated Erin.

"I hope you will keep an open mind and you will have an opportunity to hear from me again at the conclusion of the trial," Fletman said. "And at that time, I will ask you to find on behalf of Children's Hospital of Philadelphia."

• • •

DR. CRAWFORD, BEASLEY'S EXPERT WITNESS, WAS A FORMER CHAIRMAN OF THE DEPARTMENT of neonatology at Albert Einstein Medical Center in Philadelphia. Dr. Crawford was also a courtroom veteran who testified frequently as an expert witness, so the defense strategy was to portray her as a high-paid mercenary.

George L. Young Jr. got things rolling when he stood to cross-examine Dr. Crawford: "My recollection is that you have been testifying for 25 years?"

"About 25 years," Dr. Crawford said. "Yes, sir."

"You charge for your court appearances, is that right?" Young asked.

"Yes, sir," Dr. Crawford said.

Young asked if it was true that Dr. Crawford had testified during a 1991 case in Texas that she was paid "between $80,000 and $90,000" a year for testifying as an expert witness.

"Yes, sir," Dr. Crawford said. ". . . If you put everything across the board, it's probably $90,000; $95,000 would be an average."

"So you have earned approximately $2.5 million in your career?" Young asked.

"I think you're a little generous on that," Dr. Crawford replied.

"I object," Beasley said while the doctor was answering the question. Beasley didn't want the jury to think the doctor was getting rich testifying against her colleagues.

"Sustained," the judge said.

"If you said that $80,000 a year is the average, over 25 years, that's $2 million," Young said.

This time, Beasley didn't have to object.

"I just sustained that last objection," the judge said. "I'll strike that question and the answer."

Next, it was Benjamin A. Post's turn to cross-examine the witness.

"Doctor," Post said, "have you given testimony that in 2003 your most recent tax returns indicated that for plaintiff's medical malpractice work you earned close to $200,000 a year?"

Beasley: "Your Honor, I object and move for a mistrial."

The judge: "Mistrial is denied."

Beasley: "Are you allowing the question?"

The judge: "I am not allowing the question in that form, no."

"With regard to your work in litigation-related matters," Post tried again, "and your work specifically with lawyers who represent plaintiffs in cases against hospitals and doctors, is it accurate to tell the ladies and gentlemen of the jury that your last tax returns indicated that for that type of work you earned approximately $200,000 per year?"

"Your Honor," Beasley protested, "This is in direct defiance of your sustaining that objection. I again move for a mistrial."

"The mistrial is denied," said the judge, who told the defense lawyer to "just reformulate the question."

"With respect to the work you do with litigation-related matters," Post continued, "again medical malpractice, again solely for plaintiff's lawyers suing hospitals and doctors, is it accurate to tell the ladies and gentlemen of the jury that your last income tax returns would reflect earnings of $200,000 for that type of work?"

"Your Honor," Beasley said. "I move for a mistrial. This is the third time he's breached Your Honor's ruling."

"The objection is sustained," the judge said, ignoring Beasley's request for a mistrial.

But even though the judge was sustaining Beasley's objections, the defense was scoring points by relentlessly parading Dr. Crawford's earnings before the jury. And Beasley couldn't do anything to stop it.

"I think the judge was very conscious of who Jim Beasley was, and she was not going to allow Jim Beasley to run her courtroom," Mark MacDonald recalled in an interview. "He was going toe to toe with five defense counsels and a sixth one sitting on the bench."

The judge, when contacted in 2007, declined to discuss Beasley: "I don't really have much to say. I didn't really know Mr. Beasley. He had such a fabulous career. I only had that one trial with him."

Later in the cross-examination of Dr. Crawford, Beasley continued to object to the questions about her overall earnings as an expert witness. He also attacked the judge during a sidebar conference for allowing the defense to portray Dr. Crawford as a mercenary. But the judge overruled Beasley's objection and told him, "You are not allowed to lecture me." The judge then gave Post some free legal advice.

"Why don't you just ask her what did she earn this past year testifying?" the judge told Post. "Why don't you just ask her that?"

Post: "What did you earn in the year 1998 in litigation matters?"

Beasley: "Objection."

The judge: "Overruled."

The witness: "Somewhere around $200,000."

The defense lawyers had scored again, and they weren't finished. As George Young subsequently told the jury during his closing statement, "Dr. Crawford isn't an expert, she's an industry."

• • •

AS THE FIVE-WEEK TRIAL WORE ON, BEASLEY WOULD ALTERNATELY RAGE OR JUST THROW up his hands in disgust and laugh as the judge's rulings continued to go against him. At one point he even suggested as an aside that cocounsel Marsha F. Santangelo, M.D., stand up and make an argument, since she couldn't do any worse.

The only break for Beasley came when his wife, Helen, stopped by to visit him at the trial. "He just changed like that," Mark MacDonald recalled. "He'd been fighting this judge, and he was so pissed off. And he was so happy to see her [Helen]. He brought her over to introduce us. I just remember it as a sweet moment."

The trial schedule was the usual marathon: Beasley and Santangelo were in the office every morning by 5 or 6, and they would go home as late as 9 every night.

"He never offered any complaints to me," Santangelo said of her boss. "He was his usual self."

Santangelo didn't walk to court with Beasley every morning for a simple reason — she couldn't keep up. But walking back from court, she noticed, "He was still walking faster than I was walking, but not as fast as he usually did.

"But it was hot," she said. "It was the summer, and I didn't make anything of it."

MacDonald didn't notice any problems either, although Beasley had a cough and complained about a gimpy leg. "Given his age, his stamina was incredible," MacDonald said. "I have never seen a single lawyer do what he did. We usually say what we do isn't rocket science. Well, what Jim was doing was rocket science."

"Cutting edge," was how defense lawyer George Young described it. "A higher level of advocacy." Young also marveled at Beasley's stamina. "He was the lion in winter," Young said of his 78-year-old opponent. "I thought his age was showing, but he showed flashes of his old self.

"It's a 5½ week trial, and he's got six defense lawyers taking shots at him. He was remarkable."

But the case took its toll on Beasley. He kept sending out paralegal Kenneth Purpura to score energy bars and Goldenberg's Peanut Chews. Beasley was also losing weight, as he often did during a trial; but this time it was about 10 pounds off his spare 155-pound frame.

Helen was upset. "This is Dad's last case," she told her daughter, Pam, over the phone. "I don't think he's going to try another case."

When he came home from court every night and hopped out of his BMW, Beasley had a "Hi, darling" for his wife. He also downplayed any concerns over his health. Helen, however, had been worried for quite a while. A year earlier, she had tried to talk her husband into making an appointment with her doctor at Penn, an internist who was also a geriatrician. "No," her husband told her. "I see Bernie [Segal]. Bernie's my doctor."

Dr. Bernard L. Segal was a cardiologist who was also Beasley's personal physician. It made sense because of Beasley's triple heart-bypass surgery in 1992. But for almost a year now, Beasley had been short of breath. He had talked about it several times with Dr. Segal, but the doctor said it was only stress.

On Sept. 24, 2003, Dr. Segal noted in a progress report that Beasley "feels his pulse rate is more rapid than it should be. This is associated with some degree of shortness of breath. At no time has he had chest pain or angina pectoris."

The doctor made several house calls to Beasley's Villanova estate, examined the patient, and said there was nothing to worry about, it was just stress, and that Beasley needed to lighten up on his schedule. On July 3, 2004, during the MacDonald trial, Dr. Segal came out to examine Beasley one more time and left saying, "You're really fine."

But Beasley seemed to know something was wrong. When he and his son flew to Atlantic City for an air show during the summer of 2004, Beasley sat silently in back during the short, 15-minute trip and let Jim Jr. fly the Mustang. That had never happened before.

Every morning, Beasley played solitaire on the computer and timed his reactions to make sure he wasn't slipping mentally. But he was having physical problems. During the summer, down in Florida, his wife noticed that Beasley had a hard time riding a bicycle a quarter-mile on level ground, although he didn't complain about it. He also had a dry cough he couldn't shake. In August, he had a railing installed in the basement of his home, to accommodate what his son described as an "unsteady gait."

James E. Foerstner, one of Beasley's lawyers, was in the courtroom when Beasley gave his summation to the jury in the MacDonald case. "He seemed exhausted," Foerstner said.

Beasley sat and listened with a poker face on July 21, 2004, as they read the verdicts that favored the defense on all but one minor question. Beasley turned to Mark MacDonald, sitting at the table behind him and whispered, "This is not over." Beasley and Santangelo left the courtroom with their clients, without showing any emotion. Back at the office, Beasley began work on an appeal.

A few weeks after the verdict, Santangelo walked into The Beasley Building and saw something strange; Jim Beasley got on the elevator with her. "That was unprecedented," she said. Beasley always lectured the staff on the health benefits of climbing the stairs; the boss *never* rode the elevator.

Beasley looked over at Santangelo; "You got your hair cut," he said. "Yes," she said. He looked tired, Santangelo thought to herself. When he got off at the second floor, Beasley said goodbye to Santangelo, adding, "Have a good day."

• • •

BEASLEY WALKED A COUPLE OF BLOCKS FROM HIS OFFICE OVER TO THOMAS JEFFERSON University Hospital to see Dr. Segal. "The patient, age 78 [years] young, enjoys an excellent exercise tolerance," the doctor wrote in a progress note on Aug. 9, 2004. "He has no chest pain, palpitations, lightheadedness, vertigo. He states that in the early morning on getting up, his pulse rate tends to be somewhat increased."

"On examination he looks well," the doctor wrote. "His blood pressure is 120/70. Pulse is 86 and regular." Beasley's cholesterol was 211, with an LDL of 99, and his weight was 151 pounds. "First and second heart sounds are normal," the doctor wrote. "Lungs are perfectly clear."

"At some time a decision will be made regarding a CAT scan of the chest," Dr. Segal wrote. "A CAT scan was performed a number of years ago."

Beasley finally had a chest X ray on Aug. 19, 2004, almost a year after he had been complaining about shortness of breath. The X ray showed a shadow on his lungs diagnosed as pneumonia. Dr. Segal put Beasley on antibiotics. A day or so later, Beasley finally had a CAT scan, and it revealed something more extensive than an infection. This time, Dr. Segal ordered a biopsy.

The day of the biopsy, Beasley underwent general anesthesia. After the biopsy was over, Beasley realized he was so weak, he would be lucky to walk the few blocks back to the office. He staggered down the street, past three homeless men who suddenly looked menacing.

Toward the end of August, Beasley called his old flying buddy Dan Caldarale at 7 a.m. "What are you doing?" Beasley asked. "Oh, man, I'm so aggravated," Caldarale said. His grass needed cutting, Caldarale said, and he had a plane all masked, ready to paint. But Caldarale's back was killing him; so was a bum shoulder.

Beasley wasn't feeling so great himself, but he wanted to help. "I can't paint that goddamn airplane," he told Caldarale, "but you're my best buddy and I'll cut your grass." He hung up, and two hours later, he showed up at Caldarale's airport hangar. Beasley hopped a tractor and mowed seven acres.

Jim Jr. called his parents' home on Sept. 5, 2004, to wish his mother happy birthday, but when she came to the phone, Helen was grim. "You need to talk to Dad," she said.

Beasley was blunt. "I have lymphoma," he said. Jim Jr. was shocked, but he slipped into his doctor persona, not wanting to give off any expressions of alarm.

"OK," he said. "What kind?"

"Non-Hodgkin's lymphoma."

Jim Jr. tried to stay upbeat. "We'll get through this," he told his father. "What are we going to do?" They talked about how to treat the illness. They also discussed how to break the news to other lawyers at the firm. Beasley said he would call them into his office one at a time.

When his daughter, Pam, phoned later that day, Beasley was cheerful. "Hi, baby," he said. "I'm doing great." Then he blurted, "I've been diagnosed with lymphoma, but everything's going to be fine, because it's curable."

Slade McLaughlin thought Beasley looked haggard when he went in to see him.

"Hey, Tiger, I just got back from the doctor and I've got cancer," Beasley told McLaughlin. But Beasley was optimistic. "It's nothing to worry about," he said. "I've got a very treatable form."

McLaughlin shook Beasley's hand and wished him luck. "I'll be back," Beasley said as he gave McLaughlin a firm shake. "I don't need luck."

Beasley went in for a bone-marrow aspiration, which involved inserting a big long needle into his hip bone, to get a marrow sample. Jim Jr. accompanied his Dad, and watched as the doctors did the test without anesthetic, because that would have involved another deep jab with a needle. Beasley didn't flinch. "He's so fucking tough," Jim Jr. told Pam after the test.

Beasley, his wife and son went to see Dr. John Glick, a world expert on lymphoma. Dr. Glick's diagnosis was that the disease was at Stage 2, which gave Beasley a 70-percent chance of recovery. Dr. Glick talked to Beasley about chemotherapy, specifically a radioactive injection that would give him the strongest possible dose. Dr. Glick also decided to transfer the patient to the Hospital at the University of Pennsylvania, where Glick was president and director of the university's Abramson Family Cancer Research Institute.

At Penn, they gave Beasley an injection of radioactive glucose, followed by a full body scan. Cancer cells ingest glucose at a faster rate than do normal cells; with cancer cells appearing on the scan as black dots. When Jim Jr. saw the scan, he saw clouds of black dots everywhere; the cancer was so aggressive it had spread throughout his father's body. Both femurs were infested; so was Beasley's chest, abdomen and lymph nodes. There was so much cancer in the chest that Jim Jr. suspected external compression of the airways. No wonder his father had that dry cough and so much trouble breathing.

Jim Jr. was simultaneously crushed, and also disbelieving. "How is this guy doing it?" he wondered. "How did he just get through a 5½ week trial?" Jim Jr. glanced over at his father, and decided he didn't look all that bad. But he seemed like a pilot limping home with a nearly empty fuel tank. Or as Jim Jr. said to himself, "He's gonna slide home with nothing left."

Jim Jr. was also upset that Dr. Segal had blown off chronic shortness of breath in a 78-year-old man. In hindsight, the doctor should have ordered a chest X ray a year earlier.

"The moral is, don't have your friend as your doctor," Jim Jr. said. But he also blamed his father, because he had deliberately overlooked so many warning signs.

Dr. Segal defended himself in an interview by saying he hadn't seen much of Beasley in the months before his diagnosis. "He was a fellow with long-standing heart disease who was doing well. Regrettably, there was a lag of about 9 or 10 months where I didn't see him as a patient."

Beasley had gotten busy with his trials, and "he stopped thinking about himself during this time," Dr. Segal said. The doctor said he was devastated when Beasley told him he had lymphoma. "He called me after the diagnosis. He couldn't climb the stairs."

When Beasley figured how upset his doctor was, the patient tried to reassure the doctor.

"Relax," Beasley told Dr. Segal. "I've had a good life."

• • •

On Saturday, Sept. 11, 2004, it took three people to get Beasley out of the bathroom. His worried wife called Dr. Glick.

"Dr. Glick, my husband is getting weaker and weaker, and I want to bring him to the emergency room today," Helen said over the phone. The doctor said he would have a resident meet the Beasleys at the emergency room, but Beasley said forget it. "Honey, I'm not going," he said. "I have some say about my care."

Jim Jr. stopped by the house with a new *Scarface* DVD. Father and son were big fans of the movie, so they went up in his room to watch it. But Beasley was so tired he lay down and couldn't get up. He was supposed to start chemotherapy as an outpatient the following week, but his son decided why wait.

"Dad," Jim Jr. said, "you're getting in my fucking truck and we're going to the hospital." But his father was adamant. "I'm not gonna go; I'm not gonna give in to this."

"What's the downside?" Jim Jr. asked his father. "They admit you in the emergency room, and you start your chemo early." But Beasley kept refusing. "If I do it, I'm giving in," he said.

To Jim Jr., this made no sense. "I don't know who you're giving in to," he said, but he decided he wasn't going to push it any further.

The next day, father and son had two tickets for the Philadelphia Eagles 2004 home opener, but Beasley was too sick to go. So Jim Jr. took another lawyer from the firm to Lincoln Financial Field.

That night, at his home in Villanova, Beasley was having long coughing spells that wouldn't end. His face turned red as he tried to catch his breath. Then his head and upper body started to jerk back and forth, and his eyes rolled back as if he was having a seizure.

"Call 911," Helen told Pam, but Beasley said, "Call Bernie." Beasley finally made the trip by ambulance to Bryn Mawr Hospital. Dr. Segal arrived to check on his patient.

Beasley, still coughing badly, was diagnosed with Stage 4 lymphoma. The cancer had spread to the bones. His chances for survival had dwindled to less than 10 percent.

He was transferred to the Hospital of the University of Pennsylvania, at Dr. Glick's request, and Helen rode over with him in the ambulance. Beasley, dressed in a hospital gown, realized the ambulance driver was going the wrong way, so he sat up and gave the driver directions to the expressway.

At Penn, Beasley was given steroids as part of the chemo treatment, and he had a sudden burst of energy. He went to the bathroom by himself, and he watched two of his favorite movies on DVD, *Full Metal Jacket* and *To Kill a Mockingbird*. He was also making small talk with his Asian nurse, telling her, "My daughter-in-law's Asian, too."

But at 8 a.m. Wednesday, Jim Jr. got a call from the hospital. "Your dad had a tough night," Dr. Glick said. The doctors were trying to hydrate Beasley to keep the chemo from crystallizing, when he went into heart failure.

When she arrived at the hospital, Helen could see that her husband was worried. "I don't think I'm getting out of here," he said, but Helen refused to believe it. "Of course you are," she said. "You'll be around for 99 more years."

• • •

WHEN JIM JR. ARRIVED AT THE HOSPITAL WHERE HE HAD ATTENDED MEDICAL SCHOOL for four years, the doctors told him they were dealing with a very aggressive cancer that might already have invaded the heart.

Beasley was grim when he greeted his son. "This is a death watch, isn't it?" He was gasping for breath, as if on a treadmill. But his son downplayed the situation, saying, "We're just waiting for the chemo to work."

Jim Jr., however, saw that the accessory muscles in his father's neck were no longer flexing. "You're just tired," he told his father. "You need to have your strength so the chemo can work. We've got to be able to give you a break, and the only way to do that is to get you intubated."

Beasley, however, was still thinking like a lawyer. He had a breathing mask over his face now, so he couldn't talk, but he wrote in shaky handwriting on a pad, "Who's responsible for this?"

The son had no answer, so he switched subjects. "We're gonna get you as high as I was in high school," Jim Jr. joked. "How long?" his father wanted to know, writing out the question on a pad. "I don't know," his son said. "It's a function of the chemo."

As a doctor, Jim Jr. knew that once his father was intubated and tethered to a breathing machine, his life would slip away. But the son resolved to stay upbeat. He decided he wouldn't say goodbye. As they wheeled his father out of his private room, off to the intensive care unit, Jim Jr. gave him the thumb's up. And as he was being wheeled away on a gurney, Beasley looked back over his shoulder, caught his son's eye, and returned the gesture.

It was Saturday, Sept. 18. Jim Jr. made hasty calls to his father's closest friends: Dick Sprague, Dan Caldarale and Walter Woodworth. Sprague and Caldarale left immediately for the hospital; Cousin Walter, at home in San Diego, refused to believe the bad news, saying he would just have to see "Jimmie" when he was better.

Caldarale arrived first. Beasley was lying on a gurney, wearing a breathing mask, on his way to the ICU. Caldarale grabbed Beasley by the arm, and Beasley looked up. Caldarale was wearing a Beasley Law School T-shirt, which drew a faint smile from Beasley.

Caldarale held on tight to Beasley's arm and started saying Hail Marys. He looked at his old buddy, but Beasley appeared out of it. Caldarale kept thinking how, just three weeks earlier, Beasley had been riding a tractor, mowing seven acres.

Jim Jr. also called Nancy and Lynn, Beasley's daughters from his first marriage, and told them to come down to the hospital fast. He knew his father would object, but his father was no longer conscious. As Jim Jr. told himself, "This wasn't about him anymore."

They intubated Beasley in the ICU and put him on low-blood-pressure medicine. But when his heart went into arrhythmia, they had to shock him back. They gave him a low dose of dopamine to keep his kidneys working. His condition was so bad the doctors decided to give him another drug called levophed, a powerful adrenaline that clamps down on blood vessels, forcing blood into the heart and brain. The downside of the drug, however, known among doctors as "Leave 'em dead," was that it also simultaneously cut off blood supply to the extremities. Beasley's hands and feet turned cold.

The doctors gave him morphine for pain. Beasley's dopamine level went up to 85, meaning he was no longer maintaining his own blood pressure. His pacemaker sounded; his heart was going into arrhythmia again, so once more they had to shock him back to life.

As Jim Jr. conferred with the doctors, the main question was, was the chemo working? The cancer was so aggressive, the doctors needed to know how hard to push this. They wanted to put Beasley on a gurney and wheel him down for a CAT scan, to see whether the cancer was spreading, but whenever they tried to move him off his bed, the unconscious patient went into arrhythmia again.

"This is fucked up," Jim Jr. said to himself. He looked at Pam and his mother. "It's over," he said. "It's time to stop this. If they can't even move him from his bed to a gurney in spite of all the meds he's on, what are we doing?

"We've got to end this," Jim Jr. said. His sister and mother began crying, but Jim Jr. pressed on. The attending physician in the ICU agreed that there was no chance of recovery. About 12:30 p.m., the family decided to withdraw life support.

Beasley wasn't religious, but his wife, a Catholic, had asked that a hospital chaplain be summoned. A large black female Pentecostal minister showed up and volunteered to read the 23rd Psalm. "Let's all say it together," the minister said, but Helen said, "I don't think everyone knows it." So the minister took over: "The Lord is my shepherd. I shall not want."

For the next three hours, family members stood around Beasley's bed, holding his hands, stroking his face and kissing him. They murmured goodbyes and said prayers as he slipped away.

"You don't have to fight anymore, Dad," Jim Jr. kept telling him. And if Beasley could still hear, it must have been a strange request to a man who had fought so long and so passionately for so many people.

The ICU staff cranked up the morphine and cut back on the ventilator. Jim Jr. put his mother right next to his father and placed her hand on her husband's heart. It stopped beating at 3:22 p.m. Jim Jr. marked the time with a Sharpie on a white board and also on his arm.

Then, Beasley's heart started beating again. Jim Jr. couldn't believe it. His heart stopped beating again at 3:24, then at 3:26, and finally at 3:28. Jim Jr. told the nurse to turn off the monitor. His father had finally stopped fighting.

When Dick Sprague arrived at the hospital, it was too late. Sprague was crying, but Jim Jr. was already thinking of better days. His mind drifted back to when his father first taught him to fly the T-6, by hopping out of the plane while it was still on the runway. In his memory, Jim Jr. could still see his father standing on the wing of the plane, looking strong and supremely confident in his flight suit.

"Just go," he had said.

In the final years of his life, Beasley had been preparing his son to take over the law firm and fly solo. "One of these days, you're gonna look around and I won't be there," he kept saying.

As friends and family wept around him, James Edwin Beasley finally showed his age. Jim Jr. looked over at his father and realized that in his last week of his life, he had aged about 20 years.

It was just as the son had predicted. Jim Beasley slid home with nothing left.

• • •

Hours before the start of Jim Beasley's Irish wake, four pilots gathered outside Beasley's hangar at the Northeast Philadelphia Airport. Like a quarterback kneeling in the huddle, Jim. Jr. looked up at Ed Shipley, Dan Caldarale, and Dan Dameo, and gave them the flight plan.

They were to take off in four T-6s and climb to 1,500 feet. Then they would descend on Holy Sepulchre Cemetery in suburban Cheltenham Township, the Catholic cemetery five miles west of the airport where Jim Beasley would be entombed.

"I'm going to take us down to 400 feet," Jim Jr. told the pilots. About the time that a military honor guard was folding up the flag from Beasley's coffin, and presenting it to his widow, the four T-6s were scheduled to roar over the gravesite in a Missing Man formation, the traditional way to honor a fallen pilot.

It was a clear, sunny Indian summer day in Philadelphia when the temperature would hit 80. The pilots were dressed in flight suits, and Dan Caldarale's looked a little tight and short on the sleeves. That's because in honor of the missing man, Caldarale was wearing Jim Beasley's old flight suit.

The pilots took off on time from the Northeast Philly airport and climbed into a V-formation. They spread out like fingertips, with Jim Jr. in the lead. When they approached the cemetery, Dan Caldarale, on the right wing flying Jim Beasley's T-6, began trailing white smoke.

As they neared the gravesite, Jim Jr. flashed a quick hand signal, a jerk of a thumb pointing back over his shoulder, and Caldarale gracefully departed the formation. He flew straight up on a slow rise for 400 feet, leaving a white smoke trail behind him. The other three pilots held formation as they flew over the graveyard. Only the wingman was missing.

Index

Photography Credits